D1601529

The Waning
of the Communist State

This volume and the conference from which it resulted were sponsored and/or supported by the Joint Committee on Chinese Studies and the Joint Committee on Eastern Europe, of the American Council of Learned Societies and the Social Science Research Council.

The Waning
of the Communist State

Economic Origins
of Political Decline
in China and Hungary

EDITED BY

Andrew G. Walder

UNIVERSITY OF CALIFORNIA PRESS

Berkeley   Los Angeles   London

University of California Press
Berkeley and Los Angeles, California

University of California Press, Ltd.
London, England

© 1995 by
The Regents of the University of California

Library of Congress Cataloging-in-Publication Data
The waning of the communist state : economic origins of political
  decline in China and Hungary / edited by Andrew G. Walder.
      p.   cm. — (Studies on China : 21)
  Includes bibliographical references and index.
  ISBN 0-520-08851-4 (alk. paper)
    1. Communism — Hungary.   2. Hungary — Politics and
government — 1945–1989.   3. Hungary — Economic policy — 1968–1989.
4. Communism — China.   5. China — Politics and government — 1976–
6. China — Economic policy — 1976–   I. Walder, Andrew George.
II. Series.
HX260.5.A6W36   1995
335.43/09439 — dc20   94-26931
                                                                CIP

Printed in the United States of America
9 8 7 6 5 4 3 2 1

STUDIES ON CHINA

A series of conference volumes sponsored by the Joint Committee on Chinese Studies of the American Council of Learned Societies and the Social Science Research Council.

To the memory of my grandparents

Jacob Walder (b. 1893 as Jacob Voloder, Sinj, Dalmatia)

and

Mary Walder (b. 1897 as Mary Becic, Chicago, Illinois)

CONTENTS

PREFACE

History has always been far more engrossed by problems of origins than by those of decline and fall. When studying any period, we are always looking for the promise of what the next is to bring. . . . But in history, as in nature, birth and death are equally balanced. The decay of overripe forms of civilization is as suggestive a spectacle as the growth of new ones. And it occasionally happens that a period in which one had, hitherto, been mainly looking for the coming to birth of new things, suddenly reveals itself as an epoch of fading and decay.

JOHAN HUIZINGA, *The Waning of the Middle Ages* (1924)

Huizinga's observations on the writing of late medieval history bring to mind recent work on the decline and fall of communism. So many of us have scoured the record of late communism for hints of a nascent civil society, the birth of a public sphere, the rise of ethnic nationalism, the seeds of democracy, or the emergence of a market economy. In our understandable desire to chart the emergence of the new, we often relegate to an afterthought the decline of the institutions that served for so long to sustain the communist political order. This book, whose title recalls Huizinga's classic work, is in part an effort to restore some balance to our treatment of the last years of communism.

Our search for the sources of political decline is not, however, motivated primarily by a desire to restore interpretive balance; we seek a more satisfactory explanation of the decline and fall of a long-formidable and once highly centralized type of single-party state. The guiding conception in political sociology's treatment of this subject so far has highlighted the relationship between state and society. Elements in society are seen as the motive force for political change; they slowly free themselves from state control and eventually gain the upper hand through political resistance, both overt and hidden. In this volume we stress not solely the relationship between state and society but also relationships within the party-state apparatus. We highlight not only the increasing autonomy and assertiveness of ordinary citizens, but also the increasing independence of the lower elements of the party-state apparatus from their superiors. We emphasize not the new political networks among ordinary citizens, but the new political and economic ties that bind officials with private enterprises and entrepreneurs. We explore not the reorientation of interests and orientations among the citizenry, but the reorientation of interests and orientations among party-state officials. Where so much of past work has heralded what one author has aptly called "the quiet revolution from below," the essays collected here describe a "quiet revolution from within" that is equally important in understanding the epochal political changes of recent years.

Planning for the conference that resulted in this volume began in late 1987, at the suggestion of James L. Watson, then chair of the Joint Committee on Chinese Studies of the American Council of Learned Societies. That committee kindly provided funds for a planning meeting at Harvard University in the spring of 1988, at which Ellen Comisso, Susan Shirk, Theda Skocpol, David Stark, and Iván Szelényi offered valuable advice. All of us at that meeting took for granted that communist regimes were undergoing an irreversible process of political change, although I doubt that any of us sensed that the end in Eastern Europe was so near. Our main concern at that time was to identify the ways in which various economic reforms, concessions to private enterprise, and illegal but tolerated "second economies" were contributing to the process of political change. That has remained the main concern, even though these questions have acquired a more historical flavor in the context of Eastern Europe.

The conference was subsequently funded by a 1990 grant from the Joint Committee on Eastern Europe of the American Council of Learned Societies, and it convened August 25–30, 1992, at Arden Homestead, New York. In addition to the authors of the chapters in this volume, several others presented papers or served as discussants, and I would like to thank them here: John Glenn III (also our rapporteur), Joel Hellman, Kathryn Hendley, Frank Pieke, and Gordon White. I am also grateful to Jason Parker, who supported this project in many ways as the ACLS executive associate responsible for both of the committees that supported this project, and Beata Tikos, who ensured that the meetings at Arden House went off smoothly. Finally, I would like to thank the eight chapter authors, who patiently endured my criticisms and requests through the three rounds of revision that have ended in the essays published here.

Andrew G. Walder
Cambridge, Massachusetts
May 30, 1994

CONTRIBUTORS

David L. Bartlett received his Ph.D. in political science at the University of California, San Diego, and is assistant professor of political science at Vanderbilt University. He has published articles in *East European Politics and Societies* and in other edited volumes. He is currently at work on a book about the political economy of the economic transition in Hungary.

Ole Bruun received his Ph.D. in anthropology at the University of Copenhagen. He is the author of *Business and Bureaucracy in a Chinese City: An Ethnography of Private Business Households in Contemporary China* (Institute for East Asian Studies, University of California, 1993), and is a fellow at the Nordic Institute of Asian Studies in Copenhagen.

Dru Gladney received his Ph.D. in anthropology at the University of Washington, Seattle, and is associate professor of Asian studies at the University of Hawaii at Manoa and research fellow at the East-West Center's Program for Cultural Studies. He is author of *Muslim Chinese: Ethnic Nationalism in the People's Republic* (Harvard, 1991), and of several recent articles in *Journal of Asian Studies*, *Central Asian Survey*, and *International Journal of Middle Eastern Studies*.

Ákos Róna-Tas received his Ph.D. in sociology from the University of Michigan, and is assistant professor of sociology at the University of California, San Diego. His articles have appeared in the *American Journal of Sociology* and *East European Politics and Societies*. He is currently completing a book entitled *The Small Transformation: The Social Origins of the Private Sector in Hungary*.

Anna Seleny received her Ph.D. in political science from the Massachusetts Institute of Technology, and is assistant professor of politics at Princeton University. Her dissertation is about the political economy of property rights in Eastern Europe, especially Hungary, and she is currently writing in a comparative vein about the political legacies of state-socialist institutions in the Czech Republic, Hungary, Poland, and Slovakia. Her articles have appeared in *East European Politics and Societies* and *Law and Policy.*

Andrew G. Walder received his Ph.D. from the University of Michigan and is professor of sociology at Harvard University, having previously taught at Columbia. He is the author of *Communist Neo-Traditionalism; Work and Au thority in Chinese Industry* (California, 1986), and of recent articles in the *American Sociological Review Theory and Society, Rationality and Society,* and other journals.

Shaoguang Wang received his Ph.D. in government from Cornell University. He is assistant professor of political science at Yale, author of *Failure of Charisma: The Chinese Cultural Revolution in Wuhan* (Oxford, 1995), and the co-author of *A Report on the Capacity of Chinese Government* (Oxford, 1994).

David L. Wank received his Ph.D. in sociology from Harvard University. He is currently assistant professor in the Faculty of Comparative Culture, Sophia University, Tokyo. His chapter in this volume draws on his dissertation, "From State Socialism to Community Capitalism: State Power, Social Structure, and Private Enterprise in a Chinese City," and he continues to work on this subject and on the revival of Buddhism in urban China.

Yun-xiang Yan received his Ph.D. in anthropology from Harvard University, and is assistant professor of anthropology at the Johns Hopkins University. He is the author of *The Flow of Gifts: Reciprocity and Social Networks in a Chinese Village* (Stanford, 1995).

ONE

The Quiet Revolution from Within: Economic Reform as a Source of Political Decline

Andrew G. Walder

Leninist party organization and the command economy have been the two pillars of communist rule through much of this century. Although modified in the histories of regimes as disparate as those of Prague and Pyongyang, Budapest and Beijing, these two institutions nonetheless came to define, more clearly than anything else, precisely what set communist regimes apart from other modern forms of authoritarian rule. The party organization, with its hierarchy of status and command, its demands for loyalty and discipline among members, its commanding presence in workplaces and institutions of higher education, and its legendary hostility to alternative forms of political expression and activity, served for decades to weave together these polities. The command economy, at the same time, gave these parties effective control of most, if not all, significant productive assets — most important, over the right to decide how to use these assets and how income from them was to be allocated. Ruling parties turned their asset ownership to political ends when they fashioned a distinctive system of material privilege according to political rank, and of career rewards for political loyalty. By providing resources for fostering discipline and loyalty within the party organization, the command economy therefore served as the economic foundation for party rule. Departures from the practices of the command economy, by altering control over property and opportunity, brought political change in their wake. This book is a collective effort to identify those changes and to clarify why and how they occur.

Our subject is but one piece of the larger historical puzzle of the decline

I am grateful to David Bartlett, Daniel Chirot, Anna Seleny, Jon Unger, David Wank, and Yunxiang Yan for providing me with critiques of earlier drafts, and to audiences who endured various oral presentations of these arguments at the University of Copenhagen; Harvard University; the University of California, Los Angeles; and Texas A&M University. —AGW.

and fall of communist regimes. It has often been noted that the process of decline and transformation has not been the same everywhere; indeed, some argue that in no two places has it been the same (e.g., Bruszt and Stark 1992). One evident difference among regimes is in the pace and extent of change in the two institutions that I have just called the pillars of communist rule. Some regimes experienced more striking changes earlier in political, rather than economic, institutions. The Polish United Workers' party lost its political monopoly in 1980 and suffered a dramatic drop in membership in the wake of Solidarity — something from which it never recovered. Under Gorbachev's glasnost and rising challenges from the republics, the communist party of the Soviet Union rapidly lost its internal discipline and cohesion in the late 1980s. In both countries the rapid deterioration of the party's internal cohesion served more quickly to accelerate the deterioration of the command economy.

In other countries, however, relatively far-reaching reforms of the command economy, coupled with significant concessions to enterprise outside of its boundaries, proceeded long before such deterioration of the party organization. Hungary under János Kádár and China under Deng Xiaoping are well-documented examples of the latter pattern. Reforms of the system of central planning, accompanied by escalating concessions to a second economy and private enterprise, led eventually in Hungary to a negotiated transition to multiparty democracy, one already under way well before ruling parties in Berlin, Prague, Sofia, and Bucharest collapsed in such spectacular fashion in late 1989. In China, more far-reaching and sustained economic reforms have led to an equally striking process of political decline, of which the massive wave of street protests in 1989, the largest independent challenge in the regime's history, were but one symptom.

The latter historical pattern, in which changes in economic institutions bring forth a steady political decline, is the subject of this book. It is not our purpose simply to point out the importance of economic variables in bringing about the transformation of communist regimes. Few will dispute the fact that the political changes of recent years are rooted in the long-term failure of Soviet-style economic institutions. Several impressive analyses of the flaws of these economic institutions are already in print (Kornai 1992; Nove 1983; Murrell and Olson 1991; Kaminski 1991), and more are no doubt on the way. Nor is our purpose to explain *why* leaders in some communist regimes chose to reform their public enterprises and give concessions to private economic activity, while others temporized, resisted, or turned instead to political reform (see, e.g., Shirk 1993). Our piece of the puzzle is a different one: once a communist regime chooses the path of reform and concessions as a response to declining economic performance, what have been the political consequences? What political changes are attributable to change in economic organization, and what *processes* bring them about?

These questions are more easily stated than answered, because they require a sharper definition of the process of change, and impose a heavier burden of evidence about the actual workings of economic and political institutions, than many purported explanations of the decline of communism. It is relatively easy, especially in retrospect, to identify obvious macrohistorical trends that have been connected with this decline: global military and economic competition, the rigidities and inefficiencies of central planning, declining consumer living standards, a decline in the legitimacy of the party and its ideology, and the gradual emergence of oppositional move ments. It is not so very obvious, however, how (or whether) economic diffi culties weaken party cohesion, or how oppositional movements are finally able to establish themselves, and it is not easy to specify and document (as opposed to assuming or asserting) the processes whereby such changes occur. The task is made more complicated by the possibility that different processes may lead to the same outcome: the ruling party may lose its internal discipline and cohesion under the pressures of sustained and well-organized opposition (e.g., in Poland); in the face of large, but relatively unorganized, street demonstrations of limited duration (e.g., in East Germany, Czechoslovakia, and Romania); or in the relative absence of both kinds of opposition (e.g., in Hungary and the Soviet Union). To complicate matters still further, the decline of some regimes may be attributed to the *failure* to implement long-needed economic reforms (e.g., in the Soviet Union), while in others political decline may be an unexpected *result* of economic reform (e.g., in China and Hungary).

Regime changes of such historic proportions take place through a wide variety of interconnected processes, and one must make a choice at the outset that simplifies the problem and clarifies the process of interest. Such a choice inevitably narrows one's vision, but we hope it may afford us a more thorough understanding of one of the several processes thought to be at work. The choice made in this volume can be stated simply. It starts with the observation that *all* communist regimes have departed in some way from the defining features of central planning in an effort to compensate for shortcomings in the performance of these institutions. Whether such departures are planned or unplanned, the result of elite or popular initiatives, they are of equal interest. This volume's premise is that such departures set in motion a chain of consequences, usually unintended, and if the departures are extensive enough, they eventually alter political institutions and relationships to the point where Communist party rule can no longer be sustained.

In defining the problem in this fashion, we designate departures from central planning as a historical "master process" analogous to the ones Charles Tilly (1984, 1992) has identified for the rise of the modern state in Europe. We are by no means the first to point to the transformative potential of departures from central planning; this has long been a distinguishing feature of social-science scholarship on Hungary, and it has more recently become common in research on China. In many ways this volume was inspired by, and is the successor to, an earlier volume edited by Victor Nee and David Stark (see Stark and Nee 1989), also about China and Hungary, which called explicit attention to the broader political implications of often-obscure changes in the economic institutions of these regimes.

To agree that economic reform leads to political change is not necessarily to agree about *how* it does so. This book extends this tradition of scholarship while departing from its past emphases. Earlier research has worked primarily with an implicit model that posits a subterranean conflict between state and society. Research on economic institutions (and on political dissent) has sought to discover how citizens obtain greater autonomy through hidden acts of resistance and push back the boundaries, and the power, of the party state. While this depiction of change is certainly reflected in some of the papers collected here — especially in Yun-xiang Yan's portrayal of the decline of dictatorial cadre rule in a Chinese village and in Dru Gladney's study of the rise of ethnic identity and assertiveness among Chinese Muslims — our research also emphasizes a different process and a different set of causes. Instead of the relationship between state and society, and the oft-noted contest between the two, this book highlights changes wrought within political institutions themselves without the agency of citizen resistance: changes in the relationship of higher to lower levels of government, in the relations between superior and subordinate within the party and government, and in the interests and orientations of officials within the party-state apparatus, especially in its lower reaches. In the cases of China and Hungary, we find these to be the primary causes of the decline of the party state, a decline that is itself a precondition of citizen resistance so widely heralded in other writings.

Our analysis also differs from the tradition of policy-oriented studies of socialist economic reform: we argue that political decline occurs independently of the relative *success* of reform or of reigning macroeconomic trends. As David Bartlett's chapter emphasizes, and as the other chapters on Hungary make clear, the 1980s there were a period of economic recession, falling real incomes, growing foreign debt, and retrenchment in government spending, and the party declined there in part because of its narrowing economic and political options. As the chapters on China make clear, however, the period after 1980 has been one of extraordinary economic growth, rising incomes, and the opening of new opportunities in the foreign and private sectors. Despite a strikingly different economic environment, China's party-state organizations have nonetheless experienced changes that parallel, and in many ways go much further than, those observed during the last decade of communist rule in Hungary. Our analysis of regime change does not therefore center on trends in economic growth and income, or on levels of satisfaction among citizens, although we recognize that these may be important factors. The political consequences that we emphasize flow directly from innovations in economic institutions, regardless of their success or failure in stimulating the economy.

We therefore substitute a more organizational and regime-centered focus for the prevalent concern with state-society relations. Communist regimes have owed their existence to the discipline and cohesion of the party apparatus and to that apparatus's ability to avert organized political opposition. If we can uncover the processes that weaken the discipline and cohesion of the party-state apparatus, we shall have illuminated one of the main causes of the decline of communist rule, and perhaps also have helped to explain the rise of citizen resistance and changes in state-society relations.

Each of the chapters in this book examines the ways in which a certain kind of departure from central planning reallocates resources and opportunities and ushers in a process of political change. The chapters are grouped into four parts, each of which highlights a different dimension of the process of change. Part 1 is about the process of political decline, and contains two retrospective interpretations of the decline of party rule in Hungary. Anna Seleny portrays a political system that was evolving from its very inception. She emphasizes the ways in which the second economy and then economic reform, by subtly altering the property rights on which the regime was founded, led to a reallocation of political rights and capacities, as well as to progressive changes in political discourse and political mentalities within the party elite. Ákos Róna-Tas examines the ways in which the Hungarian party's progressive concessions to the second economy irreversibly eroded the party's internal cohesion and commitment to a planned economy, as the party itself came to depend upon the new sources of income generated and lost the political will to return to the status quo ante, even as its regime deteriorated visibly.

Part 2 examines the eclipse of the party center and of the central state. Shaoguang Wang documents the massive transfer of fiscal resources from the center to the regions brought about by tax reforms, which many have argued are an important cause of China's recent economic dynamism (Oi 1992, 1996). He argues carefully that this shift in fiscal resources is a good measure of the declining capacity of China's central state, and attributes a number of other symptoms of political decline to this redistribution of resources. David Bartlett's chapter illustrates the decline of the center from another angle; he shows how enterprise reform and fiscal liberalization led in an unintended way to the center's loss of political initiative. These reforms activated party-state organizations at lower levels of the hierarchy — especially state enterprises and the official trade unions — endowed them with greater political leverage, and, in the context of economic retrenchment, led to an intensified pattern of bargaining, in which the center came increasingly to react to initiatives from below instead of setting the political agenda. Bartlett portrays the decline of the party center and the rise of its former subordinate organizations as influential political actors.

Part 3 documents the ways in which the growth of a lucrative private sector in urban China transformed the local party state. David Wank shows how municipal party officials and the larger private businessmen in the coastal port of Xiamen have forged new alliances and cooperative partnerships that have drastically altered the interests, incomes, and political networks of party officials. Ole Bruun examines a parallel process on a smaller scale in one neighborhood in Chengdu, a large city in China's interior. Bruun shows the ways in which petty local tradesmen and shopkeepers have become tightly integrated into the local political hierarchy, while at the same time transforming it.

Part 4, finally, documents changes in the exercise of power and in group identity at the grass roots. Yun-xiang Yan argues that the shift from collective to household agriculture altered past patterns of peasant dependence within his north China village and have made village officials more dependent upon independent family farmers for their incomes. This, in turn, has led subtly to fundamental changes in local political mentalities and in the ways political power is exercised. Finally, Dru Gladney's essay analyzes the ways in which concessions to private enterprise, in the context of a still-traditional Stalinist nationalities policy, stimulated economic prosperity, while at the same time reinforcing long-submerged ethnic identities among Muslim communities on China's southeastern coast. Gladney portrays the rise of an increasingly self-conscious and prosperous ethnic community, along with a remarkably open and assertive new form of ethnic politics engaged in by the local officials who represent these communities in bargaining with higher levels of government.

Together, the essays in this volume suggest a more regime-centered organizational perspective on the processes of political change. Where past work on state-society relations has elaborated the gradual empowerment of citizens so well captured by Iván Szelényi's (1988) arresting phrase "the quiet revolution from below," our focus on the organization of political power leads us to emphasize a contemporaneous "quiet revolution from within." The purpose of this essay is to sketch the outlines of this broader perspective and to highlight its distinctive emphases.

THE COMMAND ECONOMY AND PARTY POWER:
THE PROBLEM DEFINED

Writers from Leon Trotsky ([1937] 1972) and Bruno Rizzi ([1939] 1985) through Milovan Djilas (1957) and Iván Szelényi (1978) have argued that a ruling Communist party's power and authority—along with the privilege enjoyed by its members—are founded upon de facto party ownership of productive assets, and an organized monopoly over the allocation of goods and career opportunities. While these writers have emphasized the ways in which political control over economic assets breeds a ruling class with interests in the perpetuation of bureaucratic power, others stress the ways in which this conjunction of political and economic power serves to organize the political order. According to this view, party authority is founded upon a citizen dependence upon officials for the satisfaction of material needs, and for access to career opportunities (Oi 1985, 1989a; Walder 1983, 1986). Such dependence is high when party officials are able to satisfy these needs and when citizens have no alternative sources of need satisfaction. It is decreased when the abilities of officials to reward subordinates declines, when alternative sources of need satisfaction are made available to citizens, or when superiors become newly dependent upon subordinates for the satisfaction of *their* needs.[1]

Despite the emphases of past work, it is not solely the dependence of citizens upon party officials in places of work and education that has promoted political order. Communist parties historically have developed elaborate monitoring practices at the grass roots to observe, report, and record citizen behavior and utterances, and have used such information systematically in allocating rewards and career opportunities. The placement of party organizations in all work, government, and educational institutions, and the placement of party members and activists in all work groups and classrooms reinforced such monitoring capacity. The maintenance of elaborate political records on all citizens, and their systematic use in reward decisions, made this information politically effective. A decline in the capacity to monitor citizen behavior and link it to material rewards and sanctions is a second possible source of institutional weakening.

Note, however, that the capacity of a party state to monitor citizens depends crucially upon the internal discipline and cohesion of party-state organizations. The agents of the party center must be induced to carry out the tasks given them by their superiors, and this is also a question of incentives and dependence. One cannot simply assume a disciplined and cohesive party-state apparatus, just as one cannot simply assume a compliant citizenry. Discipline and compliance, where they occur, must be explained. To the extent that party officials and their agents are dependent upon their

1. It should be evident that these arguments are founded in power-dependence or exchange theory (Blau 1964; Emerson 1962; Stinchcombe 1965), and in recent compatible extensions to organized groups (Hechter 1987), but there is no need to rehearse these theories here.

superiors for the satisfaction of needs, and to the extent that their superiors are able to satisfy their needs, incentives will be viable and discipline high. To the extent that party officials and their agents develop alternative sources of need satisfaction to those previously monopolized by their superiors, and to the extent that the capacity of their superiors to provide for these needs is diminished, discipline within the party apparatus declines, and officials in the lower reaches of the party state are no longer the obedient agents they were in years past.

Departures from central planning have political consequences in both these ways. First, they might interrupt the rewards and career paths formerly controlled by superiors within the party-state, or they shift the balance of dependence more in favor of subordinates within the apparatus. Second, they weaken both the incentive and the capacity of local officials to monitor and sanction citizen behavior. Explanations for political decline should therefore begin by examining the processes whereby the party's monopoly of income and opportunity is diminished by the growth of alternatives (or whereby superiors come to depend more on their subordinates than before), and the processes whereby local authorities have a diminished capacity or incentive to monitor and sanction the behavior of citizens. Note that these questions, ostensibly about the capacity of party-state institutions to maintain political order, are *simultaneously* questions about political change, whether that is conceived of as a deterioration of political hierarchies or as the emergence of conditions that facilitate effective protest and opposition.

DEPARTURES FROM CENTRAL PLANNING AS A SOURCE OF POLITICAL DECLINE

Departures from central planning take place either by design, as part of an official program of economic reform, or by evolution, as countless individuals and institutions adopt strategies to satisfy their needs in ways that are not possible within the confines of the command economy. While departures from central planning in postcommunist regimes are intended in large measure to dismantle the bases of the party's power and privilege, the effects of such departures under party rule are usually unintended, albeit no less significant.

The Growth of Economic Alternatives

The first type of departure serves to create a sphere of economic activity and sources of need satisfaction separate from those under the control of party officials. One well-known instance of this is the gradual evolution, through a series of popular initiatives and tacit official concessions, of a sphere of activity referred to variously as a "second economy," "informal sector," "black markets," or "moonlighting." Eastern Europe's "second economy" — primarily in agriculture, services, construction, repair, and commerce — has received considerable scholarly attention, and it is thought to have accounted for a large proportion of citizen income in Hungary and other countries (Kemény 1982; Gábor 1979; Feldbrugge 1984; Grossman 1977).[2]

A second type emerges when tacit official tolerance becomes explicit and legal, either through somewhat begrudging legal acceptance of "private plots," as in the former Soviet Union, or when the regime not only legalizes but encourages such independent initiatives in an effort to stimulate incomes and growth, as in China and Hungary in the late 1970s and early 1980s. The distinctive feature of these activities is that they are formally separate from public enterprise (although often interdependent with it) and are organized by households or partnerships. Well-documented examples include the rural "household" (China) or "cooperative" (Hungary) sector of family-owned service, transportation, manufacturing, and agricultural sideline enterprise (Szelényi 1988; Nee 1989a; Oi 1989a; Zweig 1986), the sale or rental of public enterprise to private entrepreneurs in China, enterprise work partnerships in Hungary (Stark 1989), household in place of collective farming in rural China and Poland, and the legalized urban private service, commercial, and manufacturing (sometimes called "cooperative") sectors of Hungary (Rupp 1983), China (Gold 1989; Wank 1993), Poland (Åslund 1984; Rostowski 1989) and the former Soviet Union (Åslund 1991), mostly in the 1980s. Such alternative forms of economic enterprise are the primary focus of the chapters by Róna-Tas, Wank, Bruun, and Yan.

A third instance is the opening up of national borders to foreign trade and investment, through the creation of alternative sources of investment capital, bank credit, or channels for sales and supply (and thereby of income). This opening can take place in a relatively centralized fashion, with national monopolies under the direction of central planners standing between enterprises and the outside world (e.g., in Poland in the 1970s). Its political impact will, however, be greater to the extent that these alternatives are directly available to localities, enterprises, and households without medi-

2. This is perhaps the area where departures from central planning were most pronounced in the former Soviet Union and other regimes in which reform programs and legal concessions to private enterprise were limited. It is well known that such departures, usually discussed under the rubric of corruption, were very widespread in the late Brezhnev era. In some regions of the USSR, such as Georgia, corruption connected to black market activity thoroughly penetrated party structures. These "departures from central planning" are conceptually not fundamentally different from the ways in which party officials in China and Hungary profit from ties to legal private firms, and it follows that we should observe a similar pattern of political decline in places where such corruption was most widespread.

ation by planning agencies. Such alternatives became most widespread in China after the mid 1980s, with the emergence of a distinct joint-venture and foreign-enterprise sector, often but not always set in local "special economic zones." These alternatives, especially along the eastern coast, have penetrated deeply into urban and rural economies, and have created lucrative new sources of income for both public and private enterprises, and important new sources of investment capital (Chan, Madsen, and Unger 1992; Pearson 1991, 1992; Zweig 1991). This kind of departure from central planning is featured prominently in Gladney's chapter, which discusses investment by and trade with Arab nations, and Bartlett's chapter, which shows how the Hungarian central government found itself increasingly constrained by a growing dependence on foreign investment and credit.

Enterprise Reform in the Public Sector

Departures of this type were once almost synonymous with "reform" in a state-socialist economy. They were fitfully discussed, debated, and implemented in a piecemeal fashion in almost all communist countries, beginning in the Eastern Bloc during the 1950s. In two countries — Hungary after 1968 and China after 1978 — they were implemented to a significant degree over a sustained period, resulting in marked changes in economic institutions.

"Enterprise reform" is intended to change the mechanisms of the centrally planned economy, and through this change the environment of the enterprise and the decision-making behavior of managers. Overall, it consists of four separate kinds of reform; in practice, the mix and extent of each kind of reform varies considerably in each nation's experience. The first is commercial reform: an end to or sharp reduction in the purchasing monopoly of state commercial and planning agencies, and a reduction of guaranteed sales and supplies; the introduction thereby of sales competition through variety and quality of product; and the increasing determination of production decisions by the demand of enterprises and individuals. The second is price reform: a shift from prices set and readjusted by planning agencies to variable prices determined autonomously by buyer and seller. The third is financial reform: an end to state appropriation of enterprise surpluses in favor of annual revenue contracts or altered systems of taxation that allow enterprises to retain increasing amounts of their surpluses. Enterprises' retained revenues are to rise with profitability and in theory may vary widely. Accordingly, working and investment capital are allocated, not through budgetary grants, but through bank loans to be repaid with interest. The fourth is wage reform: more flexibility in enterprise wage bills; greater wage variation in response to enterprise and individual productivity; reduced employment and welfare guarantees and tightened labor discipline.

These reforms have been analyzed extensively, but almost exclusively from a policy perspective: in what ways does implementation fall short of the general principles of reform (it always does); what kinds of organizational interests and systemic inertia cause implementation to fall short; have the changes implemented achieved their intended effects on productivity; and if not, why not? Perhaps because political change is seen to flow largely from the first type of departure, this type of reform has not usually been examined for its political consequences. It figures prominently, however, in the chapters by Szelény and Bartlett.

Changes in Revenue Flows: Fiscal Reform

A third type of departure from central planning is in the way that revenues extracted from enterprises are distributed among levels of government. In the traditional command economy, revenues extracted from enterprises flow into government coffers, and those revenues are divided among levels of government agencies in an annual process of budgetary bargaining. Just as the financial reform of enterprises seeks to provide an enterprise with an incentive to earn higher profits by guaranteeing it rights to larger shares of increased profit, fiscal reform is designed to give local governments both the incentive and the means to increase their revenue base by guaranteeing them rights to larger shares of increased revenues.

China's fiscal system, for example, has moved from internal transfers of profits and tax payments to new kinds of negotiated tax "responsibility contracts," thereby strengthening the rights of localities to income from their assets, by limiting their revenue obligations to higher levels of government. In many areas of the country, tax responsibility contracts have been extended down to the level of the township (a level between the county and the village). Responsibility for collecting taxes is delegated to the government jurisdiction (which has also earned new rights to add additional local taxes and levies of its own), and the jurisdiction is obligated to turn over a quota of tax revenues to the level of government above it. Revenues collected above that target level are shared according to a variety of formulae, and in extreme cases they are kept entirely by the jurisdiction that collects them. In the same way that household contracting in agriculture reassigns rights to income from assets downward to the peasant family, tax quota contracting reassigns rights to income from assets downward to local governments (Oi 1992, 1996). As enterprises held by lower-level government jurisdictions expand rapidly and compete with older state enterprises for earnings, tax revenues shift further toward the localities (Naughton 1992). A rapid redrawing of fiscal arrangements between the Soviet center and various constituent republics was a key process in the unraveling of the Soviet political order in the late 1980s (Ellman and Kontorovich 1992). The chapter by Wang analyzes the more gradual, yet nonetheless considerable, impact of fiscal reform upon the integrity of the Chinese state, especially the power of the center over the regions and localities.

THE QUIET REVOLUTION FROM WITHIN: WEAKENING THE CENTRALIZED PARTY STATE

Party-state hierarchies in communist regimes were long distinguished by the dependence of officials upon their superiors, and of lower levels of government upon higher levels. Officials' living standards were specified by rank according to *nomenklatura* standards: salary, mode of transportation, housing conditions, and consumption patterns were all closely tied to rank. Appointments and career advancement were screened carefully by officials at the next-higher level in the hierarchy (Walder 1995). Political surveillance and loyalty screening affected officials more acutely than ordinary citizens; the mass campaign and purge served to reinforce this political dependence by eliminating suspected deviants in highly public ways. Official advancement depended upon fidelity and conformity in carrying out the party's political line. It was precisely this structure of dependence and incentive that made possible some of the greatest disasters of communism — for example, the false reporting of output and overprocurement of grain that created the massive famines of 1929–33 in the Soviet Union (Conquest 1986) and of 1959–61 in China (Bernstein 1984), or the escalating search for and elimination of class enemies (Conquest 1990; Medvedev 1989). These and other disasters of communist rule were essentially phenomena of bureaucratic conformity, and in some cases *overconformity*.

It has long been noted that after the initial phase of communist rule, purges and their associated uncertainties declined, and relations among officials evolved into a more secure period of stable bureaucratic administration (Kassof 1964; Lowenthal 1970; Dallin and Breslauer 1970; Hankiss 1990). While this reduced the insecurities that had led to rigid conformity in the past, it did not change the characteristic dependence of officials upon their superiors for resources, evaluation, and career advancement. Departures from central planning served to alter these patterns of dependence in three distinct ways, and in so doing ensured not merely an end to overconforming bureaucratic responses, but increasing difficulty by the center in controlling the behavior of its presumed agents in localities.

The first change is in the creation of *firmer rights of local governments* over their productive enterprises, especially with regard to their operation and the income to be derived from them. This has served to reduce local governmental dependence upon bureaucratic superiors for government revenue and investment funds, as the chapters by Wang, Bartlett, and Gladney illustrate. In years past, assets developed by local authorities were subject to arbitrary expropriation by higher levels of government — that is, an arrogation of control rights and income rights by the higher level of government (Zweig 1989). In China, the end of these arbitrary seizures of revenue and income-bearing property was accompanied by a more careful specification of the local versus the state share of revenues collected from local enterprises. These rights, in turn, gave rise to new monitoring and information problems, as local officials were both agents of higher levels of government and beneficiaries of increased local revenues. One symptom of these monitoring problems is the rapid growth of extrabudgetary funds — revenues collected from enterprises but not calculated into the revenue base of local government budgets that is the basis for dividing revenues between the locality and the state, a phenomenon that Wang appropriately terms a "second budget."

The second change — related but not identical to the first — is the creation of *new sources of revenue* that do not depend upon the largesse or permission of superiors. For local governments, these are to be found not only in the new rights to revenue from public enterprises, but also in the lucrative new sources of revenue to be derived from a rapidly growing private, foreign, or joint-venture sector, or from foreign investment and trade. One important manifestation of this is in the use of such public property as land, buildings, or equipment by state organizations for enterprises outside of the plan. Another is found in the selling of "political insurance" to private firms, whereby they are registered as "collective" in return for larger payments to public coffers (Liu 1992). For managers of public enterprises, such sources of revenue are to be found in the opening of "branch" or "collective" enterprises wholly owned by the public firm, by establishing joint ventures, or by increasingly lucrative dealings "outside the plan," either in products or in materials. One of the messages of Gladney's chapter is that the leaders of Muslim communities have excelled in the exploitation of such independent opportunities in China.

A third change is in the creation of *new sources of personal income,* whether officially designated "corruption" or not. This is a central theme in Róna-Tas's analysis of the politically corrosive impact of the second economy in Hungary. We also observe this in the public officials who are made salaried partners of firms without making investments (Wank's chapter), in the large salaries earned by rural officials who head village "corporations" (Oi 1986, 1989a), in the officials who open their own businesses as "cadre entrepreneurs" (Nee 1991; Szelényi and Manchin 1987), in official predation upon private enterprise for payoffs or favors (Oi 1989b; Zweig 1986), in the rents extracted by public officials for the exercise of their public duties in the realm of licensing and taxation of enterprise (Oi 1989b, Zweig 1986), and in the payoffs received from foreign businesspeople and investors as a fee for official cooperation in facilitating local business operations.

All of these changes serve to open up alternative sources of revenue, income, and career advancement to officials *outside of* the hierarchies of the party and the command economy. As party-state officials are less dependent upon their superiors for revenue, income, and to some extent even career advancement, they become more interested in, and dependent upon, new economic activities emerging locally. Officials gradually become oriented more "downward" and less "upward" than at any time in the past. Success for local officials — whether measured in job performance, budgetary revenues, local economic prosperity, or personal income — is determined increasingly by local activities and opportunities outside the traditional structure and practices of central planning. The greater the departures and alternatives, the greater the change in official orientation, and the weaker the claims and the capacities of higher levels of government.

POLITICAL AUTHORITY IN LOCAL SETTINGS

With the erosion of the mechanisms that once enforced discipline within the centralized party-state apparatus, and the attendant change in the orientations of local officials, the exercise of political authority in local settings changes in profound and complex ways. Increasingly, local political authority is based on control over new kinds of resources, on the forging of new kinds of political loyalties, and on the emergence of new forms of bargaining. Increased demand-making and contestation of authority by citizens is one facet of these changes, but it is hardly the dominant one usually portrayed in writings that chronicle the rise of civil society or the triumph of society over the state.

In recent research, and in the essays collected here, one can discern five separate trends in the exercise of party authority in local settings. The first is the creation of new kinds of alliances, or enhanced mutual dependencies, between officials and entrepreneurs in household or private enterprise (Solinger 1992). This is a social-structural expression of the increased autonomy of local officials from their superiors, and the enhanced orientation of officials toward new local sources of revenue and income. In many ways, as David Wank argues, these ties of patronage and mutual benefit come to supplant the earlier ties between party officials and political activists that characterized these regimes in an earlier period of their evolution. Wank shows how the owners of private businesses in the Chinese coastal city of Xiamen actively build ties with local officials, ties that are cemented by the exchange of protection and advantage for income. Bruun also shows the ways in which petty entrepreneurs and small shopkeepers in one neighborhood in the interior city of Chengdu are closely tied to officials in the neighborhood offices. Both chapters illustrate a phenomenon widely commented upon in writing about a broad variety of settings: the close involvement of local officials in emerging market opportunities (Wong 1987; Oi 1986, 1989a; Nee 1991, 1992; Meaney 1989; Szelényi and Manchin 1987; Odgaard 1992; Solinger 1992; Staniszkis 1991; Humphrey 1991). Whereas past studies have tended to emphasize cadre predation upon successful entrepreneurs, Wank and Bruun show that such ties may also be initiated by entrepreneurs as part of their strategy for success (see also Liu 1992).

A second evident trend is the one toward some version of local "corporatism," in which local governments become intimately involved in coordinating and managing the market-oriented activities of publicly owned assets under their jurisdiction (White 1987; Oi 1986, 1988). Different analysts have stressed different reasons for this development: the incentives provided by redrawn fiscal arrangements (Oi 1992), the continuing regulative powers of local officials over an economy in transition between plan and market (Oi 1986, 1990; Nee 1989a, 1989b, 1992), or the continued control of government agencies over the supply of materials in a situation of continuing scarcity (Burawoy and Krotov 1992; Oi 1989a). All of these studies point to the consolidation of local or regional industrial empires based on public ownership and management, or some residual thereof.

A third trend is the emergence of new forms of bargaining around the enforcement of authority relationships. Within public institutions, this is seen in new patterns of "hidden bargaining" between managers and workers over questions of work and pay (Kövari and Sziráczki 1985; Sabel and Stark 1982; Stark 1985; Burawoy and Lukács 1992; Walder 1987, 1989); in relations between officials and citizens, it is seen in the complex tacit negotiations employed in dealings between local officials and private entrepreneurs over the enforcement of, and compliance with, tax and other regulations (as seen in the chapters by Wank and Bruun). These changes are often subtle and are not always clearly visible; Yan's chapter illustrates the quietly profound ways in which the shift from collective to household agriculture has reduced the power of Chinese village officials and altered the practice of local government.

A fourth trend is the emergence of new forms of collective protest and the creation of new kinds of collective group identities and antagonisms (Connor 1991; Perry 1985; Nee 1989a; Stark 1989; Walder 1991). Gladney's chapter on the intensification of Muslim identity in China is an extended illustration of the ways in which departures from central planning may promote long-suppressed ethnic identities in communist and postcommunist regimes. There is an extensive and influential literature, written from the perspective of state-society relations, and sometimes framed as a "rise of civil society" or some partial approximation thereof, that charts the emergence of citizen autonomy, public dialogue, and protest and opposition in communist regimes (Arato 1981; Frentzel-Zagorska 1990; Kennedy 1990; Ost 1990; Brødsgaard 1992; Ostergaard 1989; Sullivan 1990; Strand

1990; Brovkin 1990; Mastnak 1990; Friedgut and Siegelbaum 1990; Walder
and Gong 1993; Wank 1995).

A fifth trend is the emergence of organized vessels for the expression of
group interests — for example, the formation of new kinds of trade associations (White 1993; Pearson 1994) or the rising role of organized religion in
the community life of private entrepreneurs (Wank 1993). The private entrepreneurs' association analyzed in Bruun's chapter and the revived and
newly prosperous mosques analyzed in Gladney's might be considered manifestations of this nascent trend, although one might dispute the extent to
which, or the success with which, these organizations further group interests.

In light of the consistent emphasis in recent research upon the growing
empowerment of society vis-à-vis the state, there are two striking things about
these trends. The first is that — a structural description of local political
change, only the last two trends — the rise of new group identities and the
formation of independent organizations — are the concern of work in the
"civil society" or "public sphere" genre, while the third — the rise of bargaining in the exercise of authority — might arguably be interpreted as a shift in
power toward "society." Furthermore, the last two trends are rarely clear-cut:
the evidence for them is often disputed, leading to common debates about
whether civil society has emerged, is emerging, or might emerge, and usually
concluding with the claim that these are the seeds of future developments.

On the other hand, evidence for the first two trends — the growth of extensive ties between local officials and private entrepreneurs, and the deep
involvement of local officials in managing market-oriented enterprises — is
pervasive. These are not typically described as nascent trends, and debate
about them has centered not on their existence but on whether such phenomena will disappear as market allocation becomes more pervasive (e.g.,
Nee 1989b, 1991; Oi 1990; Stark 1990, 1992). These trends also fit poorly
with the structural image of a "society" detaching itself from, and gaining
greater autonomy and power vis-à-vis the "state." Instead, a different image
is appropriate: that of the lower reaches of a state structure gaining increased autonomy from higher reaches and forging new kinds of political
and economic ties with individuals and enterprises outside.

The second striking thing about these trends is that the process of political decline they represent cannot be understood without an appreciation of
the changing interests, orientations, and capacities of party-state officials.
Who are the political actors responsible for the decline of the centralized party-state? The pronounced past emphasis upon ordinary citizens as
agents of change who struggle with a recalcitrant state has tended to ob-
scure the crucial role played by party-state officials in the decline of the very
institutions with which they are so intimately identified. When party officials
seek new sources of income in private enterprise or build alliances with

entrepreneurs in the private economy, they act in a self-interested and "non-political" fashion, but the aggregate political consequences of these individual actions can be very large. Officials who pursue individual interests in this fashion do not need to act in a concerted fashion for their activities to have a large impact. Indeed, the processes of change emphasized in this volume underline the fact that large systemic changes can occur without the agency of citizen resistance, whether organized or not.

THE SELF-REINFORCING CHARACTER OF POLITICAL DECLINE

The process of political decline set in motion by departures from central planning is to a considerable degree self-reinforcing. As departures from central planning proceed, the costs of reversing them rise, and the party's political will, as well as organized capacity to reverse them, declines. Once these economic changes have proceeded far enough to alter patterns of dependence and sources of income among officials significantly, the costs of reversal become so large that opposition to change by hard-line communists can do little more than slow its pace. There is no feasible road back to the status quo ante, even though the effects of economic change on the political system may be widely evident and openly reviled by hard-line communists. This is true for the following reasons.

First, the new sources of income and revenue detailed earlier create powerful vested interests in the maintenance and expansion of departures from central planning. Peasant households increasingly exercise de facto property rights over land and enterprise; local governments enjoy enhanced revenues; officials gain higher personal incomes from new alternative sources; officials in one area want the expanded foreign trade and investment privileges that other areas have already been granted; the private sector supplies revenues, raises incomes, and solves unemployment problems for local governments. Retrenchment and reconsolidation of the former practices of central planning must confront powerful new vested interests in existing departures—whether from large population groups such as peasants or politically pivotal ones such as local government officials and managers of public enterprise.

Second, even should national officials seek to reverse a course of departures from central planning, they could do so only through the agency of local officials—one of the key groups who have gained the most through such departures. To ask these people to curtail departures from central planning is to ask them to cut their own lucrative sources of government revenue, organizational earnings, and personal income. Therefore in addition to the development of vested interests around these economic departures, the *organized means for the regime to implement a reversal of policy* is itself progressively undermined. What makes these departures so difficult to re-verse is not simply their popularity with citizens, but their popularity with the very agents through whom the party center must enforce its orders (see also Nee and Lian 1994).

These changes do transform—indeed undermine—the institutions upon which communist regimes were founded and long stabilized. Yet this decline in the organizational capacity of a communist regime does not lead ineluctably to any specific political outcome. In Hungary, the end came through a fundamental division within the party leadership, a split, negoti-ated transition to free elections, and electoral defeat of the reform wing of the Hungarian Socialist Workers' party (Bruszt 1990). Yet other outcomes would be equally consistent with this quiet undermining of the traditional institutions of communist rule: a coup or revolution; fragmentation of the polity along regional lines, leading either to a new form of federalism that enshrines increased local autonomy or to national fragmentation and civil war; or gradual evolution into a more fluid and contested form of authori-tarianism, which in the optimistic scenario will gradually evolve into multi-party competition. The processes we have examined here make such politi-cal changes inevitable, but whether these changes will be abrupt or gradual, violent or peaceful, is more heavily influenced by processes that are more historically contingent and short-term than the ones that are the subject of this book.

ANTICIPATIONS OF POSTCOMMUNIST TRANSFORMATIONS

At first glance, the studies collected in this volume might appear to have little direct relevance for the economic and political transformations of the postcommunist era. All of the studies in this volume are preoccupied with the effects of economic change upon communist rule. The collapse of the old regime and the uncertain transition to the new would appear to raise radically new questions and highlight new uncertainties and instabilities. Studies conceived in an effort to understand the evolution and decline of communist regimes might appear to be too focused upon historical issues to be of great relevance in understanding the new.

Such appearances are deceiving. When one takes up new questions about the postcommunist era, one defines the political outcomes differently, but departures from central planning continue to affect the path of political change. If the issue of concern in this volume is the governability of a communist regime, the question today is often how the transition to a mar-ket economy may affect the governability of a *post*communist regime. Set-ting aside for the moment questions about the economic viability of various plans for the transition to a market economy, there remains the question of how specific reallocations of rights to control and derive income from productive assets will affect the distribution of political power and the exercise of political authority, however constituted.

In this newly fluid setting, the now-familiar trends — and the questions we have sought to answer in this volume — reappear in altered form. To what extent do departures from central planning reallocate rights to households and ordinary citizens, affect a downward redistribution of political power, and promote the development of organized parties and political associations, trade unions, and representative democracy? To what extent is this trend offset by the competing development of concentrations of corporate power in the former state enterprises and corporations, or in local alliances between government officials, bankers, and entrepreneurs? It is tempting to assume the latter trends away by reference to a fuller development of a market economy, but we have already seen that party-state officials can adapt quite well to market conditions. The emergence of "civil society" today is still fraught with the same difficulties, and offset by the same competing trends, as those detailed in this volume. The same kinds of alliances between entrepreneurs and officials that lead to the emergence of "cadre entrepreneurs" or "nomenklatura capitalism," and to the consolidation of local concentrations of corporate economic power, have emerged and are widely commented upon, and lamented, in the postcommunist world. In these countries, political debate often centers on how to arrange departures from central planning to prevent these outcomes. In this sense, our analyses of the political consequences of departures from central planning under Communist party rule lead seamlessly to new questions about the construction of a postcommunist order.

REFERENCES

Arato, Andrew. 1981. "Civil Society Against the State: Poland, 1980–81." *Telos* 47 (Spring): 23–47.

Åslund, Anders. 1984. "The Functioning of Private Enterprise in Poland." *Soviet Studies* 36, 3: 427–44.

———. 1991. *Gorbachev's Struggle for Economic Reform: The Soviet Reform Process, 1985–88.* Ithaca, N.Y.: Cornell University Press.

Bernstein, Thomas P. 1984. "Stalinism, Famine, and Chinese Peasants: Grain Procurements During the Great Leap Forward." *Theory and Society* 13 (May): 1–38.

Blau, Peter M. 1964. *Exchange and Power in Social Life.* New York: Wiley.

Brødsgaard, Kjeld Erik. 1992. "Civil Society and Democratization in China." In *From Leninism to Freedom,* ed. Margaret L. Nugent, 231–57. Boulder, Colo.: Westview Press.

Brovkin, Vladimir. 1990. "Revolution from Below: Informal Political Association in Russia, 1988–1989." *Soviet Studies* 42, 2: 233–57.

Bruszt, László. 1990. "1989: The Negotiated Revolution in Hungary." *Social Research* 57, 2: 365–87.

Bruszt, László, and David Stark. 1992. "Remaking the Political Field in Hungary: From the Politics of Confrontation to the Politics of Competition." In *Eastern Europe in Revolution*, ed. Ivo Banac, 15–55. Ithaca, N.Y.: Cornell University Press.

Burawoy, Michael, and Pavel Krotov. 1992. "The Soviet Transition from Socialism to Capitalism: Worker Control and Economic Bargaining in the Wood Industry." *American Sociological Review* 57, 1: 16–38.

Burawoy, Michael, and János Lukács. 1992. *The Radiant Past: Ideology and Reality in Hungary's Road to Capitalism*. Chicago: University of Chicago Press.

Chan, Anita, Richard Madsen, and Jonathan Unger. 1992. *Chen Village under Mao and Deng*. Berkeley and Los Angeles: University of California Press.

Connor, Walter D. 1991. *The Accidental Proletariat: Workers, Politics, and Crisis in Gorbachev's Russia*. Princeton, N.J.: Princeton University Press.

Conquest, Robert, 1986. *Harvest of Sorrow: Soviet Collectivization and the Terror Famine*. New York: Oxford University Press

———. 1990. *The Great Terror: A Reassessment*. New York: Oxford University Press.

Dallin, Alexander, and George W. Breslauer. 1970. "Political Terror in the Post-Mobilization Stage." In *Change in Communist Systems*, ed. Chalmers Johnson, 190–214. Stanford, Calif.: Stanford University Press.

Djilas, Milovan. 1957. *The New Class: An Analysis of the Communist System of Power*. New York: Praeger.

Ellman, Michael, and Vladimir Kontorovich, eds. 1992. *The Disintegration of the Soviet Economic System*. London: Routledge.

Emerson, Richard. 1962. "Power-Dependence Relations." *American Sociological Review* 27, 1: 31–41.

Feldbrugge, F. J. M. 1984. "Government and Shadow Economy in the Soviet Union." *Soviet Studies* 36, 4: 528–43.

Frentzel-Zagorska, Janina. 1990. "Civil Society in Poland and Hungary." *Soviet Studies* 42, 4: 759–77.

Friedgut, Theodore, and Lewis Siegelbaum. 1990. "Perestroika from Below: The Soviet Miners' Strike and Its Aftermath." *New Left Review*, no. 181 (May–June): 5–32.

Gábor, I. R. 1979. "The Second (Secondary) Economy." *Acta Oeconomica* 22, 3–4: 291–311.

Gold, Thomas B. 1989. "Urban Private Business in China." *Studies in Comparative Communism* 22, 2–3: 187–202.

Grossman, Gregory. 1977. "The 'Second Economy' of the USSR." *Problems of Communism* 26, 5: 25–40.

Hankiss, Elemér. 1990. *East European Alternatives*. New York: Oxford University Press.

Hechter, Michael. 1987. *Principles of Group Solidarity*. Berkeley and Los Angeles: University of California Press.

Humphrey, Caroline. 1991. " 'Icebergs,' Barter, and the Mafia in Provincial Russia." *Anthropology Today* 7, 2: 8–13.

Kaminski, Bartłomiej. 1991. *The Collapse of State Socialism: The Case of Poland*. Princeton, N.J.: Princeton University Press.

Kassof, Alex. 1964. "The Administered Society: Totalitarianism Without Terror." *World Politics* 16, 4: 558–75.

Kemény, István. 1982. "The Unregistered Economy in Hungary." *Soviet Studies* 34, 3: 349–66.

Kennedy, Michael D. 1990. "The Constitution of Critical Intellectuals: Polish Physicians, Peace Activists and Democratic Civil Society." *Studies in Comparative Communism* 23, 3–4: 281–303.

Kornai, János. 1992. *The Socialist System: The Political Economy of Communism.* Princeton, N.J.: Princeton University Press.

Kővári, G., and G. Sziráczki. 1985. "Old and New Forms of Wage Bargaining on the Shop Floor." In *Labour Market and Second Economy in Hungary,* ed. Péter Galasi and György Sziráczki 133–78. Frankfurt: Campus.

Liu, Yia-ling. 1992. "Reform from Below: The Private Economy and Local Politics in the Rural Industrialization of Wenzhou." *China Quarterly* 130 (June): 293–316.

Lowenthal, Richard. 1970. "Development vs. Utopia in Communist Policy." In *Change in Communist Systems,* ed. Chalmers Johnson, 33–116. Stanford, Calif.. Stanford University Press.

Mastnak, Tomaż. 1990. "Civil Society in Slovenia: From Opposition to Power." *Studies in Comparative Communism* 23, 3–4: 305–17.

Meaney, Constance Squires. 1989. "Market Reform in a Leninist System: Some Trends in the Distribution of Power, Status, and Money in Urban China." *Studies in Comparative Communism* 22, 2–3: 203–20.

Medvedev, Roy. 1989. *Let History Judge: The Origins and Consequences of Stalinism.* Revised and expanded ed. New York: Columbia University Press.

Murrell, Peter, and Mancur Olson. 1991. "The Devolution of Centrally Planned Economies." *Journal of Comparative Economics* 15, 2: 239–65.

Naughton, Barry. 1992. "Implications of the State Monopoly over Industry and Its Relaxation." *Modern China* 18, 1: 14–41.

Nee, Victor. 1989a. "Peasant Entrepreneurship and the Politics of Regulation in China." In *Remaking the Economic Institutions of Socialism: China and Eastern Europe,* ed. Victor Nee and David Stark, 169–207. Stanford, Calif.: Stanford University Press.

———. 1989b. "A Theory of Market Transition: From Redistribution to Markets in State Socialism." *American Sociological Review* 54, 5: 663–81.

———. 1991. "Social Inequalities in Reforming State Socialism: Between Redistribution and Markets in China." *American Sociological Review* 56, 3: 267–82.

———. 1992. "Organizational Dynamics of Market Transition: Hybrid Forms, Property Rights, and Mixed Economy in China." *Administrative Science Quarterly* 37, 1: 1–27.

Nee, Victor, and Peng Lian. 1994. "Sleeping with the Enemy: A Dynamic Model of Declining Political Commitment in State Socialism." *Theory and Society* 23, 2: 253–96.

Nove, Alec. 1983. *The Economics of Feasible Socialism.* London: George Allen & Unwin.

Odgaard, Ole. 1992. "Entrepreneurs and Elite Formation in Rural China." *Australian Journal of Chinese Affairs* 28 (July): 89–108.

Oi, Jean C. 1985. "Communism and Clientelism: Rural Politics in China." *World Politics* 37, 2: 238–66.

———. 1986. "Commercializing China's Rural Cadres." *Problems of Communism* 36, 5: 1–15.

———. 1988. "The Chinese Village, Inc." In *Chinese Economic Policy,* ed. Bruce Reynolds, 67–87. New York: Paragon House.

———. 1989a. *State and Peasant in Contemporary China: The Political Economy of Village Government*. Berkeley and Los Angeles: University of California Press.

———. 1989b. "Market Reforms and Corruption in Rural China." *Studies in Comparative Communism* 22, 2–3: 221–33.

———. 1990. "The Fate of the Collective after the Commune." In *Chinese Society on the Eve of Tiananmen: The Impact of Reform,* ed. Deborah Davis and Ezra Vogel, 15–36. Harvard Contemporary China Series, no. 7. Cambridge, Mass.: Harvard University Council on East Asian Studies.

———. 1992. "Fiscal Reform and the Economic Foundations of Local State Corporatism in China." *World Politics* 45, 1: 99–126.

———. forthcoming. *Rural China Takes Off: Incentives for Reform.*

Oi, David. 1990. *Solidarity and the Politics of Antipolitics.* Philadelphia: Temple University Press.

Ostergaard, Clemmens Stubbe. 1989. "Citizens, Groups, and a Nascent Civil Society in China. Towards an Understanding of the 1989 Student Demonstrations." *China Information* 4, 2: 28–41.

Pearson, Margaret. 1991. *Joint Ventures in the People's Republic of China*. Princeton, N.J.: Princeton University Press.

———. 1992. "Breaking the Bonds of 'Organized Dependence': Managers in China's Foreign Sector." *Studies in Comparative Communism* 25, 1: 57–77.

———. 1994. "The Janus Face of Business Associations in China: Socialist Corporatism in Foreign Enterprises." *Australian Journal of Chinese Affairs* 31 (January): 25–46.

Perry, Elizabeth. 1985. "Rural Collective Violence: The Fruits of Recent Reforms." In *The Political Economy of Reform in Post-Mao China,* ed. Elizabeth Perry and Christine Wong, 175–92. Harvard Contemporary China Series, no. 2. Cambridge, Mass.: Harvard University Council on East Asian Studies.

Rizzi, Bruno. [1939] 1985. *The Bureaucratization of the World*. Translated by Adam Westoby. New York: Free Press.

Rostowski, Jacek. 1989. "The Decay of Socialism and the Growth of Private Enterprise in Poland." *Soviet Studies* 41, 2: 194–214.

Rupp, Kálmán. 1983. *Entrepreneurs in Red: Structure and Organizational Innovation in the Centrally Planned Economy*. Albany: State University of New York Press.

Sabel, Charles F., and David Stark. 1982. "Planning, Politics, and Shop-Floor Power: Hidden Forms of Bargaining in Soviet-Imposed State-Socialist Societies." *Politics and Society* 11, 4: 439–75.

Shirk, Susan. 1993. *The Political Logic of Economic Reform in China*. Berkeley and Los Angeles: University of California Press.

Solinger, Dorothy. 1992. "Urban Entrepreneurs and the State: The Merger of State and Society." In *State and Society in China: The Consequences of Reform,* ed. Arthur L. Rosenbaum, 121–41. Boulder, Colo.: Westview Press.

Staniszkis, Jadwiga. 1991. "'Political Capitalism' in Poland." *East European Politics and Societies* 5, 1: 127–41.

Stark, David. 1985. "The Micropolitics of the Firm and the Macropolitics of Reform: New Forms of Workplace Bargaining in Hungarian Enterprises." In *States versus Markets in the World System,* ed. Peter Evans, Dietrich Rueschemeyer, and Evelyne Huber Stephens, 247–73. Beverly Hills, Calif.: Sage.

———. 1989. "Coexisting Organizational Forms in Hungary's Emerging Mixed Economy." In *Remaking the Economic Institutions of Socialism,* ed. Victor Nee and David Stark, pp. 137–68. Stanford, Calif.: Stanford University Press.

———. 1990. "Privatization in Hungary: From Plan to Market or From Plan to Clan?" *East European Politics and Societies* 4, 3: 351–92.

———. 1992. "The Great Transformation? Social Change in Eastern Europe." *Contemporary Sociology* 21, 3: 299–304.

Stark, David, and Victor Nee. 1989. "Toward an Institutional Analysis of State Socialism." In *Remaking the Economic Institutions of Socialism: China and Eastern Europe,* ed. Victor Nee and David Stark, 1–91. Stanford, Calif.: Stanford University Press.

Stinchcombe, Arthur. 1965. "Social Structure and Organizations." In *Handbook of Organizations,* ed. James G. March, 142–93. Chicago: Rand McNally.

Strand, David. 1990. "Protest In Beijing: Civil Society and the Public Sphere in China." *Problems of Communism* 39, 3: 1–19.

Sullivan, Larry. 1990. "The Emergence of Civil Society in China, Spring 1989." In *The Chinese People's Movement: Perspectives on Spring 1989,* ed. Tony Saich, 126–44. Armonk, N.Y.: Sharpe.

Szelényi, Iván. 1978. "Social Inequalities under State Socialist Redistributive Economies." *International Journal of Comparative Sociology* 19, 1–2: 63–87.

———. 1988. *Social Entrepreneurs: Embourgeoisement in Rural Hungary.* Madison: University of Wisconsin Press.

Szelényi, Iván, and Robert Manchin. 1987. "Social Policy under State Socialism: Market Redistribution and Social Inequalities in East European Socialist Societies." In *Stagnation and Renewal in Social Policy,* ed. Gøsta Esping-Andersen, Martin Rein, and Lee Rainwater, 102–39. Armonk, N.Y.: Sharpe.

Tilly, Charles. 1984. *Big Structures, Large Processes, Huge Comparisons.* New York: Russell Sage.

———. 1993. *Coercion, Capital, and European States, A.D. 990–1992.* Cambridge, Mass.: Basil Blackwell.

Trotsky, Leon. [1937] 1972. *The Revolution Betrayed: What Is the Soviet Union and Where Is It Going?* New York: Pathfinder.

Walder, Andrew G. 1983. "Organized Dependency and Cultures of Authority in Chinese Industry." *Journal of Asian Studies* 43, 1: 51–76.

———. 1986. *Communist Neo-Traditionalism: Work and Authority in Chinese Industry.* Berkeley and Los Angeles: University of California Press.

———. 1987. "Wage Reform and the Web of Factory Interests." *China Quarterly* 109 (March): 22–41.

———. 1989. "Factory and Manager in an Era of Reform." *China Quarterly* 118 (June): 242–64.

———. 1991. "Workers, Managers, and the State: The Reform Era and the Political Crisis of 1989." *China Quarterly* 127 (September): 467–92.

———. 1995. "Career Mobility and the Communist Political Order." *American Sociological Review* 60, 3, in press.

Walder, Andrew G., and Xiaoxia Gong. 1993. "Workers in the Tiananmen Protests: The Politics of the Beijing Workers' Autonomous Association." *Australian Journal of Chinese Affairs* 29 (January): 1–29.

Wank, David L. 1993. "From State Socialism to Community Capitalism: State Power,

Social Structure, and Private Enterprise in a Chinese City." Ph.D. diss., Department of Sociology, Harvard University.

———. 1995. "Civil Society in Communist China? Private Business and Political Alliance, 1989." In *Civil Society: Theory, History, Comparison,* ed. John A. Hall, 56–79. Cambridge, Eng.: Polity Press.

White, Gordon. 1987. "The Impact of Economic Reforms in the Chinese Countryside: Towards the Politics of Social Capitalism?" *Modern China* 13, 4: 411–40.

———. 1993. "Prospects for Civil Society in China: A Case Study of Xiaoshan City." *Australian Journal of Chinese Affairs* 29 (January): 63–87.

Wong, Christine P. W. 1987. "Between Plan and Market: The Role of the Local Sector in Post-Mao China." *Journal of Comparative Economics* 11, 3: 385–98.

Zweig, David. 1986. "Prosperity and Conflict in Post-Mao Rural China." *China Quarterly* 105 (March). 1–18.

———. 1989. *Agrarian Radicalism in China, 1968–1981.* Cambridge, Mass.: Harvard University Press.

———. 1991. "Internationalizing China's Countryside: The Political Economy of Exports from Rural Industry." *China Quarterly* 128 (December): 716–41.

PART ONE

The Process of Political Decline

TWO

Property Rights and Political Power: The Cumulative Process of Political Change in Hungary

Anna Seleny

East European state socialist systems are said to have collapsed in 1989. The Hungarian case, however, suggests a different formulation.[1] Indeed, as this essay demonstrates, the Hungarian socialist system began transforming itself almost from its inception, and by 1989 was a hybrid produced by forty years of accommodation and compromise among the social, economic, political, and ideological forces it had suppressed or fostered.

Yet even in the late 1980s, most domestic and foreign observers doubted whether this history of compromises, typically expressed as economic reforms, would fundamentally alter Hungarian socialism. In fact, for many, the historical ubiquity of piecemeal reform seemed to confirm the system's essential stability.[2]

In a more basic sense, however, prolonged transformation was ultimately

Thanks are due the following individuals who commented on this essay, or on earlier versions: David Bartlett, Suzanne Berger, Donald Blackmer, Consuelo Cruz, Xueliang Ding, Robert Fishman, István Gábor, Péter Galasi, Atul Kohli, Andrew Koppleman, János Kornai, Mária Kovács, György Kővári, Mihály Laki, Andrei Markovits, Ákos Róna-Tas, Kathleen Thelen, Zoltán Tóth, Andrew Walder, and the participants in the 1992 ACLS-sponsored conference, Political Consequences of Departures from Central Planning, Arden Homestead, New York. The usual disclaimers apply. I am grateful to several institutions whose support made possible the dissertation from which parts of this article are drawn: the American Council of Learned Societies, the Fulbright Commission, Harvard University's Center for European Studies, the International Research and Exchange Commission, the MIT Center for International Studies, and the MacArthur Foundation. — AS.

1. The distinction drawn here between "collapse" and "transformation" is more than semantic. The institutional legacies of formerly socialist systems continue to shape the parameters of possibility today, limiting, for instance, the chances of success of some market initiatives, while creating a more hospitable environment for others. The notion of "collapse," while appealingly clear-cut, is thus misleading.

2. This was true not only of understandably cynical Hungarian citizens, but also of many

startling, because unchanging political structures hid as much as they revealed. Put another way, the Hungarian socialist system, like its Polish and
Chinese counterparts, underwent epochal internal systemic transformation
first and regime change last. In this process, cycles of economic reform both
determined change and obscured it, helping to maintain socialist political
structures even as they altered economic management and, more subtly, the
practice of politics.

This essay examines the internal transformation of Hungarian socialism,
by focusing on the systemic impact of official and unofficial departures from
central planning. It demonstrates that the sociopolitical effects of economic
reforms and informal economic activity were often more profound than any
appreciable economic improvements that flowed from them. Most analysts
agree that efforts aimed at the improved efficiency of the classical model or
the attainment of some ideal mix of plan and market failed to render socialist economies competitive. While this consensus is compelling, it tends to ignore the broader political impact of economic reforms, and is itself one reason why the complex process of socialist transformation remains so poorly
understood.

The following analysis therefore explores some of the ways in which economic reforms and informal economic activity altered the implicit and
explicit rights of the social groups that comprised the socialist system. I
advance two general claims about Hungary, one of the countries where
economic experimentation and reform under socialism went farthest. The
first is that even when accurately assessed as relatively ineffective, economic
reforms (and other departures from central planning) led to a redistribution of control over economic activities. They invariably resulted in redefined rights of particular groups to command obedience or resources as
an expression of their positions in the socialist economy; and eventually
opened up the possibility of the renegotiation of the basic assumptions of
socialist ownership and control. The essay demonstrates, for instance, how
informal relations of production fundamentally altered power relations between the larger population and the party state. It was in part these changed
relations that led the Hungarian Socialist Workers' party to accept a significant reform of property rights by 1982. The party was also forced to make
important concessions to autonomous economic actors thereafter, culmi-
nating in the new Association Law of 1989.

Reformers and second-economy participants had established less dramatic precedents long before, however. As we shall see, this extended process involved the de facto diffusion of property rights previously controlled

observers and analysts, who, as Andrew Walder 1990 has pointed out, now see these same
factors as having contributed to the transformation of socialist systems.

by state bureaucracies — and eventually, their de jure transfer — to the citizenry at large. But this was no zero-sum game in which one group always lost and another gained economic or political power, because the interests and ultimately the identities of actors were altered in the process. Socialist workers became entrepreneurs, but so did some party-state officials or their relatives. Still other officials went to work for private businesses or opened consulting companies. Later on, managers bought out their state firms, or parts of them, sometimes through spontaneous privatization. Like much of the citizenry, party and state officials followed property rights: where earlier they had acquired rights to various forms of property primarily on the basis of positions in the bureaucracy, now those same positions often helped them secure new footholds in an incipient market.

The second claim advanced here is that Hungary's economic reforms were more than either ideologically bounded or "rational," pragmatic responses to a systemic or external economic crisis. Leadership's choice of any particular reform must refer to the historical trajectory of reform in a given country, which in turn partially determines the strategies available to reformers. In Hungary, this trajectory limited the possibilities for a return to orthodoxy. Yet history, while important, is not in itself sufficient to explain divergent reform processes and outcomes within and across socialist systems. Although often overlooked, the leadership's conceptual *use* of history is crucial. Hungarian leaders, like their Chinese counterparts, generated innovative interpretations of domestic reform histories in order to increase their degrees of freedom in policymaking without appearing to betray the fundamental tenets of socialism.

Both claims — the one concerning the political character of economic reforms; the other concerning the centrality of history and its uses to the chances of particular reforms — are grounded in close analysis of what I have elsewhere called the "institutional residue" of economic reforms (Seleny 1989, 1991). Consisting of people, practices and ideas, including creative adaptations of received political discourse, the institutional residue of reform was the cumulative product of individual reforms and reform attempts — even those that were partially reversed and whose proponents were temporarily marginalized. Elements of this residue were observable in both the formal and informal institutions of the system, and came into play at critical junctures. Three stand out:

1. *Groups of reformers* and their allies who frequently remained in official positions even when reforms they sponsored were partially rescinded.
2. *Practices altered by reforms,* both within state firms and outside them, for example, in second-economy activities, not always directly associated with state firms, but that became informally institutionalized features of the system.

3. *A reform discourse* that expanded the vocabulary of reform politics, gave rise to novel conceptualizations of history, and was both cause and effect of changing identities among the leadership.

As we shall see, the formation of this institutional residue was both a manifestation of the state's inability to keep strict control of the economy in the face of systemic rigidities, and evidence of a subtle and complex subversion from within and below. Increasingly constrained to improve the performance of state firms, leaders implemented reforms in a cyclical pattern, while oscillating between repression and toleration of an expanding second economy, defined here as the sum total of all untaxed, private economic activity: licensed and informal; legal, illegal, and on the borderline of illegality, both prior to and after its legalization in 1982.[3] Second-economy activities were indirectly or directly influenced by reforms intended to improve state-firm performance, and the behavior of state-firm managers toward workers was in turn profoundly affected by second-economy expansion. Over time, this interaction fundamentally altered the substructure of state power and citizen politics.

TWO POLAR NOTIONS OF POLITICS

Through the history of Hungarian economic reform, and in the relationship between the second economy and the Hungarian socialist state, we see joined in practice the analytic duality so often posed between the economic and political realms. Moreover, we see reform-minded leaders of the Hungarian Socialist Workers' party blending two views of politics that have held sway under both capitalism and socialism.

At one extreme of this implicit polarity, the object of politics is the defense of collective identity: political decisions are ultimately reducible to the distinction between friend and foe, and political struggle inevitably pits the one against the other. At the other extreme, politics is a pluralistic contest over the allocation of goods and values enforceable by the state.[4] In the

---

3. By contrast, the state sector, or "first" economy, encompassed state-owned firms, state-controlled cooperatives, government agencies and registered nonprofit institutions. Definitions of the second economy vary significantly with the analyst's focus, assumptions, and ideological perspective. This simplified working definition draws on those used by Gábor and Galasi 1985, and Kornai 1986, 1992.

4. This insight is from Gianfranco Poggi 1978, who analyzed the polarity typically posed between the pluralist worldview exemplified by the American political scientist David Easton and that of the German legal and political theorist Carl Schmitt. He also noted commonalities between them. As Poggi points out, Marxism can be understood as a radical variant of the Eastonian view: politics is essentially concerned with allocation by command. But for our purposes it is important to see that Marxist principles — as practiced in the socialist countries — also approached the Schmittian pole. To be sure, the protagonists of Schmittian politics are

PROPERTY RIGHTS AND POLITICAL POWER   *31*

twentieth century, it has often been according to some variant of these views that practitioners have tried to shape the world and theorists to make it intelligible. Thus, beginning in the 1960s, as the rule of terror eased in the East, scholarly consensus in the West shifted from one view toward the other: moving away from totalitarian accounts of immutability and, via moderniza-tion / convergence theories, toward pluralist accounts of change.

In the totalitarian view, politics was fundamentally Schmittian: the party state subjugated society; foes were those who defied it and would pay a heavy price.[5] Modernization theorists, on the other hand, posited that with eco-nomic progress, the politics of friend and foe would be subsumed under the allocative imperative. Interest-group theorists studied bargaining relations within the socialist state and tended to describe socialist politics as corpora-tist or, alternatively, as an "institutional" variant of pluralism (Hough 1969, 1977; Skilling and Griffiths, 1971).[6] On this view, friends often fought about control over the allocative process, among other things. But this analysis of socialist political practice and struggle failed to specify the relative strengths of competing groups or the limitations and possibilities of the structure in which they operated. Class-based theories turned totalitarianism on its head: socialist politics and power structures were natural outgrowths of a prevailing logic of production and allocation that *determined* friends and foes. But such theories became entrapped in circularity, since the state itself had imposed the new economic order and set the parameters of class rela-tions through its administrative policies.[7] They simply could not explain the failure of class-based support for the classical bureaucratic socialist model (Kornai 1992), or the variation in departures from the model over the course of socialist practice in Eastern Europe and elsewhere. As a result, like the older totalitarian alternative and the present consensus on the funda-mental "unreformability" of socialism, neither interest-group nor class the-ories had much to say about the *process* of reform and transformation.

In the 1980s, new institutionalists, building on the work of Eastern Euro-pean scholars, drew attention to a variety of institutional adaptations under

---

nation-states, and the identity formation of their collectivities is inextricable from political struggle. In classical Marxian analysis, class identity is determined by the members' position in the division of labor, and long-run political outcomes are thus preordained. Nevertheless, the notion of an existential clash is central to the concept of politics itself.

5. Two classic formulations of totalitarian theory are given in Arendt 1986 and Friedrich and Brzezinski 1965.

6. For a sophisticated review of totalitarian, modernization, interest-group, neo-Marxist and other theories of socialist systems, see Comisso 1991.

7. From the very start, the state regulated class conflict through its policies of demobiliza-tion and remobilization of the labor force; allocation of opportunities for education, work-places, and housing; and redistributive fiscal measures. For a review of class-based theories as applied to socialist systems, see Szelényi 1982.

way in several socialist systems. These important studies elucidated the uniquely *socialist* institutional logic of systems that had often been treated as distortions of capitalism (Nee and Stark, 1989). Because of the shift of focus away from the Communist party, however, this approach cannot explain socialist countries' sharply different reform strategies, or the systemic political impact of these strategies. (See chapter 3 of this volume.)

THE LINKS BETWEEN SOCIALIST POLITICS AND ECONOMICS

Except for the new institutionalists, both the totalitarian and the class-based theories all tended to separate the economic and political realms. Yet as we shall see, the institutional residue of reform revealed the intimate links between politics and economics in socialism. To be sure, politics and economics are always and everywhere connected. But somewhat paradoxically, this connection was more palpable under socialism than in most capitalist systems. The latter, especially if they operate in the framework of reasonably democratic politics, allow space for public struggles over economic issues to proceed within existing legal and political-institutional structures. Governments fall, but political systems remain in place. State-socialist systems, on the other hand, officially permitted only high-level struggles over economic issues, which were eminently political — not least since oversight of the economy constituted the primary justification for a massive party-state bureaucracy. Most other debate and bargaining, and a good deal of action, therefore occurred in the informal realm.

In Hungary, for instance, the formalization of informal economic activities by the early 1980s took on much greater political significance than similar changes in capitalist systems — for example, Spanish and Italian efforts to incorporate large informal sectors into the formal economy (cf., e.g., Benton 1991). In capitalist democracies, incorporation of informal businesses through legalization programs meant an increase of government control over them, as the state gained the power to tax and regulate. At the firm level, this was true in Hungary as well. In a socialist system, however, such incorporation also signified at least a de facto loosening of the state's extremely broad claim to control the economic realm. At most, over time, it meant a de jure repudiation of that claim.

Thus, although not generally appreciable in the short run, even relatively small losses of control over the economic realm eventually had direct or indirect political repercussions. One kind of evidence for this view can be found in the frequent reversals of economic reform: in a common pattern (e.g., contemporary Russian politics), reforms from above run up against the self-preserving instincts of bureaucrats. But in Hungary and elsewhere, such reversals could not prevent the resurgence of the same systemic troubles that originally compelled radical and reluctant reformers alike to undertake reform programs. As an indirect consequence of these cycles of reform, reformers lost confidence in scientific socialism; and eventually socialism lost much of what remaining legitimacy it had in the view of the population. This process, in conjunction with social pressure from a society transformed over time partly by the experience of these same reforms, precluded the indefinite perpetuation of a zero-sum system of reform cycles.

Indeed, by the late 1970s, several such cycles had already resulted in a partially "privatized" public sector,[8] and in a differently "politicized" economy. The party had always made economic decisions on the basis of political considerations, but now economic issues were increasingly subject to the influence of actors outside the party state apparatus. The turning point in this process, however, was a 1982 restructuring of property rights that legalized much of the second economy and opened up important new channels for private and quasi-private enterprise. This reform is representative of important differences between Hungarian reform socialism and other Eastern European varieties, and of similarities to the Chinese variant. For the first time on a wide scale, the leadership felt obliged not only to acknowledge the right of individuals to own and operate private businesses but also to legitimize them through a public relations campaign that emphasized their importance to the improvement of the "market socialist" economy.

After 1982, private entrepreneurs were permitted to cooperate in various forms of partnership, and the formal private sector expanded dramatically. From 1982 on, the authorities could no longer refuse a license or otherwise prohibit any citizen from choosing to work on his or her own account, or from participating in the new partnerships, as long as certain basic legal and professional preconditions were met.[9] The new private and quasi-private companies were excluded from only a few areas, such as banking and mining.[10]

The statutes that brought these new companies into existence took effect on January 1, 1982, and specified several new forms of property, among them "business work-partnerships," "civil law partnerships," private cooperatives (known as "small cooperatives"), and quasi-private "enterprise business work-partnerships." The reform also ended restrictions on industrial production in agricultural cooperatives.

To be sure, the legalization was in some respects incomplete, and was

8. I refer here mostly to de facto and not de jure privatization of state-sector firms or their subsidiaries, although both kinds of privatization are linked to the extension of the second economy's unofficial and after 1982 official role in the state sector. See, for example, Sabel and Stark 1982 and Stark 1985.

9. The professional preconditions had to do mainly with minimum required investments for the various partnership forms and the presentation of a feasible business plan to local authorities.

10. Some restrictions on international trade also applied.

perforce based on a confusing and often self-blocking regulatory system. Numerous further refinements and amendments would follow before it was possible to speak of a reasonably unfettered private sector in Hungary. Only with the implementation of the 1989 Law on Association was the mix of de facto and de jure rights granted the private sector in 1982 codified in a uniform law passed by Parliament, not contingent on state administrative directives (Sárközy 1988, 9).

But this was merely one more case of socialist law lagging behind the reality of socioeconomic practice and attempting to rationalize its earlier piecemeal legitimation. The 1982 statutes created new forms of private enterprise, but also legalized preexisting informal activities, or included and called them "new"; the 1989 Association Law unified regulations introduced in 1982 and thereafter, and stated clearly that this was its purpose. This law was a direct continuation of the 1982 initiative (as well as of some earlier ones) and of other 1980s reforms affecting both private and state firms. Its authors in the Ministry of Finance noted that "results hitherto obtained in the field of company law enable[d] the maintenance of continuity," although it had become necessary to "place the regulations originating from different dates into a uniform context" (*Act on Economic Associations* 1988, g). In essence, and despite what it did not do,[11] the 1982 reform expanded the scope and changed the basis of entrepreneurship and private business ownership from *privilege* — small numbers of licenses granted at the discretion of local authorities — to that of a *right* based in government decree and a broad regulatory mechanism.

The following section illustrates how the 1982 and subsequent 1980s reforms were tightly linked to the historical development of economic reform and the second economy. The third part of this essay explains why the 1982 reform represented a fundamental political compromise between labor and the Hungarian socialist state. The fourth part describes the leadership's effort to redefine socialism broadly enough to permit accommodation of the greatly expanded property rights of citizens. Finally, I consider the political and economic impact of this redefinition on the Hungarian socialist system.

---

11. Many restrictions, unresolved issues, and legal ambiguities remained: for example, limited partnerships for individuals were not permitted until 1987, and then only if at least one member had juridical status; the number of employees for some forms of partnership was restricted; the manner and degree to which individual citizens could establish economic associations with private or state-owned firms was strictly regulated until 1989. In addition, until then, certain types of private partnership operated under a confusing two- and sometimes three-tier system of direct and indirect control: sectoral (e.g., retail vs. manufacturing); state administration (Ministry of Finance, the tax authorities, the economic police), and judicial (e.g. the Court of Registry).

CYCLES OF REFORM AND RECENTRALIZATION

From the start, Hungarian socialism was caught in a seemingly insoluble dilemma. On the one hand, attempts by the party state at economic and political centralization led workers (often in collusion with pragmatic managers) to defend their autonomy and standards of living through a hidden organization of work antithetical to socialist ideology: the informal economy. On the other hand, subsequent reformist attempts to use the informal economy to support a state sector increasingly afflicted by systemic rigidities provided workers with opportunities to accumulate property rights implicit in private and quasi-private work, in turn antithetical to socialism.

During the Stalinist period, and indeed until 1950, the party state was impelled by notions of revolutionary duty to create and defend a socialist collective identity: statecraft came to be synonymous with politics, and the task of politics was entwined with the eradication of intraparty and societal pluralism, private property, free association, and autonomous relation to work. The party state took decisive punitive measures against those it identified as "foes": dissidents, "bourgeois" intellectuals and professionals, and individuals engaged in all manner and scale of private economic activity. At the same time, it drafted a centrally planned economic blueprint that left minimal space for independent decision making by actors in the state sector.

While the end of the Stalin era and the Hungarian revolution of 1956 did not lead to a fundamental revision of this narrow view of politics, they did soften the draconian conception of political objectives. Another cause of this softening, however, is traceable to the leadership's pressing need for workable responses to the rigidities of the classical bureaucratic socialist system, which were becoming clear by 1953. Indeed, as we now know, such rigidities became intractable long before 1989, and gradually eroded the party's effective control over the production and allocation of goods and services. This allocative aspect of politics, which took pride of place in official rhetoric, but had in fact been subsumed by the party's politics of maximal cohesion, became a systemic problem, which left the leadership determined to regain control over production and allocation without surrendering its view of politics. Accordingly, official treatment of all private economic activity alternated between repression and relative unofficial toleration, and economic reforms moved in a fairly clear cyclical pattern of one step back, two steps forward.

The leadership was resolute in its initial attack on the private sector. The nationalization of nonfarm enterprises employing more than ten workers was completed by the early 1950s, and most of the smaller units were forced to join state cooperatives. By 1963, only a miniscule portion of the economically active population was still self-employed.[12] And the collectivization campaign of peasant farms, which began in the late 1940s after the expropriation of large landholdings, occurred simultaneously with the institution of a forced delivery system that aimed to substitute centralized redistribution for market mechanisms and ensure agricultural exports to the Soviet Union. After the 1956 revolution, however, many cooperatives broke up, and by 1959 the number of small private farms approached the precollectivization figure (Róna-Tas 1989, 17). The second collectivization campaign was completed by 1962, but in a tacit concession to peasants in the aftermath of the violence of 1956, each individual who was a full member of an agricultural cooperative was granted a small household plot for private production and consumption, and thus the opportunity to keep up with the living standard of the industrial wage earner.[13] Indeed, a vital and influential second economy eventually grew out of the relationship between the household plots and state cooperative farms.

Still, national economic management in this period aimed primarily at forced industrialization, which shortchanged both agricultural development and private consumption (Galasi and Sziráczki 1986, 3) and hinged on five-year plans that established obligatory targets in terms of macroaggregates and on annual plans for enterprises. This period of centralized planning was characterized by vertical organization of the economy and political institutions, central allocation of production inputs, and "commands" flowing from the authorities to enterprises concerning investment, employment, wages, and prices. The bias toward heavy industry and very large firm size was also clear (Galasi and Sziráczki 1986, 3–5). As long as reallocation and intensive application of previously underutilized resources made extensive growth possible, output and industrial capacity grew rapidly, but this process slowed as labor reserves were depleted and heavy industry was built up and diversified.

But even before the revolution of 1956, and long before the most dramatic expansion of the second economy, the larger society reacted against the elite politics of maximal cohesion. This was most widely evident in the behavior of individuals in the workplace, and in the behavior of firms as economic agents, which together engendered structural problems, such as the hoarding of materials and workers. Almost from the beginning, the

12. In 1963, 1.9 percent outside agriculture, 2.1 percent among peasants (Andorka 1990, 4). By comparison, when the communists took power in 1948, about half the labor force was employed in small-scale production (Donáth 1977, 38–45).

13. Andorka 1990, 4. Indications that the state would have to co-opt peasants and that dependence would run both ways appeared early on and contributed to the expansion of the second economy. For instance, allowing peasants to keep a larger number of animals was crucial, because they sometimes slaughtered their cattle rather than compulsorily give them up (Berend 1983, 287–88).

party's responses to such problems helped alter both the original economic blueprint and the political ideology underlying it. For example, the attempt to ease institutional problems led the authorities to make limited concessions to the private sector as early as 1953. Industrial cooperatives of former small firms had been so completely integrated with the state sector that they were producing almost exclusively for the large state enterprises and were thus unable to meet consumer demand (Galasi and Sziráczki 1986, 8). In one of numerous swings between orthodoxy and reform, Imre Nagy's "New Course" partially reversed the earlier attempt to abolish small-scale industry between 1953 and 1955. The new policy allowed members of cooperatives to resign and private artisans to apply for licenses; in a year and a half, the authorities issued more than 60,000 such licenses (Hegedüs and Márkus 1979, 275). But the number of employees in small-scale industry never even reached 1951 levels, a brief resurgence of the trend in 1956 and 1957 notwithstanding. By 1955, amid accusations that "speculators and former capitalists . . . [who] never pursued any productive activity" were taking advantage of liberalized licensing, increased taxation and cancellation of some licenses slowed the rapid growth of small-scale businesses (Hegedüs and Márkus 1979, 275). Economists proposed that the small-scale private sector be more actively encouraged in an effort to promote flexibility in the economy, but the party further restricted this sector after 1958, and its size consequently diminished (Galasi and Sziráczki 1986, 9).

Indeed, between 1957 and 1964, conservatism in socialist economic management predominated. Nevertheless, compulsory deliveries in agriculture were abolished in 1956–57, and by the mid 1960s, reform was high on the national agenda. In 1968, the New Economic Mechanism (NEM) introduced substantial changes. The NEM decentralized economic management to the extent that it eliminated the system of compulsory plan targets and gave state firms increased latitude in a number of areas (Kornai 1986). During the NEM period, official policy also eased some restrictions on the licensed nonagricultural private sector and on the operation of agricultural household and auxiliary plots. With the 1968 reforms, the household plots, which were supposed to have been "organically" (vertically) integrated into the state-controlled agricultural cooperatives, were encouraged to market their produce either directly or through the cooperatives, which frequently supplied the necessary inputs and technical advice, lent equipment, and often shared profits from the sale of privately or partially privately produced goods. In fact, the finances of state-controlled cooperatives and the private peasant producers were intricately intertwined, amounting to substantial symbiosis.[14]

14. For example, calves born in the cooperative were sometimes sold to individual members, who raised them on private household plots; the cooperative then bought them back and

Outside agriculture, the second economy arose, in the first instance, spontaneously and from below as a result of factors involving the worker as both producer and consumer. The worker as producer — the final arbiter in the socialist economy as in any other — responded to the need for greater autonomy, for demonstrable recognition of work through appropriate incentives, and for enhanced consumption possibilities. Thus, the workers' weak identification with work in the state sector and wish to increase earnings beyond their limited means to do so, together with the state's political decision to maintain full employment in a system characterized by firms' "soft budget constraints" and "investment hunger" (Kornai 1980, vol. A, 306–9, 189–90), gradually embroiled the state in a struggle of defensive and counterdefensive competition; firms hoarded workers and workers hoarded labor power.

This hoarding of labor power by workers prompted endless debates in the Eastern European literature concerning how best to instill "interest in property" — how to interest workers in expanding enterprise capital (Antal 1985, 279). But workers acted in light of the macroeconomic fact of labor shortage in an economy where firms, ultimately invulnerable to failure, ran at full employment even when the marginal cost of labor was higher than its output. Independent labor unions would, of course, have recognized in this fact a source of political leverage, and the authorities would have been forced, in turn, to acknowledge them as a potential political force. But under socialism, the official labor union would have repressed such organizations. Instead, workers pursued their interests informally. This usually took the form of conserving labor power for second-economy work. Workers also used materials, vehicles, tools, and personnel from state-sector jobs for after-hours second-economy projects or businesses. Even hiring practices in the "official" economic sector were affected: for example, the manager of a state plumbing firm took care to hire workers skilled in bricklaying, wiring, or painting so that the new addition to the factory could help co-workers build their own houses on weekends; later the group might hire out as informal private contractors.

State-sector employees and pensioners could legally work part-time in private small-scale industry from 1968 on. Some of the more prohibitive tax rules were also eased. But it was the varied informal, illegal, or semilegal private activities that had managed to survive that increased the most in

---

sold them to a state enterprise. Because the cooperative was considered part of the socialist sector (although nominally in cooperative ownership, it functioned essentially as a state-owned unit), it received a slightly higher price for the cattle than the peasants would have had they sold them directly to a state firm without the mediation of the state agricultural cooperative. The state cooperative farm typically split the premium with the individual cooperative members who had raised the cattle on their household plots (Andorka 1989).

response to the 1968 reforms (Galasi and Sziráczki 1986, 14–18). These activities were more severely punished at some times than at others, but in general the relatively liberal attitude of the authorities until 1972 contributed to their expansion. Private entrepreneurs in the 1960s and 1970s often operated without licenses and secured work orders through first-economy firms. Even in the more orthodox 1970s, harsh verdicts against transgressors could not stop private contracting, partly because it was either expedient or profitable for all concerned; partly because defensive networks of high trust alliances often protected the individuals involved.

In order to escape notice by anonymous informers,[15] as well as the jealousy and disapproval of neighbors and acquaintances, second-economy entrepreneurs and their clients developed a coded language of polite ambiguities, and a kind of informal referral service that, drawing on the accumulated information and experience of past transactions, identified trustworthy participants in activities ranging from the simplest exchange to the most intricate cooperative arrangement. Such informal social mechanisms further reinforced the strong incentive to private entrepreneurship born of the shortage economy, which was therefore preponderantly a seller's market (Kornai 1980, 1992). And thanks in part to informal networks of trust, the window washer and plumber, like the electrician, auto mechanic, dentist, or language instructor working after official hours, were far from paralyzed by the need for caution. A provider, to be sure, was always selective, but if satisfied with a client, might establish a durable professional relationship based on loyalty, not only to the individual, but often also to his or her close friends and relatives. Most evaded punishment for unlicensed private activity, which could be harsh: property was confiscated, heavy fines were levied, and people were sent to jail for terms of several years' duration (Hegedüs and Márkus 1979, 280).

During the recentralization of 1972–79, industrial concentration increased. The number of firms decreased, while the percentage of workers employed in firms of more than 1,000 grew as smaller firms were reorganized into larger enterprises and mammoth trusts. This was done on the theory that the bureaucratic chain of command would be simplified and macroeconomic planning rationalized, since consolidated firms would not compete against one another or duplicate productive efforts. Between 1972 and 1974, hard-liners also attempted to reverse the expansion of the agricultural second economy of household plots, citing the "threatening development of rural capitalism." A powerful agricultural lobby, which included directors of agricultural cooperatives and party leaders from agricultural

---

15. Producers, and to a lesser extent also consumers, of second-economy goods and services could be reported at any time by anonymous informers — a well-established, very common practice in Hungary, which invariably led to investigation by the authorities.

regions, fought the reversal, however, with the result that the conservatives were only partially successful (Andorka 1990, 5). By the late 1970s, the process of commercialization of private small-scale agricultural production was well under way (see Szelényi 1988).

Nevertheless, the truncated process of economic reform and partial reversals of earlier liberalization left industry poorly suited to adapt to the new, more stringent international economic environment following the first oil crisis. Hungary responded to the oil crises and ensuing trade account imbalances with an effort to extend its long-standing model of extensive growth; since domestic inputs of labor, capital, and raw materials had already been mobilized, the country turned to external credit. By 1978, however, in the context of deteriorating terms of trade (owing partly to Hungary's increasing import needs and losing some of its market shares to the newly industrializing countries) and to rising interest rates, debt service could only be met by holding down consumption and expenditures on social services, and real wages fell between 1978 and 1980 (Andorka 1990, 5–6).

A new wave of reform measures began in 1979 with the attempt to bring domestic nonagricultural producer prices in line with world market prices. The new policy, which also included reduction of some food subsidies, was implemented as part of a larger effort to reduce foreign indebtedness through the restriction of domestic demand. This in turn led to a fall in real wages and to a trade surplus that helped reduce the country's foreign debt slightly (Galasi and Sziráczki 1986, 22). And in an attempt to increase economic efficiency, a number of large companies were now reorganized into smaller ones, while other large plants were decentralized, so that some three hundred new state-sector firms were established between 1980 and 1983.

As mentioned earlier, these cyclical reforms served temporarily to maintain the socialist political structure.[16] But as we have seen, by the mid 1960s, a very real and somewhat ironic disjuncture between the "planned" and the "unplanned" economies had developed. On the one hand, the ubiquitous second economy operated on the basis of informally institutionalized high-trust alliances that entailed a retreat to seemingly antiquated forms of economic transaction, which turned on rituals of formal behavior and on the personal reputations of participants. On the other hand, the National Planning Office still struggled to construct balances with the aid of input-output models or mathematical programming in the pursuit of ever-greater plan consistency.[17]

16. For example, by solving specific problems, improving economic performance in a particular area, or at least giving the impression that the authorities understood the system's weaknesses and had the resulting problems well in hand.

17. I refer here to the various methods used to improve on the "manual" method of elaborating material, product, semiproduct, manpower, and financial balances.

The elements of future change emerged from this disjuncture and began to accumulate as an institutional residue of reform, whether the architects of reforms intended to perfect "scientific" socialism or to create a "market" variant. Indeed, as the interplay between systemic economic crisis and social pressures forced party leaders to consider new reforms, they turned, not only to stories of partial success, but also sometimes to elements of once-repudiated programs and to progressively inclined officials and scholars who had enjoyed greater influence during earlier reform campaigns.[18] All became essential components of the institutional residue that not only made imaginable and possible but also justified increasingly radical experiments: reforms like the 1982 property rights reform, further liberalization of both the state and private sectors after 1982, and, ultimately, the transformation of the system as a whole.

Often, old concessions became the basis for new reforms, like buried blueprints for change later rediscovered and adapted to new circumstances. Take the party's acceptance of private plots in agricultural cooperatives and, later, of increasingly commercialized household-plot production. Seen as necessary evils, these plots were originally meant to be tolerated only temporarily on the way to large-scale, "modern" agriculture, and in the meantime were supposed to be fully vertically integrated into state cooperatives. But as we have seen, the outcome was quite different, especially after the 1968 New Economic Mechanism. Even as a growing number produced directly for the market, many of the private agricultural activities of these plots came to be symbiotically integrated financially and administratively with the state-controlled cooperatives.

Some analysts, in fact, understand the 1982 reform of property rights as a straightforward, pragmatic extension to industry, construction, and services of reforms that had met with reasonable success in agriculture (see, e.g., Hare 1986, 35). Hungary's positive experience with household plots was indeed a crucial factor in the party's acceptance of the 1982 statutes. But the implementation of the 1982 reform proposal (or of any other advanced in the 1980s) was not assured, and a functionalist explanation based on the success of predecessor reforms cannot fully account for the party's adoption of increasingly radical reforms. As we shall see, high-level officials had to wage an intramural political struggle on behalf of the 1982 reform, and ultimately prevailed through tactical maneuvering and innovative adaptations of reform discourse that harnessed a shared experience of reform to their purposes. To make sense of this battle, however, we must focus briefly

18. A number of people in the Ministry of Finance or its associated research institute (Pénzügykutató Rt.) who were connected with the 1982 reform and other 1980s reforms had also been involved between 1963 and 1968 with the planning of the New Economic Mechanism (Székacs 1990).

on one of the principal political-economic forces that compelled these reformers to act. Specifically, we must examine how workers' second-economy
strategies forced the socialist system to begin to internalize the realistic costs
of highly motivated labor.

INTERNALIZING AN "EXTERNALITY":
THE TRUE COST OF LABOR AND APPLIED KNOWLEDGE

The most rigid structural characteristics of the socialist system at times afforded workers the opportunity for resistance, and the rapid growth of the
second economy in the 1960s both enabled and manifested this resistance
((Gábor 1988). From then until the 1982 reform, the second economy—
originally a coping mechanism for an experimenting state and a forcibly
reorganized society—served as socialism's silent counterpart to capitalism's
adversarial bargaining. The second economy is, in fact, one indication of
the limits of rationality under a centrally planned economy, much as unemployment indicates these limits under capitalism.

In the foregoing section we saw that state-firm managers tried to protect
themselves from the exigencies of the plan by hoarding workers, and workers hoarded labor power largely because the shortage economy demanded
the goods and services they could produce outside working hours and/or on
the side at state jobs. In this context, the control that managers and union
officials could exert over workers was further compromised by the expansion
of second-economy earning possibilities after 1968. On the one hand, firm
managers' ability to increase wages remained limited even after the 1968 reform, and the nonmonetary incentives they could offer workers (e.g., housing, preferred vacation slots, and desirable work assignments) were often in
short supply. On the other hand, the guarantee of full employment and the
party state's reluctance to use force, especially after 1956, blunted managers' credible threats against workers who shirked or withheld effort. Managers' ability to reward and punish was curtailed in other ways. For example,
even an openly uncooperative worker could reasonably expect that he or she
would eventually receive many of the benefits allocated through state firms.
For one thing, housing and vacations accrued as rights to state-firm employees. For another, state-firm managers who maintained good relations
with *all* available workers could expect an easier time meeting plan targets.
Finally, managers' discretionary application of incentives was restricted by
the fact that workers' "pay" came in several administratively determined
forms (guaranteed subsidized housing, free education and medical care,
subsidized food, etc.), of which wages were, in effect, a residual category: in a
sense, pocket money granted by the "paternal" state (Kornai 1993).

In short, even as the socialist system of work unwittingly provided workers
with subversive capability, the system also attempted to externalize the true

cost of labor power.[19] Although this attempt was never fully successful, workers suffered the consequences of the lack of property rights of disposal over their time and energy—or of rights poorly defined—and of firm behavior minimally constrained by markets. In a capitalist system, workers are a long way from being free to set the price of their labor power. But whatever the costs and risks, their relative freedom to relocate, to choose self-employment, to work with friends, to obtain further training without need of official permission, or to switch professions, is far greater than in the socialist system, where most labor power could officially only be sold to the monopoly buyer: the state, represented by its firms.[20] Even in relatively liberal Hungary, where especially after 1968, workers were free to change jobs and relocate, and firms had more autonomy in investment and wage decisions, serious hindrances to the institutionalization of smoothly functioning labor markets remained (Galasi and Sziráczki 1986, 14). In the context of full employment and labor shortage, firms persisted in their efforts to hoard workers in a variety of innovative ways, even as these failed to satisfy their "labor hunger."

Paradoxically, despite the lack of organized collective bargaining through independent trade unions, this situation afforded workers increased informal bargaining power as firms developed *internal* labor markets in the effort to keep them (Galasi and Sziráczki 1986, 15–16; Stark 1986): in effect, a

19. Externalities are generally understood as the beneficial or negative effects that the production activities of firms bring to bear on one another. However, I want to generalize the concept here to include the beneficial or harmful effects that a group of state monopolies—socialist firms—may have on a factor of production, in this case, labor. Here, there are several externality-generating activities that lower the production or utility of the externally affected parties, including maintenance of administrative labor markets prior to 1968, and thereafter, of firm-level and economywide wage controls by indirect means. But fundamentally, the externality-generating activity is the curtailment of workers' choice between self-employment and employment by the state—that is, the effective abolition of private entrepreneurship. For an interesting discussion of externalities, including an elucidation of the long-standing debates over the income effects of transaction costs (e.g., Coase's theorem, whether the identity of owners matters, etc.), see Demsetz 1988, vol. 1, esp. chs. 2 and 7.

20. Two distinguished Hungarian economists have summarized the pre-1968 system in this way: "Central economic management attempted to restrict the enterprises' and employees' freedom of action in the allocation of labour as well as in the determination of wages. It tried to diminish unplanned labour turnover through legal punishments against 'migratory birds', and those who quit their jobs without employers' authorization ('unjustified turnover')" (Galasi and Sziráczki 1986, 12). The point, of course, is not that capitalist labor markets function purely through the price mechanism, or that socialist ones function solely on the basis of allocation; either characterization would be overdrawn. The authors show that in socialist practice, labor allocation "from the outset included some elements foreign to the nature of a system of obligatory plan targets" (ibid.). The foregoing is simply meant to illuminate differences in the degree to which administrative versus price mechanisms controlled classical socialist labor markets, which, in practice for most socialist workers, did amount to a difference in *kind*.

kind of micro-level internalizing of the "externality" — in this case a more realistic approximation of the cost of workers' labor power. Specialized and skilled workers were best situated to bargain up their wages, but virtually all workers could conserve a portion of their energies for second-economy projects. Thus state employees, the overwhelming majority of the population, maintained informal veto power over the only resource they effectively commanded at work: their own labor power.

By the early 1960s, with the rapid growth of the informal second econ omy, rigid wage-fixing and restrictions on labor mobility had become unten able. Even the changes wrought by the 1968 New Economic Mechanism could not, however, significantly moderate firms' demand for labor, worsening labor discipline, and the reduction in the ratio of wages to living stan dards, despite increasing wages. In the early 1970s, 'drastic" direct inter vention in the labor market proved unsuccessful and temporary (Hare, Radice, and Swain 1981, 49–53).

The 1982 reform of property rights represented a partial macroeconomic internalization of the externality. Workers had previously borne the financial and opportunity costs of administratively determined wages and forced state employment. At a deeper level, society as a whole bore the costs in loss of international competitiveness and comparatively low living standards. Now the party state would officially assume the "cost" of the highly motivated labor of the significant segment of the population willing to work intensively on their own account or for private-sector employers. It would, for instance, bear the practical costs of regulatory adjustment, as well as the ideological and political costs of an expanded private sector.

It appeared that the party and second-economy participants had made a mutually beneficial trade. On the one hand, the leadership would lighten the burden of the system's accumulating incapacities by allowing private production to meet consumer demand that state firms were unable to satisfy. The state could also collect tax revenue from private firms. On the other hand, citizens achieved the absolute right to dispose of their own labor power, as well as rights of control over, residual income from, and alienability of private enterprise.

Given this apparently mutually beneficial trade, then, it may be tempting after all to view the reform as a straightforward functional response to systemic economic exigencies. But if this is the case, why did other socialist countries not pursue a similar course? A combination of conjunctural and historical factors are frequently marshaled to account for the difference in the Hungarian response. The conjunctural factors have received widespread attention, especially Hungary's onerous foreign debt;[21] among the

---

21. Fearful of the social consequences of the price hikes implemented in 1979 and thereafter, the leadership hoped that the increases would be tolerated if they were not accompanied

historical factors, the social pact struck by leaders and society in the after-math of the 1956 revolution figures prominently.[22]

However, conjunctural and historical factors amounted to necessary, but not sufficient, conditions for the implementation of institutional reform. Many of the economic pressures experienced by the Soviet Union, Czecho-slovakia, Bulgaria, Cuba, and even the much-vaunted former German Dem-ocratic Republic were as severe or worse than in Hungary, yet these coun-tries undertook no comprehensive reform of property rights. And while the 1956 revolution helps explain the initial consumerist pact, it cannot ac-count for its repeated renegotiation – for the dynamic process of reform and retrenchment, with its many points of political struggle.

Understanding what made Hungary different requires that we turn now to an analysis of a high-level reformer's perceptions of and justifications for the trade-off between decreased central control on the one hand and cit-izens' rights to engage in private enterprise on the other.

THE POLITICS OF PROPERTY-RIGHTS REFORM: TACTICAL LESSONS, DISCOURSE AND ADAPTIVE IDENTITY

In 1978, against a historical background of official denunciation and per-secution of unlicensed second-economy activities, the Central Committee identified "the utilization of leisure time" — by then an unmistakable eu-phemism for time actually or potentially spent working in the second economy — as the most likely source of improved living standards (Fekete 1990, 16). Moreover, in open contradiction to socialist ideology, the Hun-garian Socialist Workers' party legalized and began to foster the expansion of private enterprise. Why and how did the Hungarian leadership reach the

---

by serious shortages. The economic crisis made capital- or import-intensive solutions to recur-ring shortages more costly, however, and the writing on the wall was clear: they would soon be beyond reach even as temporary expedients. The assumption of a large foreign debt in the 1970s and early 1980s, for example, carried tremendous new costs of its own in the form of debt service, pressure from international financial institutions and, by 1982, near-default. In addition, despite the fact that neither actually occurred on any significant scale, anticipation of wholesale reduction of subsidies to state firms and the possibility of bankruptcies led reformers to think of private firms in terms of potential job creation in the event of state-firm layoffs.

22. The unspoken assumption of this social pact was that in exchange for its political quiescence, the population expected an improvement in the material conditions of life; that there was, in fact, an unmarked but strongly felt consumption frontier that necessarily set the broad parameters of economic policy. To be sure, these parameters were also determined by systemic pressures common to all socialist economies. But given the imperative of defending this consumption frontier, together with the fact that Hungary is a small and relatively open economy, these same systemic pressures left the leadership with *fewer* degrees of freedom than the Chinese, Soviet, Czechoslovak, or, for different reasons, perhaps even the Polish leadership to *avoid* institutional reform. See also Szelényi 1989, 221.

decision to legitimize activity that had until then been considered criminal; and, furthermore, to create new legal channels for private and quasi-private business?

Part of the answer has to do with social and political learning. By the late 1970s, experience with reform and the size and scope of the second economy had taught political leaders and academics alike new lessons about Hungarian social reality. The object of the lesson varied among groups, as did their adaptive responses. Even before 1982, party and state officials, like their Polish counterparts, sometimes helped families and friends obtain leases on state shops or licenses to open private ones. Indeed, in Budapest lore, behind every fashionable boutique hid a powerful party member or government official. And if not every introduction-pollution was actually an incipient private businessman, the infiltration of the second economy into the state sector had nevertheless already done much to change officials' calculus of private interest (Hankiss 1989, 126).

If an official also advocated reform, then he belonged to a distinguished group that included both academic economists and members of the party-state apparatus who had been associated with the stalled 1968 reform, and whose intellectual and moral authority was fortified by the severe, accumulated economic pressures that account for the timing of the 1982 decrees. But some officials had also learned the specific tactical lessons that would make them possible, and knew how to put established procedure in the service of change. It was high-level functionaries of the National Planning Office who set about the process of drafting a reform proposal that they perceived as politically risky, and that one Hungarian sociologist describes as "coup-like" (Fekete 1990, 15–16), because it involved a small, specially selected group of technocrats relieved of their regular duties, working in near secrecy and with relative speed. If not for the self-conscious political decision by this small group of high-level reformist officials in the Ministry of Planning (and later, the Ministry of Finance) to harness the history of reform to the service of their program, it is doubtful whether the wider party would have approved the 1982 reform of property rights.

This process began with the establishment in 1979 of an "expert commission" that included economists and sociologists who had undertaken extensive research on the second economy.[23] It continued in starts and stops over the next three years, and it met at various points with resistance from the central economic management and within both the party and government apparatuses. Eventually, the process broadened to include the participation of other ministries (Finance, Industry, Labor, Justice) and culminated in a proposal that, despite the best efforts of the reform's sponsors to avoid

23. Among them were the economists István Gábor and Péter Galasi and the sociologists Pál Juhász, Támás Kolosi, and Robert Manchin (Fekete 1990, 18).

controversy, ultimately became the subject of intense debate within the party and government. These debates and the public campaign[24] that followed were conducted in an idiom carefully crafted to emphasize the innocuous, "socialist" nature of the reform. To this end, its sponsors took great pains to distance the "new" private sector to be "created" by the reform from the extant second economy — until then the subject of official disapproval even as unofficial toleration increased. In this ideologically correct public discourse, the "new" private sector was repeatedly referred to as a "helper" or "background" economy for the socialist firms: private partnerships — especially the intrafirm work partnerships — would be the "household plots of industry." These terms emphasized harmony and labor exchange between the state sector and its "helper" sector, and carried the reassuring implication that the latter would be self-limiting.[25]

The redefinition of the second economy amounted to an effort to divide it into parts that would be ideologically acceptable and therefore "integratable." As mentioned earlier, the economic success of the agricultural mixed model turned out to be particularly reassuring to both reformers and conservatives among the leadership. Household plots, seen as "organically integrated" into socialist cooperatives, had not palpably upset the balance of domestic political power. Therefore, the reasoning went, the small manufacturing firms and service establishments that could be expected to grow from the 1982 reform would help industry as the household plots had helped agriculture.

For tactical reasons, the validity of the analogy, although occasionally questioned during 1981 debates within the state apparatus, was not seriously challenged. Nevertheless, the analogy was incomplete at best. Virtually all the household plots operated under the aegis of state cooperatives or other state institutions, and capital accumulation was severely restricted by their small size and because they were universally a part-time undertaking. Moreover, their "private" nature was ambiguous, since opportunities for expansion or transfer of the plots were quite limited.[26] Thus their overall effect on the property structure of the economy was hardly appreciable, even if their impact on agricultural production was striking (Andorka 1990).

There was another difference, however. A much larger segment of officialdom might now either be threatened by, or gain from, the expansion of private industry and services beyond the confines of agricultural and other

24. The purpose of the media campaign was to try to get people to accept the legalized second economy as a part of the plan to build a better socialism: it was necessary precisely because the public had become accustomed to rhetoric condemning informal private enterprise as corrupt and its practitioners as "exploitative speculators."

25. David Stark makes a similar point, and analyzes the broader significance of factory work partnerships and other "mixed property forms." See Stark 1989, esp. 142.

26. The plots could be given back to the co-ops.

state cooperatives. Depending on the position, connections, and skills of the official, granting private businessmen favors or eased access to shortage materials might now result in larger bribes, or even in a share of profits (see, e.g., Oi 1991). On the other hand, not all officials would be equally well positioned to take advantage of such rent-seeking activities, the scope for which might in any case presumably shrink as the economic and political clout of private business grew.

All of this was left unsaid, however. In fact, reformers tried hard to present the new regulations as a relatively insignificant matter. They framed the proposed reform as, at worst, a marginal expansion of the concept of state socialism. As former Minister of Finance István Hetényi, one of the chief architects of the reform, put it:

> It we had [already] been able to declare that for the state firms, the profit criterion and demand should be the engines, and not plan indicators, then it was much simpler to declare that this was so for the individual. The issue was, did private activities fit into socialism or not? They fit because by 1968 we had turned away from the Leninist conception of socialism as one large factory. What remained was that this wasn't an exploitative society. So everything that wasn't exploitative—private firms employing large numbers of people—was already included in the definition of socialism, or somehow got included. (Hetényi 1991)

However, both the secretive "coup-like" methods employed by its sponsors and their efforts to head off potential discord within the party-state apparatus suggest that at least some government and party leaders were aware that the proposed reform was an unprecedented ideological departure and a potential challenge to their authority from within their own ranks. Nevertheless, most did not seriously entertain the possibility that an expanded private sector might grow into a broader political challenge to the system as a whole. Hetényi confirmed this.

> There was serious opposition in the ministries and in state management, which in the final analysis is explained by the fact that the reform decreased their power, as did everything that was permissible to do without them . . . [the private sector] wasn't controllable like large [state] firms—which, I need not remind you, were controllable even after 1968—after the abolition of command planning. And in certain cases expansion of the private sector meant competition for the large [socialist] firms.
>
> Because of the various political considerations, great juggling and wizardry were needed to find the new socialist forms that would be appropriate for small-scale private production. [Take] small cooperatives, for example. We explained that this socialist—or a little bit socialist, or half-socialist—type of activity wasn't foreign to socialism. Certainly, capitalist organization was not included here. Because we labeled these new forms partnerships, small cooperative[s], and so on, they received a patina of socialism, and the message was

that [they] hurt no one . . . we could solve this by the forms we chose and by emphasizing that this reform really provided opportunities for the workers. This eased the fears of many politicians: it wasn't about capitalism — or about capitalist entrepreneurs, but tens of thousands of workers would be able to earn additional income. (Hetényi 1991)

We see here that, despite the efforts of reformers like Hetényi to downplay the impact of this reform proposal, nothing less than the accepted definitions of both capitalism and socialism were at stake. It is not immediately clear how we should understand the statement that "capitalist organization was not included." Certainly, the economy remained organized largely along socialist lines. It bears repeating, however, that several of the property forms instituted in 1982 were unambiguously private. Even those that were nominally "socialist" (like the "small cooperative") were privately (albeit cooperatively) held; and — the different requirements for their establishment notwithstanding — functioned exactly like private businesses.[27] No formal limits on investment were set for any of the new business forms, although some were restricted as to the number of partners or employees. No capital market existed yet, but in theory at least, private entrepreneurs would be able to obtain loans from Hungarian banks. By the late 1980s, the remaining restrictions on numbers of employees had been lifted,[28] and the difficulties in obtaining formal credit had been eased.

The organizational forms chosen by the reformers functioned like a veil that partially obscured their nature, as Minister Hetényi himself indirectly allowed. By insisting that "capitalist organization was not included," Hetényi was trying to maintain nominal conformity with an inoperative ideology: the 1982 reforms provided opportunities, not for *capitalist* entrepreneurs, but for *worker* entrepreneurs. However, this was no simple case of maneuvering or posturing. It was the adaptive response of a socialist reformer to the contradictory requirements of his position. Hetényi was not the only high-level official who over the course of a long career attempted to reconcile the conflicting goals of a system he believed he served best by trying to improve it from within. Nor was he a capitalist in socialist guise. Indeed, while a few of the most fervent advocates of private enterprise may already have been looking ahead to a market-based system, they were not the norm. Looking back in 1991, Hetényi expressed it in the following way:

If someone says that they saw a private market economy in this reform, or a mixed market economy — well, perhaps; but it wasn't of the order of a system change, although in retrospect this is less clear. What was clear *then* was that in

27. The one difference — the supposedly "indivisible capital" of the cooperatives — was easily bypassed through informal means.

28. Unless one counts as significant the limit of five hundred employees. This final "fig-leaf" restriction was also lifted after the first parliamentary elections.

Hungary, politics were highly pragmatic. Of course, we had to keep the rule: there should be no exploitation — that is, no private firms employing large numbers of people. (Hetényi 1991)

However, even if Hetényi and some of his high-level colleagues in the Planning and Finance ministries were relatively sanguine about the 1982 proposals at the time, the view from elsewhere in the bureaucracy was different. Middle-level officials of the National Planning Office who participated in the drafting of the proposal based on opinions expressed by the "name of committee" were "astonish[ed]" when in 1980, the party's Political Committee approved further work on the reform proposal (Fekete 1990, 20). These officials knew that although both licensed and informal private entrepreneurship had been increasingly tolerated since 1968, for as long as the party felt able to do so, it had resisted the step of legalizing most preexisting informal second-economy activities and creating new legal private business forms. In fact, at the eleventh hour, the party leadership allowed the project to languish because of a slight economic upturn: by the spring of 1980, the population had accepted the domestic price hikes quietly, and the balance of payments improved with a rise in convertible currency exports. But in early summer, a further deterioration in the external balance showed that the reprieve had been temporary, and the leadership demanded a stepped-up pace from the commission assigned to work with the various government agencies and ministries to formulate what would become the 1982 reform of property rights. Some in the Planning Office assigned to the project were highly skeptical about the chances of such a proposal ever being implemented, and refused to believe that it had received the "political green light" from above. Others were afraid of later political reprisal, and one department head actually refused to sign "such a document, [saying] he did not want to be jailed for ten years." Among the few officials with "informal knowledge" of the preparatory work under way, some "mocked" it ("Who is backing you that you dare such things?"), still others were concerned about the betrayal of socialist ideals, and very few openly supported the idea, although some "kept their fingers crossed in secret" (Fekete 1990, 21–22).

The party's application of historically and ideologically laden language was a reflexive process. Reformers used this language to conciliate the claim that an expanded market sector based on private ownership could coexist peacefully with the state sector and the political status quo, and their own tactical awareness that winning the larger party and government apparatus over to this viewpoint would be difficult. But peaceful coexistence seemed plausible in the first place because by the late 1970s, the Hungarian socialist system had become identified with its long history of pragmatism. The system had partially reformed itself often enough so that to most members of the party-state apparatus, the possibility of revolution seemed as remote as the possibility of actually naming a part of that system not socialist. In effect, any "pragmatic" reform that was proposed came to be viewed as yet another manifestation of a reformist socialist regime. By this time, party leaders, once impelled by a mandate of vigilance against enemies internal and external, were either uninterested in distinguishing "friend" from "foe," or unable to do so, except in the narrow sense of tactical "enemies" — those who opposed their plan of the moment. The system was even able to accommodate champions of radical reform. The institutional residue of reform had unhinged expectations to the point where, at least from the perspective of reform-minded "insiders," the essence of the system was a certain malleability. In this context, a new discourse of property-rights reform was constructed under the safe rubric of liberalization of the second economy, with virtually no reference to ownership or property rights per se. This discourse altogether avoided the fact that the 1982 reform was much more than the liberalization of supplemental earning possibilities for workers — that it was, in truth, an institutional reform of property rights with far-reaching sociopolitical effects. The reform turned out to be a watershed in the process of de-étatization of the economy. But given the institutional residue of reform in Hungary, parties to any particular reform debate could always locate the "turning point" either in the past or in the future: it never had to be the reform under discussion. For many, the real turning point that made Hungarian socialism "different" was the New Economic Mechanism of 1968; for some, it was the early reforms of the 1950s; and for still others, it had yet to occur. In any case, proponents of reforms — especially later ones — had a good chance of defusing political debate.

Accordingly, in 1981 party debates, sponsors of the reform maintained that it was not a threat to political stability and would not alter power relations in any significant way. And, since in certain aspects the reform represented an ex post facto legalization of long-standing second-economy practices,[29] some officials and potential entrepreneurs alike mistakenly dismissed it as just another phase in the familiar cycle of repression and toleration of second-economy activity.

However, by explicitly redefining both the legal limits and content of property rights, the party state effectively lost its three-decade battle to keep the second economy within boundaries it tacitly deemed "acceptable." In principle, the 1982 reform could have been rescinded, since it was not yet firmly anchored in the constitution and in the fundamental political changes of 1989.[30] In practice, unless the reform had been rescinded very

29. Notably the intrafirm work partnership, which institutionalized earlier informal bargaining between skilled workers and state-firm managers. See Stark 1989.

30. Like almost everything else about the 1982 regulations, this too was somewhat ambiguous. Ultimately the day-to-day efforts to harmonize the complex regulations fell to the Minis-

soon after its enactment into law, the party would have had to launch a new national program of expropriation to take back the property rights it granted the citizenry. This would have required that hard-liners gain the upper hand within the party, and that they be willing to use force. Such a move, in turn, would have further undermined the already weakened legitimacy of the party, and not only in the obvious sense that the use of force might have rekindled the passions of 1956. In addition, given the practical and ideological justifications for the "helper economy" that officials advanced in the aggressive media campaign to educate the population about the reform, reversal would have damaged the party's credibility beyond redemption.

HYBRID ECONOMY AND POLITY

In our story, economic reforms have figured as the formal, ex post facto expression of underlying shifts in the system of socialist dependencies. We have seen that despite the hierarchical nature of this system, workers were able to force concessions from the state by rechanneling their labor power into informal economic activities. Eventually, the leadership faced an impossible choice. Either it had to implement economywide institutional reforms like those currently under way in postsocialist countries, explicitly restructuring the state sector and inciting a broad coalition of political opposition; or do nothing and risk serious political unrest on the part of a populace accustomed to a relatively high consumption standard.

Against this background, the 1982 reform of property rights was at once plausible and radical. It was a way out of the dilemma, and could be conceived of as part of a broader effort to stimulate market competition in the state sector.[31] By adding "small enterprises on a large scale" (Buky 1981) — in short, by modernizing the second economy — reformers hoped to create a sector of small-scale firms that would increase the flexibility and efficiency of large state-owned firms.

---

try of Finance, although some types of firms were registered with the Court of Registry, bringing them under constitutional authority.

31. For example, small independent enterprises were formed by breaking off from a large trust or enterprise. The former were no longer subject to many types of detailed administrative interference and reporting requirements, and no longer received subsidies or access to materials through the parent organization, which, correspondingly, could no longer siphon off resources from the newly independent enterprises. Also, prior to 1982, only a ministry, some other national agency, or a local council could found an enterprise. After 1982, enterprises could establish subsidiary companies. See Hare 1983, 323–25; and Comisso and Marer 1986. For the rationale behind the whole range of institutional reforms undertaken in the early 1980s, a description of the "menu" of models needed to introduce flexibility into the Hungarian economy, and the legal and organizational forms employed, see Sárközy 1988, 80–103.

Party leaders attained their short-term goal of stabilizing consumption levels because the reform led to the population's almost incredible self-exploitation: in the 1980s, Hungarians worked the longest day in Europe (Economist Intelligence Unit 1990, 9). In the longer term, the reform had far-reaching, unanticipated consequences. The contention of some analysts that the 1982 statutes hardly altered the "statist character" of the Hungarian economy (e.g., Kovrig 1987, 122) is accurate only if we consider fixed capital assets or official measurements of the national product; and then only in the static sense. Although 80–90 percent of the means of production were still state owned as of 1990, it was also estimated at that time that the second economy — in all its traditional and newer manifestations — accounted for up to 30 percent of GDP.[32] Poor in capital, but rich in highly motivated and skilled labor power, this sector produced goods and services far out of proportion to its capital assets.

In addition, by 1988–89, economic work partnerships, small cooperatives, and independent craftsmen cooperated routinely in numerous ways that were important to their individual stability and growth prospects. This cooperation ranged from simple barter deals (one firm's microcomputer repaid by another's work on a rush project) and the subcontracting of overflow work, to informal information-sharing or the pooling of resources. And once the 1989 Law on Association eliminated the legal, if not all actual, discrimination against private firms, as well as the barriers to their interaction with the state sector, the earlier establishment of forward linkages with state firms began to produce new forms of cooperation between the two sectors, such as an increasing number of joint ventures.

In sum, private business expanded more rapidly and robustly than many officials expected (Fekete 1984, 28–29), and its political-institutional consequences imposed a significant burden of change on the government. The seemingly endless round of amendments, modifications, and subsequent reforms that the Ministry of Finance was forced to undertake between 1982 and 1989 indicates that once property rights are granted to groups thereby legally enfranchised, the pressure to broaden those rights grows from its own logic.

Many new issues arose in this period. If, for example, the party permitted private enterprise, it also had to allow the purchase of real estate on a commercial basis. If banks could lend the funds of private businesses to state firms and to individual borrowers, how would the party justify denying private businesses equal access to commercial loans? And if one purpose of the "helper economy" was to ease shortages and bottlenecks, on what basis would private firms be prevented from establishing joint ventures with domestic and foreign firms, or engaging in cross-border trade?

32. István Gábor, quoted in "Italy on the Danube," 1991.

We have seen that the balance of power between the ubiquitous subterranean second economy and the state had been changing prior to 1982 as well. However, as long as the renegotiation of this balance remained largely tacit, it was essentially stable within broad institutional limits. Formalization of this relationship upset the balance. Simply put, prior to 1982, the state could pursue more or less tolerant policies toward the informal sector, but the limits of its authority were substantially redrawn with the institutional reform that redefined the rights of second-economy participants. Moreover, once legalized on an expanded basis, the party took on *the official responsibility* for the mediation of the internal systemic contradictions engendered by the conflicting logics of private and state-firm activities pursued in a socialist framework. These contradictions took the form of pressing daily problems in need of immediate attention, usually from the Ministry of Finance, which issued decree after decree in the effort to resolve them. The net effect of such decrees was the broadening of second-economy entrepreneurs' property rights and space for action, and a blurring of the lines of authority within and between various government institutions previously responsible for overseeing the small pre-1982 formal private sector.

These broadened rights posed challenges that extended beyond coordination of increasingly complex economic mechanisms. Once endowed with legal status, individual entrepreneurs and various organized groups pressed for further changes. For instance, transmission-belt organizations, responsible for "representing" the interests of the small traditional legal private sector of manufacturers and retailers, were internally disrupted because the government changed the economic landscape overnight without specifying their new mandates (Seleny 1993, ch. 6). In 1987, entrepreneurs formed their own independent interest-representation organization, which helped extract concessions for the private sector (e.g., on tax policy); and a year later, entrepreneurs formed a political party.[33]

Finally, having partially internalized the cost of highly motivated labor and its applied knowledge, as well as the accountability for the systemic contradictions this implied, the government set in motion a process that would culminate in an even more radical internalization: the 1989 Association Law, whereby it all but abandoned pretense at controlling the number and organizational types of private businesses.

---

33. The Entrepreneur's party was never very large or powerful, since the entrepreneurs were not a unified political bloc in Hungary, any more than elsewhere. But in 1988, the Smallholders' party, the strongest political party from 1945 to 1948, reestablished itself and again advocated a strong private sector, especially the reprivatization of land. Over the next two years, the interests of the private sector began increasingly to figure in the platforms of the other major independent parties as well.

Still, there had been significant opposition to the 1982 reform. Progressive officials were able to overcome this opposition and implement their program because they self-consciously cast the reform as a continuation of socialist tradition. The same reform discourse, to be sure, would not have resonated in the same way elsewhere. But in Hungary, this discourse was plausible even to hard-liners, because it drew on a forty-year history of greater and lesser departures from central planning, and was eventually accepted as "fitting into" — not threatening — a "pragmatic" Hungarian variant of socialism.

This victory by reformers marked the point of no return in the long transformation. As we have seen, a new program of expropriation and nationalization would have required force, and would have seriously destabilized a regime whose legitimacy had already been eroded. Secondly, this remarkable shift in official ideology had profound consequences. To the extent that a society is shaped by a common ideology, it is effectively governed by what one scholar calls the "regnant metaphor." Such a metaphor infuses the lives and struggles of those who believe in it with transcendental meaning; even skeptics and unbelievers cannot altogether escape its influence if it is pervasively institutionalized. A society that merely dethrones its regnant metaphor risks anarchy; one that openly supplants it may undergo revolution (Cruz-Sequeira 1994). In Hungary, as elsewhere in the socialist world, the party state upheld a metaphor of social life as an existential battle between friend and foe — and private enterprise had long been regarded as an archenemy. This metaphor was partially modified early on in practice; but it was explicitly and comprehensively altered only in 1982. The "foe" became "friend" and "helper" in official rhetoric and law; private enterprise would thereafter be society's enemy only if it transgressed limits established by socialist law.

CONCLUSION

The 1982 reform of private property rights — a late manifestation of recurring reform cycles — further *destabilized* party ideology, social attitudes, and behavior, even as it proved insufficient to stabilize the economy in the long run. Like earlier reforms, once enacted, the 1982 property-rights reform narrowed subsequent choices for the leadership. *Unlike* earlier reforms, the 1982 reform created new institutions and explicitly political actors: newly legal forms of economic association, ownership, and work that enfranchised a broad, but previously vilified, social group on a very different political basis. Moreover, by enfranchising groups upon which it had, ironically, become partially dependent precisely because it had marginalized them for so long, the state surrendered its exclusive control over ownership, production, employment, and resource allocation. The system came to depend, in fact, on those it had excluded: second-economy entrepreneurs and "radical" reformers.[34]

Most profoundly, the relationship between the second economy and the socialist state led to the mutual absorption of two extreme conceptions of politics: the one a balancing of socioeconomic interests, the other having to do with the formation of essential identity and the maintenance of maximal cohesion within the party state. In Hungary, neither conception triumphed, for neither state strategies to limit private economic activity — ranging from repression to tacit toleration and reform — nor the defensive oppositional strategies of second-economy participants were entirely "successful." As we have seen, the party leadership got much more than it bargained for, and the entrepreneurs less: the former lost "control", and the private sector, however dynamic, operated under a variety of restrictions and impediments until 1989.

However, the process that culminated in a redefinition of property rights was also bound up with increasingly broad and diverse conceptions of self on the part of all involved. These conceptions often stood in opposition to official norms and thus undermined the very social categories on which the system rested. Even as they despaired at their own belief in the possibility of infinite "corruption" within the context of an "unchangeable" system, Hungarians were simultaneously drawn to what had officially been seen as "disreputable" second-economy activities. For many, such activities, initially a route to subsistence, became subtle acts of defiance, and gradually a source of self-definition and esteem, encompassing the concepts of time, knowledge, and relation to work as property. As Hungarians became housebuilders, mechanics, software designers, private marketers of their own produce — indeed, as they became astute buyers and vendors of all manner of tangible and intellectual goods and services — they also constructed parallel identities and quasi-institutionalized networks of high-trust alliances. Second-economy production and consumption came to represent an incipient alternative politic so widespread as to leave virtually no one untouched. Over time, the informal and formal private sectors merged, and a sui generis private market took shape. This hybrid private sector, which throughout its development contributed to the expansion of the range of economic and political choice for previously excluded groups, still coexists with the remnants of a large state sector, and thus sometimes faces discrimination despite laws guaranteeing a level playing field for private and state-owned firms.[35] At the same time, however, and especially in the far more transparent political and economic context following Hungary's first post-

34. Kornai 1986 distinguishes between "naive" and "radical" reformers. See esp. 1728–32.
35. Notably in credit allocation and access to scarce inputs.

socialist elections, the private sector continues to grow and to recombine creatively with privatizing state firms.

Hungary's contemporary mixed economy thus represents, in part, the historical culmination of socialist economic reforms that, as we have seen, failed in their intent to "perfect" socialism, but had profoundly transformative consequences for state and society alike. These consequences were political in the broadest sense of the word, entailing not only the diffusion and formalization of property rights but enhanced notions of work and identity born of those expanded rights.

Five years after the fall of the Hungarian Socialist Workers' party, comparative assessment of the costs and benefits of Hungary's protracted transformation is still difficult. Yet two things seem clear on this reading of late socialist and early postsocialist Hungary. First, like the other countries of the region, Hungary will almost certainly *remain* a highly mixed economy for decades to come. While the need to reduce the size and influence of the state sector and to free economic space for private enterprise is pressing for all postsocialist countries, Hungary's precocious accommodation of private and quasi-private businesses led, as we have seen, to their informal and formal cooperation with state firms. This positive legacy of reform socialism is likely to enhance the possibilities for mutually beneficial cooperation among Hungary's contemporary hybrid economic institutions.

Finally, the political process that underlay reform socialism holds useful lessons about compromise for today's leaders; and it warns against extremes of political-economic reasoning and discourse, whether of international or domestic origin. At best, policy prescriptions born of such reasoning and rhetoric are simply out of touch with the complex reality of contemporary Hungary.[36] At worst, they block efforts to use local experiences of adaptation and histories of compromise creatively.

REFERENCES

Act on Economic Associations. 1988. Public Finance in Hungary, no. 45. Budapest: Secretariat of the Ministry of Finance.

Andorka, Rudolf. 1989. Author's interview, Harvard University Center for European Studies, Cambridge, Mass.

———. 1990. "The Importance and Role of the Second Economy for Hungarian Economy and Society." MS. Budapest: University of Economics.

Antal, László. 1985. "About the Property Incentive (Interest in Property)." *Acta Oeconomica* 34, 3–4: 275–86.

Arendt, Hannah. [1951] 1986. *The Origins of Totalitarianism.* London: André Deutsch.

---

36. Several prominent Hungarian researchers have recently made similar observations. See Kornai 1993, 51.

Benton, Lauren. 1991. *Invisible Factories: The Informal Economy and Industrial Development in Spain.* Albany: State University of New York Press.

Berend, Iván T. 1983. *Gazdasági útkeresés, 1956–1965* (Searching for the Economic Path, 1956–65). Budapest: Magvető.

Buky, B. 1981. "Hungary Tries Small Enterprises on a Large Scale." Radio Free Europe Background Reports (Hungary), October 12.

Comisso, Ellen. 1991. "Where Have We Been and Where Are We Going? Analyzing Post-Socialist Politics in the 1990's." In *Political Science: Looking to the Future,* vol 2, ed. W. Crotty, 77–122. Evanston, Ill.: Northwestern University Press.

Comisso, Ellen, and Paul Marer. 1986. "The Economics and Politics of Reform in Hungary." *International Organization* 40, 2: 421–54.

Cruz-Sequeira, Consuelo. 1994. "The Political Culture of Order and Anarchy: Remembrance and Imaginative Power in Central America." Ph.D. diss., Massachusetts Institute of Technology.

Demsetz, Harold. 1988. *The Organization of Economic Activity.* London: Basil Blackwell.

Donáth, Ferenc. 1977. *Reform és forradalom: A magyar mezögazdaság strukturális átalakulása, 1945–75* (Reform and Revolution: The Structural Transformation of Hungarian Agriculture, 1945–75). Budapest: Akademia Kiadó.

Economist Intelligence Unit. 1990. *Hungary: Country Profile, 1990–91.* London: World Microfilms Publications.

Fekete, Judit. 1984. "Adalékok a kisvállalkozás jelenségrendszeréhez" (Contributions to the Phenomenon of Small Enterprise). MS. Budapest: Eotvös Lorand University (ELTE).

———. 1990. " 'Coup' as a Method of Management: Crisis Management Methods in Hungary in the Eighties." *Acta Oeconomica* 42, 1–2: 55–72.

Friedrich, Carl Joachim, and Zbigniew K. Brzezinski. 1965. *Totalitarian Dictatorship and Autocracy.* Cambridge, Mass.: Harvard University Press.

Gábor, István. 1988. "Second Economy in State Socialism: Past Experience and Future Prospects." Unpublished paper presented at the 3d Congress of the European Economics Association, Bologna.

Gábor, István, and Péter Galasi. 1985. "Second Economy, State and Labour Market." In *Labour Market and Second Economy in Hungary,* ed. Péter Galasi and György Sziráczki, 122–32. Frankfurt: Campus.

Galasi, Péter, and György Sziráczki. 1986. "The New Industrial Organization: Review of Developments in the Organization and Structure of Small and Medium-sized Enterprises." Country Report, Hungary. MS. Budapest: Karl Marx University of Economics.

Hankiss, Elemér. 1989. "Demobilization, Self-Mobilization, and Quasi-Mobilization in Hungary, 1948–1987." *Eastern European Politics and Societies* 3, 1: 105–51.

Hare, Paul. 1983. "The Beginnings of Institutional Reform in Hungary." *Soviet Studies* 35, 3: 323–25.

———. 1986. "Industrial Development of Hungary since World War II." Paper prepared for conference, The Effects of Communism on Social and Economic Change: Eastern Europe in Comparative Perspective. Joint Committee on Eastern Europe, Department of Economics, Heriot-Watt University, Edinburgh.

Hare, Paul, Hugo K. Radice, and Nigel Swain, eds. 1981. *Hungary: A Decade of Economic Reform.* London: George Allen & Unwin.

Hegedüs, András, and Mária Márkus. 1979. "The Small Entrepreneur and Social-ism." *Acta Oeconomica* 22, 3–4: 267–89.

Hetényi, István. 1991. Author's interview. University of Economics, Budapest.

Hough, Jerry. 1969. *The Soviet Prefects: The Local Party Organs in Industrial Decision-making.* Cambridge, Mass.: Harvard University Press.

———. 1977. *The Soviet Union and Social Science Theory.* Cambridge: Harvard University Press.

"Italy on the Danube." 1991. *Economist*, February 23, 48.

Kornai, János. 1980. *The Economics of Shortage.* 2 vols. Amsterdam: North-Holland Publishing.

———. 1986. "The Hungarian Reform Process: Visions, Hopes and Reality." *Journal of Economic Literature* 24, 4: 1687–1737.

———. 1992. *The Socialist System: The Political Economy of Communism.* Princeton, N.J.: Princeton University Press.

———. 1993. "Transformational Recession: A General Phenomenon Examined Through the Example of Hungary's Development." Collegium Budapest Institute for Advanced Study, Discussion Paper no. 1.

Kovrig, Bennett. 1987. "Hungarian Socialism: The Deceptive Hybrid." *Eastern European Politics and Societies* 1, 1: 113–34.

Nee, Victor, and David Stark, eds. 1989. *Remaking the Economic Institutions of Socialism: China and Eastern Europe.* Stanford, Calif.: Stanford University Press.

Oi, Jean. 1991. "Partial Market Reform and Corruption in China." In *Reaction and Reform in Post-Mao China,* ed. R. Baum, 143–61. New York: Routledge.

Poggi, Gianfranco. 1978. *The Development of the Modern State: A Sociological Introduction.* Stanford, Calif.: Stanford University Press.

Róna-Tas, Ákos. 1989. "The Social Origins of the Transformation of Socialism in Hungary: The Second Economy." Paper delivered at the annual meeting of the American Association for the Advancement of Slavic Studies, Chicago.

Sabel, Charles, and Stark, David. 1982. "Planning, Politics, and Shop-floor Power: Hidden Forms of Bargaining in Soviet-imposed State-Socialist Societies." *Politics and Society* 11, 4: 439–75.

Sárközy, Tamás. 1982. "Vállalattipusok és a jog" (Enterprise Types and the Law). *Gazdaság* 15, 32.

———. 1988. "Elöszó." In *A tarsásági törvény: Magyarázatokkal és iratmintákkal* (Introduction to the Law on Association: Explanations and Sample Documents). Budapest: Lang.

Seleny, Anna. 1989. "The Hungarian Second Economy as Political Arena." Paper delivered at the annual meeting of the American Association for the Advancement of Slavic Studies, Chicago.

———. 1991. "Hidden Enterprise and Property Rights Reform in Hungary." *Law and Policy* 13, 2: 149–69.

———. 1993. "The Long Transformation: Hungarian Socialism, 1949–1989." Ph.D. diss., Massachusetts Institute of Technology.

Skilling, Gordon, and Franklyn Griffiths, eds. 1971. *Interest Groups in Soviet Politics.* Princeton, N.J.: Princeton University Press.

Stark, David. 1985. "The Micropolitics of the Firm and the Macropolitics of Reform: New Forms of Workplace Bargaining in Hungarian Enterprises." In *States versus*

60   ANNA SELENY

Markets in the World System, eds. P. Evans, D. Rueschemeyer and E. H. Stephens, 247–73. Beverly Hills, Calif.: Sage.

———. 1986. "Rethinking Internal Labor Markets: New Insights from a Comparative Perspective." *American Sociological Review* 51, 4: 492–504.

———. 1989. "Coexisting Organizational Forms in Hungary's Emerging Mixed Economy." In *Remaking the Economic Institutions of Socialism: China and Eastern Europe,* eds. Victor Nee and David Stark, 137–68. Stanford, Calif.: Stanford University Press.

Székács, Anna. 1990. Author's interview, Ministry of Finance, Budapest.

Szelényi, Iván. 1982. "The Intelligentsia in the Class Structure of State-Socialist Societies." In *Marxist Inquiries,* supplement, *American Journal of Sociology* 88, eds. Michael Burawoy and Thoda Skocpol, 349–397.

———. 1988. *Socialist Entrepreneurs. Embourgeoisement in Rural Hungary.* Madison: University of Wisconsin Press.

———. 1990. "Eastern Europe in an Epoch of Transition: Toward a Socialist Mixed Economy?" In *Remaking the Economic Institutions of Socialism: China and Eastern Europe,* eds. Victor Nee and David Stark, 208–32. Stanford, Calif.: Stanford University Press.

Walder, Andrew. 1990. "Political Upheavals in the Communist Party-States." *States and Social Structures Newsletter* 12 (Winter): 7–9. New York: Social Science Research Council.

THREE

The Second Economy as a Subversive Force: The Erosion of Party Power in Hungary

Ákos Róna-Tas

In the past decade and a half, few scholars of state-socialist societies disputed the political significance of economic activities outside the state-organized socialist sector, the so-called second economy. Now that state socialism has collapsed in Eastern Europe and the Soviet Union, one must ask what role, if any, the second economy played in the rapid demise of these regimes.

While there has been a virtual consensus on the political importance of the second economy, by no means everyone has claimed that it was a subversive force. Some have argued that the second economy lived in organic symbiosis with the first (Grossman 1982; Ericson 1984; Mattera 1985; Gábor 1986; see also Kemény 1984). It is claimed to have been a stabilizing factor in these societies, as it kept the wheels of an ill-conceived economic system spinning by nimbly correcting the inefficiencies of central planning (Stark 1986, 1989). In political terms, the second economy was a blessing to the regime, because it kept people busy, away from politics, pursuing their individual interests without the possibility of becoming collective actors through organized political action (Burawoy 1985, 194–95).

Those who believe that the second economy was a subversive force first pointed to the ideological hostility and suspicion with which party states viewed it. They argued that the second economy upset and interfered with the process of macroeconomic planning and control by creating a segment in the national economy that was not only impossible to plan and hard to influence, but was even difficult to observe systematically (O'Hearn 1981;

I would like to thank Anna Székács, who as an architect and defender of the legalization of small private enterprise during the 1980s is one of the heroes hidden behind the abstractions of the sociological narrative, for her generous help. I have also received useful comments from David L. Bartlett, Ellen Comisso, István R. Gábor, Anna Seleny, Andrew G. Walder, and anonymous reviewers. — ART.

Galasi and Kertesi 1987). Worse yet, the alternative resources provided by
the second economy and not controlled by the center created a new space
of stratification, where new groups were forming with their autonomous
group interests, soon to be converted into a political challenge (Rakovski
1978; Bloch 1986; Kennedy 1991; Kolosi 1984). At a deeper level, the
second economy was also a force of socialization whereby people acquired
values that eventually were bound to clash with the officially promoted value
system (Szelényi 1988; Kovách 1988).

What was the role of the second economy in the collapse of communism?
In this paper, through an analysis of the Hungarian case, I attempt to answer
this question. I argue that the second economy undermined the regime's
economic power, its control over the economy as a whole. Whatever correc-
tive effect it had was very small, and even this effect resulted in unforeseen
difficulties. Moreover, I contend that the legalization of the second economy also led to unanticipated social and political consequences that made
the leadership weaker.

Admittedly, Hungary is a special case, because the second economy was
more developed there than elsewhere in Eastern Europe, with the possible
exception of Poland (Sampson 1986; Ékes 1986; Cochrane 1988; Szelényi
1988, 23–32; Łos 1990; Jedrzejczak 1991). This development gave the second economy in Hungary the visibility and, possibly, the force it did not
possess in most other countries in Eastern Europe. Yet this exceptional
strength seems to contradict our preliminary claim about the subversive
nature of the second economy. As this strength derived from the fact that
the Hungarian party state accepted and legalized many forms of the second
economy, one needs to explain why the communist party state embraced
the second economy, if indeed it was subverting communist power.

One way to decide whether the second economy was subversive or re-
medial for the system is to assume the perspective of the party state itself.
Using the expectations of the central apparatus can provide us with a convenient baseline against which the performance of the second economy can
be evaluated. Yet if we claim that the second economy failed by the very
standards of the central bureaucracy, we have to explain why the leadership
kept to a policy it had to consider a failure.

WHAT THE PARTY THOUGHT THE SECOND ECONOMY COULD DO

Through an elaborate process starting in 1976, the leadership of the Hungarian regime came to the conclusion that, all in all, a carefully limited
second economy could serve a useful purpose in the development of socialism (Fekete 1987, 1990; Berend 1990, 240–74). By 1980, the regime was in
a difficult situation. Real wages in the socialist sector began to decline in the
late 1970s (table 3.1). The economy was accumulating a foreign-debt bur-

TABLE 3.1   Real Wages from the Socialist Sector,
1967–1989

Year	Real Wages per Worker (previous year = 100)
1967	103.7
1968	102.3
1969	104.5
1970	104.7
1971	102.3
1972	102.2
1973	102.8
1974	105.6
1975	103.8
1976	100.1
1977	103.8
1978	103.1
1979	98.3
1980	98.4
1981	101.1
1982	99.3
1983	96.8
1984	97.6
1985	101.3
1986	101.9
1987	99.6
1988	95.1
1989	100.9

SOURCE: Baló and Lipovecz 1991, 606–7.

den of as yet unknown proportions (Zloch-Christy 1987, 31–42), which had to be serviced with a sclerotic and inefficient industrial structure and under constantly worsening terms of trade (Berend 1990, 234).

At the turn of the decade, the Hungarian leadership was facing a dilemma. If it did not want to return to the coercive practices of the 1950s and wanted to maintain an acceptable level of economic growth, it had only two choices. It could radically loosen state control over the entire economy by carrying out a thorough and radical economic reform, completely overhauling the socialist sector in hopes that this would result in higher efficiency, increased productivity, and a better industrial structure. Or it could try to follow its earlier path of extensive growth and increase production by drawing new resources into the economy.

Radical economic reform was politically unfeasible. In the political backlash against the liberalizing economic reforms of 1968, the position of large state companies was dramatically strengthened (Szalai 1990, 1991). Through a series of mergers in the 1970s, industrial production became highly concentrated (Kopátsy 1983), giving enormous power to company managers, who would have resisted radical changes, assuming the leadership had been willing to pursue this path.

Following its own inclinations and moving in the direction of less resistance, the regime chose the second alternative. The new resources that were needed to keep the economy going could not come from foreign sources, not just because the terms of trade had been shifting to the disadvantage of the country, but also because of rising interest rates that resulted from the tighter monetary policies of Western governments to fight inflation in the global recession (Zloch-Christy 1987, 87). In fact, Hungary had to maintain a positive balance in foreign trade — that is, allow resources to be taken out of the country — to be able to service its foreign debt. The state thus decided to draw new resources from the population in the form of labor and goods. This was very difficult. Virtually everyone who could work was in the labor force; in fact, the size of the workforce was declining (Galasi and Sziráczky 1983). Increasing labor time was politically unfeasible. Temporarily cutting consumption would have upset the bedrock principle of the Kádárist compromise, which promised slowly but securely rising living standards for political acquiescence, and was bound to create political tensions.

But while the political situation gave the leadership strong incentives to try to exploit the second economy, by the late 1970s, the reformers also had the proper ideology to frame the reform in an acceptable way. The language that was created by social scientists (Seleny 1993) allowed the leaders to think and talk about the second economy without open ideological hostility. The second economy could now be discussed as an economic rather than a political issue.

The resolution issued at the meeting of the politburo of the Hungarian Socialist Workers' party (HSWP) on February 19, 1980 (HSWP 1980b) officially endorsed an increased role for the second economy and spelled out the role the party leadership saw for it in building socialism. The document hastened to point out that the solution of the country's economic ills ultimately rested with the performance of the socialist sector, and that the interests of the socialist sector thus had to be protected above all. It would, however, be a mistake for the regime not to take advantage of the second economy — or *secondary* economy, as the party preferred to call it[1] — since over three-fourths of Hungarian families had already allegedly participated in it (a mysterious figure that was subsequently often quoted).

1. There was a heated debate in the late 1970s and early 1980s about the name that best described activities outside state-organized production. The second or secondary economy was often also called the auxiliary (*kisegítő*) economy.

The document spelled out the following goals for the secondary economy:

1. It should help to satisfy the need for consumer goods and services, and should help in the protection and expansion of the residential housing stock. On this first point, the leadership was guided by previous experience with household farming, private residential construction, and private services. In the 1970s, all three played an important role in the consumer economy, especially in the countryside.

2. The secondary economy was also to help create small units of production. This was needed because the socialist sector was overcentralized, with too many large firms. Concerning this second goal, the leadership left the most important issue ambiguous: were small units needed temporarily, or were there segments of the economy where the small would always prevail? This ambiguity is well reflected in a strictly confidential internal memo prepared for the politburo meeting by the Economic Policy Commission, which first explained that the "basis for the presence of the secondary economy is those real and differentiated needs that come with the rise in living standards [and that] cannot be met — or cannot be met with proper efficiency — by the socialist economy within the framework of large-scale production" (HSWP 1980a, 1).

This wording still left open the possibility that the problem was the fundamental incompatibility of certain "real" needs with socialist production. Yet later the memo makes a clearer statement: "A segment of needs can be met properly only by small organizations, often with a few members. *Currently*, organizations of this kind rarely exist in the socialist sector; small firms [have] more or less disappeared" (HSWP 1980a, 3; emphasis added).

Half a year later, in an action plan written in preparation for the new laws by one of the chief institutional sponsors of the reform, the Ministry of Finance, the distinction was clearly drawn (MF 1980). The new laws had a double purpose: they were simultaneously to allow the creation of smaller firms alongside the already-existing large ones *within* the socialist sector and to make it possible to take advantage of the second economy. The socialist economy was not inherently incompatible with small firms; currently, however, there happened not to be enough of them, and the second economy could act as a temporary substitute.

3. The leadership also foresaw that the necessary restructuring of the economy would result in the reallocation of workers. The secondary economy would then help by absorbing frictional unemployment. Restructuring the economy away from loss-producing, inefficient industries and toward dynamic, modern, competitive firms was a battle cry that had kept returning since the early 1960s, when Hungary stepped out of autarkic isolation.[2]

2. "Restructuring" meant, not so much a change in the organization of production, as a switch from one line of products to another one, i.e., from iron and steel to chemicals.

Each time this desire got on the political agenda, the specter of unemployment was raised, inasmuch as workers in loss-making firms were expected to be laid off. When in 1968 the leadership decided to brave this specter, a series of elaborate measures was taken to ease the decline in state jobs. However, unemployment failed to develop at that time, and the measures turned out to be completely unnecessary. Restructuring returned to the political agenda by the late 1970s.

4. The leadership expected the secondary economy to draw more labor into production. The resolution was vague about mobilizing private capital through the secondary economy, but the confidential internal memo made this need explicit (HSWP 1980a).

The leadership was very uneasy about mobilizing private capital from the population. Letting individuals invest ran against its chief principle that income must be proportionate to work and should be earned by work alone. Making money without work was an ideological anathema; rent income of any sort was strongly frowned upon.[3]

5. Finally, the new measures were to help to integrate the secondary economy into the socialist economy as a whole. It was claimed that the measures would allow better visibility, and thus more control over these activities. As the resolution put it:

> We have to make it explicit that recognizing private activities politically does not mean that we widen their realm at the expense of the socialist sector, but that we connect them better into our entire economic system, into the reach of the planned economy. We wish to make the spontaneous economic activities of the population better serve our goals of economic policy, and we make an effort to *make them more socially organized.*[4] (HSWP 1980b, section 9; emphasis added)

Illegal and invisible activities were supposed to decline as a result, making the second economy more amenable to a comprehensive system of regulation and planning. The internal memo also mentioned that new regulations should reduce monopolies in the secondary economy.

The need to control the second economy was quite obvious. Once the leadership was convinced that the second economy was not going to disappear anytime soon, it had only two alternatives: to try again to stamp it out or to make an attempt to draw it under its own supervision. The debacle of 1974, when the party state began to crack down on the second economy, which resulted in a serious meat and produce shortage by the next year, made it clear that only the second alternative was feasible (Róna-Tas 1989).

As to the social effects of these measures, the resolution suggests

---

3. The only form that was tolerated at that time was renting apartments for tourists through state agencies or subletting one's own apartment.

4. In official language, the "socially organized sector" is the sector organized by the state.

somewhat ambiguously that the secondary economy is "more usefully approached from the angle of the needs it serves than from that of the incomes [it generates]" (HSWP 1980b, section 2). Incomes earned proportionate to work were to be acknowledged. Again, the confidential internal memo was more blunt. It estimated that the number of people with very high incomes from the secondary economy was not more than a few tens of thousands; besides, very high incomes existed in the first economy as well. The memo also gave estimates about the participation of different social groups in the secondary economy. The lowest rate (10 percent) was for managers, and moving down the socioeconomic ladder, these rates increased. The memo made it clear that income earned from the secondary economy helped those worse off (people in need of housing, young couples, people with large families, and the elderly), thus relieving political tensions. Consequently, the leadership should anticipate no significant change in inequalities on the whole as a result of these measures.

Nevertheless, there was lingering nervousness about growing inequalities, so the action plan of the Finance Ministry tried to further ease these fears with the following reasoning in a discussion of the tax measures that had to accompany the new law:

> initially the measures . . . , on the one hand, will increase inequalities within the secondary economy because of competition, and [on the other] will increase differences between the secondary economy and those . . . living from wages and salaries. Because of cutting back internal consumption, incomes in this latter group will fall, and for this same reason, incomes from the second economy and the numbers of its participants will rise. . . . Labor power will be sucked into this area, as that is where differentiation will seem to happen according to one's performance. Well, if we do not obstruct this process by administrative measures, increasing competition will weed out many. Not everyone will then be able to earn [a] high income from the secondary economy. . . . All this will equalize incomes. (MF 1980, 9)

This is the classic liberal argument for equality through market competition.

Clearly, at this time, the leadership envisioned a socialist economy controlled by the state, with small private units helping out only as long as necessary. The reforms were to enhance economic performance, which, in turn, it was thought, would increase the legitimacy of the regime. It was not that the politburo and the central committee were unaware of the possible dangers. They kept pointing out that the umbrella term "second economy" was too all-inclusive. As they put it in the resolution: "The Politburo regards the comprehensive treatment and the aggregation of different activities [as] appropriate only under exceptional circumstances. . . . As these are diverse activities, which cannot be treated in a unified manner, it is more useful to review and legislate individual areas separately" (HSWP 1980b, section 10).

With this caveat, the leadership wished to retain maximum flexibility to tailor regulations according to its interests, not to allow undesirable activities to sneak in on the backs of desirable ones.

The laws of 1981, following the political decision, promoted the creation of small units in the socialist sector, allowed and encouraged private individuals to set up small work partnerships, and at the same time liberalized the licensing and operating conditions for small artisans and tradesmen working alone or with their families. The new laws somewhat relaxed the limitations on the number of people that could be employed by private employers; new partnerships could now employ up to ten people. As an important concession, the laws allowed private enterprises to engage in business with socialist firms.

These laws contained several restrictive conditions as well. No work partnership could become a legal entity, which meant that they had to face discrimination in a legal and administrative environment that favored corporate actors and discriminated against private ones (e.g., a series of activities were open only to "corporations"). Members of private partnerships bore unlimited liability for any failure. The law did not allow for members not actually working in the partnerships, and no one could thus become a member by investment only. There were severe restrictions on credit as well.

WHAT THE SECOND ECONOMY ACTUALLY DID

If the regime wanted to create a private sector that primarily attended to the needs of consumers, the reform clearly got out of hand. The majority of the new enterprises were either company work partnerships or cooperative work partnerships, partnerships founded in firms or cooperatives by employees using the resources of their mother company. These partnerships either subcontracted for their own firms or — less frequently — for other companies. In 1983, only 2 percent of their receipts came from consumers (CSO 1984). These figures did not substantially improve in the 1980s (HSWP 1985). Economic work partnerships, which were private partnerships founded solely by individuals with their own resources, and individual artisans and tradesmen also soon found out that doing business with state companies was much more lucrative than peddling to individual consumers. As a result, while consumer goods and services did improve somewhat overall, in many places their supply actually shrank as private entrepreneurs abandoned consumers to pursue more promising outlets among state firms.

As we have seen, the legalization of the second economy was intended to stimulate the creation of small companies. The predominance of large firms decreased in the 1980s, chiefly because of the multiplication of small private enterprises. Slowly the socialist sector, which included state firms and

TABLE 3.2   The Distribution of Firms
in the Socialist Sector by Size, 1982 and 1988

Firms	1982	1988
Companies and trusts	1,782	1,986
(more than 1,000 employees)		
Total no. of companies	752[a]	723
Total no. of employees (1,000s)	2,280[a]	2,126
Subsidiaries / small enterprises	25	391
Traditional cooperatives	4,132	3,772
Small cooperatives	145	3,100

sources: Calculated from CSO 1989, 120b, and CSO 1990, 120d.
[a]In 1981.

cooperatives, also began to change its face, yet not much happened to state firms. Cooperatives were the ones to shrink by spawning so-called small cooperatives, cooperatives with fewer than a hundred but more than fifteen members. The number of cooperatives of the old type declined as well. Yet large state companies prevailed; only in a few cases did local plants become autonomous subsidiaries and form small companies.[5] The socialist sector, especially the state sector, proved to be surprisingly resistant to change (table 3.2).

All in all, decentralization in the socialist sector succeeded only on its fringes, in the cooperative segment, but not in the segment where the state held direct property rights.

The expected restructuring of the economy failed to occur. There was no unemployment for the second economy to soak up. In fact, internal reports to the leadership claimed it as an achievement that private enterprises had not siphoned off labor from state firms, as they had in the late 1960s. Most of the participants in these new ventures kept their state jobs and engaged in their private activities part-time.

If anything, restructuring of the workforce was made more difficult by the reforms. Internal subcontracting made it possible for state firms to keep their workers. What attracted workers to a firm was its ability to provide lucrative subcontracting jobs, not its ability to pay higher wages.

It is also uncertain how successful the legislation was in mobilizing extra labor. The amount of time a person worked in 1986 was exactly the same as in 1977 (table 3.3). Time spent in the second economy increased, but this was counterbalanced by a two-hour cut in the work week in 1981–82. The

5. Small cooperatives and small enterprises were legal categories. Together with the limitation on their size, there were other special regulations they had to obey.

TABLE 3.3   How Hungarians Budgeted
Their Labor Time, 1977 and 1986
(Number of minutes on an average spring day)

Activity	1977	1986
Primary occupation	217	191
Conferences	1	2
Secondary nonmanual work	0	3
Secondary manual nonagricultural work	2	9
Household farming	60	74
Occasional agricultural work	1	/
All income-earning activities	281	281

SOURCE: Falussy and Harcsa 1987, 13.

main reason for this cut, originally heralded as a major step toward improving living standards, was that it had been promised much earlier, and the party had already begun phasing it in by 1980.

Yet if we look behind the number of minutes and hours counted, we find another picture. While the cut in work time in the socialist sector was two hours a week across the board, the increase in work time in the second economy was distributed very unevenly. Thus, those who worked in the second economy worked more in 1986 than in 1977, while those who did not work in the second economy worked less. As the free time of those engaged in the second economy was absorbed by that work, they increasingly began to draw on time at their state workplaces to do things they should have done after work. They would run errands, go home to receive the repairman, or even study for evening classes. This, of course, gave others license to do the same, even if they happened to have free time after work. This meant that the extra labor input in the private sector came at the expense of cutting effort in the socialist sector.[6] In other instances, people worked hard during regular hours, but on tasks for their private partnerships. This was especially common among professionals, such as engineers or architects, who could not be supervised by factory-style methods (Laky 1984). The law of 1981 did not result in more labor being drawn into the economy; it simply resulted in a redistribution of efforts.

In terms of investment, very little capital got mobilized (table 3.4). None

6. A study conducted by the Central People's Oversight Commission in 1983 revealed that half of the 8,400 surveyed clients attending to their own private business at various service outlets were doing so during the time they were supposed to be at work (Timár 1988, 115). One half of those absent from their jobs did not even bother to ask for permission. Finding reliable data on labor intensity that can be compared across years is impossible, but as discussed later, the leadership was convinced that labor discipline was not only poor but also declining.

TABLE 3-4 The Number of Small Work Partnerships Filing Taxes at the End of Each Year, Average Value of Their Assets, Average Value of Assets Per Capita, and Average After-Tax Annual Income of a Part-Time Participant

(in 1,000 Current Forints)

	1983	1984	1985	1986	1987
Economic work partnerships					
Number	4,629	7,340	9,514	10,941	11,185
Assets/enterprise	191.8	247.1	262.8	312.7	394.1
Assets/participant	32.1	37.8	40.6	47.2	58.9
Net income/part-time participant	40.3	54.1	54.5	56.5	69.4
Company work partnerships					
Number	9,837	17,775	20,267	21,490	19,117
Assets/enterprise	65.9	75.1	69.4	76.8	39.6
Assets/participant	6.2	6.6	5.8	6.2	3.1
Net income/part-time participant	28.9	35.8	35.9	37.9	42.6
Cooperative work partnerships					
Number	1,276	2,243	2,523	2,768	2,337
Assets/enterprise	454.8	570.7	554.8	621.9	752.3
Assets/participant	13.8	16.9	15.7	16.8	20.4
Net income/part-time participant	27.3	33.9	34.5	36.4	42.9
Other business partnerships					
Number	463	622	823	1,484	2,199
Assets/enterprise	266.6	284.9	222.8	178.7	528.9
Assets/participant	15.8	20.9	17.5	49.5	125.0
Net income/part-time participant	17.9	38.6	19.7	22.3	25.8

SOURCE: Calculated from Baló and Lipovecz 1988, 696–97.

of the company work partnerships needed any capital of their own, as they used their company's machines and premises. People in other types of private enterprise were reluctant to invest because of the lack of matching credit, legal limits on size of the operation, and, most important, because they did not trust the party state to keep to its political promises.

And, finally, did the reforms make the second economy easier to control? The proportion of illegal activity as a share of the gross domestic product did not decrease — in fact, it is estimated to have risen from around 15 percent in 1980 to 30 percent by 1987, the year before personal income tax was introduced. After that, this figure almost doubled in two years (Lackó 1992).

Where activities were the easiest to oversee, that is, in internal subcontracting partnerships, very serious and unanticipated difficulties arose. As early as November 30, 1982, the State Office of Wages and Labor (SOWL) critically described the practice by which firms circumvented wage regulations by giving out jobs to their workers through internal subcontracting (SOWL 1982). Because subcontracts were paid out of the expense fund and not the wage fund of companies, managers were able to pay more to their workers than they were supposed to. While workers performed quite efficiently when working under internal subcontracts, their total production on the job, which also included their inefficient and "undisciplined" regular work hours, was not proportionate to the overall income they received from their firms in two installments: as regular wages and as subcontractor fees. The memo sent to the party's Economic Policy Commission deplored the loss of control over wages and purchasing power, which resulted in inflationary pressures (SOWL 1982). This seriously upset the macroeconomic balance.

If, indeed, the reforms did not live up to the original expectations, why didn't the leadership turn around and put a stop to the experiment?

In 1984, for the first time in several years, the leadership closed the year with a foreign-trade surplus. This generated new optimism in top circles. The leadership believed that the recession was over and economic growth was back on track and felt sufficiently confident at that point to roll back the most undesirable features of the second economy.[7]

In 1985, new regulations slapped extra taxes on contracts between state companies and work partnerships. This was designed to cut down on the outflow of wages, which was most dramatic in internal subcontracting. While the initial targets were the company work partnerships, this extra tax was applied across the board. The leadership, which in 1980 was fully aware

7. "We are through with paying the penalty for our past mistakes," János Kádár reportedly said at a Central Committee meeting.

of the importance of handling parts of the second economy separately, had to realize that penalizing company work partnerships alone would simply make these partnerships turn into other forms of private work partnerships. It became clear that unless one were willing to erect an elaborate bureaucratic system of regulations and enforcement, only across-the-board measures could be successful. The extra tax was raised to 20 percent by 1987.

The leadership decided to mount an attack on a second front as well. In March 1985, the party's economic committee issued a directive in "defense of labor time." In October, in a draft for the action program that specified the steps to be taken, the State Office of Wages and Labor lamented. "In the last [few] years, several signs have suggested that labor discipline is deteriorating, and considering the past three decades, it can be stated that it is at its lowest point" (SOWL 1985, 1).

Ten months later, the final version of this document was submitted as the joint contribution of the State Office of Wage and Labor, the National Council of Trade Unions, and the Hungarian Chamber of Commerce, the organization representing company managers. A little more cautiously, but closely following the draft, and occasionally veering into metaphysical depths, the text argued that:

> In a broader sense, labor discipline is a certain mode of being of the citizen, it is a form of behavior, the substantive expression of one's relationship to labor. It reflects the wide spectrum of behavior the citizen judges permissible for himself. Labor discipline is a segment of discipline in general, of the economy and of the development of economic policy. In recent years, — as widely observed — labor discipline in its broader and narrower sense has been deteriorating in many areas of the economy. (SOWL 1986, 2)

In the summer of 1987, *Pártélet* (Party Life), the official organizational journal of the HSWP, published a roundtable discussion entitled "On Elementary Order." The participants bemoaned what they considered the complete breakdown of order, the lack of labor discipline, poor management and organization at the workplace, corruption, and the absence of discipline in society in general (Roundtable Discussion 1987). The representative of the State Office of Wages and Labor put it this way:

> We even encouraged people: work at six [different] places! Take a second job, join the company work partnerships, work on Saturdays and Sundays! This is how it happened. But scattered effort, exhaustion, and the fact that one could make more money in the second economy led to the decay of respect for the first job. There is a loosening of a solid value system that linked one's material success to the clockwork precision of labor in large-scale industrial organizations, [i.e.,] to conformity to traditional work culture. (Roundtable Discussion 1987, 44)

In July 1986, a secret resolution by the Council of Ministers was issued to clamp down on undisciplined workers.[8] This campaign, which in many respects bore the stamp of earlier discipline campaigns, replete with public exhortations and threats (Makó and Gyekiczky 1987), turned out to be the last of its kind and slowly fizzled out within a year.

WHY DID THE LEADERSHIP CONTINUE TO SUPPORT
THE SECOND ECONOMY?

In 1987, economic reform gained new impetus, partly because real wages began to decline again, and partly because foreign debt had been growing rapidly since 1985 (Zloch-Christy 1987, 42-68). In many respects, the country was back in where it had been in 1980 (footnote 1987, 310). A report by three ministries to the party leadership reiterated the original objectives of 1980, but this time they called for more radical solutions, because otherwise "the small-scale organizations may undergo a process of slow atrophy and exclusion from the economy" (MF 1987, 4). The suggestions included the introduction of private limited liability companies, joint ventures between state and private enterprises, and rules liberalizing private investment. These were the first steps toward the transition that continued in the drafting of the new Enterprise Law of 1989, which for the first time declared "sector neutrality": the legal equality of private and state-organized economic activities.

However, the reason for the leadership's failure to retreat from its liberal course was not simply that external economic conditions forced it to make concessions on behalf of efficiency. It is true that most of the debate increasingly took place within the highly bureaucratic discourse of economic policy; arguments and counterarguments were all couched in economic jargon in which the original social and political concerns were not made explicit. While the 1980 politburo resolution still spoke openly about some of the possible social and political consequences of the 1981 law, it failed to foresee the most important political developments because it was so preoccupied with the issue of income inequality.

The first unanticipated consequence was that after some initial skepticism, company managers in the socialist sector, with a few exceptions, quickly became strong supporters of work partnerships. First of all, small private partnerships were a way of avoiding decentralization in the state sector, which meant that large firms could preserve their power. State firms could also improve their economic performance by contracting with capable outside private partnerships. In these relationships, state companies

---

8. The campaign came on the heels of a similar campaign in the Soviet Union in 1985, after Gorbachev took power.

negotiated from a position of strength. Moreover, company work partnerships and cooperative work partnerships were attractive to state managers because they were instrumental in keeping the best workers in the firm satisfied. For these reasons, company managers resented the extra tax they had to pay on contracts with work partnerships.

Managers also resisted the disciplinary campaign. Despite all the complaints about increasing chaos and subsequent pressures to restore discipline, the number of disciplinary actions held steady, a little above seven thousand a year, during the early and mid 1980s, although it did slightly increase in industry (LIC 1982, 1985, 1988). This showed that company managers were reluctant to address the issue, or rather that they had other solutions to this problem.

The report filed by the State Office of Wages and Labor in July 1987, which evaluated the results of the disciplinary campaign, observed that

> the execution of the resolution in certain respects met with the disagreement of workers and company managers. This is also related to the fact that in certain cases, central regulation was taken as limiting the autonomy of the company. In our opinion, the new regulation helps bar management from granting certain, sometimes unprincipled, concessions in the process of labor market bargaining that are not in harmony with the spirit of the law. (SOWL 1987, 2)

Enterprise managers preferred "unprincipled concessions," turning a blind eye to discipline problems as long as they could bribe key workers by offering them subcontracting jobs to do what needed to be done.

But managers were prone to other forms of unprincipled behavior as well. The 1981 reform created a serious conflict of interest for company managers. Top managers were forbidden to join company work partnerships formed and subcontracted by their own firms; however, this restriction was spelled out more vaguely for managers of cooperatives. Furthermore, it was far from obvious where the dividing line ran between top managers and other employees. It was impossible to devise a hard-and-fast rule about who should be excluded from these work partnerships.[9] In the first years of the reform, the State Office of Wages and Labor was inundated with requests to evaluate the legality and appropriateness of particular cases. Seeing the impossibility of a legally coherent position, the office refused to give opinions and routinely directed applicants to consult a public memorandum published in 1976, five years before the reform had been announced. The normative void created by this sudden shift in the boundary between private and public led to general condemnations of corruption — the private mis-

---

9. People excluded from taking any second job included judges, lawyers, and members of the armed forces and the police.

appropriation of public (i.e., state) property—but very few cases of actual prosecution (Szamel 1989).

The 1981 reform also gave some of the more adventurous managers, especially those in the cooperative sector, the opportunity to split off the better-functioning part of the firm and start a small company. It is thus not surprising that top company managers, who became even more independent from the state apparatus in the mid 1980s,[10] gave their political support to small enterprises. This support found its institutional form when their political organization, the Chamber of Commerce, established a special Small Enterprise Division, which became the political voice of small companies and work partnerships.

There was a second unforeseen development that had a direct political consequence. In 1983, the Ministry of Finance asked for external opinions from all over the country for its next report on the status of the second economy. Károly Grósz, the first secretary of a northern county, who became prime minister in 1987 and first secretary of the HSWP in May 1988, wrote an eleven-page study generally supportive of small economic units, but also made the following observation:

> It is our conviction that these new opportunities can contribute to the strengthening of consumerism. It distracts a portion of people interested and potentially active in public affairs, it reduces the pool of potential cadres, and [it] raises doubts in people who are unselfishly working for the public good. (Grósz 1983, 6)

The second economy was also ruining the socialist brigade movement and eroding the trade unions:

> Many rightly see a contradiction in the fact that until now trade unions fought for shorter work hours, reduction in unhealthy jobs and in the retirement age, etc., and now workers in new enterprise forms completely ignore [these achievements] in pursuit of higher incomes and do not want them. In the long run, this can have undesirable effects for workers and can have [bad] consequences for companies and society. (Grósz 1983, 6)

The National Council of Trade Unions submitted a report voicing the same concerns about unregulated incomes and work conditions in partnerships. It also underscored the fact that the partnerships not only created tensions with the socialist work movement but weakened the "political activism" of their members, who were neglecting to attend union and party meetings (NCTU 1983).

"The new enterprise forms give two strata the opportunity of upward mobility: one is the progressive force of our society, the creative manual

---

10. From 1984 on, they were elected by the factory rather than appointed by the state.

TABLE 3.5   Relationship Between Party Membership
and Participation in the Second Economy
Among People in the Socialist Sector, 1986

	Not member of the HSWP	Member of the HSWP	
Not active in the second economy	2265 75.0%	373 68.1%	2638 74.0%
Active in the second economy	753 25.0%	175 31.9%	928 26.0%
	3018 84.6%	548 15.4%	3566 100.0%

SOURCE: 1986 Social Stratification Survey Database, TARKI (Institute for Social Research and Information), Budapest.
NOTE: Chi-square = 11.75081; D.F. = 1; significance = .0006.

workers and intellectuals; the other is that stratum that is unable to pass on to others the burden of inflation, and who must work extra in order to maintain their living standards," the Patriotic Popular Front, the official umbrella organization of all public associations, pointed out half a year later (PPF 1984, 2).

This "progressive force" was precisely the base from which the party had drawn its membership since the 1970s (Szelényi 1987). Almost a third of all party members were actively involved in the second economy in one way or another, compared with a fourth of the rest of the labor force (table 3.5), and party members were twice as likely to participate in work partnerships as those who were not members of the party (table 3.6). Small enterprises attracted party members in disproportionate numbers, as party members could take advantage of their connections in finding good contracts with socialist firms,[11] knew how to negotiate with bosses, and had organizational skills. Most of them were professionals and highly skilled workers; what had kept many of them out of the second economy before 1981 was that their specialized expertise often proved not to be very useful to individual customers, as few households needed the services of computer programmers or electrical, mining, and chemical engineers, not to speak of accountants, printers, machine-tool operators, and scientific researchers.

11. Just how important connections were was clearly spelled out in a report by the National Organization of Artisans. Most artisans who worked alone or with family for private consumers were at a disadvantage in finding contracts in the socialist sector. As the report put it: "Many [artisans] felt 'on their own skins' the lack of proper personal connections, which had a strong influence on their abilities to cooperate with large firms" (NOA 1983, 2).

TABLE 3.6   Relationship Between Party Membership
and Participation in Work Partnerships
in the Socialist Sector, 1986

	Not member of the HSWP	Member of the HSWP	
Not work partnership member	2843 94.2%	485 88.5%	3328 93.3%
Work partnership member	170 5.8%	63 11.5%	238 6.7%
	3018 84.6%	548 15.4%	3566 100.0%

SOURCE: 1986 Social Stratification Survey Database, TARKI (Institute for Social Research and Information), Budapest.
NOTE: Chi-square = 24.17333; D.F. = 1; significance = .0000.

The opening up of the socialist economy to the private economy made the character of labor more alike in the two sectors. Now the person who made valuable contributions in his state company could make valuable contributions in the private sector by performing a similar job for better pay. The same person whom the party needed on the shop floor could find opportunities in the private sector, and his interests were no longer tied to those of the party leadership.

The party very soon found that many of its best activists were deeply involved in the second economy and had little time for public affairs. As another strictly confidential memorandum to the politburo euphemistically put it in 1985, "the activities of work partnerships — according to the experiences of meetings of local party cells — make leisure time more valuable, and that sets higher standards for the quality of political and voluntary work" (HSWP 1985, 3).

Acutely aware of this problem, the party conducted a study in 1986 that showed that it was hard to get people to enroll in party schools and other political training courses, and that it had become difficult to recruit young people into the party (Székács 1987, 40). Party members had an influence not only by "exit" — by not participating in party life — but also by "voice," letting their party bosses know what their preferences were.

The reforms of 1981 thus created a constituency that had a vested interest in their continuation. Worse yet, this constituency was recruited from among company managers and activists on whom the party depended for its local presence.[12] Discontinuing the reforms would have meant that the leadership would have had to turn against the party's own ranks.

CONCLUSION

The role of the second economy in Hungary was clearly a subversive one. It accomplished very few of the objectives the leadership had set for it, it destroyed the leadership's control over labor, and it upset its ability to plan the macro-balance of income flows. Moreover, it deprived the party leadership of its social base.

The New Economic Mechanism, introduced in 1968, was the first substantial departure from central planning in Hungary. It aimed at revamping the internal mechanisms of the socialist sector. Within five years, party hardliners in the leadership were able to mount a successful assault on economic liberalization. Conservative spokesmen claimed that the reformist course had dealt a blow to the flagships of the socialist economy — the large industrial state firms — and undermined the economic position of the cornerstone of communist power — the urban industrial workers. They also mounted a successful attack on "petit bourgeois" behavior that sacrificed the collective good to petty egotism. At that time, party hard-liners were successful in rallying workers and managers of large companies to their cause, and as a result, economic reforms were halted and reversed (Hegedüs 1984; Berend 1990). Despite this reversal, the balance of power between the central apparatus and the companies, which the 1968 reforms tilted in favor of the second, never returned to where it had been before 1968.

The 1981 reform was initially an attempt to avoid more substantial reforms in the state sector, but instead inadvertently further weakened the power of the party state. This occurred, not simply through the strengthening of civil society vis-à-vis the party state, but by a reconfiguration of the division between the party state and civil society. By redrawing the boundary between private and public, the 1981 reform uncoupled the interest of company managers and the party membership from the power interests of the party. Worse yet, since the party initiated the reforms, managers and party members could argue that by following their new interests they fol-

---

12. There were some company managers who were less supportive. A manager who complained that work partnerships disorganized the wage structure explained why he nevertheless allowed them to operate in his company and was waiting for the top authorities to ban them. "By now the party secretary, the trade union representative, the party steward, and the majority of the union stewards are all members of work partnerships. This has become a political issue; without a high-level political decision, there is little I can do about it" (quoted in Pongrácz 1990, 115).

lowed the party line. As a result, conservatives in the party were paralyzed from within the party and it became impossible for them to repeat their earlier success. Like Cassandra and Laocoön, hard-liners tried to warn the party of the impending dangers, but this time the Trojans liked the big horse too much to heed their advice.

It has been pointed out all too frequently that scholarship on Eastern Europe overestimated the stability of these regimes. The literature on the second economy allows us to pinpoint some of the reasons why. These reasons are both theoretical and political.

The theoretical compass for most of the research on the second economy was provided by a new institutionalist framework (Nee and Stark 1989; Gábor 1980). This framework was developed in opposition to totalitarian and modernization theories of socialism at a time when empirical research became possible in these countries, and it greatly contributed to our understanding of the inner workings of socialism by discovering the diversity of its institutional forms and by providing a glimpse of socialism from below. However, its focus on the diverse institutional logic of particular areas of socialist societies deflected attention from the centrality of the party state — a principle at the heart of totalitarian theories — and from the historically cumulative changes in the system as a whole due to large-scale unintended consequences — a point emphasized by modernization theory. There is no doubt that on the first point, the new institutionalism was also hampered by the empirical inaccessibility of the party state. Since the party state was the linchpin of the socialist regime, the demise of socialism had to occur through the demise of the party state. The cost of ignoring the party state as an institution was to miss observing the disintegration of socialism.

Once the party state as an institution was reduced to insignificance in its theoretical framework, the new institutionalism lost the key to the process by which unintended consequences accumulated and acquired large-scale importance. The institution that had to manage all institutions was the party state, and it had the task of negotiating the immense variety of institutional outcomes with one another and with its own power interest. Without insight into the internal mechanisms of the party state, the new institutionalism had to abandon macropolitical concerns for a kaleidoscope of diverse institutions.

The political reason for underestimating the subversive force of the second economy was that the political consequences of depicting the second economy as a useful and integral part of the socialist economy were more acceptable to most researchers. The best scholars on this topic in Hungary were strongly involved in pushing for the legalization of private activities, and so it was imperative for them to argue that the second economy had few undesirable political side effects. Scholars in the West, who often relied heavily on the work of Eastern European researchers, were also reluctant to supply arguments for alarmist communist hard-liners.

While the second economy could not play a direct role in the rapid finale of the communist regimes, and thus will not supply either the final cause or an explanation for the timing of the collapse, it contributes to our understanding of how the collapse happened. It can partially clarify why the regime in Hungary was willing to give up its power with such surprising ease.

REFERENCES

Balo, György, and Iván Ipovecz, 1988. *Tények könyve '89* (The Book of Facts '89). Budapest: Computerworld Informatika.

———. 1991. *Tények könyve '91* (The Book of Facts '91), Budapest: Rácio.

Berend, Ivan T. 1990. *The Hungarian Economic Reforms, 1953–1988.* Cambridge: Cambridge University Press.

Bloch, Andrzej. 1986. "The Private Sector in Poland." *Telos* 66 (Winter): 128–32.

Burawoy, Michael. 1985. *The Politics of Production: Factory Regimes under Capitalism and Socialism.* London: Verso.

Cochrane, Nancy J. 1988. "The Private Sector in East European Agriculture." *Problems of Communism* 37, 2: 47–53.

CSO [Central Statistical Office]. 1984. *A kisszervezetek 1983-ban és 1984 I. félévében* (Small-scale Organizations in 1983 and the First Half of 1984). Budapest: KSH.

———. 1989. *Piaci szereplők a magyar gazdaságban, 1982–1989: A kisvállalkozások szerepe, fejlödése* (Market Actors in the Hungarian Economy, 1982–1989: The Role and Development of Small Ventures). Budapest: KSH.

———. 1990. *The Situation, Working Conditions, and Possibilities of Further Development of Small Ventures in Hungary.* Budapest: KSH.

Ékes, Ildikó. 1986. "Jövedelemszerzési lehetöségek egyenlötlensége és a munkaeröpiac megosztottsága" (Inequalities of Income Earning Opportunities and the Segmentation of the Labor Market). *Közgazdasági Szemle* 33, 4: 415–21.

Ericson, Richard. 1984. "The 'Second Economy' and Resource Allocation under Central Planning." *Journal of Comparative Economics,* 8, 1: 1–24.

Falussy, Béla, and István Harcsa. 1987. *Idömérleg: A magyar társadalom életmódjának változásai az 1977 tavaszi és az 1986 tavaszi idömérleg felvételek alapján* (Time Budget: Changes in the Ways of Life of the Hungarian Society According to the Spring 1977 and Spring 1986 Time Budget Studies). Budapest: KSH.

Fekete, Judit. 1987. "Kriziskezelésünk krizise" (The Crisis of Our Crisis Management). Diss., Hungarian Academy of Sciences.

———. 1990. " 'Coup' as a Method of Management: Crisis Management Methods in Hungary in the Eighties." *Acta Oeconomica* 42, 1–2: 55–72.

Gábor, R. István. 1986. "Reformok, második gazdaság, 'államszocializmus': A 80-as évek tapasztalatainak fejlödéstani és összehasonlitó gazdaságtani tanulságairól" (Reforms, the Second Economy, 'State Socialism': The Developmental and Comparative Economic Lessons of the Experiences of the 1980s). *Valóság* 7: 32–47.

Galasi, Péter, and Gábor Kertesi. 1987. "The Spread of Bribery in a Centrally Planned Economy." *Acta Oeconomica* 38, 3–4: 371–89.

Galasi, Péter, and György Sziráczky. 1983. "Gazdasági fejlödés és munkaeröpiac Magyarországon, 1968–1982: Az 'aranykortól' a válságig" (Economic Development and the Labor Market in Hungary, 1968–1982: From 'Golden Age' to Crisis). MS.

Grossman, Gregory. 1982. "Comment on 'The Second Economy in the CMEA: A Terminological Note' by Frank Holzman." ACES Bulletin 24, 1: 111–14.

Grósz, Károly. 1983. "Tájékoztató az új kisüzemi formák müködésének Borsod megyei tapasztalatairól" (Report on the Experiences of Small Businesses in Borsod County). MSZMP Borsod-Abaúj-Zemplén Megyei Bizottsága, August 31.

Hegedüs, András. 1984. "A nagyvállalatok és a szocializmus" (Large Firms and Socialism) Könyvdapgéri Kiemölay t, 11 l. j 66.

MSWP [Hungarian Socialist Workers' party]. 1980a. "Elöterjesztés a Politikai Bizottságnak a másodlagos gazdaság szerepéröl és fejlesztéséröl lehetöségéröl (Proposal for the Politburo on the Secondary Economy and the Possibility of Its Further Development). MSZMP KB Gazdaságpolitikai Osztály, February 19.

———. 1980b. "Határozat (a másodlagos gazdaság szerepéröl és fejlesztésének lehetöségéröl)" (Resolution on the Role of the Secondary Economy and the Possibility of Its Further Development). MSZMP PB, February 19.

———. 1985. "Jelentés a kiegészitö gazdasági tevékenységek helyzetéröl" (Report on the Situation of Complementary Economic Activities). MSZMP KB, July 31, 1985.

Jedrzejczak, Grzegorz T. 1991. "Privatisation and the Private Sector." In Poland into the 1990s: Economy and Society in Transition, ed. G. Blazyca and R. Rapacki, 107–17. London: Pinter.

Kemény, István. 1984. "A második gazdaság Magyarországon" (The Second Economy in Hungary). In Nemzet és demokrácia Kelet-Európában (Nation and Democracy in Eastern Europe), 18–30. Paris: Magyar Füzetek.

Kennedy, Michael D. 1991. Professionals, Power and Solidarity in Poland: A Critical Sociology of Soviet-Type Society. Cambridge: Cambridge University Press.

Kolosi, Tamás. 1984. "Status and Stratification." In Stratification and Inequality, eds. R. Andorka and T. Kolosi, 51–104. Budapest: Institute for Social Sciences.

Kopátsy, Sándor. 1983. Hiánycikk: a vállalkozás (A Good in Short Supply: Entrepreneurship). Budapest: Közgazdasági és Jogi Kiadó.

Kovách, Imre. 1988. Termelök és vállalkozók (Producers and Entrepreneurs). Budapest: Social Science Institute.

Lackó, Mária. 1992. "Az illegális gazdaság aránya Magyarországon 1970 és 1989 között: Egy monetáris modell" (The Proportion of the Illegal Economy in Hungary Between 1970 and 1989: A Monetarist Model). Közgazdasági Szemle 39, 9: 861–82.

Laky, Teréz. 1984. "Small Enterprises in Hungary: Myth and Reality." Acta Oeconomica 32, 1–2: 39–63.

LIC [Labor Information Center]. 1982, 1985, 1988. "A munkaügyi döntöbizottságok adatai" (Data on Labor Arbitration). Budapest: Munkaügyi Informatikai Központ, Allami Bér- és Munkaügyi Hivatal.

Łos, Maria, ed. 1990. The Second Economy in Marxist States. London: Macmillan.

Makó, Csaba, and Tamás Gyekiczky. 1987. "Szociológiai szempontok a munkafegyelem problémáinak elemzéséhez" (Sociological Aspects of Labor Discipline). *Közgazdasági Szemle* 34, 5: 562–76.

Mattera, Philip. 1985. *Off the Books: The Rise of the Underground Economy.* London: Pluto Press.

MF [Ministry of Finance]. 1980. "A kisüzemi termelés és kiegészitö tevékenységek továbbfejlesztésének kérdései" (Problems of Further Developing Small-scale Production and Auxiliary Activities). Budapest: Pénzügyminisztérium.

——— 1987. "Jelentés (tervezet) a Gazdaságpolitikai Bizottság részére a kiegészitö és kisegitö tevékenységek helyzetéiöl" (Draft Report for the Economic Committee on the Situation of Complementary and Auxiliary Activities) Budapest: Pénzügyminiszter, Ipari Miniszter, Mezögazdasági és Élelmezésügyi Miniszter, April.

NCTU [National Council of Trade Unions] 1983. "Levél dr Meggyessy Péter elvtáisnak, minis/rerhclyettes, Pénzügyminisztérium" (Letter to Comrade Dr. Pétor Meggyesy, Ministry of Finance). Szakszervezetrk Országos Tanácsa, Fötitkárhelyettes, September 1.

Nee, Victor, and David Stark. 1989. *Remaking the Economic Institutions of Socialism: China and Eastern Europe.* Stanford, Calif.: Stanford University Press.

NOA [National Organization of Artisans]. 1983. "Levél dr. Meggyessy Péter elvtársnak, miniszterhelyettes" (Letter to Comrade Dr. Péter Meggyesy, Deputy Minister of Finance). Kisiparosok Országos Szervezete, Országos Központ, Elnökhelyettes, August 29.

O'Hearn, Dennis. 1981. "The Second Economy in Consumer Goods and Services." *Critique* 15: 93–109.

Pongrácz, László. 1990. *Bérszabályozásaim* (My Wage Regulations). Budapest: Közgazdasági és Jogi Kiadó.

PPF [Patriotic People's Front]. 1984. "Levél dr. Hetényi István elvtárs, pénzügyminiszternek" (Letter to Comrade Dr. István Hetényi, Minister of Finance). Hazafias Népfront Országos Tanácsának Titkára, March 16.

Rakovski, Marc. 1978. *Towards an East European Marxism.* London: Allison & Busby.

Róna-Tas, Ákos. 1989. "Everyday Power and the Second Economy in Hungary: Large Consequences of Small Power." Center for Research on Social Organization Working Papers. Ann Arbor: University of Michigan.

Roundtable Discussion. 1987. "Kerekasztal beszélgetés az elemi rendröl" (Roundtable Discussion about Elementary Order). *Pártélet* 7 (July): 43–54.

Sampson, Steven L. 1986. "The Informal Sector in Eastern Europe." *Telos* 66 (Winter): 44–66.

Seleny, Anna. 1993. "The Long Transformation: Hungarian Socialism, 1949–1989." Diss., Department of Political Science, Massachusetts Institute of Technology.

SOWL [State Office of Wages and Labor]. 1982. "Észrevételek a kisgazdaságok, a kisüzemi termelés tapasztalatairól a GPB részére készitett jelentés tervezethez" (Observations on the Experience of Small Firms and Small-scale Production for the Draft of the Report to the Economic Policy Committee). Budapest: Allami Bér- és Munkaügyi Hivatal, November 30.

———. 1985. "A munkaidöalap védelmét szolgáló átfogó cselekvési program" (The Comprehensive Action Program to Protect Labor Time). Budapest: Allami Bér- és Munkaügyi Hivatal Foglalkoztatáspolitikai és Területi Föosztály, October 17.

———. 1986. "Javaslat a munkafegyelem javítására teendö intézkedésekre, a munkaidöalap védelmére: Elöterjesztés a Gazdaságpolitikai Bizottság részére" (Proposal for Measures to Improve Labor Discipline and to Protect Labor Time: Proposal to the Economic Committee. January.

———. 1987. "Tájékoztató a Minisztertanács részére a munkaidö jobb kihasználására, a munkafegyelem javitására hozott 3253/1986. Mt.h. számu határozat végrehajtásáról" (Report to the Council of Ministers on the Execution of the Resolution Number 3253/1986 to Enhance the Utilization of Labor Time and Improve Labor Discipline). Budapest: Allami Bér- és Munkaügyi Hivatal, July.

Stark, David. 1986. "Rethinking Internal Labor Markets: New Insights from a Comparative Perspective." *American Sociological Review* 51, 4: 492–504.

———. 1989. "Coexisting Organizational Forms in Hungary's Emerging Mixed Economy." In *Remaking of the Economic Institutions of Socialism: China and Eastern Europe*, eds. Victor Nee and David Stark, 137–68. Stanford, Calif.: Stanford University Press.

Szalai, Erzsébet. 1990. *Gazdaság és hatalom* (Economy and Power). Budapest: Aula.

———. 1991. "Integration of Special Interests in the Hungarian Economy: The Struggle Between Large Companies and the Party and State Bureaucracy." *Journal of Comparative Economics* 15, 2: 284–303.

Szamel, Lajos. 1989. *A korrupció, a protekció és a többi . . .* (Corruption, Pulling Strings, and So On . . .). Budapest: Kossuth.

Székács, Anna. 1987. "A kisüzemi szervezetek müködéséröl" (The Operation of Small-scale Organizations). Internal study for the Ministry of Finance, Budapest, April 15.

Szelényi, Iván. 1988. *Socialist Entrepreneurs: Embourgeoisement in Rural Hungary.* Madison: University of Wisconsin Press.

Szelenyi, Szonja. 1987. "Social Inequality and Party Membership: Patterns of Recruitment into the Hungarian Socialist Workers' Party." *American Sociological Review* 52, 5: 559–73.

Timár, János. 1988. *Idö és munkaidö* (Time and Labor Time). Budapest: Közgazdasági és Jogi Kiadó.

Zloch-Christy, Iliana. 1987. *Debt Problems of Eastern Europe.* Cambridge: Cambridge University Press.

PART TWO

The Eclipse of the Center

FOUR

The Rise of the Regions: Fiscal Reform and the Decline of Central State Capacity in China

Shaoguang Wang

Analytically, central planning has three distinct characteristics. The first is the state monopoly that emerged when the private sector was eliminated and the collective sector was brought under tight state control. The second is omnipresent regulation, which, by leaving little space outside of plans, straitjackets economic agents' decision making. The third is the concentration of authority in the hands of the central government. Local governments are granted little discretion over resources and decision making and are allowed to act only as "transmission belts" for the central government.

While central planning provides communist regimes with a high degree of control, it has two fatal defects. One is information dependence: the center has to rely upon agents spread widely across the nation for information. In a hierarchical system, those at the bottom have little choice but to pursue their objectives by manipulating the supply of information to the center. Therefore there is always the danger of information transmitted to the center being distorted. As economic development multiplies the volume of information that central planners have to process, the information supremacy of agents over their principals tends to be enhanced. The other defect of the centrally planned economy is its neglect of agents' incentives. Agents are assumed to have no goals other than those that are set at the top of the hierarchy; but they do have their own objectives, which are not always in line with their principals'. This is an important cause of "slack" in the system.

Deborah Davis, James Scott, Ian Shapiro, Andrew Walder, and participants at seminars at Columbia University, Duke University, and the University of Washington have commented on this paper. I wish to thank them for their helpful criticisms. I also wish to acknowledge the financial support for this project of the Yale Center for International and Area Studies Research Fund, the Yale Social Science Research Fund, and the Center for Modern China Research Fund. — SW.

Departures from central planning are an effort to overcome these two defects. Departures may take any of the three forms Andrew Walder discusses in the introduction to this volume, which we may term decentralization (fiscal reform), deregulation (enterprise reform), and demonopolization (alternative economic sectors). Whereas demonopolization reinvigorates the nonstate sector, decentralization and deregulation mainly involve changes in various relationships within the public sector. Indeed, the success or failure of a country's departure from central planning to a large extent hinges on its reform of the public sector. It is therefore important to understand the political consequences of decentralization and deregulation.

This chapter examines the growth of extrabudgetary funds in China, which I believe clearly gauges the extent of decentralization and deregulation. Extrabudgetary funds are funds in the public sector that are not subject to central budgetary control. In an ideal-type centrally planned economy, nothing should escape central control. Nevertheless, extrabudgetary funds have existed in China since the establishment of the People's Republic. They are funds in the public sector, in that they include only funds at the disposal of government agencies and state enterprises, not funds belonging to collective enterprises, private firms, and households. These extrabudgetary funds are not subject to central budgetary control, because they are retained by government agencies and state enterprises and are not recorded in formal budgets. Since they are not subject to central budgetary scrutiny, they are also outside of central plans. The expansion and contraction of extrabudgetary funds has mirrored changes in the role of central planning over the past forty years. Whenever Beijing has adopted measures to decentralize, local governments' extrabudgetary funds have grown; and whenever Beijing has adopted measures to deregulate, state enterprises' extrabudgetary funds have expanded. As a result of drastic decentralization and deregulation in the 1980s, almost as much "public money" is circulating outside the state budget as within it today. In many provinces, extrabudgetary revenues and expenditures have surpassed even their budgetary counterparts. Given their magnitude, some Chinese economists and policymakers now refer to extrabudgetary funds as China's "second budget."

The central argument of this chapter is that the rise of the "second budget" after the late 1970s has contributed to the decline of central state capacity in China. What do I mean by "state capacity"? Why is state capacity important? How do we measure it? What causes state capacity to vary? I address these issues in the first part of the chapter. In the second part, I apply the concepts developed in the first to an analysis of the rise of extrabudgetary funds. I attempt to show the causal connections between the rise of extrabudgetary funds and the weakening of state capacity. In the last part, I examine the socioeconomic and political consequences of declining state capacity. I argue that the crises we witnessed in China in the late 1980s were attributable, at least in part, to the political weakness of the center vis-à-vis its own agents.

STATE CAPACITY

Definition

State capacity is one of the defining characteristics of any political system (Almond and Powell 1966; Katzenstein 1978; Zysman 1983; Migdal 1988; Ikenberry 1988; Organski and Kugler 1980). By "state capacity," I refer to the ability of a government to administer its territory effectively (Skocpol 1985). In the modern world, the survival and functioning of a political system depends on four basic state capacities: the capacity to mobilize financial resources from the society to pursue what the central policymakers perceive as the "national interest" (extractive capacity); the capacity to guide national socioeconomic development (steering capacity); the capacity to dominate by using symbols and creating consensus (legitimation capacity); and the capacity to dominate by the use or threat of force (coercive capacity).

These four capacities are conceptually distinct but interrelated in practice. For instance, the legitimation of a regime is dependent on its performance. If the state is able to produce and deliver economic and social goods at the level its subjects expect, or at least as its rulers promise, it should have no legitimacy problem. On the other hand, if the state apparatus cannot adequately steer the economic system, this is likely to result in a decline in its legitimacy. With legitimation capacity, the state can effectively steer activities without the necessity of constantly deploying coercion. Without legitimacy, however, the state would find it much more difficult to extract resources from the society, and would have to bear much higher costs for maintaining law and order (Habermas 1975). An overloading of control problems would weaken the state's coercive capacity, which in turn would lower the expected cost of joining the opposition. Of course, the decline of the four capacities rarely occurs simultaneously or in the same sequences in different cases. But their changes do tend to reinforce one another. Once overall state capacity falls below a certain threshold, the regime would be in serious trouble, if not in danger of collapse.

Measurement

State capacity is more easily asserted than measured. Indeed, the concept of overall state capacity as discussed above is too complicated for ready measurement. In this chapter, extractive capacity is therefore selected as a key indicator of overall state capacity. The substitution is based on the assumption that an effective political system should be able to extract resources, aggregate them, and use them for national purposes; a government that is unable to generate sufficient resources for realizing its policy goals is less effective. Extractive capacity is arguably the most fundamental of state capacities. The availability of resources permits the state to carry out its other tasks. Many empirical studies have shown that the government's political-capacity-as-fiscal-extractive-capacity provides a useful analytic tool for explaining such divergent phenomena as the outcomes of wars among major powers (Organski and Kugler 1980), demographic transitions (Organski, Kugler, Johnson, and Cohen 1984), the probability of developing countries suspending their external debt payments (Snider 1990a), and domestic political violence (Snider 1990b).

To construct an indicator of the state's extractive capacity, we need two points of reference. The first is the absolute value of the actual revenue captured by the public sector. The other is gross domestic product (GDP) or national income, which measures the total volume of the nation's financial resources. The two reference points enable us to define state extractive capacity as the ratio of the former to the latter:

$$\text{State extractive capacity} = \frac{\text{Size of public sector}}{\text{Total financial resources}} = \frac{\text{Budgetary funds}}{\text{National income}} \quad \text{[I]}$$

Since extrabudgetary funds are an additional source of public expenditure and investment in China, they should be included when we measure the size of the public sector. Definition II may thus provide us with a better tool for measuring the extent to which the national income is captured by the public sector in China.

$$\text{State extractive capacity} = \frac{\text{Budgetary funds} + \text{Extrabudgetary funds}}{\text{National income}} \quad \text{[II]}$$

The Determinants of State Capacity

As a dependent variable, what are the determinants affecting longitudinal variation in the extractive capacity of the state? What factors influence the executive's ability to allocate resources in pursuit of its policy objectives? In discussing the conditions underlying the effectiveness of the state, emphasis has been laid on "state autonomy." Many believe that the state as a corporate entity is unlikely to be capable of formulating goals or implementing them unless it is somewhat insulated from the surrounding social structure. Here societal resistance is considered the primary obstacle to the effectiveness of state actions (Krasner 1978a).

While there is no doubt that state autonomy is necessary for effective state intervention, it is mistaken, however, to think that autonomy is in itself sufficient for effective state action, because the state is not monolithic. Instead, it has a complex structure both horizontally in terms of numerous ministries and vertically in terms of different levels of government. Central ministries and local governments, although supposedly the rulers' agencies, do not always share their principals' aims. It is probably more realistic to assume that they have goals other than those imposed by the rulers. If they do, they could be competing extractors. In analyzing political constraints on the extractive capacity of the state, we thus need to distinguish between *resistance* by private citizens who are directly affected by the extractive policies of the state, and *competition* among state agents who desire control over the resources already extracted in the name of the state. While resistance occurs mainly at the extraction stage, competition is more likely to appear at the allocation stage (Lamborn 1983).

Having intentionally destroyed all competing societal centers of power, the communist state is no doubt much more insulated from societal pressures than its counterparts in the West or in the Third World. Authoritarian statism does not, however, correspond to a univocal strengthening of the state. To enforce authoritarian rule, the state has to construct an elaborate set of agencies throughout the nation. These agencies may over time develop their own preferences. The unique preferences these agencies assume create in them centrifugal tendencies. These state agencies could become "power centers" competing with central rulers and threatening the coherence and the stability of the state as a corporate whole. The principal weak point in the state socialist system is thus more likely to lie "within the regime itself, within the apparatus of the state" than "outside it in its relations with civil society" (Schmitter 1975).

Distance usually makes it much more difficult for national leaders to monitor local governments' activity than that of central ministries. This study will therefore focus on subnational governments.[1] The extent to which local governments are able to compete with the rulers over resources, and thereby weaken overall state capacity, depends on two variables: their preferences and the resources already at their disposal. *The desire to compete* depends on how far local governments' preferences deviate from the center's. When local governments have no preferences of their own, or their preferences largely converge with those of the rulers, we should expect subnational governments to act as central decision makers' deputies, imple-

---

1. For the sake of convenience, this study treats the central government as a homogeneous entity, represented by what Levi calls "the rulers" (1988), what Zysman calls "the national political executive" (1983), what Krasner calls "central decision makers" (1978b), and what Chinese call "the center" (*zhongyang*). It needs to be emphasized that, composed as it is of hundreds of agencies and thousands of bureaucrats, the central government as such is also internally fragmented; and that conflicts between different central agencies, like those between the central government and local governments, could compromise the ability of the central government to pursue coherent policies.

menting whatever orders they receive from the center. Local governments would not seek to capture resources for themselves unless they have interests that diverge from their superiors'. However, it is one thing to have a desire to compete, while it is another to have the ability to do so. *The ability to compete* is a function of local governments' control over relevant power resources and their ability to influence central decision making. Local governments could improve their situations by employing the resources already under their control to gain control over other (and more) resources.

The distinctive sense of identity and the independent ... tend to reinforce ... The growing consciousness of self interest is likely to enhance local governments' desire to grasp more resources into their own hands; with more resources under their control, subnational governments ... to develop new independent preferences. The process of mutual reinforcement could result in a centrifugal tendency among local governments.

Since the state is not a monolithic entity, we need to modify definitions I and II. These definitions assess the extractive capacity of the state by breaking the state into its components, assessing the capacity of each part, and then summing the capacity of all components for the total capacity of the state. But, as often happens, the value of a whole is sometimes less than the sum of the values of its parts. When local governments pursue goals running contrary to the center's interest, for instance, the financial resources at their disposal will undermine rather than enhance the overall capacity of the state.

I am not suggesting that local governments always use their share of budgetary income and extrabudgetary funds under their control to pursue interests at odds with the center's. Nor should we assume that every yuan extracted in the name of the state serves to strengthen state capacity. It should be clear by now that when I speak of state capacity, I am referring to the aggregate capacity of the state as a corporate whole, which is definitely weaker than what definitions I or II suggest. How much weaker? There is no way to give a precise answer. In fact, we do not need a precise answer so long as we are able to gauge a longitudinal trend. For these reasons, I give the following three definitions to approximate the real extractive capacity of the central state. Definitions III, IV, and V are based on a truism: at least, central planners are able to employ the center's share of budgetary revenues at will to pursue what they believe to be the national interests.

$$\text{State extractive capacity} = \frac{\text{Central budgetary funds}}{\text{Total budgetary funds}} \quad\quad [\text{III}]$$

$$\text{State extractive capacity} = \frac{\text{Central budgetary funds}}{\text{Budgetary funds} + \text{Extrabudgetary funds}} \quad\quad [\text{IV}]$$

$$\text{State extractive capacity} = \frac{\text{Central budgetary funds}}{\text{National income}} \qquad [V]$$

Definitions III, IV, and V are indispensable supplements to definitions I and II. When the preferences of the central and local governments are convergent, definitions I and II should be able to serve as a good indicator of state extractive capacity. However, definitions III, IV, and V better measure state extractive capacity when the preferences of the central and local governments diverge.

THE RISE OF THE SECOND BUDGET

The Evolution of Extrabudgetary Funds before the Reform

China came closest to the ideal model of central planning during the first five-year plan (1953–57). Under the unified fiscal system adopted in the early 1950s, the scope of the Chinese budget was even broader than that of the Soviet Union. While the Soviet Union allowed enterprises to retain a substantial portion of their profits and depreciation funds, the Chinese budget centralized virtually all enterprise profits and depreciation funds through the state budget. Enterprises had to rely on the state budget not only for investment but also for working capital (Lardy 1978).

During this period, only a few insignificant sources of funds were left outside the state budget. Among them the most important were major repair funds and bonus funds controlled by enterprises; and the agricultural surtax, surcharges on industrial and commercial taxes, and miscellaneous fees controlled by local governments (Lardy 1978). Those funds were called "extrabudgetary funds." Throughout the first five-year plan, the size of the extrabudgetary funds was very small, ranging from 4.2 percent to 8.5 percent of budgetary revenue, and the use of those funds was generally subject to strict central regulations (Du 1984; Deng 1990) (see table 4.1).

A number of observations about the prereform period are worth notice. First, during Mao's era, departures from central planning took the form of administrative decentralization. Every time the center decided to decentralize control over resources and decision making to governments at lower levels, extrabudgetary funds expanded quickly. There were two such upsurges of extrabudgetary funds in the prereform period, both of which were the results of Mao's decentralization drives. The first hike occurred during the Great Leap Forward (1958–60). In a matter of three years, the extrabudgetary funds registered a 447 percent increase, climbing from 2.6 billion yuan in 1957 to 11.8 billion in 1960. The other hike took place when Mao launched his second decentralization drive in the early 1970s. Between 1970 and 1977, while the budget revenue grew only 31.9 percent, extrabudgetary funds tripled, reaching 31 billion yuan in 1977.

TABLE 4.1   Growth of Budgetary Funds,
Extrabudgetary Funds, and National Income
(in 100 million yuan)

Year	B Income	E Income	N Income
1952	173.94	13.62	589
1953	213.24	8.91	709
1954	253.53	14.23	748
1955	255.46	17.02	788
1956	286.26	21.42	882
1957	310.04	26.33	908
1958	387.60	55.99	1118
1959	487.19	66.55	1224
1960	572.29	117.78	1220
1061	356.06	57.40	996
1962	313.55	68.00	991
1963	342.25	51.85	1000
1964	399.54	65.86	1166
1965	473.32	75.56	1387
1966	558.71	81.13	1586
1967	419.36	83.61	1487
1968	361.25	77.44	1415
1969	526.76	87.42	1617
1970	662.90	100.94	1926
1971	744.73	118.56	2077
1972	766.56	134.24	2136
1973	809.67	191.29	2318
1974	783.14	219.72	2348
1975	815.61	251.48	2503
1976	776.58	275.32	2427
1977	874.46	311.31	2644
1978	1121.12	347.11	3010
1979	1067.96	452.85	3350
1980	1042.22	557.40	3688
1981	1016.38	601.07	3941
1982	1040.11	802.74	4258
1983	1169.58	967.68	4736
1984	1424.52	1188.48	5652
1985	1776.55	1530.03	7020
1986	2122.01	1737.31	7859
1987	2199.35	2028.80	9313
1988	2357.24	2360.77	11738
1989	2664.90	2658.83	13176
1990	2937.10	2708.64	14384
1991	3149.48	3243.30	16117

SOURCE: General Planning Department, Ministry of Finance 1992,
13–14, 19, 339.

NOTE: B Income = budgetary income; E Income = extrabudgetary
income; N Income = national income.

Second, subsequent recentralization never succeeded in returning fiscal flows to their prior state, because local forces that warmly embraced decentralization resisted recentralization. Despite the center's intense efforts, for instance, its recentralization program of the early 1960s could not bring extrabudgetary funds down to the level of the mid 1950s. Although the ratio of extrabudgetary to budgetary funds often fluctuated in the pre-reform period, the direction of change was unmistakable. It grew from an insignificant 6.5 percent during the mid 1950s to 35.6 percent in 1977 (General Planning Department, Ministry of Finance 1992). Correspondingly, central control over regional economic activity declined. With more resources under their control, localities found that they did not have to take central plans as seriously as in the past; some even acted contrary to central plans and discontinued cooperation with other localities mandated by central planners (Lyons 1987). The late Mao era, from the mid 1960s to the mid 1970s, was thus characterized by two seemingly contrasting trends: At the same time that the state was becoming increasingly repressive, the state organizational structure was gradually being fragmented, with lower levels of government gaining at the expense of the center (World Bank 1990a).

Third, in the Mao era the institution of extrabudgetary funds was mainly used to address just one of the two main defects of the centrally planned economy—information dependency. This was reflected in the fact that the most important components of extrabudgetary funds had been major repair funds and depreciation funds. Such funds were used primarily to give enterprises and local administrative authorities some flexibility in maintaining and improving their production capability. The incentive function of extrabudgetary funds was very weak. Bonus funds were nonexistent in many years. When they existed, they were awarded only to enterprises that over-fulfilled output and profit plans; and their volume was small, in general no more than 1 to 3.5 percent of the total profits (Lardy 1978). Under such an institutional arrangement, although enterprises or local governments might have an organizational interest in expanding the size of extrabudgetary funds, factory managers and local government officials as individuals did not have a personal stake in doing so. Since they could not gain much personally from the expansion of extrabudgetary funds, they tended to give in when facing great pressure from Beijing. That was an important reason why the centrifugal tendencies, although growing, were still limited in the late Mao era.

The Expansion of Extrabudgetary Funds after the Reform

Deng's decentralization differs from Mao's in that it attempted to address both information and incentive problems, emphasizing the latter. The essence of Deng Xiaoping's far-reaching economic reform can be summarized in one Chinese phrase, *fangquan rangli*—that is, devolve control over resources and decision-making power to subnational governments on the one hand and to enterprises on the other (Li 1990). It was hoped that *fangquan rangli* would motivate enterprises and local governments to pursue greater efficiency; greater efficiency would generate more profits; more profits would enlarge the tax base; and eventually the enlarged tax base would bring about a higher level of revenues for the central government.

Fangquan rangli involves changes mainly in two respects. On the one hand, "eating in separate kitchens" (*fenzao chifan*) was introduced in 1980 to expand local governments' fiscal autonomy. On the other hand, state enterprises were allowed to retain a larger proportion of profit for their own uses. Since many authors have discussed in detail changing central-local fiscal relations (Oksenberg and Tong 1991, Oi 1992; Shirk 1993), I need not repeat them here. In what follows, I shall focus on the second development, which is the explosion of extrabudgetary funds in the 1980s.

The Explosion of Extrabudgetary Funds.   There are three primary ways for enterprises to retain profits. First is depreciation funds, which existed before the reforms. However, there were important policy changes concerning the rate of depreciation and the management of depreciation funds after 1978. In 1978, the rate of depreciation was only 3.7 percent, but it increased gradually to 5.3 percent by 1985. As the size of China's fixed assets grew at a fast pace in the 1980s, the higher rates of depreciation allowed enterprises to retain billions more yuan a year (Deng 1990; Feng 1990). "Retain" is a term that needs some qualification. Before 1978, enterprises usually had to surrender a large percentage, and in some cases even all, of the depreciation funds they had retained to government agencies (in most cases, local ones). In this case, enterprises had no discretion over the use of funds retained in their names. On the eve of the reform, as a measure of recentralization, the central government decided to collect 50 percent of depreciation funds for the central treasury. After 1979, however, central policies began to grant enterprises larger and larger shares of the funds. Finally, in 1985, the central government gave up its share altogether, leaving all depreciation funds to enterprises (Li, Fan, and Cong 1987).

Major repair funds are the second main source of enterprise income. Set at a certain percentage of the depreciation funds, the major repair funds grew along with depreciation funds (Deng 1990).

Enterprises' retained profits are the most important source of extrabudgetary funds. Before 1978, enterprises remitted almost all their surplus funds to the state, and in return the government provided financing for the enterprises' production requirements and investment. As a result, state firms were not motivated to maximize profit. Profit retention was designed to foster state-owned firms' profit maximization incentive. Since 1978, there

have been four regimes of profit retention: "enterprise fund," "profit retention," "tax-for-profits," and "tax contracting" (Lee 1991).

We need not go into details of those schemes. Suffice it to say that they all
shared a common feature: the profit-retention rate of an enterprise was set
on the basis of periodic negotiations between the enterprise and its administrative overseer rather than strictly according to its performance. In the
early years of the reform, the negotiability of an enterprise's financial obligation to the state budget was partially attributable to China's distorted
price structure. Since the prices of almost all products and production
factors were then set by planners, it was almost impossible to establish a clear
linkage between the level of an enterprise's profits and its real performance.
Negotiation was supposed to work as a mechanism for determining how
large a proportion of the profits an enterprise deserved to retain. The negotiability, however, gave the enterprise an incentive to divert its resources
more to rent-seeking activity (e.g., striving for a higher rate of profit-
retention in its bargaining with the superior government agency) than to
the improvement of its efficiency. As a result, the initial reform was not
successful. "State revenue decreased significantly, while performance of
state enterprises did not improve significantly" (Lee 1993, 181).

One may expect that as China's price reform proceeded, the negotiability would recede into the background. But that did not happen. If the
negotiability was a bad design, then why did the government allow it to
persist? In fact, the central government made numerous attempts to reduce
the negotiability. The tax-for-profits system implemented from 1983 to
1986 was such an attempt (Bachman 1987). Under this system, a state
enterprise was supposed to pay its income tax according to a stipulated and
nonnegotiable tax rate. Only the enterprise's share of the remaining profits
was still subject to bargaining, and the central government hoped to wipe
out all vestiges of arbitrary bargaining eventually. But local governments did
not like the tax-for-profits system, because it threatened their discretionary
control over local enterprises, and their resistance forced the central government to abandon the tax-for-profits system, replacing it with the tax-
contracting system in 1987.

The new system was entirely based upon bargaining. The enterprise was
required to deliver a tax or taxable profit quota in lieu of income tax, but
there was no stipulated formula for determining the amount of profit remission. The negotiability of tax contracts created opportunities for the enterprise and the local government to collude to increase their own revenues at
the expense of the state budget (Lee 1993).

Through these schemes of profit retention, enterprises were able to retain larger and larger shares of their profits in the 1980s. In 1978, the ratio
of retained profits to total profits was lower than 5 percent. But more recently estimates ranged from 33.7 percent to 62.2 percent (Deng 1990; He

TABLE 4.2 Extrabudgetary Funds by Ownership
(in 100 million yuan)

Year	Local Government	Administrative Agency	Enterprise
1952	12.53		1.09
1953	1.40	2.07	5.44
1954	2.07	3.34	8.82
1955	3.27	3.68	10.07
1956	5.00	3.85	12.57
1957	5.66	3.80	16.87
1958	17.59	9.29	29.11
1959	35.39	11.70	(illegible)
1960	(illegible)	23.13	71.26
1961	13.29	15.61	28.50
1962	20.60	15.91	(illegible)
1963	(illegible)	11.99	32.67
1964	8.87	16.07	40.92
1965	9.47	18.74	47.35
1966	10.36	20.00	50.77
1967	9.72	22.00	51.89
1968	9.96	24.00	43.48
1969	12.19	26.00	49.23
1970	13.45	28.00	59.49
1971	14.72	30.00	73.84
1972	23.28	31.66	79.30
1973	24.14	32.57	134.58
1974	22.65	34.60	162.47
1975	27.86	42.30	181.32
1976	28.35	48.81	198.16
1977	30.76	56.84	223.71
1978	31.09	63.41	252.61
1979	39.94	68.66	344.35
1980	40.85	74.44	442.11
1981	41.30	84.90	474.87
1982	45.27	101.15	656.32
1983	49.79	113.88	804.01
1984	55.23	142.52	990.73
1985	44.08	233.22	1252.73
1986	43.20	294.22	1399.89
1987	44.61	358.41	1625.78
1988	48.94	438.94	1872.89
1989	54.36	500.66	2103.81
1990	60.59	576.95	2071.10
1991	68.77	697.00	2477.53

SOURCE: General Planning Department, Ministry of Finance 1992, 188–89.

1987; Cai 1988; Ning 1990). Even if we take the conservative estimation, enterprises' retained profits still increased 14-fold, while total profits grew only 170 percent between 1978 and 1987 (Deng 1990). Obviously, retained profits eroded government revenues from state enterprises: what the state budget received was a declining share of enterprise income.

Owing to these changes, the volume of extrabudgetary funds controlled by state enterprises underwent a phenomenal increase. In 1978, extra-budgetary funds controlled by enterprises accounted for only about 8.4 percent of national income. By 1991, the ratio had risen to more than 15.4 percent. That addition, 7 percent of national income, amounted to 112.8 billion yuan in revenues lost to the state budget, the equivalent of five times China's fiscal deficit in that year (State Statistical Bureau 1992).

Like the extrabudgetary funds controlled by state enterprises, those controlled by administrative agencies have also grown at a high rate. Between 1978 and 1991, such funds grew elevenfold (see table 4.2).

On paper, the extrabudgetary funds of the third category—those directly under the control of local governments—do not appear to have grown much (also see table 4.2). But as I detail below, local governments had no difficulty capturing some of the resources retained by the enterprises under their jurisdiction. What local governments actually controlled was thus much larger than what was nominally under their names.

Together, the three categories of extrabudgetary funds reached 324.3 billion yuan in 1991, exceeding budget revenues (314.9 billion) for the same year. For this reason, many Chinese scholars and policymakers call extrabudgetary funds China's "second budget." Before 1978, the growth rates of extrabudgetary funds often oscillated greatly over short intervals, which meant that extrabudgetary funds were sensitive to central policy changes and that central policymakers had some control over the size of extrabudgetary funds. After 1978, however, the fluctuation began to flatten out and there were no longer any instances of negative growth. Moreover, the growth rate of extrabudgetary funds has been consistently higher than that of national income, GDP, or budgetary incomes (Wang 1989). Given the central government's countless efforts to arrest the growth of extra-budgetary funds, the secular trend of sustained increase reveals how ineffective the central control over extrabudgetary funds has become.

Control and Resistance.   In the early 1980s, when extrabudgetary funds grew to roughly half the size of budgetary revenue, some Chinese economists and policymakers already realized that the growth of extrabudgetary funds could get out of hand (Contemporary Chinese Public Finance Editorial Group 1990). Beijing then faced a delicate task: to limit the negative impact of growing extrabudgetary funds on macroeconomic stability without hindering the incentive effects of the funds. In the past, whenever the center wanted to confine negative effects of extrabudgetary funds, it simply resorted to administrative measures, such as moving some funds from the extrabudgetary category to the budgetary category. In the 1980s, Beijing sought to deal with problems caused by oversized extrabudgetary funds by imposing taxes on them. At the end of 1982, the State Council introduced a 10 percent energy and transport surcharge on all extrabudgetary funds. The next year, the surcharge was increased to 15 percent (Contemporary Chinese Public Finance Editorial Group 1990). At first, the energy and transport charge was said to be levied for only three years. By 1985, however, the growth of extrabudgetary funds had not been contained. Beijing accordingly declared that the charge would become a permanent tax in 1986 Meanwhile, the State Council put out sterner regulations about the collecting and use of extrabudgetary funds (State Council 1986). In 1986, the central effort seemed to have some effect. The ratio of extrabudgetary funds to budget revenues fell for the first time since 1978, although the magnitude of change was very small. But the success proved to be short-lived. The ratio went up by 10 percent in 1987, which was the biggest annual leap in six years. In the following years, more control mechanisms were tried. In 1989, another tax, "a budget adjustment charge," was imposed on extrabudgetary funds (State Council 1989). Despite all those efforts, extrabudgetary funds have continued to expand.

In the early 1960s, the central government cut the volume of extrabudgetary funds in half. Why wasn't the central government able in the 1980s to repeat what it had done two decades before?

First, monitoring problems are far more intractable than before. In the prereform period, when enterprises were forced to disburse 95 percent of their profits to government and receive allocations to cover their operational costs, there were scant funds to hide and it was difficult to hide them. Profit-sharing has exceedingly complicated the monitoring process. No matter what form profit-sharing took, it had to be implemented according to some elaborate formulas, which necessarily required a larger volume and better quality of information for central controllers to detect noncompliance. Since such information was hard to come by, local units had much less difficulty than before in generating extrabudgetary funds through various legal, quasi-legal, and illegal ways.

Second, the incentives of managers and local officials to increase extrabudgetary funds have increased greatly. Before the reform, as pointed out above, extrabudgetary funds were mainly designed to overcome central planners' information-dependence problem. After the reform, instead, extrabudgetary funds were allowed to grow in order to provide incentives to state agents and primary producers. Extrabudgetary funds could now be used to sponsor housing projects, to increase bonuses, to provide various forms of local collective welfare, and the like. Obviously, the larger the volume of extrabudgetary funds under local discretion, the more local people, especially officials and managers, benefit. Since personal interests are now at stake, enterprise managers and local government officials have become more energetic and innovative in expanding extrabudgetary funds and more determined to resist Beijing's attempts to recentralize.

Third, and most important, local governments, which are supposed to police noncompliant behavior by enterprises in acquiring and using extrabudgetary funds, have become noncompliant themselves. Under the "eating from separate kitchens" system, local governments' objective is to enhance their own revenue base. Therefore, they tend not to enforce central guidelines strictly when this means reducing the amount of extrabudgetary funds left in the local economy (Oi 1992).

Local government would generally rather see enterprise earnings retained than transferred to the center by way of taxes, because as long as money is kept within the localities, they benefit from it in one way or another. Three mechanisms have often been used by local governments to let local enterprises expand their extrabudgetary funds by diverting budgetary funds. First, local authorities often wink at the enterprises' practice of tax evasion. A check conducted in 1987–88 under the auspices of the State Council, for instance, uncovered fiscal fraud amounting to 10 billion yuan (4.2 percent of the budgetary income of 1988). That was probably just the tip of the iceberg. It was estimated that at least a half of state enterprises were engaged in some forms of avoidance, and that revenue equivalent to about 2–3 percent of national income was lost in fiscal fraud.[2]

Second, local governments often grant local enterprises tax holidays and ad hoc tax relief (Walder 1992). In many cases, such authorizations exceed their statutory rights and contravene tax laws. In 1978, exempted or relieved taxes amounted to only 600 million yuan nationwide. In 1988, however, 10 billion yuan of taxes were exempted. Between 1978 and 1988, a total of 48.6 billion yuan of taxes were not collected, which was equivalent to 83 percent of the deficits occurring in the same period (Wang 1990).

Third, the shift to tax contracting in 1986 made it easier for local governments to leave a much larger share of profits to local enterprises. Unlike the tax-for-profit reform, the contracting system relies on ad hoc negotiation of profit remission or tax assessments between enterprises and their supervisory bodies, which allows local governments to continue acting as "patriarchs" in their regions. Indeed, more often than not, local governments are very lavish in negotiating contracts with their subordinate enterprises. Small wonder a World Bank study finds that whatever forms of contracting were adopted, the effective rates of income tax were always much lower than the nominal rate (World Bank 1990b).

2. *Caizheng* 12 (December 1989): 8.

Local governments benefit both directly and indirectly from what local enterprises have retained. Direct benefits usually take the form of what is known in Chinese as *tanpai*—the imposition of various fees on enterprises in addition to formal tax obligations (Huang 1990). Without any statutory basis, such ad hoc charges are a main vehicle for local governments to appropriate local enterprises' retained profits. A nationwide survey conducted in 1990 found that there were altogether more than 50,000 varieties of such charges (Enterprise Management Yearbook 1991), from which local authorities extracted at least 20 billion yuan a year (Wang 1988). A large percentage of enterprises' extrabudgetary funds was sucked away by *tanpai*. Empirical studies suggest that somewhere between 20 and 60 percent of extrabudgetary funds originally retained in the name of enterprises eventually ended up in the coffers of local governments (Liang 1989; Zhu 1990; Li 1991; Wang Yunguo 1992). Some enterprises complain that the burden of *tanpai* is twice as heavy as that of formal income taxes (Wang and Xiao 1992).

Even if extrabudgetary enterprise funds don't change hands, local governments can still dictate how such funds are used. A strategy for local governments to do so is *pingpan* (assortment plate), which refers to schemes in which various local enterprises are "invited" to invest in projects local governments consider vital for regional development. It is hard for enterprises to reject such "invitations." On the one hand, the local government generally has fairly good information about the financial strength of every enterprise within its jurisdiction. Therefore, lack of funds cannot serve as a sufficient excuse for not accepting such "invitations." On the other hand, as centralized material allocation is withering, a substantial portion of the materials falling outside central purview is managed by local governments (World Bank 1990a). Moreover, banking institutions have also increasingly come under the control of local governments. Depending on local governments for allocating cheap inputs and credit, enterprises cannot afford to offend local bosses by not following their guidance.

Even if enterprises spend their extrabudgetary funds on housing projects or distribute them as bonuses, local governments would still benefit, in the sense that their burden of financial expenditures in those areas would be lightened.

Under a situation in which local forces have strong incentives to maximize extrabudgetary funds, the center needs an effective apparatus for policing local forces if it hopes to control the size of those funds. Measures that were once effective in containing local forces prior to the reform have become increasingly irrelevant in the postreform era. New control mechanisms, however, have yet to be developed. The result is what we have observed—the explosion of extrabudgetary funds in the 1980s.

The Decline of State Capacity

The explosion of extrabudgetary funds represents a significant erosion of the state's extractive capacity. In table 4.3, I use the five definitions developed above to estimate the changes in the Chinese government's political-capacity-as-fiscal-extractive-capability in the past four decades.

From column II of the table we find that, contrary to conventional wisdom, the size of the public sector has expanded rather than contracted during the reform era, if extrabudgetary funds are included. Of the enlarged public sector, however, the portion under the center's control has been significantly reduced (columns III and IV). In market economies, the ratio of central-state revenues to total state revenues is normally higher than 50 percent. Even in the United States, a very decentralized system by world standards, the federal government's tax income accounts for about 60 percent of the total tax revenues (World Bank 1990b). But in China, the central government's share (28 percent) is now only half that of the federal government of the United States. In theory, owing to its major role in the national economy, the central government in a socialist country should command a substantially larger share of GDP or national income than in a capitalist setting (Musgrave 1969). However, the share of national income controlled by the central government of China (column V) has declined from 24 percent in the 1950s and 1960s to 13 percent in the 1980s, much lower than what central governments in developed countries (24.2 percent of GNP) and middle-income countries (24 percent of GNP) were able to capture, and even lower than what central governments in Third World countries were able to get (15.4 percent of GNP) (World Bank 1990b).

Is the rise of the "second budget" an important factor causing the decline in central extractive capacity? The five columns suggest that the decline of the central state's extractive capacity is as much because of a declining share of budgetary revenue in national income as of the accelerating growth of extrabudgetary funds. If there were no extrabudgetary funds, both the share of national income collected as taxes by the state (25 percent, column I) and the center's share of total budget revenues (50 percent, column III) would have been considered comparable to other countries'. Only when taking into account extrabudgetary funds held by lower levels of government and state enterprises do we find that the center's share is too small.

A correlation analysis of the relations between the growth of extrabudgetary funds and budgetary funds produces the results shown in table 4.4.[3] Here we find that the growth of extrabudgetary funds and the growth of

3. The idea of conducting this type of analysis comes from Deng Yingtao (1990, 278–79).

TABLE 4.3   Changes in PRC State Extractive Capacity, 1952–1989

Period	I $\dfrac{BI}{NI}$	II $\dfrac{BI + EI}{NI}$	III $\dfrac{CBI^a}{BI}$	IV $\dfrac{CBI}{BI + EI}$	V $\dfrac{CBI}{NI}$
1952–66	0.35	0.40	0.67	0.59	0.24
1967–77	0.33	0.41	0.62	0.50	0.20
1978–89	0.25	0.45	0.50	0.28	0.13

SOURCE: General Planning Department, Ministry of Finance 1992 13 186, 330,

NOTE: BI = budgetary income; CBI   (I III II budgetary) income; EI = extrabudgetary income NI = national income.

[a]According to some authoritative Chinese sources, the center's share in budget revenues has been declining in the past four decades. In the first three years of the PRC the center's share was as high as 80 percent. It stabilized at about 70 percent in the first five-year plan, and then fell to about 50 percent during the Great Leap Forward before it rebounded to around 65 percent in the rest of the 1960s. In the 1970s, Mao's second decentralization caused the center's share in revenues to drop again, down to just slightly over 60 percent. Deng Xiaoping's reform has driven the ratio further downward to about 50 percent on average for the whole decade of the 1980s (see Yun, Wang 1990, and Wu 1990). In 1989, the center's share was only 45.2 percent (see Yuan Dong 1992). For the sake of convenience, I put the center's share of budget revenues at 67 percent for the entire 1952–66 period, 62 percent for 1967–77, and 50 percent for 1978–89 in this column.

TABLE 4.4   Correlation between BI/NI and EI/NI

Period	Cor. coeff.	Std. error	t-stat
1952–66	0.841	0.14	5.614[a]
1967–77	0.143	0.27	0.433
1978–91	−0.714	0.24	3.531[b]

SOURCE: General Planning Department, Ministry of Finance 1992, 319–20.
[a]Significant at the .001 level
[b]Significant at the .01 level

budgetary funds were positively correlated in the early years of the People's Republic, not correlated in the chaotic Cultural Revolution period, and negatively correlated in the reform era. When the preferences of the central and local governments were largely convergent, local governments did not try to increase extrabudgetary funds at the expense of budgetary funds. That is why the correlation was positive in the first period. The absence of correlation in the second period was probably because in this period the preferences of the central and local governments began to diverge, but the center was still able to maintain a degree of extractive capacity. The negative correlation in the reform era indicates that local forces have gotten the upper hand in their competition for resources with the center. Indeed, since the reform started, extrabudgetary funds have grown at much higher rates than budget income. While the former grew around 9.3-fold between 1978 and 1991, the latter increased less than 2.8-fold. Huge financial resources that would have been appropriated by the state budget have thus either been "given" willingly by the center to enterprises and local governments or "taken" by the local forces against the center's will.

POLITICAL CONSEQUENCES OF THE DECLINE OF CENTRAL EXTRACTIVE CAPACITY

The decline of central extractive capacity has had three important political consequences: decline of central state steering capacity; decline of legitimation capacity; and growth of the power of local government.

The Decline of Steering Capacity

In any economic system, a careful management of effective demand is crucial for macroeconomic stability. Such a function must primarily be performed at the central level (Oates 1988). To perform the role of stabilization, however, the central government has to have sufficient financial resources at its disposal. Without the support of sufficient resources, its policy instruments are not likely to be effective. The declining extractive capacity has weakened Beijing's steering capacity.

First, both individual and public consumption have expanded more rapidly than central leaders would like. Between 1978 and 1987, the income of urban residents increased at an average annual rate of 17.2 percent, and public consumption 16.3 percent, both much more rapidly than national income (13.4 percent). Since the early 1980s, the central government has adopted numerous measures to curb the expansion of consumption, but so far they have had little effect, because most of the money has come from extrabudgetary funds (Deng 1990).

Enterprises are the driving force in the explosive growth of consumption. They have good reason to divert as much extrabudgetary money as possible to current consumption. First of all, enterprises are granted only the right to dispose of extrabudgetary funds; they do not have ownership. If they invest such funds in productive projects, at best they would be allowed to retain a part of the profits produced by the projects. In other words, they would have only a partial ownership of what the funds would bring about. If they consume those funds now, however, they in effect enjoy a full ownership. Moreover, if enterprises accumulate extrabudgetary funds, their savings may be tapped to satisfy the revenue needs of the local government in forms of *tanpai*. Furthermore, what a single enterprise retains after taxes is generally too small to be used for meaningful investments (Li, Fan, and Cong 1987; Deng 1990). For these reasons, enterprises' best strategy in handling extra-

budgetary funds is to consume them. Numerous studies have shown that
70–80 percent of enterprises' retained profits were spent on consumption
(Song 1989; Bi, Ren, and Tie 1991).

Second, Beijing has largely lost control over the level and structure of
investment. Between 1978 and 1987, China's capital investment grew at an
average annual rate of 21.9 percent, much more rapidly than the targeted
rate and the growth rate of national income (Qiu 1991). Local governments
have been the driving force behind the capital expansion. Most of the local
projects are orchestrated by local governments (Deng 1990). Local governments' favorites are high profit promising projects, which they expect to
become lucrative sources of future local income. Despite discouragement
from Beijing, the decade of the 1980s saw small cigarette factories, small
breweries, small textile mills, small home electronic appliance plants, and
the like springing up throughout China. In sectors that produce positive
externalities, however, local governments have little incentive to invest, and
the level of investment has thus been too low. Investment in energy, raw
materials, transportation, and communication, for instance, has lagged far
behind that in processing industries, thus creating many "bottlenecks" in
the economy (Xiao and Wan 1992; Chen 1993).

In theory, the central government could solve the problem of structural
imbalance by investing to fill the structural gaps, but to do so it has to have
sufficient investable funds at its disposal. But that is exactly what the central
government has found difficult to obtain. Since the early 1980s, extrabudgetary funds and bank loans, both of which are controlled by local
governments, have underwritten most capital construction. The proportion
of capital investment financed through the state budget has been falling
since the start of the reform. By the end of the 1980s, it may have dropped to
below 10 percent (Yao 1991). Therefore, it is not surprising that the central
government has been able to control neither the level nor the structure of
capital investment.

Owing to the runaway increase of both consumption and investment, the
aggregate demand for consumer goods and capital goods persistently ex-
ceeded the supply capacity of the economy throughout much of the 1980s,
which posed an enduring threat to macroeconomic stability.

A sign of macroeconomic instability is inflation. From 1951 to 1978, the
average annual inflation rate was just 0.7 percent. In the first five years of the
reform, inflation remained mild, rising annually 2.6 percent on average
from 1979 to 1984. After 1984, prices started to rise at an accelerated rate.
In 1988, the inflation rate climbed to 18.5 percent, and in the first six
months of 1989, it reached 25.5 percent. The urban costs of living increased
even faster. As the inflation rate rose to levels that had been unknown in
decades, the whole nation was thrown into panic. Dissatisfaction with the
high inflation rate was an important factor that brought millions of people

to the streets in 1989 (Wang Shaoguang 1992). In 1992 and 1993, when a new round of "investment fever" (*touzi re*) and "consumption fever" (*xiaofei re*) engulfed China, inflation again quickly climbed to the double-digit level, thus giving rise to concerns about political stability (Yuan 1993).

In addition, the continuing lags in infrastructural development pose a threat to China's future development. As pointed out above, the expansion of the processing sector has constantly outpaced the development of the country's infrastructure in the past decade. Given the existing distribution of resources, it is unlikely that the center's investment in energy, transporta tion, and raw-materials industries would be able to offset the pressure exerted by growing local investment in processing industries. If the existing "bottlenecks" persist or take a turn for the worse, it is doubtful whether China's impressive growth record of the past fifteen years or so will last (Wang and Hu 1993).

The Decline of Legitimation Capacity

Two factors have contributed to the decline of legitimation capacity: inequality and corruption. The explosive growth of funds outside central control has resulted in growing interregional, intersectoral, and interunit inequality. In theory, the central government should have the prime responsibility for distribution policies (Oates 1988), but in today's China, immense financial resources are not subject to central redistribution; and what is available to the center is not sufficient for it to perform the function of redistribution. Extrabudgetary funds simply stay where they are created. Enormous gaps thus exist between units, sectors, and regions in terms of how much extrabudgetary money they obtain (General Planning Department, Ministry of Finance 1992). Since extrabudgetary funds tend to be self-multiplying, the gaps are likely to be perpetuated and widened. The eleven coastal provinces, for instance, procured 55 percent of all local extrabudgetary funds in 1985. Two years later, their share went up to over 70 percent (Deng 1990). As mentioned above, enterprises are inclined to divert most of their retained funds toward increasing bonuses and other forms of welfare; and local governments tend to spend extrabudgetary funds on projects providing local public goods. As a result, the quality of life for people working in different units or living in different regions differs a great deal (He and Tang 1992; Zheng and Zhang 1992; Li and Shang 1993; Zhang 1994), and the gaps are going to persist and widen unless the center's ability to perform the function of redistribution is enhanced.

The augmentation of extrabudgetary funds has also facilitated corruption. Since it has become a common practice for enterprises and local governments to file false reports about their extrabudgetary incomes and to misrepresent their extrabudgetary expenditures, doors are open for corrupt local officials to spend public money for their personal enjoyment. Extrabudgetary funds enable enterprises and government agencies to establish what Chinese call "little pots of gold" (*xiaojinku*). From such "little pots of gold," corrupt officials can draw money to buy fleets of foreign cars, pay their travel expenses in China or abroad, purchase apartments for their families, and entertain themselves in luxurious restaurants.

Not only are existing extrabudgetary funds likely to be misused, power is often misused to create extrabudgetary funds. Ad hoc charges are a case in point. Because funds allocated through money-tight budgetary processes are not adequate for government use in less to support their routine operations, not to mention providing competitive earnings for their staff, those agencies have become desperate to explore new sources of income. The ad hoc charges are a means through which they can make extra incomes. Facing mounting fiscal deficits, the central government has also been compelled to legitimate such practices (An 1992). Such "profit-making" activities have further distorted the roles of those state agencies. Instead of seeing the corporate goals of the state as the best means of maximizing their individual self-interests, Chinese bureaucrats are becoming increasingly dependent on "rents" and therefore increasingly committed to the expansion of "rental havens." As a result, not just individual bureaucrats, but also whole bureaucratic institutions are becoming corrupted (Lan 1993; Yu and Yang 1993). Corruption has enabled some officials and their relatives to become super-rich overnight, thus further widening the gap between the "haves" and the "have-nots" (Zhu and Zhu 1993).

The widening inequality and rampant corruption have considerably undermined the legitimacy of the communist regime. Were one to single out one factor underlying the support of the Chinese for the communist regime, it would be their expectation of a society in which people are equal and the government is honest. But now, despite the improvements in the living standards of almost everyone, people feel that their society is becoming increasingly "unjust." A 1988 public opinion survey found that 88.7 percent of urban residents believed that social inequalities were "great" or "very great" in China. That was another of the main reasons why millions of Chinese took part in the protest movement of 1989 (Wang Shaoguang 1992).

The Fragmentation of the State

Mounting social and economic problems are symptoms of the inability of the central government to guide societal development. Central control capacity is apparently not sufficient to resolve those problems. However, the weakening of central control should be attributed, not so much to challenges from what many now call the rise of "civil society," as to the fragmentation of the state. Thanks to Deng's fiscal decentralization, the state apparatus in China has gradually been fragmented. The central government at first intentionally "withdrew" from some of the areas where it had intensively intervened in the past, hoping that the autonomy granted to lower levels of government and enterprises would improve the efficiency of the system. Local forces exploited the opportunity to appropriate every bit of resources and power given up by the center and thereby gradually strengthened their ability to compete with the center for control over even more resources. As the center's extractive capacity declined, its policy options became increasingly limited, and the effectiveness of its policy tools was greatly impaired. Thus, in effect, the center was "pushed out" of some of the areas in which it wanted to retain firm control. In a space of fifteen years or so, the Chinese political structure has been transformed from one that was once reputed for its high degree of centralization and effectiveness into one in which the center has difficulty coordinating its own agents' behavior. Because power and resources are dispersed, the exercise of central control now depends to a large extent upon the consent of the subnational units whose actions are slipping from central control. Beijing no longer has undisputed authority over local forces; the center is just one level of decision making, and not necessarily the one with guaranteed access to channels of effective control down to the grass roots. Subnational units are, of course, still under the nominal control of the center, but they have their own agendas and, more important, they have the resources to pursue those agendas even in defiance of central guidance. The corporate coherence of state organizations, which is imperative if the state is to play its roles, has been greatly weakened.

REFERENCES

Almond, Gabriel A., and G. Bingham Powell, Jr. 1966. *Comparative Politics: A Developmental Approach.* Boston: Little, Brown.

An Tifu. 1992. "Guanyu zhenxing woguo caizheng de ruogan sikao" (Reflections on How to Develop the Fiscal System of Our Country). *Caijing yanjiu* (Research in Finance and Economics) 1 (January): 8–16.

Bachman, David. 1987. "Implementing Chinese Tax Policy." In *Policy Implementation in Post-Mao China,* ed. David Lampton, 119–53. Berkeley and Los Angeles: University of California Press.

Bi Da, Ren Qing, and Tie Ying. 1991. "Guanyu guoyou zichan suoyouquan yueshu jizhi de tantao" (A Study of Property Rights of State Enterprises). *Jingji guanli* (Economic Management) 8 (August): 13–16.

Cai Yin. 1988. "Gaige guojia yusuan guanli tizhi de shexiang" (Suggestions Concerning the Reform of Our Budget Management System). *Caimao jingji* (Economics of Finance) 2:28–31.

Chen Leyi. 1993. "Lun 'jichu pingjing'" (On "Bottlenecks"). *Caijing wenti yanjiu* (Studies of Financial Problems) 5 (May): 16–21.

Contemporary Chinese Public Finance Editorial Group. 1990. *Zhongguo shehui zhuyi caizhengshi cankao ziliao, 1949–1985* (Historic Financial Data of Socialist China). Beijing: Chinese Financial Economics Press.

Deng Yingtao. 1990. *Zhongguo yusuanwai zijin fenxi* (An Analysis of China's Extra-budgetary Funds). Beijing: Press of Chinese People's University.

Du Linfeng. 1984. *Zhongguo shehui zhuyi caizheng guanli* (Financial Management in Socialist China). Beijing: Press of Chinese People's University.

Enterprise Management Yearbook. 1991. *Zhongguo qiye guanli nianjian 1991* (Enterprise Management Yearbook of China 1991). Beijing: Enterprise Management Press.

Feng Baoxing. 1992. "Dui caizheng guize shifu de tantao" (Discussion on the Financial Reform Guideline). *Jingji zhongheng* (Economics Tribune) 11 (November): 44–51.

General Planning Department, Ministry of Finance. 1992. *Zhongguo caizheng tongji, 1950–1991* (China Finance Statistics, 1950–1991). Beijing: China Finance Press.

Habermas, Jürgen. 1975. *Legitimation Crisis*. Boston: Beacon Press.

He Minsheng and Tang Kuiyu. 1992. *Shehui fenpei de dingxin yu bianyi* (Changes in the Distribution of Social Wealth). Harbin: Heilongjiang People's Press.

He Zhengyi. 1987. "Caizheng gaige jiben silu de ruogan sikao" (Reflections on the Main Problems of Fiscal Reform). *Caimao jingji* 9: 37–42.

Huang Yasheng. 1990. "Web of Interests and Patterns of Behavior of Chinese Local Economic Bureaucracies and Enterprises During Reforms." *China Quarterly* 123 (September): 431–58.

Ikenberry, John. 1988. *Reasons of State*. Ithaca, N.Y.: Cornell University Press.

Katzenstein, Peter J., ed. 1978. *Between Power and Plenty*. Madison: University of Wisconsin Press.

Krasner, Stephen D. 1978a. *Defending the National Interest*. Princeton, N.J.: Princeton University Press.

———. 1978b. "United States Commercial and Monetary Policy: Unraveling the Paradox of External Strength and Internal Weakness." In *Between Power and Plenty*, ed. Peter J. Katzenstein, 51–87. Madison: University of Wisconsin Press.

Lamborn, Alan C. 1983. "Power and the Politics of Extraction." *International Studies Quarterly* 27, 2: 125–46.

Lan Ye. 1993. *Zhongguo zhengfu dacaiyuan* (Cut Down the Size of the Chinese Government). Chongqing: Chongqing University Press.

Lardy, Nicholas R. 1978. *Economic Growth and Distribution in China*. Cambridge: Cambridge University Press.

Lee, Keun. 1991. *Chinese Firms and the State in Transition: Property Rights and Agency Problems in the Reform Era*. New York: M. E. Sharpe.

———. 1993. "Property Rights and Agency Problems in China's Enterprise Reform." *Cambridge Journal of Economics* 17, 2: 179–94.

Levi, Margaret. 1988. *Of Rule and Revenue*. Berkeley and Los Angeles: University of California Press.

Li Nianhua. 1991. "Shuilianjiao huanshi lianjiaoshui" (Why Is It So Hard to Collect Taxes). *Liaowang* (Outlook [domestic ed.]) 27 (July 8): 18.

Li Qinting, Fan Yong, and Cong Yanzi. 1987. "Dangqian caizheng mianlin de zhuyao wenti ji duice" (The Main Problems in Public Finance and Policy Options). *Caimao jingji* 4 (April): 40–43.

Li Shi and Shang Lie. 1993. "Guoyou dazhong xing qiye jian zhigong shouru chaju de fenxi" (Analysis of Employees' Income Differences Among Medium- and Large-sized State-owned Enterprises). *Jingji yanjiu* (Economics Research), no. 3 (March 20): 32–40.

Li Xianglu. 1990. "Weishenmo shuo fenquan gaige fangzhen shi zhengque de" (Why Is the Reform Guideline of Decentralization Correct?). *Zhishi fenzi* (Chinese Intellectual), Fall, 3–6.

Liang Huaping. 1989. "Jiaqiang yusuanwai zijin guanli gaohao zhonghe caili pingheng" (Strengthening Control over Extrabudgetary Funds and Striking a Fiscal Balance). *Jianghuai luntan* (Jianghuai Tribune) 4 (April): 18–24.

Lyons, Thomas P. 1987. *Economic Integration and Planning in Maoist China.* New York: Columbia University Press.

Migdal, Joel S. 1988. *Strong Societies and Weak States.* Princeton, N.J.: Princeton University Press.

Musgrave, Richard A. 1969. *Fiscal Systems.* New Haven, Conn.: Yale University Press.

Ning Xueping. 1990. "Shidang jizhong caili shi yixiong zhongda de zhanlüe juece" (Recentralization of Financial Resources Is an Important Strategic Decision). *Jingji zhongheng* (Economics Tribune) 5 (May): 16–19.

Oates, Wallace E. 1988. "Public Finance with Several Levels of Government." MS. Department of Economics, University of Maryland.

Oi, Jean C. 1992. "Fiscal Reform and the Economic Foundations of Local State Corporatism in China." *World Politics* 45, 1: 99–126.

Oksenberg, Michel, and James Tong. 1991. "The Evolution of Central-Provincial Fiscal Relations in China, 1971–1984." *China Quarterly* 125 (March): 1–32.

Organski, A. F. K., and Jacek Kugler. 1980. *The War Ledger.* Chicago: University of Chicago Press.

Organski, A. F. K., Jacek Kugler, J. Timothy Johnson, and Youssef Cohen. 1984. *Births, Deaths, and Taxes: The Demographic and Political Transitions.* Chicago: University of Chicago Press.

Qiu Huabing. 1991. "Dangqian caizheng kunnan de chengyin yu duice" (The Causes of the Current Fiscal Difficulties and Policy Suggestions). *Xiamen daxue xuebao* (Journal of Xiamen University) 1 (January): 25–31.

Schmitter, Philippe C. 1975. "Liberation by Golpe: Retrospective Thoughts on the Demise of Authoritarian Rule in Portugal." *Armed Forces and Society* 2, 1: 5–27.

Shirk, Susan L. 1993. *The Political Logic of Economic Reform in China.* Berkeley and Los Angeles: University of California Press.

Skocpol, Theda. 1985. "Bringing the State Back In: Strategies of Analysis in Current Research." In *Bringing the State Back In,* ed. Peter B. Evans, Dietrich Rueschemeyer, and Theda Skocpol, 3–37. Cambridge: Cambridge University Press.

Snider, Lewis W. 1990a. "The Political Performance of Third World Governments and the Debt Crisis." *American Political Science Review* 84, 3: 1263–80.

——. 1990b. "The Political Performance of Governments, External Debt Service, and Domestic Political Violence." *International Political Science Review* 11, 3: 403–22.

Song Yunzhao. 1989. "Zhongguo tonghuo pengzhang chengyin de fenxi" (An Analysis of the Causes of China's Inflation). *Fudan xuebao* (Journal of Fudan University) 2 (February): 1–6.

State Council. 1986. "Guanyu jiaqiang yusuanwai jijin guanli de tongzhi" (Directive Concerning the Strengthening of the Center's Control over Extrabudgetary Funds). *Caizheng* (Public Finance) 6 (June): 11.

———. 1989. "Guojia yusuan tiaojie jijin zhengji banfa" (Method for Collecting Budget Adjustment Tax). *Caizheng* 4 (April): 10.

State Statistics Bureau. 1992. *Zhongguo tongji nianjian, 1992* (China Statistical Yearbook, 1992). Beijing: Chinese Statistics Press.

Walder, Andrew G. 1992. "Local Bargaining Relationships and Urban Industrial Finance." In *Bureaucracy, Politics, and Decision-Making in Post-Mao China*, ed. Kenneth G. Lieberthal and David M. Lampton, 308–33. Berkeley and Los Angeles: University of California Press

Wang Mengkui. 1990. "Gaishan guomin shouru fenpei geju" (It Is Necessary to Change the Current Pattern of the Distribution of National Income). *Jingji ribao* (Economics Daily), October 20 9

Wang Shaofei. 1988. "Zhongyang he difang caizheng guanxi de mubiao moshi" (The Target Model of Central-Local Fiscal Relations). *Caimao jingji* 6 (June): 22–7.

Wang Shaoguang. 1992. "Deng Xiaoping's Reform and the Chinese Workers' Participation in the Protest Movement of 1989." *Research in Political Economy* 13: 163–97.

Wang Shaoguang and Hu Angang. 1993. *Zhongguo guojia nengli baogao* (A Report on China's State Capacity). Shenyang: Liaoning People's Press.

Wang Wentong and Xiao Houxiong. 1992. "Guanyu 100 hu qiye shuifei fudan qingkuang de diaocha baogao" (Enterprises' Burden of Taxes and Charges: Results from an Investigation of 100 Firms). *Hubei caizheng yanjiu* (Hubei Research in Public Finance) 1 (January): 56–9.

Wang Yuanzeng. 1989. "Kongzhi shehui jituan goumaili yin zhonghe zhili" (We Need to Have Comprehensive Control over Public Consumption). *Caijing yanjiu* (Research in Public Finance) 4 (April): 21–4.

Wang Yunguo. 1992. "Dui dangqian qiye fudan zhuangkuang de fenxi he jianyi' (An Analysis of Enterprise Financial Burden and Suggestions). *Hubei caizheng yanjiu* 4 (April): 27–31.

World Bank. 1990a. *China: Macroeconomic Stability and Industrial Growth under Decentralized Socialism.* Washington, D.C.: World Bank.

———. 1990b. *China: Revenue Mobilization and Tax Policy.* Washington, D.C.: World Bank.

Wu Mingyi. 1990. "Guanyu difang zhengfu xingwei de ruogan sikao" (A Study of Local Governments' Behavior). *Jingji yanjiu* 7 (July): 56–60.

Xiao Qiu and Wan Donghua. 1992. "Xiaochu 'pingjing' yueshu" (Breaking the Bottleneck Constraints). *Zhongguo tongji* (Chinese Statistics) 12 (December): 9–12.

Yao Zhanghui. 1991. "Guomin shouru fensanhua yu hongguan tiaokong" (The Dispersion of National Income and Macroeconomic Management). *Jingji kexue* (Economic Science) 2 (February): 25–8.

Yu Qiao and Yang Zi. 1993. *Kuangbiao xia de Zhongguo* (China in the Storm and Stress of Rapid Change). Chengdu: Sichuan University Press.

Yuan Chen. 1993. "Mingnian tongzhang yinyou youcun" (Concerns about Inflation in the Next Year). *Zhongguo shibao zhoukan* (China Times Weekly) 99 (November 21–27): 48–9.

Yuan Dong. 1992. "Zhongyang he difang caizheng guanxi zhong cunzai de wenti he jiejue tujing" (Problems in Central-Local Fiscal Relations and Policy Options). *Zhongguo jingji wenti* 1 (January): 10–13.

Yun Zhiping and Wang Hong. 1990. "Nuli tigao caizheng shouru he zhongyang caizheng shouru de bizhong" (Striving for Increasing Budget Revenue and the Central Government's Share of Budget Revenue). *Qiushi* (Seeking Truth) 4 (February 16): 39–42.

Zhang Changliang. 1994. "Dongbu yu zhongxibu jingji chaju kuoda" (The Economic Gaps Between the Coastal Provinces and the Interior Provinces Has Been Widening). *Zhongguo shibao zhoukan* 109–10: 58–61.

Zheng Jinping and Zhang Yingxiang. 1990. "Dui woguo shouru fenpei xianzhuang de tantao" (A Study of the Income Distribution Patterns in Our Country). *Jingji yu guanli yanjiu* (Research in Economics and Management) 5 (May): 13–17.

Zhu Wei. 1990. "Zhouqian guojia yusuan lun—dui yusuanwai zijin de xin renshi" (On Balanced Budgets—A Reflection on Extrabudgetary Funds). *Caijing yanjiu* 7 (July): 30–32.

Zhu Youdi and Zhu Xiaoli. 1993. *Zhongguo dalu xinfuhao* (The New Rich of Mainland China). Chengdu: Sichuan University Press.

Zysman, John. 1983. *Governments, Markets, and Growth.* Ithaca, N.Y.: Cornell University Press.

FIVE

Losing the Political Initiative: The Impact of Financial Liberalization in Hungary

David L. Bartlett

Hungary undertook a series of financial reforms in the 1980s, including the establishment of a securities market, creation of commercial banks, liberalization of foreign exchange, loosening of wage controls, and decentralization of the budgetary system. While the technical design of these reforms bore some similarities to those initiated in China after 1978, their politico-economic circumstances differed decisively. China's financial reforms were part of a broader strategy of rapid economic growth, and the political dynamics attending their implementation resembled a positive-sum game to the extent they provided benefits to all relevant actors (Byrd 1983; De Wulf and Goldsbrough 1986; Naughton 1987; Shaoguang Wang, chapter 4 in this volume; Zhou Xiaochuan and Zhu Li 1987). By contrast, financial liberalization in Hungary was the central component of an externally imposed program of economic austerity. Here, the introduction of market mechanisms was intended to force a reallocation of capital and labor and curtail domestic demand in order to promote structural adjustment and macroeconomic stabilization. Thus, the politics of financial reform in Hungary more closely approximated a zero-sum game in which enterprises, banks, trade unions, and Hungarian Socialist Workers' Party (HSWP) authorities clashed over the distribution of economic resources.

In this chapter, I explore the political consequences of financial liberalization in Hungary during the late socialist period. I argue the following. The ruling party's employment of market-type financial mechanisms as instruments of austerity simultaneously produced economic distortions that forced the authorities to reimpose central controls and enlarged the capacity of local actors to resist such recentralization. The internal contradictions of Hungary's market socialist system induced banks, enterprises, and workers to behave in ways contrary to the goals of stabilization and adjustment, thereby generating strong pressures on the party to recentralize financial policy. At the same time, financial reform transformed the resources and incentives of those very same actors to a degree that prevented the center from fully restoring the status quo ante. This peculiar push-pull dynamic severely weakened the party's collective authority and undermined its ability to manage the economy. The failure of market-type instruments to elicit the desired responses from local agents compelled the center to intervene in microeconomic decision making, thereby ensnaring party authorities in politically damaging disputes over bank credit, wage regulations, and foreign exchange. But the prior devolution of authority to the factory level sharply circumscribed these attempts to restore central administrative controls on market processes. In short, recentralization was both economically ineffectual and politically costly to the HSWP. Caught between the dual imperatives of decentralization and recentralization, by the late 1980s, the HSWP faced a deteriorating economy, diminishing political authority, and mounting distributional clashes. Its inability to cope with the contradictory effects of financial liberalization hastened the collapse of the one-party system at decade's end.

THE CONTRADICTIONS OF FINANCIAL REFORM

The final round of Hungary's New Economic Mechanism (NEM) differed from previous phases in that its departures from central planning were integrally linked to the problems of economic austerity. By the mid 1980s, it was apparent that the program of market-type reforms initiated in 1968 had not yielded any appreciable improvement in the performance of Hungarian state enterprises, the economy's main source of foreign exchange. In 1986, the balance of payments in convertible currency plunged into the largest deficit since the 1970s. Meanwhile, the gross hard currency debt approached $20 billion, the highest in per capita terms in Eastern Europe. These circumstances compelled the leadership of János Kádár to reorient reform policy away from economic growth and toward stabilization and adjustment.

The centerpiece of the program undertaken in the latter half of the 1980s was an ambitious reform of the system of financial regulation. This program had three primary components. First, the monobanking system would be transformed into a two-tiered system. The function of credit allocation, heretofore the monopoly of the National Bank, would be devolved to a set of commercial banks. The banks, organized as joint stock companies and enjoying operational autonomy from the central authorities, would base their lending decisions on considerations of profitability and hence generate a more efficient pattern of credit distribution. Freed of the obligation to supply state enterprises directly with credit, the National Bank could then regulate the aggregate supply of liquidity through Western-type monetary instruments.

Second, the complex set of regulations prescribing wage rates for various categories of Hungarian workers would be dismantled, empowering trade union organizations and enterprise management to negotiate their own wage contracts. This, economists argued, was the essential step toward the creation of a real labor market, which would heighten allocative efficiency by enabling highly profitable enterprises to offer the most generous wage rates, and thereby attract the most highly skilled workers.

Finally, Hungary's elaborate array of foreign exchange controls would be liberalized. This entailed deregulating the import licensing system to allow enterprises to exchange their surplus forints for convertible currency and gradually transferring authority over allocation of foreign exchange from the National Bank to the new commercial banks. Like the reforms of the banking and wage systems, these measures would in theory raise efficiency and productivity in the state sector. With profitability, not political or administrative criteria, determining access to hard currency, the most successful enterprises possessing the largest forint surpluses would be the ones best positioned to import high technology products from the West.

Recentralization versus Decentralization

The fact that these reforms were designed to reallocate capital and labor within the Hungarian state sector distinguished them from earlier phases of NEM, whose distributional effects were far less salient. This created new sorts of political challenges for the HSWP, which now had to deal with the competing claims of the winners and losers from financial liberalization in an economy undergoing externally mandated stabilization and adjustment. Equally important, the financial reforms of the 1980s sharpened the tension between the recentralizing pressures of market socialism and the decentralizing "ratchet effects" of departures from central planning. Specialists on the Yugoslav and Hungarian reforms have amply documented the self-reproductive logic of the "socialist halfway house" (e.g., Bauer 1978, 1981; Comisso 1979; Kornai 1980; Laky 1980; Milenkovitch 1971; Tardos 1986; Tyson 1983). The stop-go patterns, the periodic reinterventions characteristic of those reforms result not merely from shifting political currents within the ruling party, but from the systemic peculiarities of market socialism. Such reforms delegate decision-making authority to factory-level agents, while preserving the dominant position of socialist ownership of the means of production. Possessing greater control over economic resources, but still lacking strong incentives to use them efficiently, enterprise managers and workers replicate and even intensify the same behavioral patterns that characterized the prereform system. They bid up wages and prices,

procure excess credit, purchase unneeded imports, begin dubious investment projects, and build up inventories of unusable capital goods. These
distortions eventually compel the authorities to restore elements of the old
central planning system.

The internal contradictions of market socialism become even more vexing when the reforms are implemented under conditions of economic austerity, as in Hungary during the 1980s. Josef Brada, Ed Hewett, and Thomas
Wolf (1988) show how stabilization, adjustment, and reform operate at
cross-purposes. The market-type instruments of austerity commonly prescribed by the International Monetary Fund (price adjustment, currency
devaluation, monetary contraction, etc.) often fail to work properly in so
cialist economics, forcing the center to reimpose quantitative restrictions
on investment, consumption, and imports. While such measures may well
restore short-term equilibrium, they are likely to impede the structural
changes needed to raise industry to world standards of competitiveness.
Financial reforms of the sort undertaken in Hungary further complicate
matters in that they decentralize control on the microeconomic side without strengthening control on the macro side. Absent monetary instruments
capable of restraining domestic purchasing power, the loosening of regulations on bank credit, wages, and foreign exchange merely generates an
increase in aggregate demand and forces a return to administrative-type
controls.

But the center's ability to restore such controls is constrained to the
extent that the decision-making authority already relinquished to local
agents cannot easily be recovered. To take the example of wage liberalization: the initial devolution of control empowered a large and strategically
vital constituency of actors (workers), who now possessed both a compelling
interest in retaining that authority and the resources (the power of collective bargaining and capacity to organize strikes) to resist the HSWP's efforts
at recentralization. The burgeoning wage bill compromised the macroeconomic balance, but the authorities could no longer implement the measures needed to restore equilibrium. The center now faced both deteriorating economic performance and rising mobilization from below. For the
HSWP, whose reputation and authority hinged on its capacity to manage the
economy, the political implications of this dilemma were ominous.

Summary of the Cases

As the forthcoming case studies demonstrate, all three spheres of Hungary's
financial reforms exhibited these tensions. The primary aim of the banking
reform was to transform the role of credit and make it an active instrument
of structural adjustment rather than the passive support of the central plan.
However, the new commercial banks proved unwilling to use the credit

instrument to discipline their clients, and indeed took pains to sustain credit lines to the weakest enterprises in their portfolios. The earlier decision to relinquish the crediting function deprived the center of the means of intervening in a manner that would induce the banks significantly to shift their lending policies. The commercial credit instrument thus proving ineffectual, the authorities turned to political/administrative methods of economic adjustment. The result was to shift the locus of distributional conflict over industrial restructuring away from the new banks and toward the center, entangling the party leadership in a series of disputes over capacity reductions and labor dislocations in large industrial firms.

In the case of wage reform, attempts at liberalization repeatedly ran up against the exigencies of economic stabilization. Loosening of central controls emboldened Hungarian workers, already agitated over years of stagnating real income, to press their wage claims. Lacking compelling incentives to contain labor costs, enterprise managers offered little or no countervailing pressure, and indeed shared the interest of workers to promote the liberalization of wage controls. The resultant surge in domestic demand compromised the macroeconomic balance and created pressures on the authorities to recentralize wage policy. Workers, whose capacity for collective action had been considerably bolstered by the prior decentralization, resisted and forced the center to relax wage controls. The upshot of this tug-of-war was the emergence of a strong trade union movement that expedited the party's fall from power in 1988–89.

A different politico-economic dynamic obtained in the case of foreign-exchange reforms. The center's efforts to widen access to foreign exchange for Hungarian households and enterprises resulted in deterioration of the balance of payments and depletion of the country's hard-currency reserves. For technical and political reasons, the center could more easily recentralize control of foreign exchange than commercial bank credit and wages. But while the center could reimpose controls on domestic actors with comparative ease, its efforts in the foreign-exchange area created a new constituency, Western investors, whose interests and resources strongly militated against recentralization. The HSWP was thus placed in the politically awkward position of retaining foreign-exchange controls on domestic actors while virtually eliminating them for foreign investors. This bifurcated pattern of foreign-exchange liberalization became a major source of political contention during the negotiated transition to democracy at the end of the 1980s.

Political Consequences for the Communist Party

The tensions illustrated in these cases had important consequences for the HSWP during its final years in power. As part of its post-1956 strategy of consolidation, the Kádár regime staked its legitimacy on improvements in the population's standard of living. In this respect, the program of reforms launched in 1968 was aimed at strengthening the party's political position by raising economic growth. The onset of austerity in 1979 forced a shift in the regime's strategy: market-type reform was now geared toward the goals of stabilization and adjustment. But while the measures undertaken in the 1980s went well beyond earlier phases of NEM, they remained bound by the systemic constraints of market socialism, generating a variety of distortions that could only be corrected through reimposition of central controls. Yet those very same measures endowed key economic agents with the resources to thwart recentralization. For the Kádár leadership, the result was the worst possible combination of diminishing political authority and deteriorating economic performance. These were the principal factors leading to Kádár's ouster in 1988. The successor regime of Károly Grósz proved little more successful in stemming either the economy's decline or the unraveling of the party's power. Facing a well-organized labor movement that repeatedly foiled his efforts to implement an austerity program, Grósz entered the 1989 roundtable negotiations with a very weak political hand. The result of those talks was an agreement to hold parliamentary elections the following year, and the disintegration of the party itself into separate parties. The largest of those splinter parties was headed by the reformist faction of the old HSWP. However, it fared badly in the elections owing to its association with the failed economic policies of the communist regime, as well as the controversy surrounding foreign capital's highly visible role in the privatization program initiated by the outgoing socialist government.

BANKING REFORM AND STRUCTURAL ADJUSTMENT

The creation of a two-tiered banking system in 1987 was closely tied to the problems of both macroeconomic stabilization and structural adjustment. Separating the functions of currency issue and credit allocation would allow the National Bank to focus on curtailing growth of the aggregate money supply, a central objective of the IMF-supervised stabilization program. Meanwhile, the commercial banks, now operating under joint stock ownership and hence driven by the incentive to maximize returns to the shareholders, would redirect the flow of capital within the Hungarian state sector from weak to strong enterprises. In this way, commercial credit would become an instrument of structural adjustment: the banks would supply credit on favorable terms to their best-performing clients, while compelling loss makers to implement restructuring programs as the condition for restoration of credit lines. With heavily indebted enterprises unable to take the steps necessary to restore themselves to profitability, the banks could resort to Hungary's bankruptcy law and seek liquidation of the clients' assets.

In addition to raising allocative efficiency, the banking reform would be politically beneficial to the ruling party. Industrial restructuring entailed significant socioeconomic costs: downsizing of state enterprises long accustomed to soft budget constraints; sizable reductions of a blue-collar labor force long habituated to the full-employment guarantee; and dislocation of local communities whose livelihood depended on the targeted enterprises. To the extent that the new commercial banks used the market-type instruments at their disposal, it was thought, the center would be relieved of the political burden of economic adjustment.

However, the ultimate result of the reform was to heighten the party's political liabilities. The banks, unwilling to use commercial credit as a restructuring tool, turned the problem back to the center. The central authorities, having already devolved the credit function to the banks, could not effectively intervene to redirect capital flows. The center then resorted to political/administrative instruments of industrial restructuring, sharpening distributional conflicts between state, government, and local party organizations and deepening the HSWP leadership's own engagement in the adjustment process.

Credit Allocation in the Two-Tiered Banking System

Ronald McKinnon (1991, 1992) and other scholars have noted the risks of premature liberalization of banking in socialist market systems, whose perverse incentive structures create a moral hazard of overlending to loss-making enterprises. Yugoslavia's 1965 reform permitted workers' councils and local political organizations to become the principal capital subscribers of commercial banks, thereby providing labor-managed firms with highly elastic credit lines and depriving the National Bank of Yugoslavia of effective control of the money supply (Dimitrijevic and Macesich 1973; Furubotn 1980; Furubotn and Pejovich 1973; Gedeon 1986, 1987; Hauvonen 1970; Pejovich 1973; Tyson 1977). The main problem confounding Hungary's experiment with commercial banking in the late 1980s was the large number of bad loans the new banks inherited from the National Bank. The designers of the two-tiered system had expected that the profit orientation of the banks would induce them to redirect credit flows to the strongest enterprises in the state sector. However, their loan portfolios created incentives for them to sustain credit lines to their weakest clients. A major portion of those portfolios consisted of loans to the mining, metallurgy, and other loss-making sectors over several decades during the prereform period. Both the central authorities and the commercial bank managers understood that many of those loans would never be repaid. The key issue at hand was who would absorb the financial impact of disposing of these nonperforming assets.

The authorities argued that the banks should bear final responsibility. From the center's perspective, the fact that the banks were saddled with a large amount of dubious assets was a regrettable but unavoidable consequence of the transition to the two-tiered system. The high profits of the banks would allow them gradually to build up their loss reserves and write off the loans. The bank managers countered that the party was shirking responsibility for its own financial imprudence over past decades. Furthermore, the political authorities were pressuring the banks to write down their loan portfolios at the same time that the Hungarian state was sustaining the flow of subsidies to the very same enterprises that had fallen in arrears on those debts. To begin writing down the portfolios before the state terminated budgetary support of the loss-making sectors and initiated a restructuring program would simply prolong the process and confront the banks with the need to make repeated loan write-offs (Bartlett 1993). The willingness of the commercial banks to use market instruments to discipline loss-making enterprises would thus depend chiefly on the degree of resolve the party leadership demonstrated in structural adjustment policy.

The first test of this resolve came in January 1987. The managing director of the Hungarian Credit Bank, the largest of the new banks, announced his intention to initiate bankruptcy procedures against the Veszprém Construction Company. Veszprém turned out to be the first liquidation of a major state enterprise under Hungary's 1985 bankruptcy law.

While there were a number of other clients in the Credit Bank's portfolio equally deserving of liquidation, this particular company was an especially suitable test case. It did not have a large number of outstanding international contracts, minimizing external claims on the company's assets and simplifying liquidation procedures. Moreover, it was not a major employer in the local community, which would help contain the socioeconomic fallout of bankruptcy. But despite these factors that rendered Veszprém a convenient target, the political authorities in Budapest proved leery of supporting the Credit Bank's efforts to shut down the company, underscoring their sensitivity to the political problems of industrial restructuring. The case dragged on for months, with the center repeatedly erecting obstacles to the bank's pursuit of a liquidation (interviews 5, 7, 9, 10, and 14).[1]

The Veszprém episode transformed the Credit Bank's business strategy. By the time the legal proceedings against the company were concluded, the bank managers had decided not only to forgo any further bankruptcies but to disengage the bank from restructuring policy altogether. If the party leaders refused to back up the commercial banks on a single construction company such as Veszprém, they could hardly be expected to show greater resolve in far more difficult sectors like mining and metallurgy. With regard

1. Interviews conducted by the author are listed in the Appendix.

to the loan portfolio problem, the bank managers determined they would make no agreements until a structural adjustment program was under way with the full backing of the party leadership. In the meantime, they would keep the bad loans on their books as performing assets, rescheduling and refinancing them as necessary to allow the debtor enterprises to make payments (interview 8).

The banks' refusal to use commercial credit as a restructuring instrument left the center with the option of intervening in lending policy so as to redirect capital flows in a manner consistent with the goals of adjustment policy. But having already relinquished the power of credit allocation to the banks, the Hungarian political authorities faced major obstacles to financial recentralization.

Limits on Central Intervention in Commercial Credit Policy

Under the two-tiered system, the center retained a formidable array of regulations governing the commercial banking sector: refinancing quotas, legal reserve requirements, rates of taxation, loan classification rules, and so on. But while these devices could powerfully influence the overall financial position of the new banks, they did not allow the center to intervene in specific lending decisions. The only exception was long-term refinancing credit for fixed capital investment, applications for which underwent individual scrutiny by the National Bank of Hungary. But even this regulatory instrument proved of limited usefulness, as the National Bank allowed the commercial banks to fill up their long-term refinancing quotas within a few months of the start-up of the two-tiered system (interview 14).

The center could also use its voting power as majority shareholder in the banks to redirect credit flows. But this likewise proved of limited utility. The boards of shareholders of the banks met only infrequently, and on those occasions their formal sphere of authority extended only to appointment of the management, determination of the annual dividend, and approval of the bank's general business plan. Obviously, bank managers could not be wholly indifferent to the preferences of the senior party and state officials who figured so prominently on the boards of the new banks. But the high degree of separation of ownership and control characteristic of joint stock ownership did not readily permit central intervention in the individual lending decisions of the banks.

Beyond these impediments to intervention, the political resources of the banks limited the center's capacity to reshape credit policy. The banks vividly demonstrated their political clout in early 1988, when the National Bank enacted deep cuts in refinancing quotas in an attempt to force a redistribution of commercial credit. The banks responded by appealing directly to the HSWP's central committee to intercede on their behalf. They also took steps aimed at provoking other actors to enter the fray. In direct contradiction to the objectives of the monetary authorities, the banks enlarged credit lines to their weakest clients, while cutting those to their strongest ones. As a result, well-performing enterprises, which might otherwise have supported the National Bank's position if the banks had reacted to the liquidity squeeze by diverting credit to more efficient sectors, were moved to join in opposition to the bank. Under pressure from the commercial banks, large state enterprises, farm cooperatives, and senior party leaders, the National Bank yielded and restored the refinancing lines to their previous level (interviews 1, 2, 4, 7, 8, 10, 15, 22, and 23).

The Party's Resort to Nonmarket Mechanisms

The Hungarian banking reform thus induced economic agents to reproduce the same inefficient credit flows that had prevailed under the old monobanking system. At the same time, it endowed those actors with the technical, legal, and political resources to resist the center's efforts to correct those distortions via recentralization. Facing a recalcitrant commercial banking sector, continued deterioration of the balance of payments, and mounting pressure from the international lending agencies to initiate a restructuring program, the party leadership was forced to resort to nonmarket mechanisms of structural adjustment.

Foremost among these political/administrative instruments was the Planned Economy Committee, a new intragovernmental body charged with overseeing restructuring of key industries in the Hungarian state sector. The main intent of this institutional innovation was to accelerate the restructuring process by detaching primary decision-making authority from the Ministry of Industry, whose organizational interests were too closely tied to the targeted enterprises, and investing it in a national-level body capable of transcending narrow sectoral interests.

But these expectations were dashed. The consequence of the commercial banks' disengagement was to draw state enterprises, trade unions, local party committees, state and governmental organizations, and the HSWP leadership into highly public clashes over the course of adjustment policy. The political ramifications of the center's use of nonmarket mechanisms of structural adjustment were particularly evident in coal mining and steel, two of the biggest loss-making sectors in Hungarian industry.

Structural Adjustment in the Mining Industry

In June 1988, the Planned Economy Committee announced its plan to restructure the coal industry, proposing to phase out all state subsidies to the sector over a two-year period. The committee's program appeared to gain momentum after a special conference of the HSWP in May 1988. The replacement of Kádár by Károly Grósz as the party's general secretary reflected the latter's success in cultivating the image of a tough, decisive leader willing to take the painful measures needed to pull Hungary out of its economic morass.

But Grósz quickly yielded when the first test of his resolve occurred three months after his ascension to the party leadership. A group of miners at the Mecsek pits in southern Hungary staged a walkout to protest the management's decision to reduce the so-called fidelity bonuses allocated to employees annually on the basis of years of service. Although the direct motive of the strike was the dispute over the bonuses, it was widely understood that the underlying issue was the miners' anxiety over the proposed restructuring of the Mecsek operations. The walkout was intended less as a challenge to the Mecsek management than as a message to the Grósz regime that the miners had no intention of bearing the entire burden of economic adjustment by themselves. Grósz was sufficiently exercised about the affair to hasten down to the Mecsek mine and personally negotiate a settlement (FBIS/EEU: d, e, f, g).[2]

Grósz's decision to intervene and accommodate the miners' demands was not motivated by any particular concern about the economic impact of the strike. One of the chief aims of the restructuring program was precisely to reduce capacity at Mecsek and other loss-making mines. The risk of diminished production resulting from a prolonged strike was thus hardly a credible threat, since this was what the authorities intended anyway. Rather, the walkout by the Mecsek miners was politically effective because it presented the danger of sparking similar actions by workers at other, larger Hungarian enterprises targeted for restructuring. With news of massive strikes by Polish workers in the Baltic ports filling the newspapers in the summer of 1988, and with the debate over industrial restructuring dominating the political agenda at home, Grósz feared that a strike at a single enterprise would stimulate labor mobilization in the loss-making sectors as a whole (interviews 6, 11, and 19).

The result was to send exactly the wrong signal to the opponents of restructuring in the branch ministries, trade unions, and local party committees: that the party leadership would relent if subjected to a very modest degree of pressure. If Grósz yielded so quickly to a handful of miners at a single small mine, there was little reason to expect that he would demonstrate any greater resolve if confronted by labor unrest in other, more strategically vital enterprises, such as the giant steel plants in northeastern Hungary.

---

2. Citations of documents from FBIS/EEU (Foreign Broadcast Information/Eastern Europe) are indexed in the References at the end of the chapter.

Structural Adjustment in the Steel Industry

Steel did indeed present an array of problems. Much of the industry operated with open-hearth blast furnaces and other turn-of-the-century technologies. This meant not only the production of low-quality products, but also rising labor costs and extravagant levels of energy consumption that required massive subsidies to keep the enterprises afloat.

Against this background, in April 1988 the Planned Economy Committee issued a resolution setting down the following general goals: reduction and ultimate suspension of state subsidies to the steel sector, elimination of redundant capacity, regearing of the product mix to follow prevailing trends in world markets. The committee's plan displayed a prudent sensitivity to the socioeconomic consequences of restructuring. The total projected displacement in the steel sector amounted to ten thousand workers. This seemed a fairly modest number relative to total employment in the industry. And in view of the fact that implementation would be spread over a four-year period, with a concurrent expansion of unemployment benefits and retraining programs, the plan appeared to have a reasonable chance of gaining broad political acceptance.

But despite the committee's efforts to scale down the program to politically manageable proportions, the plan immediately provoked strong resistance by workers and managers at the affected plants, as well as by their allies in local party committees and the Ministry of Industry. Exemplary of the steel lobby's political strategy was the decision by the Ózd Metallurgical Company, the industry's biggest loss maker, to negotiate a joint venture with the West German firm Korf KG that would enable it to maintain current production capacity. Auditors dispatched to the plant to evaluate the progress of the restructuring program got wind of the scheme and reported it to the Planned Economy Committee, which prevailed upon the Minister of Industry to initiate disciplinary action against the Ózd management for violating the terms of the restructuring plan. The industry minister acceded, but not before privately assuring the Ózd managers of his continued support of the venture with Korf. Keenly aware of the potential political fallout from industrial downsizing, the party leadership declined to back up the committee, and so the joint venture proceeded (Bányai 1989; interview 13).

The Political Consequences of Adjustment via Nonmarket Means

This episode was striking for the conspicuous disengagement of the Hungarian Credit Bank, the main commercial creditor of the steel companies. The adjustment program included provisions for the disposition of the old steel loans as well as the resumption of credit lines to the targeted enterprises, conditional on their attainment of specific restructuring goals. The Credit Bank's stake in the matter was considerable, as it supplied more than 90 percent of total commercial credit to the metallurgical sector, representing over 10 percent of its assets. The future of the bank itself was thus inextricably linked to the fate of the restructuring program. But despite the bank's vital interest in the case, the management was determined to minimize its involvement and shift the political onus of structural adjustment back to the center.

The banking-reform case well illustrates the political repercussions of attempts to use Western-type financial mechanisms as instruments of structural adjustment in market socialist systems. The loan-portfolio problem induced the new commercial banks to sustain credit lines to the moribund firms of the state sector, precisely contrary to the aims of the banking reform and adjustment policy. The prior devolution of the credit function to the banks limited the possibilities for financial recentralization, as the nature of the regulatory system and the structure of joint stock ownership militated against central intervention in individual lending decisions. The unwillingness of the banks to use commercial credit as a restructuring tool effectively placed the ball back in the center's court. The ironic result of the introduction of market-type mechanisms into the financial sector was thus to reinforce the ruling party's reliance on nonmarket methods of adjustment and deepen its involvement in distributional conflicts.

The politicization of structural adjustment seriously undercut the bargaining position of party chief Grósz when he entered into formal negotiations with the Hungarian opposition in summer 1989. The very political hegemony on which the HSWP based its rule proved to be its greatest liability: while the leadership could delegate policymaking authority to the Planned Economy Committee and other subordinate organizations, the nature of the one-party system prevented it from evading ultimate responsibility for the restructuring program and the general state of the Hungarian economy. With the party's authority declining, but its responsibility for the stagnating economy undiminished, Grósz could scarcely claim to his interlocutors that he possessed a credible plan of economic rejuvenation.

THE DILEMMAS OF WAGE LIBERALIZATION

In no other financial sphere was the tension between recentralization and decentralization more acute than in wage reform. As with the banking reform, economists saw wage liberalization as essential to improving the performance of the Hungarian state sector. Under Hungary's rigid income-regulation system, wage rates were poorly differentiated. By the mid 1980s, the wage differential between Hungarian white-collar and blue-collar workers varied from 5 to 10 percent, compared with 30 to 70 percent in Western market economies (RFE/RL: a).[3] Wage leveling was one of the main factors underlying the rising absenteeism and declining productivity that plagued the Hungarian state sector. Labor productivity in Hungary was estimated to be 40–50 percent below that of the industrialized West (RFE/RL: b). By conferring wage control on trade unions and enterprise management, the authorities hoped to create a more highly differentiated wage scale that would promote labor mobility and boost worker productivity.

But in the context of market socialism, wage liberalization was highly risky. With neither workers nor managers facing effective inducements to control labor costs, the likeliest outcome of the reforms was growth of the total wage bill, and hence expansion of domestic purchasing power. Reimposition of wage controls would then become necessary in order to restore macroeconomic equilibrium (interview 12). Yet once they took the initial step of loosening wage controls, the authorities faced a number of obstacles to recentralization. The prior devolution of authority to the factory level catalyzed a large group of actors, workers, who would resist any attempt to reimpose central controls on their incomes.

The economic circumstances in which Hungary undertook wage liberalization magnified the consequences of labor mobilization. By the time wage reform began in the late 1980s, Hungarian workers had endured nearly a decade of stagnating real income. For this reason, they not only seized upon the opportunity of the initial decentralization to secure compensatory wage increases, but staunchly protected those gains whenever the center tried to recentralize. Moreover, the decline of household income after 1979 solidified the collective interest of workers from different industrial sectors in obtaining across-the-board increases in wage rates. Workers' mobilization on a cross-sectoral basis worked to the detriment of wage differentiation (and hence structural adjustment) and stimulated growth in the aggregate wage bill (thereby impeding macroeconomic stabilization).

The collective bargaining power of organized labor was further strengthened to the extent that enterprise management failed to supply countervailing pressure against workers' efforts to bid up wages. The weak impulse of state enterprise managers to contain their wage bills was yet another manifestation of the perverse incentives of market socialist economies. With plant directors in Hungary's "plan bargaining" system still evaluated according to their fulfillment of the center's production objectives, enterprises continued the practice, long characteristic of centrally planned economies, of sustaining a labor slack, keeping superfluous workers on the payroll for deployment during rush periods (Antal 1983, 1985; Sipos and Tardos 1986). Consequently, labor demand remained very high under

3. Citations from RFE/RL (Radio Free Europe/Radio Liberty, Hungarian Situation Reports) are indexed in the References at the end of the chapter.

NEM, even as the center was seeking to reduce capacity in loss-making sectors through its restructuring campaign. At the same time, the soft budget constraints of state enterprises relieved managers of the liquidity constraints that might otherwise have induced them to economize on labor costs. Hikes in their wage bills gave plant directors little cause for concern, as they were confident of eventually obtaining whatever credits or subsidies were needed to cover the increase in labor costs (interviews 18 and 24).

Finally, labor mobilization created serious problems for the HSWP leadership and the National Council of Trade Unions, the party's official union organization. The Trade Union Council was unccomfortably wedged between two opposing forces: (1) a ruling party obliged by economic circumstances to implement a harsh austerity program, the centerpiece of which was a cut in the level of real household income, and (2) an increasingly agitated working class, whose interests the official union supposedly represented. The party could never gain the cooperation, much less the approval, of Hungarian workers for economic adjustment as long as they were deprived of effective means of interest representation. The upshot of these pressures was the emergence of independent trade unions, as well as the transformation of the Council of Trade Unions itself into an organization willing and able to defy the party to which it had long been allied.

Wage Reform versus Macroeconomic Stabilization

At several junctures during the early 1980s, the HSWP leadership proclaimed its intention to reform the wage regulation system, only to retreat in the face of a deteriorating balance of payments. The political authorities conceded that long-term economic development required a thoroughgoing overhaul of the maze of rules and restrictions, which created a variety of distortions in the labor market. But the exigencies of macroeconomic stabilization required the center to maintain strict controls on wage payments in the state sector (FBIS/EEU: a).

In mid 1988, the authorities announced their intention to launch a comprehensive wage reform the following year. They proposed to abolish all central regulations on wage setting, leaving wage determination entirely in the hands of the unions and enterprise management. At the same time, the center would introduce an "entrepreneurial tax," whereby all increments to the enterprise wage bill would be added to profits and taxed at 50 percent. The aim of this tax scheme was to induce enterprise managers to hold down increases in aggregate labor costs.

Even as the political authorities were announcing this plan, there was deep skepticism within official circles as to whether economic circumstances would permit its implementation. The skeptics argued that the new entrepreneurial tax would not induce enterprise directors to economize on wages. With labor costs and profits subject to the same unified tax, managers would have every incentive to permit their wage bills to rise without limit. Any increases in wage disbursements would reduce net profits; if wages went up, taxable profits would go down, and the net effect on the enterprise's total tax liability would thus be zero (interview 20).

But the continued insensitivity of state-enterprise managers to labor costs was not the most important factor jeopardizing the party's plans for wage reform. The deterioration of Hungary's terms of trade and expansion of its hard-currency debt after 1983 had brought the country to the brink of insolvency. The economic crisis was the key factor leading to the ouster of János Kádár and his allies in the spring of 1988. In an attempt to halt the economy's slide, the new Grósz regime negotiated a three-year standby agreement with the IMF. The central element of this stabilization program was a reduction in household income and domestic consumption.

Economic data from the first year of the standby indicated that the program was biting: real per capita income declined by 2 percent in 1988, while retail trade turnover contracted in absolute terms for the first time since 1952 (*PlanEcon Report* 5, 18 [May 5, 1989]: 1–3). While the IMF standby included caps on domestic credit and deficit spending aimed at squeezing liquidity in the enterprise sector, Hungarian households were now bearing the brunt of macroeconomic stabilization.

The party's decision to shift the main burden of stabilization onto the household sector had a major impact on the political environment in Hungary during the final years of communist rule. Its most important effect was to catalyze a previously compliant labor force to push aggressively for compensatory wage increases. Rising labor mobilization magnified the contradictions between wage reform and stabilization policy: to the extent that workers succeeded in bidding up the total wage bill, the center could not proceed with wage liberalization without compromising the macroeconomic balance. But the ability of the authorities to restore wage controls was now limited by the growing power of organized labor.

It is noteworthy that the transformation of Hungarian labor, long pacified under Kádár's post-1956 compromise, into an active movement for political change began within the party-controlled National Council of Trade Unions. Whereas worker mobilization in Poland involved the emergence of a fully independent trade union movement that challenged the Communist party's political hegemony, in Hungary it was manifested by the disintegration of the party's internal mechanisms of labor control.

Transformation of the Party-Controlled Trade Union

The leaders of the Trade Union Council had on previous occasions defended Hungarian wage laborers against the effects of market-type reforms.

In 1969, they allied themselves with local party secretaries and ideological conservatives on the central committee to push for restoration of price controls, the first of a series of reversals leading to the suspension of NEM in 1972 (Soós 1987). In late 1983, they pressed for wage indexing and pension increases to compensate for the IMF-sponsored austerity program launched the previous year (Noti 1987). In December 1985, they secured the party's assent to a 23 percent increase in industrial wages (RFE/RL: a).

But in no sense had the Trade Union Council functioned as an independent political actor. The presence of the president of the council on the politburo of the ruling party gave the organization considerable influence over reform policy, but also signified the fact that its political clout was largely derivative of the party itself. The council's role under NEM was less to represent members' interests than to advance the party's goal of perpetuating a politically quiescent labor force. To that end, the chain of command within the council remained highly centralized after the launching of the reforms in 1968. Until the mid 1980s, factory-level union organizations enjoyed little say over incomes policy, as branch-level representatives of the Trade Union Council continued their traditional practice of negotiating wage contracts with the Ministry of Industry and the State Office of Wages and Labor (Noti 1987). The Kádár regime's determination to maintain tight reins on labor reflected its sensitivity to contemporary developments in Poland, as well as its memories of 1956, when independent workers' councils played an integral part in the popular uprising that nearly destroyed communist rule in Hungary. The episodes cited above did not demonstrate the Trade Union Council's capacity to stake out policy positions independently of the party. Rather, its efforts to reverse reform policy in 1969 and the early 1980s converged with prevailing political currents within the party leadership.

The political and economic developments of 1988 prompted a transformation of the role of the council. Among the victims of the spring purge of the party old guard was Sándor Gáspár, the longtime president of the council. The fall of Kádár and the shake-up of the council leadership emboldened rank-and-file members to press for democratization of the union's internal structures and procedures. Gáspár's successor, Sándor Nagy, would prove far more sensitive to the demands of the membership and more willing to challenge the HSWP leadership over economic reform and stabilization policy. At the same time, the IMF standby agreement negotiated by the Grósz regime significantly raised the stakes for Hungarian workers by requiring deep, sustained reductions of real household income.

These circumstances triggered a series of highly public confrontations between the party and the new leadership of the Trade Union Council. In September 1988, the council and the Hungarian government began negotiations for a new wage agreement. Breaking sharply from its subservient position in the one-party system, the union leadership publicized its demands in advance of the meetings, claiming that higher-than-anticipated inflation necessitated retroactive wage increases in certain sectors. The union further insisted that the party move quickly on the long-delayed reforms of the wage system. Reacting angrily to the council's publicity campaign, the Grósz regime insisted that the Hungarian state was in no position to give the unions a blank check. By placing workers' needs ahead of the interests of the national economy, the council was putting Hungary at risk of international insolvency.

In addition to demonstrating the Trade Union Council's newfound assertiveness, the September negotiations were politically significant, in that they revealed the growing cleavages within the HSWP leadership. The head of the center's negotiating team was Imre Pozsgay, a politburo member and head of the reformist wing of the party. In his opening statement, Pozsgay noted that the council had historically served as an integral player within the one-party system and therefore shared some of the blame for Hungary's economic predicament. This underscored the need for a genuinely independent trade union organization answerable to the workers and not to the party. To that end, Pozsgay encouraged the council to implement internal reforms and asked the union leaders how they intended to deal with the growing pluralism within the Hungarian trade union movement (RFE/RL: d).

Tensions within the Trade Union Movement

Pozsgay's remarks underscored the uneasy duality of the Trade Union Council's position, the contradiction between its traditional role as vassal of a party leadership that was now implementing a strict austerity program and its putative responsibilities as representative of workers' interests. His mention of "pluralism" was an unmistakable reference to the recent emergence of new trade union organizations outside of the council, the most visible of which was the Democratic Union of Scientific and Academic Workers, established in May 1988 by research scholars from the Hungarian Academy of Sciences to protest the Trade Union Council's failure to represent their professional interests. The Democratic Union condemned the council for its role in the economic crisis and claimed that the official union's position on wage reform had helped thwart attempts to widen income differentials between blue- and white-collar workers (RFE/RL: d, h).

The leaders of the council at first refused to recognize this independent organization, but then retreated to a strategy of containing its growth by establishing a parallel union of professional and scientific workers. They meanwhile set about instituting the internal reforms deemed necessary to restore the confidence of the rank and file: elections by secret ballot, limitations of tenure in office of union leaders, right of factory-level units to determine the composition of higher bodies within the organization. At the same time, the council leadership formally proclaimed its independence from the center, claiming that the HSWP's subjugation of the union had distorted the goals of the organization and prevented it from effectively representing the interests of Hungarian workers (RFE/RL: f).

Armed with its revamped policy platform, in December 1988, the council negotiated a new agreement with the center. The political authorities committed themselves to holding the inflation rate for 1989 to 12 percent. An compensation for the rise in consumer retail prices, they conceded to the council's demand for a 23 percent increase in the minimum wage. The authorities meanwhile announced their intention to proceed with the progressive reform of the wage regulation system. On January 1, 1989, the center formally released large-scale enterprises, representing some 60 percent of the Hungarian state sector, from all wage regulations (RFE/RL: g).

The main intent of this measure was to heighten labor productivity within the state sector by encouraging enterprise managers and unions to formulate more highly differentiated wage scales. But because it was undertaken in the face of eroding household income, rising labor mobilization, and cost-insensitive state enterprises, wage reform produced wholly different effects. Far from promoting greater income differentiation, wage liberalization stimulated Hungarian workers, long deprived of effective means of collective bargaining, to agitate for ad hoc wage increases aimed at neutralizing the distributional effects of macroeconomic stabilization.

Conflict Between the Party and the Unions, 1989

In early January 1989, the center initiated the first of its planned price increases. A few weeks later, council chief Nagy declared that the January price hikes already surpassed the yearly inflation target agreed upon in December. Nagy emphasized that the union agreed in principle with the center's policy of freeing up prices, so long as nominal wages increased accordingly. In view of the higher-than-expected price increases, the union leadership now regarded the December agreement as null and void, proclaiming that either the minimum wage would have to be raised by more than the amount previously negotiated, the wage hike would have to be introduced ahead of schedule, or both. Nagy noted that the council presidium had recently disassociated itself from the HSWP, and that the union leadership regarded strikes as a justifiable method of achieving its demands. "It would be useless if the trade union movement had finally assembled a gun but did not have the ammunition for it" (FBIS/EEU: j). Within a few days of Nagy's statement, the party acceded to both of the union's demands (RFE/RL: i).

Its hand clearly weakened, the Grósz regime soon yielded to the unions' calls for legalizing labor strikes. In the aftermath of strikes in the coal-mining sector and other industries the previous fall, the authorities prepared a draft of a law legalizing certain types of strikes. The draft narrowly circumscribed the range of legal strikes to those related to grievances within a specific enterprise. Sympathy strikes and work stoppages undertaken to protest broader economic policies (e.g., consumer price increases) would remain illegal. Under the draft, only official trade union organizations under the umbrella of the Council of Trade Unions would be permitted to organize strikes. Both the council and the independent unions promptly rejected the draft law. The party quickly conceded, offering a revised version that legalized sympathy strikes and granted both official and independent unions the right to initiate work stoppages. (FBIS/EEU: iii, RFE/RL: j).

It was not long before the unions availed themselves of the opportunities presented by the new strike law. In April, the political authorities announced another set of utility rate hikes. The council leadership responded by demanding the suspension of the price increases. The union leaders protested that they had sought for months to engage the party in serious discussions, to no avail. At the same time, the Grósz regime was contemplating measures that threatened certain strata of the population with "mass impoverishment." Now, the council would refuse all negotiations until Grósz provided the public with detailed information about Hungary's hard-currency debt and the state budget. Only when it was generally understood what commitments the party had undertaken could a new social consensus over stabilization policy emerge. In the meantime, the unions would have to make use of "other tools of interest coordination." To this end, the council leaders declared the upcoming May Day ceremony as a "mass demonstration of employee interests." The trade union threats again compelled the center to back down: a few days after the May Day demonstration, the authorities rescinded the utility price hikes and granted the council's request for an across-the-board increase in pensions and wage hikes for selected categories of workers (FBIS/EEU: o).

By summer 1989, Grósz was engaged in the roundtable negotiations with the Hungarian opposition that would culminate in the party's assent to multiparty elections. The unions chose this occasion to escalate their ongoing dispute with the center, calling a general strike to protest proposed hikes in meat prices. This event, the first general strike in Hungary since the 1956 revolution, attracted a large number of followers but failed to compel the center to back off the meat price increases. The union leadership then announced a shift in strategy: rather than seeking to rescind price increases, the unions would dedicate their efforts to securing compensatory wage increases. The unions charged that Grósz's austerity program was assigning higher priority to price reform than to wage liberalization; the long-promised reform of the wage-regulation system should proceed immediately. In a jab at the newly legalized opposition parties, the unions noted they were still waiting for a party that offered an alternative to the HSWP's stabilization program and showed due concern for the interests of Hungarian wage earners (FBIS/EEU: p, q, r).

In addition to damaging the bargaining position of party chief Grósz, the decision of the trade unions to face down the party on the eve of the roundtable negotiations enhanced the leverage of the political opposition Labor's demands for pluralization of the union movement paralleled and fortified the opposition's push for broader political democratization.

It is noteworthy that the Hungarian Chamber of Commerce, the chief lobbying organization of the enterprise sector, remained generally mute throughout the conflict between the party and the trade unions. Its role was limited to the issuance of broad statements asserting the desirability of holding inflation to the planned levels (FBIS/EEU: b). The refusal of Hungarian managers to exert offsetting pressure to contain wage costs simultaneously strengthened the collective power of labor and complicated the center's task of restoring macroeconomic balance. The end result was to reinforce the already strongly held perception, shared by both the IMF and the Hungarian political opposition, that the HSWP was incapable of formulating a credible stabilization program.

Political Repercussions of Wage Liberalization

The original objective of the wage reform was to raise labor productivity within the Hungarian state sector by widening income differentiation. Instead, the reform provided workers with the resources to bid up total labor costs, boosting aggregate purchasing power in the economy and compromising the macroeconomic balance. Fulfilling the conditions of the IMF-supervised stabilization program now necessitated the restoration of central controls on wages. But as in the banking case, the party's opportunities for recentralization were limited once the process of wage liberalization was under way.

The main impediment to recentralization of incomes policy was the growing power of organized labor. The trajectory of the Hungarian labor movement in the late socialist period was distinct from that in other East European countries. Labor mobilization did not begin in Hungary until the end of the 1980s and never reached the levels attained by Poland's Solidarity, whose capacity to shut down major portions of industry ultimately forced the Polish United Workers' party to the bargaining table. The power of Hungarian labor derived less from its capacity to limit production than from its ability publicly to defy the ruling party, whose presumed raison d'être was representation of workers' interests. What made the comparatively limited mobilization of Hungarian workers in 1988–89 politically consequential was the fact that it was spearheaded by the party's own official trade union. The public confrontations between the National Council of Trade Unions and the Grósz regime revealed the decomposition of one of the pivotal internal structures of authority of the HSWP, whose consolidation of power after 1956 hinged on its co-optation of labor, the Catholic Church, the intelligentsia, and other social groups.

The loss of control of its own labor organization deprived the party of its primary means of recentralizing incomes policy. The wage hikes resulting from the initial liberalization now represented currency in circulation. The center was thus left with the problem of mopping up the excess liquidity the wage reform had already released into the economy. Having surrendered its capacity to manage wage bargaining through a centralized trade union apparatus, the only way the party could absorb this excess purchasing power in the hands of the population was to employ currency conversions, compulsory bond sales, freezing of personal savings accounts, and other ex post measures. But while such tools were readily available to party leaders in traditional centrally planned economies, their efficacy in socialist market economies like Hungary was highly dubious. Not only would their implementation antagonize a household sector already pressed to the limit by economic austerity, the expansion of the second economy, the decentralization of the financial system, and other departures from central planning that the party had previously undertaken restricted its ability to use ex post income-withdrawal devices to contract domestic purchasing power.

In short, wage liberalization simultaneously weakened one of the party's key instruments of political control and undermined its capacity to execute stabilization policy and thereby meet the conditions of the IMF standby agreement.

LIBERALIZATION OF FOREIGN EXCHANGE

The economic risks of liberalizing foreign exchange were at least as great as in banking and wage regulation: drainage of convertible currency reserves as enterprises, households, and foreign investors were granted rights of convertibility; expansion of the country's external debt as banks were given foreign-exchange licenses; deterioration of the balance of payments as import licensing was loosened; higher inflation as the central bank devalued the currency in preparation for convertibility.

But while the liberalization of foreign-exchange regulations generated similar sorts of contradictions between microeconomic incentives and macroeconomic control as other financial reforms, several factors distinguished it from the banking and wage cases. To begin with, foreign-exchange liberalization was unique in the nature of the political mobilization it triggered.

When the National Bank of Hungary engineered a succession of devaluations in the late 1980s, the Hungarian trade unions registered their sharp disapproval of the resultant rise in consumer prices. But whereas the unions could compel the center to roll back proposed price increases by threatening strikes or neutralizing such increases by extracting wage concessions, their political influence over exchange-rate policy was limited. A currency devaluation, once enacted, was a fait accompli; the trade unions could not compel the center to rescind it by threatening to organize strikes. Moreover, trade union opposition to currency devaluation was partially offset by support for this measure among Hungarian enterprises, particularly those engaged in convertible currency export. In contrast to wage reform, where the preferences of labor and management generally converged, in the foreign-exchange sphere there was little basis for unity.

The inability of domestic actors to bring effective influence to bear on foreign-exchange policy meant that the ratchet effects of financial liberalization were weaker than those arising from the banking and wage reforms. In the latter cases, the initial decentralization caused an inadvertent loss of control that restricted the party's capacity to correct subsequent economic distortions via financial recentralization. By contrast, the party retained the technical and political resources to reimpose controls on local agents if liberalization of foreign exchange generated deleterious effects on the macroeconomic balance.

But foreign-exchange reform was also distinguished from the other cases in that it activated a new set of players — Western investors — who were not encumbered by the same political and economic constraints as Hungarian state enterprises and households. In contrast to domestic actors, foreign capital enjoyed high mobility and multiple alternative investment sites. These resources gave Western investors considerable leverage over the HSWP leadership, which depended on the continued inflow of foreign capital to service hard-currency debt and spur economic modernization. Whereas the authorities could recentralize foreign-exchange policy in the household and enterprise sectors at relatively low cost, reimposition of controls on Western investors created a high risk of capital flight that would severely impair the party's ability to extricate Hungary from its economic crisis.

Because of the asymmetrical positions of domestic and foreign capital, the foreign-exchange sphere exhibited divergent rates of liberalization. In the domestic arena, the party made only tentative movements toward loosening controls on Hungarian enterprises and households, whose behavior continued to be shaped by the weak proprietary interests, supply shortages, and other distortions of market socialism. In the foreign arena, the party quickly dismantled barriers to private Western investors. The consequent rapid penetration of foreign capital became a highly contentious political issue during the transition to democracy in 1989–90 and remained a major source of dispute under the successor government headed by the Hungarian Democratic Forum.

Foreign-Exchange Liberalization: The Enterprise Sector

Foreign-exchange reform in the enterprise sector had two principal aims. The first was to dismantle the cumbersome import-licensing system and allow Hungarian enterprises to exchange their surplus forints for the hard currency needed to modernize their plants and equipment. The second was to expand the foreign-exchange activities of the new commercial banks. Eventually, Hungarian enterprises would be allowed both to buy foreign exchange from the banks and to deposit their retained convertible currency earnings with them (FBIS/EEU: h).

Successful implementation of these reforms presupposed two things. First, the National Bank had to contract the money supply. If enterprises were to enjoy the right automatically to convert their surplus forints into hard currency, the bank had to manufacture a shortage of local currency in the enterprise sector. Failing this, conversions of forints into hard currency by the enterprise sector, and hence purchases of Western imports, would skyrocket. Second, the National Bank had to undertake a substantial devaluation of the forint. Unless import prices were sharply increased through devaluation, broadening enterprises' access to Western import markets would merely drive up domestic demand and worsen the balance-of-payments deficit (interviews 16 and 17).

The danger was that in the socialist context, even a sizable devaluation might not have the desired impact on enterprise behavior. With state enterprises operating under soft budget constraints, demand for convertible-currency imports would remain undiminished despite substantial increases in prices. Import liberalization coupled with devaluation would then produce the worst possible scenario: both the volume of Western imports and their prices would increase, generating a rapid drain on hard-currency reserves, a dramatic deterioration of the balance of payments, and a sharp rise in the domestic inflation rate (Tarafás 1985; Wolf 1985, 1988).

Against these constraints, in the summer of 1988, the National Bank began a series of cautious, incremental currency devaluations. By the time of the commencement of the roundtable talks the following year, the forint had been devalued by some 17 percent, enough to prompt a rise in the inflation rate, but still well below what experts had deemed necessary to proceed with full import liberalization. The combination of mounting inflationary pressures, a deteriorating external balance, and undiminished import demand by cost-insensitive state enterprises circumscribed the center's range of movement in the foreign-exchange area. Even as the center granted partial foreign-exchange licenses to the commercial banks, it announced that 80 percent of Hungary's hard currency transactions would remain with the National Bank (FBIS/EEU: c, l, n; interviews 2, 3, and 18).

The absence of strong ratchet effects in the foreign-exchange area gave the political leadership greater latitude for ex post adjustments than it enjoyed in other financial spheres. In contrast to the banking reform, where the delegation of authority over credit allocation gave the commercial banks resources to resist reintervention by the center, the National Bank retained an assortment of regulations over the banks' foreign-exchange operations. This allowed the party to proceed with limited liberalization without risking a progressive and unintentional unraveling of central control.

Foreign-Exchange Liberalization: The Household Sector

The chief aim of foreign-exchange reform in the household sector was less economic than political. Broadening the population's access to foreign exchange would enable citizens to travel abroad and purchase Western products unavailable in Hungary. In this way, the party leadership hoped to alleviate some of the pain of economic austerity at home.

Unlike state-owned enterprises, Hungarian households operated under "hard" budget constraints: their liquid resources placed effective limits on their ability to purchase commodities. Thus, deregulation of foreign exchange in the household sector did not face the problem of perverse incentives that so complicated liberalization in the enterprise sector. However, it did run up against persistent shortages and pent-up consumer demand within the Hungarian economy. Those factors generated powerful pressures for recentralization in the late 1980s as the center began to widen the opportunities for Hungarian households to undertake foreign-exchange transactions.

On January 1, 1988, the Hungarian government eased restrictions on foreign travel. For the first time since the communist takeover in 1948, Hungarian citizens possessing a valid passport and the required amount of foreign exchange were allowed to travel to the West without restriction. At that point, Hungarians were allowed to exchange $400 worth of forints into hard currency per person over a three-year period (RFE/RL: c).

The world passport proved phenomenally popular with Hungarian citizens, as it gave them access to videocassette recorders, stereos, television sets, automobiles, and other products that were either in short supply or of poor quality in Hungary itself. Between January and August 1988, Hungarians made more than 1.4 million trips to Austria alone, nearly a 400 percent increase over the same period the previous year. The exodus of tourists reached unprecedented levels in November and December, as Hungarians surged across the border to indulge in spending sprees in Vienna and other Austrian cities (RFE/RL: e).

But the drainage of hard currency had serious repercussions for the country's balance of payments. By summer 1989, it was apparent that Hungary's current-account deficit for the year would be more than double the center's target. The deterioration of the external balance provoked the IMF to suspend its standby agreement with Hungary, jeopardizing the country's access to commercial credits and raising the specter of debt rescheduling (RFE/RL: k).

The situation worsened in fall 1989. In November, lame-duck Prime Minister Miklós Németh announced that both the domestic budget deficit and the hard-currency debt were much larger than the HSWP had previously acknowledged. He explained that the Kádár leadership had taken the decision to conceal this information in the early 1980s for fear that disclosure of the true status of Hungary's finances would endanger its application to join the IMF and hence its access to badly needed Western capital. Németh added that he himself had known about the party's decision to cook the financial figures, and that he was utilizing the occasion of the impending political transition to effect a general clearing of Hungary's economic and political accounts. Insofar as Hungary's international financial position was concerned, Németh's announcement meant that the country was technically on the verge of insolvency (FBIS/EEU: s, t).

Against this backdrop, the central authorities and the IMF began negotiations for another stabilization program. The suspension of the earlier standby agreement and the disclosure of the debt had stiffened the IMF's resolve. In addition to deep subsidy cuts, a stringent monetary squeeze, and other stabilization measures, the Hungarian authorities agreed to reimpose foreign-exchange controls on the household sector. The amount of foreign exchange Hungarians could purchase was sharply reduced to $50 allotments for the next two years (Okolicsanyi 1989; interview 21).

And so while the worldwide passport removed essentially all legal constraints on the ability of Hungarians to travel abroad, the exigencies of economic austerity compelled the center to deprive households of access to the foreign exchange needed to enjoy that opportunity. In contrast to the banking and wage cases, the prior devolution of authority was of little use to the affected actors. The commercial banks, once established, could divert credit flows in ways contrary to the center's restructuring program. Workers, once granted the power of collective bargaining, could organize strikes to thwart the center's income policies. Hungarian households lacked any such leverage. Not only did the size and diversity of the household sector militate against collective action, it did not possess the economic and political resources needed to defeat recentralization. Thus, while the party's decision to reimpose foreign-exchange controls on the population was politically unpopular, it did not stimulate effective resistance.

Foreign-Exchange Liberalization: Western Investors

The structural position of foreign capital was fundamentally different. The distortions of market socialism did not impede the center's attempts to loosen controls on Western investors, whose behavior was driven by the profit motive and not a skewed incentive structure or domestic shortages.

Put while liberalization in the foreign sector did not encounter the same systemic constraints as in the enterprise and household spheres, it *was* politically risky. Like their counterparts in China, Hungarian party leaders had to weigh the developmental benefits of direct foreign investment against its political costs. Not only did the rapid penetration of foreign capital affect national and cultural sensibilities, it also implied a diminution of the party's capacity to control the economy. The degree to which the political leadership mitigated such adverse consequences depended on its ability to negotiate effectively with Western investors. Here, the HSWP was at a distinct disadvantage. Unlike China, Hungary lacked the bargaining chip of a large domestic market. At the same time, foreign capital possessed several important advantages — namely, high mobility and a multiplicity of alternative investment sites in Eastern Europe and elsewhere. This asymmetrical bargaining relationship ultimately induced the party to dismantle virtually all barriers to foreign capital.

For many years preceding the collapse of the one-party system, Hungary had had the most lenient foreign-capital regulations of any socialist country except Yugoslavia. Foreign direct investment dated back to 1972, when the Kádár leadership approved a law permitting minority foreign ownership of Hungarian-based joint ventures. But despite the looseness of the regulations and the evident eagerness of the central authorities to attract foreign capital, few Western investors availed themselves of these opportunities.

In an effort to attract more foreign capital, in 1986 the party introduced some important modifications in the joint-venture code. Foreign participants could now exercise majority ownership of Hungarian-based joint ventures. The revised law also gave foreign investors tax holidays and simplified the rules concerning repatriation of profits. Foreign partners could now convert significant portions of their forint-denominated earnings back into convertible currency.

These measures did have a salutary effect on foreign direct investment in Hungary, as scores of joint-venture projects emerged in light industry, agriculture, and food processing. But foreign investment in large-scale industry still fell short of expectations, reflecting complications stemming from Hungary's obligations to the COMECON, as well as from excessively cumbersome bureaucratic procedures for approving investment applications. Moreover, Hungarian law still restricted foreign direct investment to participation in newly created joint ventures: it was not yet legally possible for Western investors to undertake equity investments in existing Hungarian state enterprises.

That barrier was removed in January 1989 with the party's approval of the landmark "Law on Economic Association." In addition to legalizing private capital ownership by Hungarian citizens, the new law entitled foreign investors to acquire up to 100 percent equity ownership of Hungarian state enterprises. The law also granted foreign investors highly favorable tax holidays, as well as legal guarantees concerning nationalization. Moreover, conversion of forint-denominated earnings, previously determined through ad hoc agreements between the foreign partner and the National Bank of Hungary, was now completely up to the discretion of the investor: foreign investors could freely convert and repatriate all of their after-tax profits (FBIS/EEU: i).

This opened the floodgates to Western investors, who would end up spearheading the privatization campaign initiated by the outgoing Németh administration and continued by the successor government headed by the Hungarian Democratic Forum (Marrese 1992). But while foreign capital assumed a dominant position in Hungary's privatization process, domestic actors remained hamstrung by an array of constraints, despite the fact that the 1989 legislation had removed most legal barriers to equity ownership by Hungarian investors: the general shortage of domestic capital, the population's unfamiliarity with equity investment, the lack of a well-developed system of financial intermediation, and the absence of an extensive secondary market that would permit households and enterprises easily to liquidate their shareholdings.

The Political Consequences of Asymmetric Liberalization of Foreign-Exchange Policy

The dilemma confronting the HSWP in the banking and wage-reform cases stemmed from the fact that financial liberalization created distortions that necessitated reimposition of central controls while simultaneously providing economic agents with the resources to resist recentralization. The party faced a different problem in the foreign-exchange arena. Here, the asymmetric positions of foreign and domestic actors compelled the central authorities to pursue a trajectory of liberalization that favored the former over the latter. This had important political repercussions both for the HSWP during its final years in power and for its democratically elected successor.

The fact that the measures taken by the HSWP placed domestic and

international actors on an uneven playing field was one of the many liabilities hampering its renamed successor organization, the Hungarian Socialist party, during the run-up to the spring 1990 elections. The ultimate
victor, the Democratic Forum, and other opposition parties charged that
the liberal foreign investment laws promulgated by the communists in the
late 1980s were allowing Western investors to buy up national assets on the
cheap (Bartlett 1992).

The political controversy over foreign capital's prominence in Hungarian privatization did not cease with the parliamentary elections. The leadership of the Democratic Forum soon faced charges from populist elements of
its own ruling coalition that the government was allowing Western investors
favored access to the Hungarian market. In spring 1993, the Forum expelled one of its senior members for publicly accusing the government of
selling "whole industrial sectors complete with their markets, with huge
discounts" to foreign buyers (*Budapest Week*, May 6–12, 1993).

But notwithstanding the adverse political fallout from foreign capital's
domination of the privatization process, restoration of controls on Western
investors was a very costly option for the HSWP, as well as for the successor
government. In contrast to the enterprise and household sectors, where
recentralization entailed minimal political or economic risk, the central
authorities enjoyed little flexibility in the external sector. Owing to foreign
capital's high mobility and the availability of many other investment opportunities, ex post amendments of the rules governing foreign direct investment were highly risky. Not only would such measures spur capital flight,
but the transformation of the regulations would cast a chill over the general
investment climate and discourage future investors from entering the Hungarian market. For these reasons, the center's influence over foreign capital
was concentrated at the bargaining stage.

Here, Hungary operated at a disadvantage relative to other capital-
importing countries. As Margaret Pearson (1991) shows, the Deng Xiaoping regime skillfully exploited the pull of China's vast market to cut favorable deals with foreign capital in the 1980s. By offering preferential access
to the local market and certain regulatory incentives, Chinese negotiators
were able to extract concessions from foreign investors on export production, technology transfer, domestic content requirements, and other issues
vital to the party's economic development strategy. By contrast, the Hungarian authorities faced major handicaps. While Hungary's long history of
market-type reforms gave it important advantages over other Eastern European countries, its small domestic market seriously weakened its negotiating
position in a highly competitive international investment environment. The
center was thus compelled to admit foreign capital on terms extremely
favorable to Western investors.

CONCLUSIONS

This chapter has addressed the following question: What happens when departures from central planning simultaneously devolve political power to local agents and create distortions that compel the center to reimpose controls? That question has special resonance in the politico-economic context of Hungary in the 1980s, when deterioration of the economy compelled the Hungarian Socialist Workers' party to shift from a growth-oriented reform policy to one based on austerity. The use of market-type financial mechanisms as instruments of stabilization and adjustment produced a variety of effects that compromised the party's ability to execute the austerity program and undermined its collective political authority. The contradictions of financial liberalization in Hungary manifested themselves in interesting ways in the three cases discussed above.

The banking reform, intended to place credit flows under the discipline of market forces, instead created a group of actors unwilling to serve as agents of economic adjustment. The portfolios of the new commercial banks, burdened by a large number of bad assets accumulated during the prereform period, gave loan officers strong incentives to sustain credit lines to loss-making enterprises. Thus, far from precipitating a redistribution of capital within the Hungarian state sector, the banking reform ended up reproducing the same patterns of credit allocation that existed before 1987. But once the crediting function was delegated to the commercial banks, the center had few means left at its disposal to redirect credit flows in a manner consistent with the aims of adjustment. While regulatory tools and equity ownership gave the Hungarian state considerable influence over the banks, such means were not amenable to intervention in individual lending decisions. The ineffectiveness of commercial bank credit as a restructuring instrument forced the center to resort to political/administrative devices to carry out restructuring policy. Thus, the unintended consequence of the introduction of market instruments into the Hungarian financial sector was to deepen the center's reliance on nonmarket mechanisms of structural adjustment, whose use drew HSWP leaders into conflicts over the pace and extent of industrial restructuring.

In the wage-reform case, the center's movements toward liberalization generated immediate pressures for expansion of the total wage bill. These pressures emanated from two sources: (1) the incentive structure of Hungary's hybrid economy, which deprived both workers and managers of strong inducements to contain wage costs, and (2) the pent-up demand for compensatory wage increases accumulated during years of declining real income. But once it began the process of wage reform, the center's capacity to recentralize control was severely limited. Not only did the party face technical restrictions on its capacity to neutralize excess household liquidity through ex post income withdrawal measures, but the initial liberalization of wage controls opened up political space for Hungarian workers, who were determined to protect the gains they had already achieved. While the fully independent trade unions that appeared at the end of the 1980s spurred this development, the most important manifestation of worker mobilization in Hungary during the late socialist period was the transformation of the ruling party's own labor organization. The Trade Union Council's shift to an opposition role removed one of the party's foremost mechanisms of political control and the crisis regime's efforts to implement an IMF-supervised stabilization program. By 1989, the trade union movement had acquired sufficient strength to force the party leadership to back down from its attempts to contract domestic purchasing power via consumer price hikes. The clashes between the center and the unions visibly weakened the party's hand precisely when it was entering into negotiations with the opposition over Hungary's political future.

Foreign-exchange liberalization, while generating recentralizing pressures as great as those produced by the banking and wage reforms, had different effects on the political capacities of the relevant actors. Foreign-exchange reform produced relatively weak ratchet effects in the domestic sphere, as the initial decentralization of control did not significantly enlarge the resources of local agents. The insulated nature of the issue area and impediments to collective action prevented enterprises, trade unions, and households from mobilizing in resistance to the center's restoration of controls. This allowed the party to proceed cautiously toward loosening foreign-exchange regulations in the enterprise sector and to retreat abruptly in the household sector. Yet recentralization was extremely difficult in the foreign sector, where liberalization stimulated a new set of actors, Western investors, who enjoyed strong bargaining leverage over the center. The consequent surge of foreign investment proved a highly contentious political issue both before and after the demise of the one-party system.

Hungary's experience with financial reform in the 1980s illuminates the unique dilemmas that arise when socialist market economies undergo externally imposed austerity. In full-fledged capitalist economies that face stabilization problems, the market serves as the primary means of redistributing capital and labor. The degree to which political leaders intervene to mediate local distributional conflicts depends on (1) the level of aggregation of the affected agents, and (2) the extent to which the structure of the state permits those actors access to the policymaking process (Lowi 1964). In traditional centrally planned economies, market forces are essentially nonexistent. This means, on the one hand, that political authorities need only resort to their existing repertoire of policy instruments to carry out the austerity program. On the other hand, it means that no prior decentralization of control to the factory level has occurred that might impede the authorities' efforts to correct economic imbalances via centrally administered cuts in bank credit, wages, and imports. As Romania's experience in the 1980s demonstrated, such methods of stabilization are crude, but effective, insofar as they enable the center sharply to contract domestic consumption.

The political economy of stabilization and adjustment in market socialist systems like Hungary is distinct from that of both capitalist economies and Soviet type planned economies. Here, neither the market nor the central planning apparatus are effective mechanisms of resource allocation. Market instruments do not induce local actors to redeploy labor and capital resources for more efficient purposes, but they do augment the capacity of those agents to resist attempts by the center to reclaim decision-making authority. Restoration of financial order thus requires the center to restore its jurisdiction in areas where it has already relinquished a significant measure of control. This places political leaders in socialist market economies in a peculiar quandary: the failure of market mechanisms to elicit the desired responses at the factory level pulls the authorities directly into distributional conflicts. But the prior introduction of those very same mechanisms prevents the authorities from employing standard central-planning tools to mediate these disputes.

All three cases illustrate the broader political dynamics underlying the collapse of state socialism in Hungary in the late 1980s. The demise of the HSWP resulted from the complex interaction of "bottom-up" and "top-down" forces: devolution of control simultaneously strengthened local agents and weakened the capacity of central authorities to correct the economic distortions arising from the initial decentralization. But the contrasts between the cases are equally illuminating, underscoring the differences and similarities in the political challenges of economic transformation confronting the successor government.

What gave leverage to the Hungarian commercial banks during the period preceding the political transition was the fact that bank credit was the primary "market" mechanism of structural adjustment then available. The banks' refusal to use it left the center with few alternatives but administrative devices whose employment unavoidably enmeshed the authorities in costly distributional conflicts. Both the banks' political influence and the center's role in the restructuring process changed markedly in the aftermath of the dramatic events of 1989–91. On the one hand, the rapid influx of foreign capital, which included a sizable number of commercial banks under full or partial Western ownership, whose portfolios were not burdened by large stocks of bad assets, transformed the competitive structure of the financial sector and reduced the relative weight of the Hungarian-owned banks. On the other hand, the abrupt collapse of the Soviet Union and the CMEA

generated a massive exogenous shock to Hungary and the other Eastern
European economies. The upshot was a de facto adjustment involving deep
reductions in industrial output and forced reorientation of trade. While the
successor government of the Hungarian Democratic Forum assumed responsibility for subsidy cuts and other distributional issues requiring official
policy decisions, its political burden was lightened to the degree that much
of the process of structural adjustment was now driven by the logic of the
world market.

The political power of Hungarian labor during the late socialist period
stemmed not from its capacity to limit production, but rather from its ability to challenge the ruling party, which had long co opted workers through
the National Council of Trade Unions. As noted in the Mersek case, the
political efficacy of production strikes is apt to be limited in an economy
undergoing restructuring, particularly when the striking workers are situated in enterprises already targeted for capacity reductions. The main exception here is Poland, where Solidarity was so well mobilized that it succeeded in virtually shutting down the Polish economy in late 1988 and
forcing the ruling party to negotiate a political transition. The fact that a
fully independent trade union organization was already well ensconced by
the time of the transition to democracy has since given Polish workers a degree of economic and political power unmatched in the rest of Eastern
Europe. The position of Hungarian workers in the postcommunist period is
quite different. The political clout wielded by Hungarian labor in 1988–89
derived from the fact that the main thrust of mobilization occurred through
the party's own trade union organization. The movement of the Trade
Union Council into an opposition role hastened the progressive unhinging
of the internal authority structure of the HSWP. But while that development
played a key part in the demise of the one-party system, it did not leave
Hungarian workers with a well-institutionalized, politically autonomous
base for collective bargaining comparable to Solidarity's. With the transition to multiparty democracy, the political power of the Hungarian labor
movement appreciably declined. The acceleration of industrial restructuring and the growing absorptive capacity of the private sector sapped the
cohesion of blue-collar workers, while the splintering of the political left
deprived organized labor of effective representation via the party system.

Foreign exchange shows a greater continuity of political and economic
effects across the pre- and post-1989 periods. The extent to which the admission of foreign investors led to loss of economic control *did* have unique
significance to a regime whose power resided in the system of central planning. Likewise, the rapid penetration of foreign capital had special ideological import for a ruling party anchored in Marxist-Leninist theory. But once
the decision was made to liberalize foreign exchange in Hungary, the same
structural factors that favored foreign over domestic capital during the

HSWP's final years in power prevailed in the posttransition phase. Thus, the trajectory of foreign-exchange liberalization after 1989 followed the general pattern of the late socialist period: full external currency convertibility for Western investors, combined with limited internal convertibility for local agents. The populist right's adverse reaction to foreign capital's privileged position, based on appeals to national and cultural values rather than socialist ideology, proved no less politically vexing to the successor government, which unlike its predecessor faced an electoral constraint.

REFERENCES

Antal, László. 1983. "Conflicts of Financial Planning and Regulation in Hungary." *Acta Oeconomica* 30, 3–4: 341–68.
———. 1985. *Gazdaságirányitási és pénzügyi rendszerünk a reform utján* (Our Economic Management and Financial System on the Reform Path). Budapest: Közgazdasági és Jogi Könyvkiadó.
Bányai, Miklós. 1989. "Hungarian Steel Sector: The Restructuring Syndrome." MS.
Bartlett, David. 1992. "The Political Economy of Privatization: Property Reform and Democracy in Hungary." *East European Politics and Societies* 6, 1: 73–118.
———. 1993. "Banking and Financial Reform in a Mixed Economy: The Case of Hungary." In *Capitalist Goals, Socialist Past: The Rise of the Private Sector in Command Economies*, ed. Perry Patterson, 169–92. Boulder, Colo.: Westview Press.
Bauer, Tamás. 1978. "Investment Cycles in Planned Economies." *Acta Oeconomica* 21, 3: 243–60.
———. 1981. *Tervgazdaság, beruházás, ciklusok* (Planned Economy, Investment, Cycles). Budapest: Közgazdasági és Jogi Könyvkiadó.
Brada, Josef, Ed Hewett, and Thomas Wolf. 1988. "Economic Stabilization, Structural Adjustment, and Economic Reform." In *Economic Adjustment and Reform in Eastern Europe and the Soviet Union*, eds. Josef Brada, Ed Hewett, and Thomas Wolf, 3–36. Durham, N.C.: Duke University Press.
Byrd, William. 1983. *China's Financial System: The Changing Role of Banks*. Boulder, Colo.: Westview Press.
Comisso, Ellen. 1979. *Workers' Control under Plan and Market*. New Haven, Conn.: Yale University Press.
De Wulf, Luc, and David Goldsbrough. 1986. "The Evolving Role of Monetary Policy in China." *IMF Staff Papers* 33, 2: 209–42.
Dimitrijevic, Dimitrije, and George Macesich. 1973. *Money and Finance in Contemporary Yugoslavia*. New York: Praeger.
Foreign Broadcast Information Service/Eastern Europe (FBIS/EEU):

 a. "Official Comments on Wage Reform Issues," October 28, 1987, 18.
 b. "Chamber of Commerce Comments," March 14, 1988, 31.
 c. "Bank Official on Devaluation of Forint," July 20, 1988, 34.
 d. "Miners Get Bonuses, Agree to Resume Work," August 25, 1988, 17–20.
 e. "Work 'Undisturbed' in Mecsek Mines," August 26, 1988, 26.
 f. "More on Aftermath of Miners' Strike," August 29, 1988, 9–11.

g. "Pécs Strike Blamed on Company Management," August 30, 1988, 24–25.
h. "National Bank Head on Plans for 1989," October 6, 1988, 20–21.
i. "Foreign Investment Protection Bill Formulated," December 15, 1988, 34–35.
j. "SZOT Chief Nagy on Trade Unions' Role," February 14, 1989, 26–28.
k. "Interest Coordination Council Views Wage Raises," February 14, 1989, 26.
l. "National Bank Devalues Forint to Boost Exports," March 21, 1989, 35.
m. "State Secretary Halmos Presents Strike Bill," March 28, 1989, 22–24.
n. "Government Devalues Forint by 6 Percent," April 14, 1989, 16.
o. "Trade Union Council Calls for 'Discussions,'" April 18, 1989, 31.
p. "Trade Union Council Considers Economic Policy," October 4, 1989, 33.
q. "Trade Union Council Announces Strategy Shift," October 1, 1989, 33–34.
r. "Trade Unions Reject Government Economic Program," November 21, 1989, 55.
s. "Nemeth Addresses Parliament Session," November 30, 1989, 69–70.
t. "Premier Németh Interviewed on Economy," December 6, 1989, 61–62.

Furubotn, Eirik. 1980. "The Socialist Labor-Managed Firm and Bank-Financed Investment: Some Theoretical Issues." *Journal of Comparative Economics* 4, 2: 184–91.
Furubotn, Eirik, and Svetozar Pejovich. 1973. "Property Rights, Economic Decentralization, and the Evolution of the Yugoslav Firm." *Journal of Law and Economics* 16, 2: 275–302.
Gedeon, Shirley. 1986. "The Post Keynesian Theory of Money: A Summary and an Eastern European Example." *Journal of Post-Keynesian Economics* 8, 2: 208–21.
———. 1987. "Monetary Disequilibrium and Bank Reform Proposals in Yugoslavia: Paternalism and the Economy." *Soviet Studies* 39, 2: 281–91.
Hauvonen, J.J. 1970. "Postwar Developments in Money and Banking in Yugoslavia." *IMF Staff Papers* 17, 3: 563–601.
Kornai, János. 1980. *The Economics of Shortage.* 2 vols. Amsterdam: North-Holland Publishing Co.
Laky, Teréz. 1980. "The Hidden Mechanisms of Recentralization in Hungary." *Acta Oeconomica* 24, 1–2: 95–109.
Lowi, Theodore. 1964. "American Business, Public Policy, Case-Studies, and Political Theory." *World Politics* 16, 4: 677–715.
Marrese, Michael. 1992. "Hungary Emphasizes Foreign Partners." *RFE/RL Research Report* 1, 17: 25–33.
McKinnon, Ronald. 1991. *The Order of Economic Liberalization: Financial Control in the Transition to a Market Economy.* Baltimore, Md.: Johns Hopkins University Press.
———. 1992. "Taxation, Money, and Credit in a Liberalizing Socialist Economy." In *The Emergence of Market Economies in Eastern Europe,* eds. Christopher Clague and Gordon Rausser, 109–27. Cambridge, Mass.: Blackwell.
Milenkovitch, Deborah. 1971. *Plan and Market in Yugoslav Economic Thought.* New Haven, Conn.: Yale University Press.
Naughton, Barry. 1987. "Macroeconomic Policy and Response in the Chinese Economy: The Impact of the Reform Process." *Journal of Comparative Economics* 11, 3: 334–53.
Noti, Stephen. 1987. "The Shifting Position of Hungarian Trade Unions Amidst Social and Economic Reforms." *Soviet Studies* 39, 1: 63–87.

Okolicsanyi, Károly. 1989. "Growing Shortage of Convertible Currency." *Radio Free Europe/Radio Liberty Background Report*, no. 233, 29 December, 1–2.

Pearson, Margaret. 1991. *Joint Ventures in the People's Republic of China: The Control of Foreign Direct Investment under Socialism.* Princeton, N.J.: Princeton University Press.

Pejovich, Svetozar. 1973. "The Banking System and the Investment Behavior of the Yugoslav Firm." In *Plan and Market: Economic Reform in Eastern Europe,* ed. Morris Bornstein, 285–311. New Haven, Conn.: Yale University Press.

Radio Free Europe/Radio Liberty, Hungarian Situation Report (RFE/RL)ı

    a. "Attempt to Freeze Wages in Response to Worsening Economic Indicators," December 29, 1986, 19–24
    b. "Full Employment Versus Economic Efficiency," February 25, 1987, 33–36.
    c. "Restrictions on Foreign Travel to Be Eased," November 28, 1987, 47–51.
    d. "Tension Mounts Between State and Unions as Workers Press for Change," November 7, 1988, 13–17.
    e. "Hungarians 'Celebrate' the October Revolution in Capitalist Austria," November 17, 1988, 23–24.
    f. "Trade Unions' National Conference," December 15, 1988, 37–41.
    g. "Wage Ceilings for 1989 Lifted," January 12, 1989, 23–26.
    h. "Hungary's First Independent Trade Union Holds Its Founding Congress," January 12, 1989, 27–30.
    i. "Massive Price Hikes Polarize Trade Unions and Government," February 8, 1989, 21–25.
    j. "A Law to Legalize and Regulate Strikes," May 9, 1989, 35–38.
    k. "IMF Forces Economic Changes on Hungary," June 16, 1989, 15–17.

Sipos, A., and M. Tardos. 1986. "Economic Control and the Structural Interdependence of Organizations in Hungary at the End of the Second Decade of Reform." *Acta Oeconomica* 37, 3–4: 241–65.

Soós, Károly. 1987. "Wage Bargaining and the 'Policy of Grievances': A Contribution to the Explanation of the First Halt in the Reform of the Hungarian Economic Mechanism in 1969." *Soviet Studies* 39, 3: 434–51.

Tarafás, Imre. 1985. "The Possibility and Conditions of Anti-Inflationary Economic Policy in Hungary." *Acta Oeconomica* 34, 3–4: 287–97.

Tardos, Márton. 1986. "The Conditions of Developing a Regulated Market." *Acta Oeconomica* 36, 1–2: 67–89.

Tyson, Laura. 1977. "Liquidity Crises in the Yugoslav Economy: An Alternative to Bankruptcy?" *Soviet Studies* 29, 2: 284–95.

———. 1983. "Investment Allocation: A Comparison of the Reform Experiences of Hungary and Yugoslavia." *Journal of Comparative Economics* 7, 3: 288–303.

Wolf, Thomas. 1985. "Exchange Rate Systems and Adjustment in Planned Economies." *IMF Staff Papers* 32, 2: 211–47.

———. 1988. "Devaluation in Modified Centrally Planned Economies: A Preliminary Model for Hungary." In *Economic Adjustment and Reform in Eastern Europe and the Soviet Union,* eds. Josef Brada, Ed Hewett, and Thomas Wolf, 39–71. Durham, N.C.: Duke University Press.

Zhou Xiaochuan and Zhu Li. 1987. "China's Banking System: Current Status, Perspective on Reform." *Journal of Comparative Economics* 11, 3: 399–409.

APPENDIX: INTERVIEWS CONDUCTED BY THE AUTHOR
IN BUDAPEST, HUNGARY

Central Committee of the Hungarian Socialist Workers' Party
   1: 7 July 1988
   2: 30 August 1988
   3: 8 September 1988
Ministry of Commerce
   4: 15 July 1988
Council of Ministers
   5: 14 April 1988
   6: 5 September 1988
Hungarian Credit Bank
   7: 27 May 1988
   8: 8 July 1988
Karl Marx University
   9: 8 July 1988
Ministry of Finance
   10: 28 June 1988
   11: 6 September 1988
   12: 13 July 1988
Ministry of Industry
   13: 24 August 1988
National Bank of Hungary
   14: 12 April 1988
   15: 18 May 1988
   16: 15 July 1988
   17: 22 July 1988
   18: 12 August 1988
   19: 26 August 1988
   20: 8 September 1988
   21: 21 May 1991
National Commercial and Credit Bank
   22: 9 September 1988
National Planning Office
   23: 21 April 1988
   24: 10 May 1988

PART THREE

Remaking Local Political Networks

SIX

Bureaucratic Patronage and Private Business: Changing Networks of Power in Urban China

David L. Wank

China's command economy gave rise to a clientelist political order. This order had several distinct features (Oi 1985, 1989; Walder 1986). First, the command economy gave lower-level officials a monopoly in the allocation of resources on which citizens were dependent. Officials had wide discretion in the allocation of material goods and career opportunities. Individuals could gain access to these resources through particularistic ties with officials. This created networks of patron-client ties across local boundaries between state and society. Second, relations between patrons and clients were stable over time. This stability was because of the closed nature of the workplace: goods and opportunities were distributed within the work unit and movement between workplaces was extremely rare. Stability was also reinforced by emotional bonds of loyalty and obligation that developed in many patron-client relations. Third, dependent clientelism was the foundation of what Michael Mann (1986) would call the state's "infrastructural power": its ability to penetrate and coordinate society. Clients helped officials mobilize compliance with central policies and directives. Clientelist networks also created social cleavages between clients and nonclients, inhibiting the development of organized opposition to the state.

What have been the consequences of China's commercial reforms for

Research in China was supported by the Committee on Scholarly Communication with the People's Republic of China. My host institution in China, Lujiang College, provided much support, including arranging interviews in bureaus. An early draft of this chapter was written while I was an academy (Kukin) scholar at the Harvard Academy for International and Area Studies. I am grateful for the extensive comments by Andrew Walder on each draft, as well as for the insights and suggestions of Ole Bruun, Gordon White, and the other participants in the conference on which this volume is based, and an anonymous reviewer for the University of California Press. — DLW.

this clientelist political order? Commercialization undermines the monopoly of officials over the allocation of goods and opportunities and should serve to undermine the basis of dependent clientelism. The reemergence of private business would appear to be especially consequential, inasmuch as it operates outside the command economy.

Debate about the consequences of private enterprise reflects three distinct views. The first view, most fully elaborated by Victor Nee (1989a, 1989b, 1991), sees private business as eroding dependent clientelism by undermining the basis of patron-client exchange. In the command economy entrepreneurs depend on officials for resources, but private business creates new resources, access to which is through markets rather than bureaucratic allocation. As markets develop, therefore, the resource dependence of entrepreneurs on officials is reduced. Nee makes a distinction between long-term and short-term consequences. In the short-term, during the transition to a market economy, officials use their remaining power and influence to force a one-sided predatory extraction. "The niches in which peasant entrepreneurs operate and compete are typically crisscrossed by patronage networks dominated by local cadres who can use their power and influence to pressure, bully, and squeeze entrepreneurs" (Nee 1989a, 172). However, in the long-term, markets have a "subversive effect . . . on established social relationships such as patron-client ties" (Nee 1991, 279), leading to the declining power of officials and enhanced autonomy of society from arbitrary state power.

This view is contradicted by a second found in studies documenting new patterns of cooperation between local officials and entrepreneurs running larger private enterprises. Noting how the tax revenue generated by private business fills local government coffers, Liu Yia-ling (1992) describes a new "interest convergence" between officials and entrepreneurs. In the effort to stimulate private business, local officials shelter it from restrictive central policies and let entrepreneurs register their enterprises as collectives in order to bypass restrictions on private business. Dorothy Solinger describes a "symbiotic relationship" between entrepreneurs running larger private firms and officials staffing the lower bureaucracy; entrepreneurs give officials income through bribes and other payments, while officials give entrepreneurs access to capital in the state structure (Solinger 1992, 128–30). In this view, private business creates new interests at the local level for entrepreneurs and officials to cooperate in ways that deviate from central-state intentions.

A third view is found in studies of clientelism in China's commercializing economy (Oi 1985, 1986; Paltiel 1989). The emergence of markets in the context of uncertainties regarding the control of assets, restraints on state power, and fluctuating state support for private property rights engenders patron-client ties among local actors in state and society to reduce these uncertainties. Clients seek patrons in the bureaucracy for political protection as well as for commercial advantage. This chapter furthers this view by extending it to a hitherto unexamined commercial activity, private capitalist business; by describing the strategies through which patron-client ties are built; and by analyzing the role of these ties in the local political order. This third view diverges sharply from the first view in arguing that there is no necessary correspondence between the emergence of markets and the decline of patron-client relations. The third view also encompasses the second view in emphasizing local cooperation between officials and entrepreneurs, but differs in its emphasis upon the individualized exchanges between officials and entrepreneurs for personal advantage that are often blatantly illegal. The distinctive contribution of this third view is therefore to emphasize the *particularistic* basis of the emerging alliance between entrepreneurs and officials in China's market economy.

In this chapter, I refer to the alliance between entrepreneurs and officials as "symbiotic clientelism." This new relationship is unquestionably clientelist: it involves an imbalance of power between official patrons and entrepreneurial clients, it involves the exercise of discretion by officials in allocating resources and opportunities, and it is embedded in personal ties. The key change from the earlier form of clientelism is that the *degree* of client dependence is greatly reduced, as the entrepreneur-clients have resources upon which officials now also depend.

In the next section of this chapter, I document the rise of private capitalist business in one Chinese city. In the succeeding sections, I in turn explain why capitalist entrepreneurs need bureaucratic support; clarify ways in which officials are able to support entrepreneurs; describe the strategies used by entrepreneurs to influence officials to help them; and describe how the resulting clientelist ties evolve and change. In the conclusion, I examine the political consequences of private capitalist business by contrasting dependent and symbiotic clientelism. The analysis is based on data from fieldwork conducted in the southeastern city of Xiamen, Fujian Province, during eighteen months of residence between June 1988 and June 1990. I interviewed entrepreneurs running one hundred private capitalist firms.[1]

THE DEVELOPMENT OF URBAN PRIVATE BUSINESS

Private business was revived beginning in 1979 after more than two decades of suppression. The state's intention was similar to that of reformers in Hungary, as described in chapter 3 of this volume. It was to supplement the

1. I conducted all the interviews myself in Mandarin Chinese. Introductions to entrepreneurs were provided by bureaus, private individuals whose friends and relatives were entrepreneurs, employees of public units who had business contacts among private entrepreneurs, and

production and circulation of consumer goods and services, create jobs, and stimulate economic competition. Private business has grown rapidly both by reviving licensed private business and by innovating within the "collective" sector.

Licensed private business first revived under the individual business family policy (see Gold 1989; Hershkovitz 1985). This permitted petty private enterprises and limited them to a maximum of seven employees and to nonmechanized forms of production and transport in a narrow range of businesses. Most of these original restrictions were subsequently eliminated in 1981. The limit on employees was politically sensitive and was not removed until the 1988 Private Enterprise Interim Regulations, which permitted private enterprises with eight or more employees (see Young 1989).

Innovations in the collective sector began with policies in the early 1980s that let groups of four or more unemployed individuals pool private capital to set up a collective enterprise (see Wank 1993, 75–85). The "public" status of these privately run collective enterprises — hereafter called cooperatives — enabled entrepreneurs to bypass restrictions faced by licensed private business and enjoy public enterprise advantages such as lower taxes and easier access to bank loans. Although cooperatives are formally classified as publicly "owned," they are considered private by entrepreneurs and the officials who regulate them, in that they are not managed by officials or people appointed by them.

Private business has grown rapidly. The number of petty private businesses grew from 150,000 in 1978 to 15.3 million in 1993. There were also 225,000 larger private enterprises, including 50,000 cooperatives by 1988, that hired on average sixteen employees (Zhang and Qin 1988). However, official figures for the larger enterprises are only an estimate; their number is probably much greater. One reason for this underestimation is that many cooperatives are counted as part of the collective rather than private sector.[2] A significant portion of collective-sector growth is thus owing to private business. From 1978 to 1992, the private sector's share of total retail sales grew from 0.1 to 20 percent, while the collective sector's share of industrial output grew from 23 to 38 percent (State Statistical Bureau 1993, 23).

The development of private business varies regionally because of local

---

through referrals from other entrepreneurs. I also interviewed officials in administrative bureaus, state commercial bureaus, public manufacturing enterprises, and state banks, as well as the officers of residents' committees.

2. The official figure of 50,000 cooperatives in 1988 is admittedly conservative (Jia and Wang 1989). Yet according to a survey published in 1989, 60 percent of all the collective enterprises in Fujian province alone are privately run cooperatives (Lin 1989, 34). The Xiamen Bureau of Industry and Commerce determined that 20 percent of the 6,324 collectives in the Greater Xiamen Municipality were really cooperatives.

differences in geography, history, and government policy. The situation in Xiamen, the field site for this study, reflects the rapid growth of private business in the southern coastal region, which enjoys more liberal economic policies and easier access to financial capital and trade through connections with Chinese in Taiwan, Hong Kong, and overseas. Xiamen, a former British treaty port, is the commercial hub of Fujian Province, has the same local dialect as in Taiwan (which is one hundred miles across the Taiwan Straits), and is in the ancestral region of one-fifth of the world's overseas Chinese.[3] These favorable conditions led to the city's designation in 1980 as one of China's five special economic zones to take the lead in creating a market economy and attracting foreign investment. In contrast to other local governments, which restrict private wholesale trade in order to control the local circulation of commodities and prices, Xiamen is one of the few local governments to issue private business licenses to general trading companies. This is because the main concern of the Xiamen government is to hasten the circulation of commodities between domestic and international markets through Xiamen in order to spur the economy of the special economic zone.

Private business in Xiamen has grown rapidly. By 1988, there were 15,254 private businesses registered under the individual business family policy, mostly in commerce and trading in consumer commodities. There were also 621 private capitalist trading firms by 1989, with 180 in the licensed private sector and 441 cooperatives.[4] The entrepreneurs who run these capitalist firms have no jobs in the state structure. They hire from eight to several hundred employees, provide their own start-up capital, keep account books, and reinvest profits for expansion. They pursue national and international trade in such consumer commodities as home appliances, car parts, and designer clothing, and in such producer commodities as chemicals, metals, and construction materials. A number of firms have diversified into manufacturing ventures in areas such as textiles, foodstuffs, handicrafts, and assembly of imported computers and medical equipment, or have established restaurants, automotive repair firms, scientific institutes, or computer software development companies. Many have also launched joint business ventures with public agencies or enterprises, and a few with overseas Chinese and foreign businesses. Their annual sales volume (at the time of the fieldwork) ranged from 1 million to 120 million yuan.[5]

3. Xiamen's registered urban population was 579,510 in 1988. Like other prosperous Chinese cities, Xiamen had an unregistered population of migrant laborers estimated at from one-quarter to one-third of the registered population.

4. All statistics were obtained through interviews with the Bureau of Industry and Commerce, which licenses private businesses. The figure for cooperatives is a bureau estimate.

5. In mid 1989, 1 yuan equaled U.S. $0.27.

WHY ENTREPRENEURS NEED BUREAUCRATIC SUPPORT

The strong desire of entrepreneurs for support from the bureaucracy was apparent during interviews. Particularly revealing was their response to an open-ended question on the prerequisites for business "success." I did not define *success*, but in interviews entrepreneurs consistently defined it in terms of business scale. To be successful was to be a boss (*laoban*) running a company (*gongsi*) and doing business in a big way (*zuò da shengyi*) as opposed to being a peddler (*shangfan*) running a shop (*shangdian*) and doing petty trade (*xiao shengyi*). The most successful entrepreneurs run enterprise groups (*qiye jituan*) diversified not only across business lines but across the formal categories of the economy into the collective and state sectors through various joint-venture arrangements. Achieving this success requires the support of officials in a wide range of matters. Some entrepreneurs talked about this support in terms of access to profit opportunities. For example, one said, "Your skill and ability as an entrepreneur are less important than having proper support [*zhichi*] from the local government. With proper support you can get whatever you need. If you don't have capital, then you can get capital. If you need scarce goods, then you can get scarce goods" (informant no. 27).

Others talked about support in terms of protection from arbitrary sanctions and regulations. Another entrepreneur said, "Everything depends on personal ties [*guanxi*]. If you have good ties with officialdom [*guanfang*], everything is easy to deal with. If you do something wrong, your friends in the relevant bureau will see that the matter is forgotten. But if your ties are bad, then officialdom will make trouble for you even if you've done nothing wrong" (informant no. 17). Ideal bureaucratic support is provided by patrons (*houtai laoban*) and backers (*kaoshan*). These are officials highly placed in public units who use their discretion regarding decisions over the allocation of resources and in administrative matters to create opportunities and overcome problems for entrepreneurs. This kind of support is considered "solid" (*ying*). Lower-ranking officials and public-unit employees with narrow spheres of discretion can also provide support, and, indeed, entrepreneurs running smaller capitalist enterprises rely entirely on these kinds of support.

An entrepreneur in the construction trade (whom I shall refer to as Zhang) shows how entrepreneurs draw bureaucratic support from a range of officials and public employees. Zhang manufactures and sells tiles, as well as a peel-resistant paint he developed for Xiamen's humid climate. He employs about sixty workers in several factories that are subsidiaries of his licensed private trading firm. My interview with him was interrupted by numerous visitors and at lunch together afterward I found out more about those who were officials and public employees. Below is an edited excerpt from my field notes on some visitors, which illustrates the extent of his ties with local officials:

The first visitor was an out-of-uniform official from the Bureau of Industry and Commerce. He wanted to buy a certain color of tile. Zhang had only one lot in stock and had already promised it to another customer. But Zhang went ahead and sold it to the official at only slightly above his production cost. It turns out that the bureau issues Zhang's business license, which lists the commodities that he can legally sell. Since the license was issued, changes in state policy have banned several of the listed commodities for private trade. However, in Zhang's case, the bureau interpreted the policy in his favor by not deleting these commodities from his license, on the grounds that the policy was not retroactive. To ensure this kind of support from the local bureau, Zhang gives its officials "special treatment" (*teshu youdai*). . . . The fourth visitor was an employee in the Railroad Bureau and former co-worker of Zhang's father, who passed away several years ago. He wanted some tile for the floor of the house he was building. Zhang sold it to him at cost and gave him some paint as a housewarming present. This individual works in the freight depot assigning freight space in railroad cars in the state-run railroad. Because there is only one railroad track through Xiamen, freight space is at a premium. Good relations with this individual assure Zhang of space when he has to ship his manufactured products to customers. . . . The eleventh visitor was a uniformed official from the local Public Security Bureau substation. He sat for a long time and smoked his way through half a pack of Zhang's imported Marlboro cigarettes lying on the coffee table in front of the sofa. When he got up to leave, Zhang took the remaining cigarettes out and pushed them into his hand. Zhang later told me that the substation officials look the other way when he does not register his nonlocal workers at the substation. Zhang prefers nonregistration, because it is then easier to fire workers. It also minimizes the apparent scale of his factory, thereby reducing taxes.

The business activities of an entrepreneurial couple give insight into higher levels of bureaucratic support. The husband had been a highly regarded mechanic in a local army unit who had left in the mid 1980s to set up his own car-repair garage. By the time I met the couple in 1989, they were running an enterprise group that consisted of the original garage, a trading firm dealing in car parts, and a transportation firm with trucking and taxi operations. They lived in a suburban four-storey mansion, where I visited them several times. During the first visit, they attributed their success to the capital provided by overseas relatives of the wife, who came from a pre-revolutionary business family, as well as to "support from the social environment" (*shehui huanjing de zhichi*). I subsequently found out the nature of this support. On my next visit, as I was being entertained in the family's private quarters by the wife, teenage children, and visiting relatives, the boisterous sounds of drinking and feasting one floor below could be heard. It turned out that the husband was entertaining officers from the local army unit, in which he had previously worked. After the husband left the army in the early 1980s, he continued to repair army vehicles in his former unit on a contract basis. When he set up a cooperative repair garage in 1985, he gave shares in the firm to these army officers, who arranged for the site for the garage and sold the entrepreneur practically brand-new equipment, at much lower prices, as damaged second-hand goods. During another visit, I literally stumbled into another form of the couple's social support when I bumped into an official wearing plastic slippers and an unbuttoned tunic emerging from the bathroom. His wet hair was plastered down, he was carrying a wet towel and a washbasin, and it turned out he was from the Transportation Bureau next door, whose personnel had a standing invitation to take hot-water baths in the entrepreneurial couple's house — a luxury, since most houses lack hot water. Needless to say, the couple had few problems regarding drivers' licenses and the registration of trucks and taxis. Near the close of my fieldwork, I was invited to the wedding of their daughter to a young official from the bureau.

In sum, the development of private business is embedded in bureaucratic support. This support consists of decisions by officials and public employees to enhance or "maximize" profit and protection for entrepreneurs. Individuals in the bureaucracy give entrepreneurs access to various resources that they control. The next section examines these various resources and the ways they enhance profit and protection in private capitalist business.

HOW OFFICIALS SUPPORT ENTREPRENEURS

Access to Profit

The resources controlled by the local bureaucracy are vast. They include previously unpriced assets, such as commodities that formerly circulated only in the planned economy and publicly owned real estate. Commercialization has given these assets a market price, thereby increasing their value. Other resources include access to financial capital, permission to trade in restricted products and engage in direct foreign trade, and advantages in the handling of routine administrative procedures that can confer competitive advantage. These resources all support the development of private business and are energetically sought by entrepreneurs.

First, entrepreneurs seek access to scarce commodities and raw materials. This scarcity often stems from a two-track price system that restricts the market circulation of commodities and raw materials. Before 1980, the prices of commodities produced by public enterprises were set by administrative fiat. Also, raw materials and commodities in scarce supply, such as steel, rubber, fertilizer, and lumber, were produced and supplied to factories according to state plan and at administrative prices; public enterprises were not permitted to exchange or resell these commodities. Beginning in 1980, commodities were gradually released from regulation and enterprises could sell or purchase them at market prices. Market prices are usually much higher than administrative prices, which do not reflect actual production costs or market demand. Thus any individual or enterprise that can obtain valuable commodities at administrative prices can reap large profits by re-selling at market prices. Many officials divert quantities of administratively priced commodities that they control to sell at market prices for their own gain. Through relations with officials, entrepreneurs can obtain access to these scarce goods.[6] Although access might include price discounts, the officials may take the lion's share of this administratively generated rent. However, for entrepreneurs to obtain scarce commodities, even at market prices, is often valuable enough.

A second source of profit is the vast amount of real estate owned by public units and controlled by the officials in them. Real estate values have sky-rocketed since the late 1970s. According to official figures, land prices in Xiamen rose approximately 900 percent from 1979 to 1986 (Xiamen City Real Estate Company 1989, 96). In interviews, entrepreneurs told me of much higher actual increases, including one of 26,566 percent.[7] Bureaucratic support in this regard can consist of access to business sites at below market prices. For example, in 1983 an entrepreneur leased a store owned by a street committee at a monthly rental rate of 1.10 yuan per square meter. In 1990, the store next door was leased to another entrepreneur for 56 yuan per square meter. However, the entrepreneur who had signed the lease in 1983 was able to avoid a lease renegotiation to reflect the increased market value because he had regularly given sums of money to the officers staffing the committee.[8] For the officers this under-the-table cash was easily diverted to personal uses and therefore preferable to contracted rental income, which would have generated greater cash flow into public coffers, but would be more difficult to pocket. Bureaucratic support can also consist of prefer-ential access to choice real estate. For example, urban school playgrounds and the large tracts controlled by the suburban village and township govern-ment are highly desired by entrepreneurs for factories.

6. Goods exchange hands many times before reaching their final market at prices far above the administrative price. One example told to me was of beer acquired by an official for 1.70 yuan a bottle and resold at 2.50, a price markup of 68 percent. In another case, fertilizer that was resold three times underwent a markup of 94.4 percent (*China News Analysis* 1988, 4).

7. This involves an individual renting a small apartment just off the main commercial street. The apartment was publicly owned, and the administrative rent was 3 yuan a month. The individual renting it then subleased it to an entrepreneur for 800 yuan a month.

8. I refer to the individuals staffing the residents' committee as "officers," as distinct from officials. The latter have formal bureaucratic careers, whereas the former are local residents, often elderly men and women, staffing this most local level of government.

A third profit opportunity is access to financial capital. Bank officials have wide discretion both in approving loans and in setting the interest rates. For example, when I asked entrepreneurs the monthly interest they paid on commercial loans, they mentioned rates of from 4 to 20 percent. Support from officials is crucial to obtaining loans and at preferential rates. The case of Xiamen's largest private firm in the late 1980s illustrates this form of bureaucratic support. The entrepreneur had high backers in the city government who arranged a large loan from a state bank in 1985. He used the loan to buy a controlling share of a newly established district-level cooperative bank. He then obtained further loans from the cooperative bank that made his private firm Xiamen's largest and gave him a national reputation. Bureaucratic support regarding access to capital is often forthcoming through the various forms of public-private business ventures discussed below.

Fourth, access to restricted trade opportunities is another source of profit. For example, only state foreign-trade corporations have the legal authority to conduct foreign trade. However, many entrepreneurs get them to sponsor their direct private trade with overseas businesses. The entrepreneurs pay foreign-trade corporation officials commissions in return for the necessary customs certificates and the use of the corporation's foreign-exchange bank account to receive payment from overseas. Commissions range from less than 1 percent in the highly competitive seafood business to more than 4 percent in the more administratively restricted trade in raw materials.[9] Another method involves discretionary access to local exemptions from state policy restrictions. For example, in Xiamen it was initially prohibited for private enterprises with private business licenses to trade in cement. In order to ensure a steady supply of cement for the local construction boom, the city government authorized a few private enterprises to trade it. As these exemptions were limited in number, access to them depended entirely on official discretion.

Fifth is access to public customers. Because public units are large in scale and have easier access to bank loans, they are potentially much larger customers than private firms. They are also more reliable trading partners, inasmuch as they are less likely to disappear or go bankrupt after taking delivery of commodities. The largest capitalist firms all conduct the bulk of their domestic trade with public units. Much of this trade takes advantage of Xiamen's geography and status as a special economic zone. A number of entrepreneurs import car parts, designer clothing, and home appliances to sell to public units in northern cities such as Beijing and Shenyang. In

9. For example, during the 1989 student movement, students charged that the China National Coal Import/Export Corporation, presided over by Deng Xiaoping's daughter, charged a commission of 4.7 percent on coal exported to Hong Kong businessmen (Han 1990, 30).

return, these trade relations give them access to the restricted commodities that officials in these units control such as cable and construction materials.

Sixth, entrepreneurs seek public status through joint public-private enterprises. These are legally licensed as "public" enterprises, enabling entrepreneurs to bypass restrictions on licensed private business such as proscriptions on the sale of wire, cable, pipes, and other scarce and lucrative commodities. Public enterprises also have advantages such as lower tax rates and larger tax breaks, have easier access to bank loans, are considered more trustworthy, are less subject to bureaucratic harassment, and are less likely to be suspected of illegal activities. Joint public-private enterprise takes several forms. One is the cooperative firm. Larger firms are sponsored by district level urban governments and smaller ones are sponsored by lower levels, such as residents' committees. Entrepreneurs pay monthly management fees to their sponsoring public units, ranging from several hundred to a thousand yuan in the late 1980s, in return for a free hand in doing business. Another form is the jointly run (*lianying*) firm. Entrepreneurs provide a share of start-up capital, and management expertise and market connections, while the public unit provides a share of start-up capital, the business site, and a public registration. Leased (*zulin*) commercial firms are a third form. These are collective firms leased by entrepreneurs. In the late 1980s, leasing contracts were for three to five years, and the monthly rents paid to parent units ranged from one to three thousand yuan. Entrepreneurs provide the commercial capital and have a free hand to conduct business, with public status. A fourth form is village and township enterprise (*xiangzhen qiye*). These are usually manufacturing firms set up with rural local governments and are registered as collectives. Entrepreneurs provide the start-up capital, while the rural government provides the site, employees, and public status, and its officials often serve as the managers.

A seventh way involves discretionary decisions in routine administrative matters in practically all administrative bureaus, one example being the regulation that entrepreneurs must obtain a temporary residence permit for nonlocal workers by registering them at the closest public security substation. Some entrepreneurs prefer not to register workers, in order to keep down tax assessments by minimizing the apparent scale of their businesses, and to make it less administratively cumbersome to fire workers. Other entrepreneurs prefer to register nonexistent workers, a form of payroll padding that lets them launder money. They withdraw money from the bank as wages for these ghost workers, which is then used to pay off officials. These misrepresentations of the size of the workforce would seem to be impossible without at least the tacit consent of officials in public security substations. The Tax Bureau was also often mentioned as the site of crucial discretionary decisions. It is no secret that entrepreneurs keep two account books, and that the ones given to the tax authorities are doctored. Charges of tax evasion are therefore less a question of whether the evasion occurred (of course it did!) than of whether the tax officials decide to accept the doctored books.

Access to Protection

The bureaucracy can interfere with or obstruct private business in many ways. Some involve the harassment of entrepreneurs by administrative measures and sanctions. Others include policy actions emanating directly from the central state, such as sudden policy shifts and extraordinary bureaucratic campaigns, the implementation of which is in the hands of local officials. Bureaucratic support in these matters consists of discretionary decisions by officials that protect entrepreneurs from these hazards.

First, entrepreneurs seek protection from local bureaucratic harassment. Harassment consists of the use of administrative procedures to make life difficult for an entrepreneur who has displeased officials in some way. It is referred to colloquially as being made to "wear small shoes" (*chuan xiao xiezi*). For example, entrepreneurs who protest about the Bureau of Industry and Commerce's licensing fee might have the fee raised or their legal business scope—the commodities they can legally trade in—reduced. Entrepreneurs who do not comply with the edicts and demands of other bureaus can be harassed by summoning them at short notice for meetings, charging them surcharges and fees, and making them strictly adhere to rarely enforced regulations regarding sanitation, working conditions, and exterior decorations. By cultivating ties with officials, entrepreneurs seek to ensure both that these officials will not harass them and that they will intervene to protect them when other officials do so. Intervention can be highly effective, as illustrated in the case of one entrepreneur running a cooperative. He purchased an expensive imported car for his exclusive use as head of the firm. The Tax Bureau sought to tax the car as private income, but the entrepreneur insisted it was public property that belonged to the cooperative. His sponsoring public unit intervened on his behalf, as he describes: "I called my mother-in-law [*popo*][10] and she came and told the Tax Bureau, 'This is a publicly owned firm and the car belongs to the firm. There is nothing in this for the Tax Bureau.' So everything was all right. If I have a problem and call mother-in-law, everything is all right" (informant no. 2).

Second, entrepreneurs seek protection from arbitrary local sanctions. Officials can impose fines and confiscate goods, regardless of whether an entrepreneur has committed an infraction or not. Indeed, sanctions are often used to generate an income for bureaus by selling confiscated goods (*neibu chuli*). The Bureau of Industry and Commerce can confiscate goods

---

10. Slang for a bureaucratic sponsor.

not in a firm's legal business scope, the Tax Bureau can seize goods in lieu of unpaid taxes, and the Customs Bureau can seize smuggled goods.[11] Officials also warn entrepreneurs of impending regulatory actions against them. One example involves an entrepreneur who set up a jointly run firm in Xiamen with a rural township government. An official from the township government who was a firm manager absconded with the firm's cash, and the entrepreneur was unable to make interest payments on loans. When the city procuratorate placed a lien on the firm, a friendly official tipped the entrepreneur off, giving him time to hide his inventory and office equipment.

Third, central-state policies are subject to sudden change. Practices that have been condoned and encouraged are suddenly proscribed and condemned. For example, in late 1988 the practice of letting entrepreneurs privately manage collective firms, such as cooperatives, was condemned by the central state. Previously, entrepreneurs running cooperatives had been praised in the state-run media for using private resources to solve public problems such as unemployment. Now they were condemned for using public status for private gain. Locally, the Bureau of Industry and Commerce tried to get cooperatives to reregister as licensed private firms. But most entrepreneurs successfully resisted reregistration through the intervention of their bureaucratic sponsors. In another case, an entrepreneur purchased a large quantity of beer in another province, where lower taxes made it cheaper, and chartered a boat to ship it to Xiamen. Shortly after leaving port, the Fujian provincial government issued a new regulation prohibiting shipments of cheaper beer into the province. A friendly official in the Customs Bureau informed the entrepreneur that the boat would be seized and its goods impounded as smuggled contraband upon arrival in Xiamen harbor. This enabled the entrepreneur to unload the boat secretly along the coast.

Fourth, entrepreneurs seek protection from bureaucratic campaigns. These are extraordinary central-state interventions targeted at problems that have defied solution through more routine regulatory measures. They unfold like the political campaigns of the Mao era: a problem is first identified by the central state; its extent is determined by several spot investigations, and a quota of transgressors is established for the local bureaucracy to fill; local results go back to the central state, which then sets punishment and quotas for each degree; and finally the local level metes out punishment according to quota. While quotas have to be filled, officials have discretion in deciding which entrepreneurs and firms are actually labeled transgres-

11. Confiscated merchandise is sold quickly at bargain prices. One entrepreneur obtained smuggled television sets, VCRs, and refrigerators confiscated by the Guangdong Provincial Customs Bureau at 15 to 20 percent below the market price.

sors. Needless to say, entrepreneurs seek to cultivate officials who can warn them of upcoming campaigns and ensure they are not labeled transgressors. There are several such types of campaigns. One is the economic rectification (*jingji zhengdun*) campaign that targets problematic economic institutions. For example, among other things, the campaign launched in September 1988 targeted activities that complicated state regulation of the economy by blurring the boundaries of public and private enterprise, such as cooperatives. Other forms are clean government (*lian zheng*) campaigns that focus on corruption and economic crimes committed by individuals, and tax-investigation campaigns (*shuishou dajiancha*). Officials in a wide range of bureaus can provide support. For example, officials in the Tax Bureau can give advance warning of spot checks and show discretion in whom they target as transgressors in tax-evasion campaigns. In another example, the sudden flight abroad (to Bolivia) of one of Xiamen's best known private entrepreneurs shortly after the start of the Economic Rectification Campaign in September 1988 was reputedly aided by an official in the city procuratorate, who had warned him of his impending arrest on bribery and smuggling charges.

HOW ENTREPRENEURS INFLUENCE OFFICIALS

I have just described the kinds of bureaucratic support that entrepreneurs seek in order to enhance the profits and protection of their businesses. All these forms of support depend on the exercise of discretion by officials. Furthermore, much of it is dubious or blatantly illegal, and is therefore more likely to be forthcoming among individuals who know and trust one another. For any single entrepreneur, the task is therefore to ensure that specific officials and public employees make decisions that support his or her firm (and not competitors'). This is achieved by strategies of personal influence that involve the cultivation of ties with individuals in the bureaucracy. Broadly speaking, entrepreneurs use three such strategies: payoffs, employment, and partnerships. Each strategy involves a distinct level of bureaucratic power and distinct mode of institutionalization. Payoffs involve street-level officials and public employees, while the other two strategies involve higher-ranking officials and greater institutionalization of exchange within the firm structure.

Payoffs

This strategy involves buying off the street-level officials and public employees whose duties bring them into contact with entrepreneurs and other citizens on a regular basis. Their power stems from their position as the most local implementors of state policies: they enforce regulations in society; take care of public assets; and gather information on society to inform higher levels of the local situation. They have some discretion in this local implementation, which entrepreneurs seek to influence by buying them off with cash payments and gifts. This strategy is indicated by various terms used by entrepreneurs. Terms such as "kickbacks" (*huikou*) and "red envelopes" (*hong bao*) refer to cash payments, while expressions such as giving officials "convenience" (*fangbian*) and "special treatment" (*teshu youdai*) refer to gift-giving.

The terms of exchange in cash payments are relatively clear-cut. For example, entrepreneurs encourage public-unit purchasing agents to place orders with their private firms through kickbacks. This practice is especially important in such highly competitive lines as auto parts. As such commodities all originate from a few Hong Kong–based suppliers, there is little variation in price, and purchase orders depend on the side benefits that an entrepreneur can give purchasing agents. One entrepreneur organized an exhibition of car parts and invited purchasing agents from public units from all over China. He put them up in local hotels and used kickbacks to land large orders from them.

Payments are also made in response to requests by officials in bureau substations for "donations." These payments assure that the officials will not cause trouble, an arrangement verging on extortion. One entrepreneur explained this as follows:

> Only those organizations that have some connection with me will ask for money. It could be a new building for the Self-Employed Laborers Association, the retirement fund for the public security substation, [or] the social welfare fund for the residents' committee. The amount is not that much, twenty yuan here, forty yuan there. It is a token sum. Of course, if you don't want to give money, they will not force you to do so. But there is a saying, 'You can get by the first of the month, but perhaps you won't be able to get through the 15th of the month.' Who knows? If you don't give money, maybe they will never make trouble for you in the future. I have never encountered this trouble yet. I have never met with any difficulty. But I have never refused to donate. (informant no. 17)

Other payoffs appear more as gifts. Gifts differ from payments in that they are actively given by an entrepreneur. However, many so-called gifts are actually given in response to hints and indirect demands by officials. This can be seen in the comments by an entrepreneur running a transportation firm:

> The local head of the residents' committee is like the Kitchen God. He has been the head since 1952. . . . I am doing business on a large scale. Now he

comes to me and says, 'Aiya, you have quite a lot of money. The country has asked me to sell these bonds, so could you help me out and buy a few extra?' He has a quota to sell. It is difficult for him to ask those old grannies and mothers with children to buy them, because they barely have enough money to fill their market baskets. So I asked the head how much the quota was. '1,000 yuan,' he said. So I said, 'Forget about asking the others. I'll take them all.' So he was very happy. It was as if a weight had been lifted from his shoulders. (informant no. 36)

In this kind of gift-giving, the terms of exchange are less clearly defined. This serves to build up reservoirs of gratitude and obligation (*han*) on the part of the receivers, which entrepreneurs can tap to deal with future uncertainties. For example, one entrepreneur gives to the local residents' committee so that its officers will be favorably disposed to him. This can be useful during bureaucratic campaigns. As he says:

> The old ladies on the street committee are really fierce. You should not take them lightly. They are all tongues and lips when it comes to gossip. They are also very important for how people think of me. . . . If there is a campaign, the cadres from the bureau always come to the residents' committee to understand the local situation. . . . So I need them to say good things about me. So I told the old wives to just let me know when they have some need. I give them some money on my own every month, and when they have special meetings, I give them forty, fifty or sometimes one hundred yuan. If you give them a little money, they will practically die of joy. (informant no. 19)

This kind of gift-giving involves numerous bureaus and their substations. One entrepreneur sold construction materials at cost to a public security substation when it was renovating its facilities. Another entrepreneur, who runs a garage, does free repairs on the motorcycles owned by substations that have jurisdiction over him.

Gifts can also be given to officials as individuals rather than as representatives of bureaus. When officials visit firms, entrepreneurs are quick to note which items they express an interest in and let them "borrow" the goods indefinitely. One entrepreneur described this as follows: "They will never say, 'Give me this' or 'Give me that.' Instead, they will say, 'This is very pretty,' and so you then say, 'Take it home and show your family.' Or they will say, 'This is quite interesting,' and so you say, 'Go ahead and borrow it' " (informant no. 23). Officials who drop by private restaurants are treated to free meals. Gifts can also be given to officials on opportune occasions. They are treated at banquets during the feasting that occurs during the summer Ghost-feeding Festival. During the winter Spring Festival, officials are treated to nightclub entertainment and banquets at the year-end business parties held by firms. The Spring Festival is also a convenient time to give gifts of cash. Large amounts are placed in the red envelopes traditionally

given to children with small sums of money in them and presented to officials under the guise of gifts for their children's education.

Employment

Another strategy is to hire officials to work in private firms. These officials
occupy the more middle echelons of public-unit hierarchies and have less
regular contact with citizens during the course of duty. They have a greater
range of discretionary authority and useful contacts with other officials in
the bureaucracy. This strategy is indicated by terms such as "advisors"
(*guwen*) and "managers" (*jingli*). There is a basic distinction in this strategy
between kin and nonkin officials.

There are several ways to employ nonkin officials. In some cases, officials
who have ties in bureaus critical to the firm's business are hired as advisors.
Such officials do not work regular hours, but only when needed. One entrepreneur explained the work of an advisor as follows: "If there is a problem,
he invites the relevant officials out for dinner. This is all he does" (informant
no. 25). In some cases, these advisors are paid fees and given company
shares, generating incomes several times their public salaries. For especially
useful information or actions, they can be given bonuses or commodities
(e.g., television sets, refrigerators, etc.). Because of policy prohibitions
against moonlighting by officials in private firms, entrepreneurs prefer to
hire recently retired officials. These officials have strong personal ties with
the bureaucracy accumulated during their long careers, which are still
fresh, because their retirement is recent.

In another pattern, nonkin officials are hired for their business skill and
acumen as well as for their personal ties. I encountered several former
manager-officials of collective trading firms in their late thirties who had
been hired as full-time managers in private firms. These former manager-
officials possess substantial business experience and personal ties in district
governments. Entrepreneurs became acquainted with them during business and lured them from public employment with offers of monthly salaries
five to six times their public ones, commissions on sales, health insurance,
and other social benefits that entrepreneurs provide for key employees. In
good business times, they can realize monthly incomes of two to four thousand yuan, roughly eight to sixteen times their former public salaries. Entrepreneurs also hire other public employees who have accumulated extensive
commercial connections in the public sectors. This usually involves public-
unit purchasing agents who work as salesmen for entrepreneurs. Their personal ties with the heads of public-unit purchasing departments can dramatically expand the market connections of the private firm. In some cases, they
still hold public-unit jobs and do private business for the entrepreneurs on
the side, in effect giving entrepreneurs well-connected sales personnel who

travel at public expense. Other purchasing agents resign their public jobs to work in private firms. They are paid base salaries of four to five times their public salaries, receive sales commissions, and are reimbursed for traveling expenses on successful deals. In good times, this can generate an income dozens of times their public salaries. One former purchasing agent I talked with boasted that his monthly income regularly exceeds ten thousand yuan (more than 50 times the average urban wage).

A less direct strategy is to hire nonofficials who have personal ties with officials. The largest private firms have "brain trusts" of economics and international finance professors from the locally based national university. They are paid retaining fees for advice on business strategy. Many of them are the former classmates and teachers of officials in strategic bureaus such as the Foreign Trade Bureau, the Tax Bureau, and the Policy Research Institute. These professors therefore have valuable ties with these bureaus which they use to influence officials on behalf of the entrepreneurs who hire them. Another example concerns retired auditors from the Tax Bureau who work in private firms. They have former colleagues in the Tax Bureau whom they can influence to accept the account books of the firms, and from whom they receive warnings of upcoming campaigns against tax evasion. One accountant can manage the books for up to half a dozen firms at the rate (in 1989) of 200 yuan per month per firm, thereby earning four to five times his or her former public salary.

Officials who are immediate kin can also be "hired" to work in the firm. I encountered numerous instances of entrepreneurs who were recently retired officials working in their offsprings' firms. In one pattern, the parent is an ad hoc advisor who dispenses advice and introductions when needed. Some instances I came across involved fathers who had worked in city government bureaus and who were well versed in bureaucratic procedure, but had few ties with public enterprises and bureaus. In another pattern, the parents who "work" in the firm are the de facto entrepreneurs. This involves parents who previously worked in public agencies that distribute commodities, such as state commercial bureaus, and who now use the personal ties accumulated during their public careers for private business. By designating their children the legal owners of the firms, they seek to deflect criticism that they are cashing in on bureaucratic connections. For example, in one firm ostensibly run by a woman in her mid twenties, the top managers are her parents, who have retired from bureaus that allocate textiles and chemicals in the command economy. Not surprisingly, the firm trades heavily in textiles and chemicals. Other examples I encountered included parents working in their offsprings' construction firms who had previously been employed by city or district construction companies; former officials in bureaus allocating foodstuffs working in their children's seafood and foodstuffs firm; and former State Foreign-Trade Bureau officials working in firms belonging to their children that exported raw materials and minerals.

Partnerships

This strategy involves officials who occupy high leadership positions. Those in public manufacturing enterprises and state commercial bureaus have wide discretion over the resources of their units, while those in administrative bureaus have the discretionary power to interpret and adapt central-state policies to fit local contexts. Terms such as *patrons* and *backers* refer to this bureaucratic support. There is also a basic distinction in this strategy between kin and nonkin.

Partnerships can be secured through material incentives. Officials are given shares in the company—referred to as "power shares" (*quanli fen*) because the officials invest their bureaucratic power rather than financial capital in the firm—and positions on the board of directors. These practices integrate powerful officials into the firm's structure and give them a vested interest in the well-being of the firm, improving the likelihood that they will actively intervene on behalf of the entrepreneur. The case of an entrepreneur in the highly competitive construction trade is a case in point. In order to guarantee a source of cement, the entrepreneur gave a 15 percent share in his firm to a cement factory run by a suburban township government in exchange for an agreement to make the firm the sole Xiamen distributor of the factory's cement output. At the onset of the 1988 Economic Rectification Campaign, when new restrictions on the private sale of cement appeared imminent, the official managing the factory leased its trucking fleet to the entrepreneur. This enabled the entrepreneur to continue the private trade under the guise of public trade, protecting it from policy shifts. The entrepreneur was also permitted to use the factory's bank account to receive payments for the cement, a practice that further obscured the private nature of the business.

Partnerships can also be forged through family ties. For example, one entrepreneur returned to his ancestral village along the coast to set up a fish farm. The fish farm is registered as a village enterprise and managed by a cousin of his, who is the village Communist party secretary, while the entrepreneur devotes his time to drumming up sales from luxury hotels. In another case, an entrepreneur's brother, sent to a suburban village in the 1960s during the Cultural Revolution campaign to rusticate urban high school graduates, had become the manager of a township factory in the village. Through this brother, the entrepreneur was able to contract with a workshop in the factory to manufacture goods for export. More highly placed officials tend to support private firms only at crucial stages. For example, in a cooperative garage, one of the founding partners has a father who heads a city government bureau. The firm received its big break in 1985, when the father leaned on a friend heading another bureau to send its vehicles to the garage for repairs. This was the beginning of a business relationship with the bureau that has enabled the firm to become one of the largest of its kind in Xiamen. In the mid 1980s, when this happened, the status of private business was low and the father's intervention was crucial in overcoming the resistance of the bureau to doing business with the private garage, although subsequent business has depended on the quality of goods and service.

SHIFTING INFLUENCE STRATEGIES AND BUSINESS GROWTH

The three strategies I have just described are not mutually exclusive: an entrepreneur may deploy them simultaneously. However, the mix of strategies shifts in the course of private business growth. This section will examine several principles that underlie this shift. One concerns the levels of bureaucratic support: entrepreneurs seek ties with more highly placed officials. The other concerns the nature of the personal tie: entrepreneurs shift away from blatantly instrumental ties to more enduring ones.

Shifting to Higher Levels of Bureaucratic Support

An entrepreneur forges alliances with higher-level officials in order to reduce the cost of obtaining bureaucratic support. First, low-level officials control few, if any, profit-enhancing assets, while their protection extends no further than their own actions. The relationship is often little more than extortion: an entrepreneur makes payments to such officials in order to avoid further costs directly threatened by them. In contrast, higher-level officials provide more bureaucratic support. Such official patrons control significant profit-enhancing assets and provide protection, not only from their own actions, but from those of other officials as well. This can be seen in the case of an entrepreneur who is the son of a high city-government official. After moving to a new business site, he was repeatedly visited by officials from a local bureau substation demanding payment of ad hoc taxes. The entrepreneur complained to his father, who in turn complained to a friend who was a vice-head of the bureau in question. The harassment stopped immediately.

Second, having higher levels of support reduces the time an entrepreneur must spend cultivating ties with officials. The gift-giving that characterizes ties with lower-ranking officials is especially time-consuming. The demands of these officials can be indirect, and entrepreneurs have to spend time figuring out just what they want. As the presentation of a gift is as important as the content, entrepreneurs have to select an opportune occasion to present it, and go through the giving ritual. In this regard, I was struck by how much time entrepreneurs running smaller capitalist firms spend interacting with lower-level officials by visits to their offices and to their houses at festivals. In contrast, payments to higher officials are routinized in the firm structure as salaries and dividend payments disbursed by the cashier, obviating entrepreneurial concern with the content, timing, and form of the exchange.

Third, higher levels of support are more "efficient." Higher-level officials have greater discretionary power than lower-ranking officials. Also, a higher-level official can usually offer both profit and protection, in contrast to a lower official, who can usually offer one but not the other. To achieve the same outcome, an entrepreneur with higher support therefore needs to rely on fewer officials than an entrepreneur with lower support. The former expends less time and money cultivating strategic officials than the latter.[12] This logic is illustrated by the example cited above of the entrepreneur engaged in the cement business with a township government, a reasonably high level of bureaucratic support. The partnership enhanced his profits by providing access to public status and scarce commodities, making it possible to evade regulations, and enhancing his protection from central-state policies. This wide range of support was achieved by entrepreneurial cultivation of only one individual in the bureaucracy, the township official managing the cement factory.

Shifting to More Enduring Ties

There are more and less instrumental strategies for exerting influence. Payoffs can be through either highly instrumental cash payments or less brazen gifts. Employment and partnerships can be through either businesslike relationships involving salaries and stock dividends or less instrumental relationships involving kinship ties. Entrepreneurs prefer less instrumental strategies, because they are more enduring.

One reason is that less instrumental strategies enhance the depth of support. For example, a highly instrumental strategy such as cash payment is based on a clear quid pro quo. The terms of exchange are known ahead of time, and the cash payment is for a specific discretionary act on the part of the official or public employee. Subsequent support is unlikely to be forth-

---

12. This is not to say that entrepreneurs with higher support cultivate fewer officials in absolute terms. These entrepreneurs engage in business activities that are more far-flung and diverse than those of entrepreneurs with lower levels of support, and their overall ties with officials are probably greater in number. Rather, I am arguing that entrepreneurs with higher support pay less for each individual tie with an official, relative to business profits, than entrepreneurs with lower support: in this sense, higher support "costs" less.

coming until new terms of exchange have been negotiated. However, many problems faced by entrepreneurs are uncertainties stemming from future shifts in central-state policies or harassment from other bureaus. Since the occurrence of these problems is unpredictable, it is impossible to negotiate bureaucratic support ahead of time. To refer to a previous example, when officials from a bureau come to the residents' committee during a campaign for information on an entrepreneur, the officers staffing the committee do not have time to bargain with the entrepreneur about the committee's response to the officials. The solution is for entrepreneurs to ensure that individuals in the bureaucracy support them of their own volition. Gift-giving is more useful than cash in achieving this, since it cloaks the payoff as kindness (renqing) rooted in concern for the officials in question as human beings, engendering feelings of gratitude and obligation on their part, which are more likely to result in decisions on behalf of the entrepreneur.

A second reason why entrepreneurs favor less instrumental exchanges is that they avoid the blatant appearance of corruption and economic crimes associated with instrumental strategies such as cash payments. An entrepreneur who relies heavily on payments is more likely to be identified as a transgressor during bureaucratic campaigns and be charged with corruption and economic crimes. In contrast, when an entrepreneur donates commodities to a local bureau without specifying anything in return, this is less likely to be labeled corruption. The same is true with employment and partnerships. An official on the payroll or board of directors can more easily be accused of abusing bureaucratic authority when supporting a firm than a family member, who might only receive a nominal salary.

Finally, a third reason for the shift away from cultivating support through instrumental personal ties is that they create tensions in the bureaucracy between officials who benefit from the firm and those who do not. This exacerbates competition between the officials that can engulf the entrepreneur in intrabureaucratic conflict. The career of an entrepreneur running Xiamen's largest private firm in the late 1980s is a case in point.[13] Originally a stevedore, he set up a grocery shop in 1979, when he was in his mid twenties. In 1982, he set up a cooperative firm sponsored by a district government. In 1985, his patrons arranged large loans from state banks for him to purchase the controlling share in a newly established savings and loan cooperative. He then took out large loans from the cooperative and organized a national car-parts exhibition, using kickbacks to land orders with public units all over China. He caught the eye of city-government officials, who arranged for his election in 1988 as a model national youth

13. He was jailed soon after my fieldwork began, and I could not interview him. However, I talked to family members, his employees, and entrepreneurs and officials who knew him.

entrepreneur. During the awards ceremony in Beijing, he met the leader of a state factory in Manchuria, who sold him cable and other scarce products. In fall 1988, at the onset of the Economic Rectification Campaign, he was arrested on charges of bribery and smuggling, his downfall being rumored to have been engineered by jealous officials not on his payroll. He was jailed for two years while his patrons tried to prevent a trial to save their skins. Because of the number of high officials involved, his trial was held in secret and he was sentenced to six years in prison.

The Logical Extreme of Bureaucratic Support

The most powerful and least instrumental type of bureaucratic support is to have a parent in the highest levels of the state structure. It is by far the most effective and efficient, inasmuch as it ensures the support of extremely powerful officials without the expenditure of any time or resources to cultivate it. It is also noninstrumental, and the support is therefore deeper, less risky, and unlikely to cause intrabureaucratic competition. Ironically, this kind of support may not involve any patron-client tie. Entrepreneurs may never communicate with the parent about business matters, and the parent may never make a single decision in support of the entrepreneur. However, everyone knows that the entrepreneur is related to the official, inducing them to open doors for the entrepreneur "voluntarily" out of awe of his family background and fear of possible reprisals for "noncompliance."

Among the entrepreneurs I interviewed, such support is illustrated by an entrepreneur related through marriage to a family of leading officials in Guangdong province. She acknowledged the importance of the tie as follows: "I use their name in doing business, and so people know that I belong to this lineage. I don't actually have to use their power in business, as people trust me because of the family connection" (informant no. 12). This family tie enables her, among other things, to purchase commodities confiscated from smugglers by the Guangdong province customs authority at bargain prices. The so-called "princes' party" (*taizi dang*), consisting of children of the central-state elite, epitomizes this kind of support. Its most illustrious members include the offspring of Deng Xiaoping, Premier Li Peng, and the deposed party leader Zhao Ziyang, as well as the families of other prominent or recently retired members of the old guard, such as Chen Yun, Hu Yaobang, and Liu Shaoqi. They were held up by the students during the 1989 student movement as exemplars of the bureaucratic corruption and profiteering flourishing during market reform. In the aftermath of the student movement, the central state launched a bureaucratic campaign against both corruption in the bureaucracy and economic crimes in private business, motivated in part by the popular outrage over these matters that surfaced during the movement. Not surprisingly, this bypassed the "princes' party" and fell on entrepreneurs with lower levels of bureaucratic support, such as those I met in Xiamen.[14]

FROM DEPENDENT TO SYMBIOTIC CLIENTELISM

Although dependent clientelism cannot be found in private capitalist business, this does not mean that patron-client ties are irrelevant to the new commercial environment. On the contrary, such ties are essential to the operation of a successful private business, but they take a new form of symbiotic clientelism. This symbiotic clientelism is a far-reaching departure from previous forms of dependent clientelism: it constitutes a major transformation *within* a clientelist political order.

Transformations in Clientelist Exchange

In dependent clientelism, officials extend material and career advantages to individuals who work within public units. In symbiotic clientelism, this exchange has in some key respects been stood on its head. First, the material basis of exchange has altered radically. Entrepreneurs no longer rely on officials for access to the necessities of daily life, but rather acquire them through their incomes. Most entrepreneurs own their own homes or apartments and have a full set of consumer appliances, as well as cars or motorcycles, while food, medical care, and educational opportunities can all be purchased.[15] Instead, it is now the entrepreneur-citizen who gives officials access to material necessities through bribes, salaries, and dividends. This income exceeds public salaries many times over. Moreover, it is an increasingly crucial form of income for officials given double-digit inflation and the increasing commodification of resources, such as education and foodstuffs, formerly provided by bureaucratic redistribution. In the late 1980s, the salaries of officials in Xiamen were between two hundred and four hundred yuan, even including the special subsidies for individuals on the public payroll in the special economic zone. In contrast, officials who work in private firms enjoy base salaries of at least several times this amount. With

14. Entrepreneurs in Xiamen generally did not support the student movement, because they were concerned that student demands for the state to suppress bureaucratic corruption would target their beneficial alliances with officials. They also feared, correctly as it turned out, that state actions to defuse popular outrage over the princes' party would lead to a crackdown on entrepreneurs at lower levels who were not connected to the central elite (see Wank 1995).

15. In my sample of one hundred entrepreneurs, thirty-nine had bought houses or apartments or had them under construction, and thirty owned houses that had been confiscated from their families in the 1950s and 1960s and returned to them in the 1980s. Thirty-one still lived in public housing, but most intended to purchase private housing. Forty-six entrepreneurs had motorcycles, while thirty-two had cars, trucks, and/or vans.

bonuses and commissions, those with business acumen and good personal ties can realize monthly incomes up to twenty or more times their former public salaries. Entrepreneurs also entice officials and other talented public employees by giving them one-time lump-sum payments when they come to work in the private firm that are equal to the sum of the public wages they would have earned had they remained in their public jobs until retirement. Entrepreneurs also provide medical insurance and pension plans to core employees comparable to such benefits in the public sectors.

A second aspect of this transformation concerns access to career opportunities. In dependent clientelism, officials gave subordinates in their organizations opportunities for career advancements through promotions and Communist party membership. Promotion is no longer an issue for entrepreneurs who run private firms. Furthermore, while officials still control access to the party, membership has little appeal to entrepreneurs, who regard it as burdening them with time-consuming meetings and the need to uphold selfless standards of behavior incompatible with private business.[16] In this new form of symbiotic clientelism, entrepreneurs can now give officials significant career opportunities through employment as managers and sales personnel.

Finally, in dependent clientelism, clients held up their end of the exchange by providing officials with intangible resources. Clients served as the eyes and ears of party officials, providing valuable information on possible sources of local opposition and discontent that helped officials in governing. Now patrons in the bureaucracy often serve as the eyes and ears of their clients, providing valuable information on policy shifts, local administrative matters, insider information on prices and auctions of public enterprises and confiscated goods, and regulatory loopholes, all of which help entrepreneurs to conduct business. Also in dependent clientelism, clients helped officials implement policies that came down from above, by taking the lead in the efforts to mobilize societal compliance. In symbiotic clientelism, officials draw on their personal ties with other officials to mobilize support for an entrepreneur within the bureaucracy.

Transformations in Clientelist Networks

The patron-client relations of dependent clientelism had a certain stability. One reason for this was organizational; they were enclosed within work units. As the work unit was the basis of bureaucratic redistribution, and transfer out was extremely difficult, clientelist relations were necessarily

---

16. Several prominent entrepreneurs I interviewed had in fact been asked to join the Communist party but refused. Only two entrepreneurs (2 percent) in my sample were party members, a figure consistent with national statistics showing only 1 percent of private business owners were party members in the late 1980s (*China Daily* 1989).

long-term. In symbiotic clientelism, patron-client relations no longer occur within work units, but between private firms and public organizations. This organizational openness has reduced the stability of patron-client ties. While the bureaucracy provides the best opportunities for enhancing profit and protection in private business, the new organizational openness means that entrepreneurs are no longer limited to one set of officials, but can pick and choose their patrons. However, two caveats must be made here. First, although the stability of patron-client ties has been reduced, their necessity has not: a patron is essential to business success. Entrepreneurs who do not cultivate a patron or some other kind of bureaucratic support are unlikely be successful. Second, despite the greater freedom to change patrons, entrepreneurs still prefer to forge long-term ties with patrons, because culti- vating a new patron is costly and long-term relations, by increasing the degree of trust and concern for mutual benefit, reduce the likelihood of opportunistic behavior by official-patrons vis-à-vis entrepreneur-clients.

A second reason for the stability of the patron-client relation in depen- dent clientelism was its embeddedness in "human feeling" (*ganqing*). In- strumental ties were overlaid with bonds of loyalty, gratitude, and obliga- tion. In contrast, relations in symbiotic clientelism can be more blatantly instrumental and involve much larger sums of money and valuable com- modities. This transformation can be seen in entrepreneurs' frequent refer- ence to "personal ties of money" (*jinqiandi guanxi*), a term that did not exist in the Mao era. The emergence of these money ties reflects the shifting relationship of material wealth to political power. In the planned economic order, wealth was a reflection of an individual's connections to power, but now money can be used to build these connections to power (Meaney 1991, 138). New patron-client relations based on a cash nexus have thus prolifer- ated. Yet narrowly instrumental ties are widely viewed by entrepreneurs as problematic, as explained above. They still prefer noninstrumental ties rooted in kinship relations (real or fictive) and strive to impart a "human feeling" dimension to "money" ties so as to make the patron-client relation- ship more enduring.

Another transformation involves the emergence of new forms of compe- tition. In dependent clientelism, individuals competed for official favor, successful ones being drawn into patron-client ties, leading to admission into the local elite. In symbiotic clientelism, officials now compete to be- come linked to the larger private firms.[17] Entrepreneurs running the larger and wealthier firms are the most desired clients, inasmuch as they can pay more for the discretion of highly placed officials. However, such competi- tion may backfire, as illustrated by the case described in the previous section of the entrepreneur arrested in 1988. His problem stemmed precisely from

17. I thank Dorothy J. Solinger for bringing this point to my attention.

the fact that competition and jealousies among officials over the rewards and opportunities stemming from his firm grew out of control. His arrest was initiated by officials outside his firm's patronage networks. The emergence of competition among patrons for clients thus adds a new form of instability to clientelist networks.

Transformations in Clientelism and State Infrastructural Power

Dependent clientelism reinforced state infrastructural power, whereas symbiotic clientelism undermines it in several ways. First, dependent clientelism reinforced the hierarchical lines of authority within the bureaucracy. Holding out the promise of reward and opportunity was an important way for the central state to ensure the loyalty of officials and for superiors to ensure the compliance of subordinates. Officials were loyal and compliant in order to attain the rewards and opportunities over which superiors had discretion. In contrast, in symbiotic clientelism, the rewards and opportunities for officials available outside the bureaucracy now far exceed those within it. As the value of the bureaucracy's reward structure declines, lower-level officials increasingly seek incomes in the market economy through the exercise of their bureaucratic discretion. Having lost control over the most lucrative rewards and opportunities, the central state is less able to maintain the loyalty of officials and responsiveness of its bureaucracy.[18]

Second, dependent clientelism gave officials a societal constituency that facilitated the implementation of state policies. Clients (activists) took the lead in setting compliance standards for society, a role that assisted officials in orchestrating acceptance of state policies. In contrast, patrons and clients in symbiotic clientelism no longer interact in ways oriented to fulfilling state goals. Instead, interaction usually involves willful deviations from central-state policies. Entrepreneurs and officials seek commercial gain through dubious and illegal practices, which they conceal from central-state supervision. Officials sell administratively priced goods obtained in the planned economy at market prices and then declare them as lost or spoiled; they lease real estate and public firms at below market value in exchange for bribes and shares in firms, and they give entrepreneurs low-interest loans in exchange for kickbacks. These activities undeniably enrich officials and stimulate private capitalist business, but they also squander public assets and deprive the state of revenue.

Finally, dependent clientelism supported state infrastructural power by creating a deep political cleavage in society between clients and nonclients, which inhibited the expression of popular dissatisfaction against the state.

---

18. The shifting orientation of officials is suggested by the statistic that 70 percent of economic crimes in 1987–88 were committed by officials (Chang 1989, 25).

Indeed, popular dissatisfaction with the state and local officials was often vented against clients (activists). In contrast, symbiotic clientelism creates a new cleavage between the central state on the one hand and communities composed of local state and society actors on the other. The actors in this community increasingly cooperate to generate prosperity through locally based resources rather than looking to the state hierarchy to provide these resources through bureaucratic redistribution. This new orientation leads local actors to cooperate in releasing the market value contained in local public resources even when this deviates from central-state policies and intentions.

CONCLUSION

Scholarly analysts widely expect the erosion of patron-client relations to be furthest advanced in locales that are highly commercialized and have many overseas contacts. Yet the symbiotic clientelism described in this chapter is pronounced in Xiamen, which is just such a locale. How can this be explained? By examining this question in a speculative fashion, I shall offer some reflections on capitalism and clientelism in China's departure from central planning *thus far.*

China's departure has emphasized a gradual path of state-initiated economic reform without corresponding political reforms (Shirk 1993). Several features of this path have been so pervasive since the late 1970s as to be stable features of the departure itself, rather than a corruption of an as-yet-unrealized "complete" or "true" market economy. These features include the two-track pricing system, unstable state policies, ambiguous property rights, and minimal legal restraints on lower officials. In such an institutional environment, the logic that drives entrepreneurs to seek bureaucratic support is reinforced through greater commercialization. This is because as commercialization drives up prices, it also raises the gap between the market prices and administrative prices. This in turn raises the value of these resources to entrepreneurs and leads to a corresponding rise in the price of officials' control over these profit opportunities. Furthermore, as the scale of private business is greater in more commercialized areas, the need of entrepreneurs for guarantees that officials will not give them trouble is correspondingly greater, driving up the value of officials' discretionary protection. In short, the link between business success and bureaucratic support intensifies in more commercialized areas.

In such an institutional environment, the salient feature of the social structure in more commercialized areas is not, as some have argued (e.g., Nee 1989a, 206; Nee 1991, 279), the reduction of dependent patron-client ties, but rather the rise of symbiotic ones. In areas characterized by petty private business, the smaller scale of commercial activity may erode dependent patron-client ties without engendering new symbiotic forms. This is because for petty private business, resource requirements are fewer and more easily available without bureaucratic discretion, thereby obviating the need for patron-client ties. In contrast, in areas of greater commercial activity, the resource requirements linked to bureaucratic discretion are also greater, obliging entrepreneurs to cultivate official patrons. In other words, it seems that greater commercialization is more likely to transform the dependent-clientelist order into a symbiotic one.

The dense overseas connections found in the southern coastal regions are another potential reason for the erosion of dependent clientelist relations between officials and entrepreneurs. In one line of reasoning, entrepreneurs who receive capital from abroad are more autonomous of state power, inasmuch as they are less dependent on officials for access to capital (see, e.g., Solinger 1992, 137). However, a somewhat different logic seems to operate in Xiamen. Thirty-five of the entrepreneurs I interviewed had relied on start-up capital from overseas relatives. While this reduced their dependence on officials for capital, the infusion of overseas capital led them to expand into business activities that *did* require bureaucratic support. Foreign capital enabled them to set up capitalist firms, which then needed bureaucratic support for access to business sites, direct foreign-trade opportunities, raw materials, and so on. In other words, access to foreign capital reduces dependence on the bureaucracy for one resource, but appears to generate a need for bureaucratic support in acquiring other resources. Thus it can be said that connections with overseas Chinese, rather than reducing the overall dependence of entrepreneurs on officials, stimulates symbiotic relations between them.

In conclusion, China's gradual departure from central planning has created a commercial economy with distinctive institutional features. Private business has emerged as a form of symbiotic clientelism. Private entrepreneurship in such an economy has an ironic political consequence: as it undermines the infrastructural power of the central state, it perpetuates a pervasive bureaucratic presence in the market economy.

REFERENCES

Chang, Maria Hsia. 1989. "The Meaning of the Tiananmen Incident." *Global Affairs* 4, 4: 12–35. Cited in Chalmers Johnson, "Forward," in *The Broken Mirror: China after Tiananmen,* ed. George Hicks, x. Essex, U.K.: Longman, 1990.

China Daily. 1989. "Business Lures Party Members." March 11, 3.

China News Analysis. 1988. Hong Kong. No. 1399a (August 15).

Gold, Thomas B. 1989. "Urban Private Business in China." *Studies in Comparative Communism* 22, 2–3: 187–201.

Han, Minzhu. 1990. *Cries for Democracy: Writings and Speeches from the 1989 Chinese Democracy Movement.* Princeton, N.J.: Princeton University Press.

Hershkovitz, Linda. 1985. "The Fruits of Ambivalence: China's Individual Urban Economy." *Pacific Affairs* 58, 3: 427–50.

Jia Ting and Wang Kaicheng. 1989. "Siying qiyezhu jieceng zai Zhongguo de jueqi he fazhan" (The Rise and Development of the Private Enterprise Owner Stratum in China). In *Zhongguo shehui kexue* 2 (February): 89–100.

Lin Jincheng. 1989. "Jiantan 'jia jiti' de ruogan wenti" (A Discussion of Some Problems of the "False Collectives"). *Jingji fazhi* 8: 34–36.

Liu, Yia-ling. 1992. "Reform from Below: The Private Economy and Local Politics in the Rural Industrialization of Wenzhou." *China Quarterly*, no. 130 (June): 293–310.

Mann, Michael. 1986. *The Sources of Social Power: A History of Power from the Beginning to 1760, vol. 1*, Cambridge: Cambridge University Press.

Meaney, Connie Squires. 1989. "Market Reform in a Leninist System: Some Trends in the Distribution of Power, Status and Money in Urban China." *Studies in Comparative Communism* 22, 2–3: 203–20.

Nee, Victor. 1989a. "Peasant Entrepreneurship and the Politics of Regulation in China." In *Remaking the Economic Institutions of Socialism: China and Eastern Europe*, eds. Victor Nee and David Stark, 169–207. Stanford, Calif.: Stanford University Press.

———. 1989b. "A Theory of Market Transition: From Redistribution to Markets in State Socialism." *American Sociological Review* 54, 5: 663–81.

———. 1991. "Social Inequalities in Reforming State Socialism: Between Redistribution and Markets in China." *American Sociological Review* 56, 3: 267–82.

Oi, Jean C. 1985. "Communism and Clientelism: Rural Politics in China." *World Politics* 38, 2: 238–66.

———. 1986. "Commercializing China's Rural Cadres." *Problems of Communism* 35, 5: 1–15.

———. 1989. *State and Peasant in Contemporary China: The Political Economy of Village Government*. Berkeley and Los Angeles: University of California Press.

Paltiel, Jeremy T. 1989. "China: Mexicanization or Market Reform?" In *The Elusive State: International and Comparative Perspectives*, ed. James A. Caporaso, 255–78. Newbury Park, Calif.: Sage Publications.

Shirk, Susan L. 1993. *The Political Logic of Economic Reform in China*. Berkeley and Los Angeles: University of California Press.

Solinger, Dorothy. 1992. "Urban Entrepreneurs and the State: The Merger of State and Society." In *State and Society in China: The Consequences of Reform*, ed. Arthur Rosenbaum, 121–42. Boulder, Colo.: Westview Press.

State Statistical Bureau. 1993. *China Statistical Yearbook 1993*. Beijing: China Statistical Information and Consultancy Service Center.

Walder, Andrew G. 1986. *Communist Neo-Traditionalism: Work and Authority in Chinese Industry*. Berkeley and Los Angeles: University of California Press.

Wank, David L. 1993. "From State Socialism to Community Capitalism: State Power, Social Structure, and Private Enterprise in a Chinese City." Ph.D. diss., Department of Sociology, Harvard University.

———. 1995. "Civil Society in Communist China? Private Business and Political Alliance, 1989." In *Civil Society: Theory, History, Comparison*, ed. John A. Hall, 56–79. Cambridge, Eng.: Polity Press.

Xiamen City Real Estate Company. 1989. *Xiamen shi fangdichan zhi* (Annals of Real Estate in Xiamen City). Xiamen: Xiamen University Press.

Young, Susan. 1989. "Policy, Practice, and the Private Sector in China." *Australian Journal of Chinese Affairs,* no. 21 (January): 57–80.

Zhang Houyi and Qin Shaoxiang. 1988. "Siying jingji zai Zhongguo de shijian" (The Practice of Private Enterprise in China). *Jingji cankao,* November 14.

SEVEN

Political Hierarchy and Private Entrepreneurship in a Chinese Neighborhood

Ole Bruun

This chapter addresses changes that economic reform has brought about in a Sichuan urban neighborhood, with particular focus on the reemergence of a private sector in the 1980s.[1] By including street-level bureaucracy in a framework for appraising the overall significance of these changes, the chapter seeks to demonstrate some innate contradictions at the basic level of an urban Chinese community, and their impact on political processes and institutions in the broadest sense.

The legalization and subsequent growth of private enterprise is the most striking departure from central planning at the local level in China. With the rapid development of private enterprise in practically every urban neighborhood, and the rising numbers of nouveaux riches that have followed, powerful new actors have emerged in local politics. The new entrepreneurs are a potentially powerful group in any local community, but the Chinese state has throughout attempted to maintain its political control and secure continuity in political institutions while invigorating the economy and bringing about higher living standards.

As opposed to a large body of literature contributing to the "civil society" discourse, in which an emerging autonomous society is attributed the potential for the ultimate overthrow of the (communist) state,[2] this chapter questions the applicability of that notion on the basis of observations in an

1. I conducted anthropological fieldwork in Chengdu, Sichuan, during parts of 1987, 1988, 1989, and 1991, including intensive interviewing with private business managers, their family members, their employees, customers, market vendors, and local authorities. The neighborhood contains over three hundred private businesses, a few thousand ordinary citizens, and various public bureaucracies. For a full account of the fieldwork, see Bruun 1993.

2. Although the civil society discourse originates in Eastern European studies (e.g., Szelenyi 1988; Hankiss 1988), a large number of writers view the reemergence of the private

urban Chinese community. Widespread interaction between the new entrepreneurs and the lower echelons of the bureaucracy, in the form of both
enduring relationships and more casual individual agreements, leads me to
question the crucial antagonism so often asserted between "state" and "society." I argue that even though competition over basic resources has sharpened, there is strong continuity in fundamental ideologies, values, and orientations among the social groups within the locality, all of whom seek to
establish and utilize connections to the bureaucracy. In fact, a large number
of ordinary households may temporarily use segments of the local state
apparatus to their own ends. For this and other reasons, much of the political struggle in the local community is absorbed by the bureaucracy and its
web of informal ties.

Avoiding the abstractions "state" and "society," I suggest a more fundamental distinction between two segments of the local community: *formal*
and informal hierarchies, which refer to the vertical ties of local participants.
The use of this conception will allow us to see structural continuity in the
context of rapidly changing economic institutions. Below, I first introduce
the neighborhood setting and then separately analyze the micropolitical
processes observed in this setting: taxation, exchange relations, and entre-
preneurial-bureaucratic alliances. Subsequently, I make some suggestions
about the overall importance of these findings.

PRIVATE ENTERPRISE IN THE LOCAL COMMUNITY

Our setting is the neighborhood of Bin Shen, which is administered by a
street committee (*jiedao weiyuanhui*), the lowest level of urban administration in China. It is located in the western district of Chengdu City between
the huge Temple Street and halfway through the old Manchu quarters, of
which it constitutes the southern half. Its streets are narrow and unimpres-
sive, lined with old, mainly wooden houses mostly of pre-Liberation origin.
Bin Shen is well known to shoppers, however, as it contains a free market,
where several hundred peasants sell their produce during the day, and
approximately three hundred private businesses are found side by side
there in every possible house or stall that can provide even minimal facilities. The main street of the area bustles with activity throughout the day and
is always crowded with shoppers, farmers, itinerant peddlers, and local people. When the reforms began, the one- or two-storeyed wooden houses
flanking the street quickly regained their original function, combining private businesses with dwellings behind or above them. Shops facing onto the

economy in China in a similar light, emphasizing its capacity for social change (e.g., Young
1989; Gold 1990; Nee 1991; Odgaard 1992).

street that had been boarded up and converted into living quarters some thirty years previously were reopened as restaurants, workshops, and businesses. In most cases, it was an easy operation, since the façades and wooden shutter boards had been left untouched since the collectivization drive of the 1950s.

The few thousand inhabitants of Bin Shen pursue a variety of professions, since the area was never integrated into a work unit (*danwei*), and the houses, bought from defeated landlords after 1949, remained private. Thus the inhabitants attended to their assigned jobs in state and collective units elsewhere in the city, but resided here. Many of the households had been engaged in private business before the large scale collectivization drives after 1949 and 1956. These households were incorporated into collectives, which turned out to be highly unstable units, regularly rejecting large numbers of workers. For this and other reasons, a substantial number of individuals always remained outside the planned economy. Today the people in Bin Shen are a cross-section of the city's population: there are workers, administrative staff, shop assistants, and teachers, and in addition to these employees of the planned economy, there are an increasing number of self-employed people, mainly in small-scale private business. Over the life span of the present inhabitants, a number of historical events, such as the Japanese bombing of the area in the early 1940s, the Liberation of 1949, and the long series of political campaigns since, have scattered the original population and brought in many new families. The present inhabitants do not form any villagelike community, and few kinship bonds between households exist, although many of those who are now elderly residents were born here or in neighboring areas.

Small-scale private business never needed government support to develop either in Bin Shen or elsewhere in Chengdu. There were 50–100 private businesses in Bin Shen in 1982, approximately 200 in 1985, 270 in 1987, 290 in 1989, and 330 in 1991. The total number of people registered as owners or employees in the private businesses in the area rose from approximately 100 persons in 1982 to an estimated 1,200 persons in 1991 (approximately 25 percent of the adult population). Although the average number of household members registered as business operators was only 1.3 per business in 1987, approximately one additional member per business was found to participate on a full-time basis. However, in most households, all members (on average four to five) are somehow involved in business.

Private businesses have tended to appear in waves, frequently with dozens of identical concerns. A number of the early ones were groceries, since this was an obvious niche where state shops were hopelessly ineffective, and small kiosks soon followed. Other shops became numerous, selling mainly kitchen utensils, plastic goods, and clothes. After a few years, businesses diversified when a large number of primarily elderly craftsmen, incorporated into collective units mainly in 1953, returned to the private sector in order to run their own small workshops. They were tailors, smiths, a traditional doctor, and makers of signboards, kitchen cutting boards, and bags. Restaurants were among the earliest private businesses, since it was easy to compete with those in public ownership, and in the late 1980s, a new wave of restaurants propagated into Bin Shen. Recently, modern hairdressing salons have also appeared, and in a matter of six months, nine such places were opened, four of them occupying neighboring lots.[3]

In terms of local social change since the reforms, private enterprise has played a crucial role. Small-scale private business has affected a rapidly growing proportion of city dwellers since its legalization in 1979.[4] In the early 1980s, apart from urban youths returning from the countryside and setting up small stalls, people were hesitant to register as *getihu* (individual households), the new stamp put on both the people in private business and their families.[5] In Bin Shen, the legalization of business implied the registration of a number of people who were already doing minor business on the fringes of the established community: primarily small vendors, repairmen, and barbers. Private business also attracted a number of other people who had never held official positions, but had survived on occasional jobs and temporary employment in collectives, interrupted by long periods of unemployment, mostly owing to chronic illnesses, physical handicaps, criminal records, or political stigmatization. When, soon after the reforms, a pre-Liberation market was officially reestablished in Bin Shen, this similarly legalized an activity already taking place. Even during the Cultural Revolution, vegetables were traded here, although on a much smaller scale. Apparently, small entrepreneurs were always one step ahead of regulations.

Considerable wealth has been generated in the new sector. At the lowest level, consisting of people trading in the street, private enterprise yields profits in the range of 100–500 yuan per month. For business people in rented premises or their own houses, profits grew during the 1980s to ap-

---

3. A common expression for such model-following is *gan chaoliu* (catch the flood). This phenomenon is reported from all parts of the Chinese world: see, e.g., Ma 1988 on Chinese rural areas; Liu 1992 on a southeastern city; and Niehoff 1987, who cites the Taiwanese expression "a swarm of bees" (*yi wo feng*). This phenomenon in itself contests the development of a "civil society": private enterprise usually builds on strictly local reference and *guanxi* agreements without any form of trans-area class consciousness.

4. When private business was legalized, it was already a social fact. Particularly in the years 1976–78, large numbers of returned "educated youth" started small businesses as a means of survival in the cities. For the history of private business since, see, e.g., Hershkovitz 1985; Yudkin 1986; Rosen, 1987–88; Ma 1988; Taubman and Heberer 1988; Young 1989; Kraus 1991. Specifically on its social impact, see Gold 1989, 1990.

5. The concept of *getihu* has a strong negative tone in ordinary language, since it is associated with the unwanted qualities of individualism: selfishness, a low level of culture, and social deviation. Being marginal implies low social status.

proximately 200–1,000 yuan for the smaller businesses, and reached several thousands for the larger businesses.[6] The explosion of private enterprise even demanded a new frame of reference for ordinary people. The old expression for the newly rich, "10,000-yuan households" (*wan yuan hu*) gave way to "1,000,000-yuan households" (*yibaiwan yuan hu*), since the former level could almost be reached in a single month by certain restaurant keepers, long-distance traders, private brokers, and other successful entrepreneurs.

While private enterprise became increasingly lucrative and secure during the 1980s, state wages lost much of their attraction. In the period 1984–90, wages in the public sector barely kept pace with inflation, For instance, in 1987, when earnings were generally low, a number of people in the neighborhood were left with standard wages as low as 35–40 yuan. In 1991, state wages ranged between 80 and 150 yuan. Even senior officials in local bureaus rarely earned more than 120–140 yuan per month. Even when the state employees' access to social services was taken into account, the majority of them were economically surpassed by people in the private sector. Serious grudges and social tension arose from the fact that social status and monetary wealth became increasingly discrepant in the local community. While the educated and upstanding members of state units frequently had to tighten their belts during the reforms, an increasing number of private entrepreneurs engaged in reckless and conspicuous consumption.

One significant social and political development is the fact that private sector employment expanded beyond the marginal social groups that embraced it in its initial phase. Increasingly, ordinary citizens began to move into the sector in the late 1980s. Some were hunting for quick wealth, but falling bonuses and the closing of collective, and in some cases even state, enterprises squeezed most out of the public sector.

Beyond this, the forces set free by the market did not give rise to an entirely "new" sector of free enterprise. There was a considerable continuity with pre-Liberation Chinese society (as Szelényi [1988] found in rural Hungary in the 1970s). As already noted, many of the people who joined in had previous experience, and a few even resumed family businesses that had occupied the same lots before Liberation: a restaurant, a bicycle repair shop, and a barbershop. Moreover, the inferior social position of these households continued, and in the city at large, the social disregard for the small private business households rapidly reproduced the pattern of the old society. Despite extensive state propaganda to heighten its status, private business became a disparaged sector of "wealth without social standing." Within the business households, the traditional hierarchy was typically

6. See Bruun 1988. This report includes statistical material on the household businesses in Bin Shen interviewed in 1987–88 and discusses development issues related to private business.

strengthened (in contrast to families where all adults earned wages outside the home) under the leadership of the eldest male and with a distribution of authority in terms of conventional family roles. To assist in the shops and perform all manual labor, low-paid rural hands and apprentices were hired, constituting a new underprivileged group in urban China.[7] In 1987, businesses in the area on average employed one person from outside the family. The relatively stable political environment and the abundance of cheap labor encouraged business owners to draw further on this resource, so that in 1991, the average number of employees had reached nearly two. The recruitment of labor in private businesses did not create a new open job market, but largely followed the extension of kinship relations and private networks (*guanxi*). Private entrepreneurs relied exclusively on local references when launching businesses. The model of a thriving business was usually a concrete local one, which scores of new businesses would imitate until profits were reduced by a saturated market.

PRIVATE BUSINESS IN THE LOCAL POLITICAL PROCESS

When investigating the impact of private business on basic "political processes," we should put the term in a proper perspective. How can we comprehend and interpret political processes so as not automatically to transfer institutions from the Western heritage, and instead to investigate how they are implanted in Chinese thought and practice? Chinese political reality is not one of democratically elected forums, political representatives responsible to parties, ideological debate over abstract issues and social visions, or established pressure groups—none of this exists in Bin Shen. In the local community, not even a formal structure allocates elective power to ordinary citizens, who thus have no connection to "politics" if defined in conventional terms. This does not, however, mean that people are not actively contesting which groups are to benefit from the reforms and fighting to maintain or change the distribution of wealth within their local spheres of reference. The most important political processes take place within informal political institutions and consist of individual actions, which nevertheless always connect to those of others.

7. Rural personnel are regarded as inferior to urban employees. The term *birth ascribed stratification* is used by Sulamith Potter 1983, 465, who argues that after 1949, the distinction between the urban and rural populations may even have increased. William Hinton 1966, 287 speaks of a "concept of hereditary social status." *Caste society* is the term used by Lucian Pye. "Moreover, by preventing people from moving freely to find better employment, he (Mao Zedong) could not help but increase inequalities by preventing the development of a true labor market," Pye observes (1988, 18). Whatever the term, such assumptions about hereditary social positions are ironic in a communist society and an aspect of the discrepancy between ideals and social practices.

The task is thus to identify concrete actions of political significance, examine the institutions in which they are embedded, and then suggest how the larger processes operate. For that purpose, we must break down the areas of obvious conflict into the concrete strategies adopted by different groups of people to solve problems and secure the largest share of a given resource. Urban bureaucrats' strategies tend to center on various ways to transform power into wealth. The new entrepreneurs' strategies are more complex, since they must to a larger extent take the current political climate, as well as customary codes or rules of action, into account. These strategies may be arranged according to the following areas of institutionalized political behavior: household strategies, bureaucratic commitment, collective passive resistance, systematized exchanges, and the building and manipulation of authority.

HOUSEHOLD STRATEGIES

When inquiring into the social significance of small-scale private business, the basic unit of analysis is evidently the Chinese household (*hu*). Focus on the domestic group instead of on individuals will provide a different perspective on basic ideologies; there is profoundly less variation among households in their collective aspirations than among individuals in this respect.

Practically all businesses in Bin Shen involved several household members and largely duplicated the organization of the household itself. However, the new market opportunities allowed the household to aggregate its individual members' social and economic capital. The strategies adopted clearly sought to maximize the use of every member's position in the simultaneous pursuit of both new material wealth and maintenance of social status, and if possible social ascendence, thus bridging several sectors of employment.

The continuing value of state employment is emphasized in one widely adopted practice. Many households with both husband and wife in official employment had difficulties making ends meet, and thus considered opening a private business to supplement their income. To maintain the status and security of the household in the transitional period, they started business with only one household member registered, frequently the wife or an unemployed son. Letting the wife run a private business while the husband maintains his position in a state unit has been extremely common; in fact, half of the locally registered business managers in Bin Shen are women. Yet this has also proved problematic, since the wives' incomes rapidly come to exceed the husbands', threatening the status of the male household heads, and thus prompting them sooner or later to take the leap into private business in order to reestablish "harmonious relations" within the household.[8] In the late 1980s, when private business seemed secure, a number of such husbands in the local area chose to leave their state work units in order to become managers of household businesses (by 1991, the average number of registered household members participating in business had risen to approximately 1.6). They were, however, mainly people in ordinary state jobs, often in workplaces with dwindling bonuses. Through the 1980s, the leap into private business continued to bring a marked decline in social status, something evidently compensated for only by a severalfold increase in income.

Thus, although private business became increasingly lucrative and secure, it did not threaten the superior security and status of state employment, and there was still a strong incentive to have one household member placed in a secure state job, particularly the household head, which granted social esteem to the entire household. In the outlook of ordinary families, private business provided an opportunity for increasing material welfare, and also for some more freedom, but it never replaced official employment as a provider of basic services, security, and social respectability.

Another common way of bridging the benefits from official and private employment is making use of connections with state units in order to create advantages in business. Retired cadres[9] are numerous in private businesses, usually being the true managers pulling the strings behind registered wives, sons, or daughters-in-law. Having lifelong pensions, they are legally barred from doing business, but street committees frequently grant them permission for a fee. Their *guanxi* with former colleagues enables them to establish profitable niches in production or specialized services, including signboard production for a large state unit, delivery of equipment, brokerage services, and translations. A few former craftsmen who had retired with cadre status had easy teaching jobs in state units while also running private businesses.

Connections can also be essential in obtaining restricted materials from the storerooms of public firms — for instance, rare metals for highly specialized production — or deliveries of goods in short supply — for instance, cooking oil and sugar, or the best brands of clothing, cigarettes, and liquor.

---

8. Numerous field accounts mention that maintaining "harmony" necessitates a higher male contribution to household income. In Chen village, for example, the men insisted that no man should be allowed to slip below any woman in the scale of prestige as defined by work points in the commune (Chan, Madsen, and Unger 1984, 92). In Sandhead, women could never reach the number of work points assigned to men, in spite of their often harder work. Attempts at equal pay were met with resistance from the men, who were afraid of losing face (Mosher 1983, 204–5).

9. The term *cadre* tends to be misleading, however, since only workers, peasants, and the jobless are not cadres; its derivations, such as *cadre entrepreneurs,* tend to present an especially distorted picture of what is usually small cadres' transfer to private enterprise (see Song Bing 1992).

Merchants with good connections gained an enormous advantage over those who could only obtain the popular brands from the state wholesale departments by accepting "compensation purchases," implying the additional purchase of loads of unpopular goods, which were otherwise left in the warehouse forever. In fact, a large number of small businesses in the neighborhood were established with such personal connections as their main assets. Connections to state units also have advantages in regard to stability in business. In several cases, the local authorities were reluctant to close down businesses that did not comply with regulations if they flaunted powerful connections: for example, a local smithy that the City Reconstruction Bureau wanted removed from the city area could point to the unique repair jobs it did for an adjacent army unit.

Another aspect of the household's optimum mixing of resources concerns its internal organization. In all spheres of social life, formal principles are coupled with an informal social reality. The domestic organization among the private entrepreneurs is often highly pragmatic, with flexible arrangements allowing for considerable adaptation to economic circumstances (Bruun 1993, 59). In order to restore the household as an economically viable unit, an estimated 15 to 20 percent of local business households had incorporated distant relatives or even nonkin—mainly young but in a few cases elderly people—as full "family members." For example, a number of elderly couples without children at home brought in adolescents to help in their shops who lived in as family members.

Enterprising households tend to be more fragmented and incomplete in relation to Chinese ideals than other sorts of families—for instance, they frequently consist of lonely elderly couples; families containing individuals without spouses; or entrepreneurial, freedom-loving young people, for whom a major advantage of individual business is the opportunity to break free from the control of family elders. In terms of basic ideologies, however, such variation does not express differing social values; neither is it seen to characterize particular social identities or professions. Rarely, if ever, is deviation in domestic organization openly displayed or emphasized in the household's identity. On the contrary, serious deviation tends to be hidden—for instance, in the application of kinship terms to newly incorporated members—and in all respects tends to be made up for whenever possible in order to restore "completeness" according to Chinese family ideals. There is only a tenuous link between household identity and a concrete profession. Even though dress, consumption, and modes of speech may contribute to distinguishing present social positions—for instance, between business people and bureaucrats—these individual expressions are not indicative of the long-term aspirations of the household as such.

On the whole, we may regard the present state and position of a given household as a point of departure in the pursuit of commonly shared values, far more than denoting a specific set of values. It goes for all aspects of life that quick moves are attempted whenever circumstances inspire them — as illustrated by the unstable business environment, with the constant abandoning and launching of businesses that came to prevail after the reforms.[10] Few households are content with their current status, as is evident from the unwavering pursuit of divorce from manual labor[11] and social ascendence, which is true of almost all households. Strong competition is seen for what is perceived as a common pool of limited resources: against the background of an unpredictably changing political situation, a higher position is sought in order to increase both the status and the security of the household, since these are perceived to coincide. Moreover, all groups also put great emphasis on the accomplishments of the next generation, a value the reforms have left intact, usually aiming at official employment.

BUREAUCRATIC COMMITMENT

Not only ordinary local citizens resumed activities from before the communist epoch. With the decline of state-sector bonuses in the mid to late 1980s and soaring inflation after 1985, many state employees were heavily hit. Of particular relevance to private business households was the fact that an increasing number of administrative staff, and subsequently entire local bureaus, adopted ways of boosting incomes that were commonly described as "traditional" (*chuantong*). The collection of taxes and levies by the local bureaucracy has again become a subject of controversy in the local community, as was the case in the precommunist era. During the latter half of the 1980s, the number of taxes and levies rose from three or four to approximately ten, and the collected sums increased from an average of 30 yuan per month per household in 1987 to an estimated 100 yuan in 1989. State taxes rose only slightly; local, mainly extralegal, charges made up most of the increase. Private businesses had become the happy hunting ground for officials seeking supplements to their meager official wages, and particularly for bureaus losing out in the new economic order, which sought to redress the balance by imposing new taxes on those unable to defend themselves. In 1991, approximately twenty different taxes and levies were collected, to the bitterness particularly of the smaller business owners (Bruun 1993, 182).

---

10. The average "lifespan" of a household business is hardly more than four to five years (Bruun 1993, ch. 7).

11. For instance, the effort to evade manual labor is expressed in the common proverb, "People who work with their minds rule, people who work with their brawn are ruled" ("Laoxinzhe zhi ren, laolizhe zhi yu ren," a classical epigram by Mencius). Since the saying has strong associative value for common people and has been impossible to eradicate, the Chinese authorities have been much aware of it; see e.g., Hu Yaobang: "an obsolete and wrong way of thinking" (*Renmin ribao*, March 14, 1983).

Bureaucratic authority over the new private entrepreneurs in terms of licenses, protection, and so on is still exclusive, and bureaucratic power is consistently abused.

So what did people do to defend themselves? Complaining to higher-level authorities was out of the question, since these were either unwilling or unable to interfere. Private entrepreneurs are barred from organizing themselves, and exhibit little interest in doing so.[12] However, bureaucratic exploitation of local enterprise is only one side of the story. In fact, the local bureaucracy also offers opportunities for a wide range of ordinary people, who may engage in work for the local bureaucracy in order to obtain privileges, manipulate or negotiate rules, or reduce bureaucratic harassment.

After a decade of reform, the street-level bureaucracy is still a large and complex structure, embracing both salaried formal employees and unsalaried informal assistants and volunteers, whose activities penetrate every aspect of daily life. These latter "petty bureaucrats" receive no regular payment, but they frequently have small monetary benefits from the "social work" (*shehui gongzuo/shehui fuwu*) they perform—for instance, three yuan per day for organizing meetings or a small sum for performing neighborhood committee work. Equipped with a semi-official status, they are an extension of the bureaus, which are already strictly hierarchical. They are employed in all areas of public administration: public security, health and hygiene inspection, all sorts of registration, propaganda, mediation, and taxation. The street committee, neighborhood committees, and Self-employed Laborers' Association are the main institutions for which they work. The street committee has a substantial number of people assisting the regular employees for shorter or longer periods of time—for instance, during campaigns. The neighborhood committees are exclusively manned by volunteers. Each committee, which typically has three to eight members, is in charge of twenty to a hundred households (there are approximately twenty neighborhood committees in Bin Shen). Altogether, an estimated one out of every three households in the area has one or more members with semi-official duties.

Since the street and neighborhood committees are integral parts of the civil administration, with firm control and intimate knowledge of every household under their jurisdiction, these "social workers" (*shehui fuwuzhe*) are indispensable. The simplest tasks of "social work" involve being aware of certain affairs in one's environment, like the cleanliness of streets or courtyards. Others involve a few hours every day, or regular shifts during the night

---

12. Neither could secret societies, guilds, or informal organizations influencing prices be traced in the area. The Self-employed Laborers' Association presumably rests too heavily on all businesses and certainly has the eradication and prevention of all other organizations among its purposes. In 1991, however, criminal gangs attempted to establish themselves in the area.

for those on the public security line, on guard for thieves or irregular activities. Other assistants are fully occupied throughout the day. These are association organizers, tax collectors, and mediators and volunteer workers in the street committee's offices. In practice, they perform the greater part of the actual work in the relationship between the bureaus and the public, and in case of conflict, they tend to act as buffers.

Although this petty bureaucracy carries little significance in the formal structure of the city government, its local political role may be very large. In the case of private enterprise, the petty bureaucracy constitutes a large field of interaction between structurally opposed sectors of the local community. Private entrepreneurs of any scale are members of the Self-employed Laborers' Association (Geti laodongzhe xiehui).[13] The association is divided into branches of businesses, of which some are again divided to reach a convenient size, usually ten to fifteen people. Such groups are endowed with a group head (*zhuren*) and two deputy group heads (*fu zhuren*) responsible to the Industrial and Commercial Administration Bureau (ICB).

Volunteer work as an institution appears deeply embedded in Chinese culture; motivation for engaging in local community life among the elder generation is positive compliance with "tradition" and orthodox thought: an expression of surplus in one's own household that allows for donating one's time and energy to something that, in the phrase of the present leadership, is "to benefit the masses." It may support personal fulfillment and a sense of totality: authority is supposed to be achieved steadily through life, and old age without authority is easily associated with failure. However, since only a small group of old people were brought up before Liberation, the encouragement for continuing such a "tradition" of devoting work to the "common good" must be sought in the conditions of the present social reality. One such condition is the fact that private business people are compelled to collect taxes among themselves. Contrary to regulations stipulating authorized tax officials to do the job, it is the association representatives, or other "volunteers," who do it on their behalf. The officials are thus shielded from charges of extortion when exorbitant taxes are collected. The tax collectors, on the other hand, are granted a certain leniency in the taxation and control of their own businesses, and any collector of levies from their businesses will face colleagues who themselves also serve as petty bureaucrats. For example, a woman running a textile shop, in which two

13. The Self-employed Laborers' Association was established in 1980 as a local initiative on the part of eight hundred businesspeople in Harbin, in northeastern China, and quickly spread to other cities. In the process, the organization metamorphosed: by being incorporated into the formal structure of society, it came under the control of the Industrial and Commercial Administration Bureau, which manned its posts (Yudkin 1986). The association is now a "mass organization" of businesspeople with compulsory membership.

young apprentices from the countryside do the actual work, is occupied with "social work" most of the day. She is at the same time mediator, association representative, and assistant tax collector. Her own business has a registered turnover of a few hundred yuan, which she states yields her a profit of only 100 yuan. When they were alone in the shop, however, her employees inadvertently put her profit at about 1,000 yuan. Similarly, a rural hand takes care of all manual work at a small bakery under the control of the wife of another association representative, who is away most of the day doing various jobs for the association. His business, which supports his household without burdening it with much work, has a registered turnover far lower than its actual level, and the tax is consequently insignificant. This petty official formerly ran a large restaurant in a building that was demolished, and he is awaiting compensation so as to start up elsewhere.

What further adds to the complexity of local bureaucracy is the practice of rotating the posts among volunteers — for instance, as association representatives — thus providing opportunities for a substantial number of people. A representative is "appointed by the ICB and elected by the masses," usually for a three-year period. Some representatives say "everyone has the right to elect, and the right to be elected." Thus everyone without grave conflicts with the bureaucracy has a chance of attaining semibureaucratic status for a three-year term, potentially boosting his or her own business. Volunteers tend to be people over fifty years and supporters of "tradition" in family affairs, but the institution of petty bureaucracy as such reinforces the basic characteristics of political struggle in Bin Shen, which is individualized and oriented toward concrete material benefits. The merging of orthodox thought and tangible benefits is conspicuous: individuals and households performing jobs for the bureaucracy are granted tax reductions, smooth access to licenses, small allowances, and political and economic protection.

From the viewpoint of business people, local bureaucracy is the main opponent of private enterprise. Encroachment on profits and obstruction of the expansion of business is perpetuated by "bureaucrats shielding one another" (*guan guan xiang hu*). Local bureaucracy is a unified structure, in that its departments all operate according to the same conventional, if unwritten, rules and have fairly predictable responses. Yet the local-level administration consists of a series of individual bureaus, which all need to be dealt with separately: the ICB and the Self-employed Laborers' Association, the street committee, the Tax Bureau, and the Public Security Bureau. Informal networks operate around each of them, involving a wide range of people. All politically significant struggle in the local community therefore tends to be absorbed into this vast arena, which ties together the opposing interests of bureaucrats, petty bureaucrats, and entrepreneurs, and within which struggle, negotiation, and compromise take place.

As private business spreads, monetary wealth is playing an increasingly dominant role. Bureaucratic authority has been challenged in this process: changes in the economic base have had a profound impact on the entire institutional setup of the local community by altering the role and authority of some key neighborhood institutions. In Bin Shen, private enterprise rapidly created a powerful Tax Bureau (Shui wu suo), brought considerable authority to the Industrial and Commercial Administration Bureau (Gong shang ju), and reinvigorated the Public Security Bureau (Gongan ju), including local police stations (*pai chu suo*), since the last two began to charge entrepreneurs for maintaining law and order. Those bureaus directly involved in the taxation and control of private enterprises gained significant power, easily transformed into monetary benefits. On the other hand, the street committee (*jiedao weiyuanhui*), formerly a stronghold of party interests and a linchpin of neighborhood governance (see Whyte and Parish 1984), encountered a decline in its authority: partly owing to the central government's deliberate attempt to reduce party power, partly because the street committees were only granted a minor role in the economic revival. Except for certifying the identity and formal status of applicants for business licenses, all responsibility for private and collective enterprise has been placed with the ICB, in principle reporting directly to the government.

Cooperation between various departments of the local administration has become increasingly problematic. The tremendous size of the local administration itself suggests a need for rationalizing, especially where local bureaus work in related fields, carrying out similar central-government programs aimed at job creation, education, or the control of individual businesses. Faced with this prospect, local departments, prominently including the street committee and the ICB, are competing to maintain their authority in a struggle between the party and the civil administration.[14] The authority of the one over the other has very concrete implications. After 1987, the central government repeatedly emphasized the correct classification of private businesses into either smaller "individual households" (*geti hu*) or larger "private enterprises" (*siying qiye*), which had not been implemented by local authorities. In 1991, the street committee and the ICB were pressured to comply. The two bodies reacted by registering the larger enterprises as "collective" rather than "private," because in such an arrangement a percentage of the turnover is usually procured by a local bureau in return for the favor. However, the street committee and the ICB disputed which of them was to be responsible for these enterprises, with the result that the larger business owners were able to play the two off against each other and thus remained "individual households," until at least the next round of rectification.

14. In 1987 and 1988, several central-government initiatives were aimed at separating party and state interests in administration — for instance, the August 1, 1988, proclamation to abolish party cells in every ministry under the state council (see, e.g., Manoharan 1990).

COLLECTIVE PASSIVE RESISTANCE

Apart from themselves engaging in efforts to work for the bureaucracy for advantages, entrepreneurs may use passive resistance. In 1988, the Public Security Bureau's new "security charge" met considerable resistance; the charge was felt to be both unfair and blatantly illegal, since people were asked to pay for what the Public Security Bureau was already supposed to have been funded for. A number of the more outspoken and articulate shopkeepers confronted the collectors — for example, by arguing that when anything was stolen, the bureau usually remained passive — and bargained the charge down. Apparently, social position became a distinguishing feature in the actual amounts paid, since the better-educated, who would point out media proclamations about the need to promote the individual economy, frequently got away with lower charges. When word spread, however, the charge was soon resisted by the majority of shopkeepers. Realizing the scale of the protests, the Public Security Bureau retreated. The bureau's original claim was twenty-five yuan per month (at that time, state taxes averaged forty yuan per month), but it was lowered to fifteen yuan per business household. The amounts paid varied greatly, however, and after the crushing of the uprising of 1989, which inspired more cautiousness on both sides, the charge fell to approximately twenty-five yuan every three months.

In early 1989, the introduction of a new charge after a series of others, an "education fee" paid to municipal authorities, was simply resisted by many business people. Word quickly traveled that some had refused to pay, and most others followed. To meet the challenge, the Self-employed Laborers' Association called a general meeting.[15] The association's claim to be the business people's own mass organization is contradicted by the conduct of such assemblies, as in the case of one I witnessed (see Bruun 1993, 119–20).

All shopkeepers were summoned to a meeting to be held at 9 A.M. in a large tea salon on the first floor of a state restaurant on a main street, 500 meters from the Bin Shen area, which had no accommodation of this size. It was a gray, dreary hall, with a dirty concrete floor, hard wooden benches, and no decoration on the old walls, which badly needed paint. The association treated everyone to tea, served by a grubby old employee from the

---

15. Monthly meetings are held in all groups, and in addition regular assemblies are held for the whole Bin Shen area. Participation is compulsory for all shopkeepers, who are here informed of government policies, new regulations concerning private business, and new taxes and charges by the ICB. These meetings are considered the basis of the political education given to shopkeepers. When the central government demands that the masses study certain topics, as was the case in 1988, when all were to "study the law," and in 1989, when political study classes were reestablished, the association is the organization through which individual households are reached.

restaurant below. The business people started coming in around nine, one by one or in small groups, engaged in animated conversation about business affairs. Many were late for the meeting, and even after its start, several groups of young people lingered near the entrance, refusing to sit down in front, where the speakers could be heard. Out of the roughly 250 people obliged to attend, about 170 actually appeared. And it quickly became evident that many shopkeepers had sent substitutes: elderly grandparents, spouses, sons and daughters, distant relatives, and even employees were numerous; actual shopkeepers probably made up only a small minority of the participants. Especially those in the larger businesses were nowhere to be seen. The main topic of the meeting was the introduction of the education fee, a compulsory one-time sum to be paid by all citizens in Chengdu. The organizers of the meeting talked at length about the necessity of this charge. The main speaker at the meeting was a Mr. Wei, an individual shopkeeper who had been promoted to volunteer for the West City level of the ICB. For half an hour, he spoke wholeheartedly about the need to educate the young and with equal enthusiasm asked the shopkeepers not only to pay the compulsory charge but even to exceed it.[16] While he talked, people were yawning, chatting, and walking in and out of the lavatory; their attitude collectively expressed the triviality of these matters, as new charges were constantly being introduced. Many had placed themselves behind pillars or in distant corners of the room, where they could not possibly follow the speeches. After Wei had finished his monologue, he rushed off to repeat his performance in another area. A local representative took over, but some shopkeepers had already started leaving before the show ended. "Time is money in private business," as one of the youths near the entrance said, using an entirely new phrase, taken from newspaper accounts of the capitalist West.

All such meetings in the local community consist exclusively of one-way communication, in the sense that only one view is propagated from the platform. Comments from the floor or open criticism are unheard of. Yet in this case the absent-minded participants created an atmosphere clearly expressive of their opinion and their degree of tolerance in the matter in question, turning the meeting into a trial of strength. The collective resistance to the new charge resulted in the compulsory sum being lowered, whereafter everyone paid. At these meetings, the association representatives are all dressed as cadres in gray or blue suits, clearly distinguishable from the individual shopkeepers. The prestige gained from performing these semi-official duties is of a kind that may allow for conversion. As one of the

16. Articles were simultaneously published in a local newspaper about (unnamed) shopkeepers donating large sums of money for this purpose (e.g., *Chengdu wanbao*, April 13, 1989).

shopkeepers put it: "Yes, it gives them a certain prestige, but they also do it to protect their own businesses. You cannot criticize officials. If we criticized an official, we would not be able to face him afterward, even these small ones."

SYSTEMATIZED EXCHANGES BETWEEN BUSINESS AND BUREAUCRACY

The coordination between the central government and the bureaucratic institutions is hardly more than desultory.[17] Judging from local experience, the implementation of central policies is highly selective, since the leading local actors are preoccupied with framing of evolution in coordinating their interests. From the grass-roots perspective, a precondition for even the state's limited control of the local bureaucracy appears to be the maintenance of exchange relations, securing extralegal privileges for the officials. Petty officialdom is important in this game, since it enters into a long series of exchanges at the lowest level. The system transmits two currents. Loyalty and expression of conformity travel upward, while the countercurrent is one of privileges — administrative freedom that is easily converted into material benefits. Successive levels of the bureaucracy employ similar means to secure their positions, turning the power structure of the local community away from any legal order, in which individuals are equally positioned. Moreover, there are both top- and bottom-level interests in safeguarding bureaucratic power. Because political and material pursuits are openly allowed to coincide, bureaucracy becomes an instrument for broad interests stretching across conventional boundaries.

The vast majority of private enterprises do not depend on the local bureaucracy for anything other than registration. The vast field of interchange is caused by the interest that the bureaucracy takes in private business. Various means to protect a thriving business against infringement exist. The orthodox strategy, to become a petty bureaucrat, tended to be used mainly by the smaller business owners. The large business owners, however, had easier access to privilege through the establishment of regular alliances with powerful officials.

In both an abstract and a material sense, exchange relations between private business and local officials appear to be firmly institutionalized. Restaurant owners had by far the highest earnings in the area, with monthly profits ranging from 1,000 to 5,000 yuan, and they routinely offered free meals to officials from local bureaus in an attempt to win their goodwill.

---

17. On the basis of material from Wenzhou, Zhejiang province, Liu 1992 introduces the concept of the "sporadic totalitarian state" to account for the local leadership taking the law into their own hands when liberalizing the economy.

Conversely, many officials occasionally simply demanded huge meals free of charge. Of greater impact, however, are cash payments to emissaries of the pertinent bureaus. The bigger businesses are generally able to reach agreements on taxation far lower than their estimated legal obligations. I estimate that these businesses pay tax on only half of their turnover. Indisputably, it is the state that loses out in the trade-off between big businesses and the local bureaucrats. In terms of additional charges, the large businesses are favored even more. They generally spend equal sums on state taxes and local charges, whereas the smaller businesses tend to spend twice as much on local charges as on state taxes.

Alliances between entrepreneurs and officials tend to be unstable and shifting, however. Relations tend to be focused on cash payments or goods given to officials, who either show an openness to such offerings or explicitly demand them in exchange for a friendly handling of the business owners' affairs. Since cooperation among different departments of the local administration tends to be minimal, a business owner can rarely count on a friendly official in one bureau to smooth relations with other bureaus. Thus the entire structure of local administration tends to create an array of casual alliances (which the business owners can only hope will be effective) and depress the development of an extensive, powerful organization across institutional and occupational boundaries.

In the 1980s, new social hierarchies were generated spontaneously. The notion of hierarchical positions now penetrates every aspect of private business. Despite the fact that private entrepreneurs are regarded as belonging to the lowest social stratum by the general populace, evident status differences are found within the private sector itself. Internally, each business displays a strongly hierarchical organization, with labor being distributed according to kinship relations, gender, and place of birth. Among owners, there is a strong avoidance of manual labor, and of any responsibility except for guarding the cash box and perhaps long-term planning, in an attempt to compensate for an inferior social standing. Conspicuous consumption among private business people is equally prominent. Moreover, testifying to the fact that exchange relations are more complex than payments in cash and kind is the fact that there is sharp competition to attract customers with high social standing. Restaurants, for example, solicit banquets held by officials or other important figures. In Bin Shen, actors and celebrities from the nearby Sichuan television station were also targeted restaurant customers, as were rich Taiwanese tourists. Similar considerations were evident in other businesses: a dealer in second-hand books, for instance, found it more worthwhile to sell a certain book to a scholar than to a commoner, irrespective of price, and a private doctor would prefer prominent patients anytime; apparently, such business can better satisfy the business owners' own aspirations to upward mobility.

BUILDING AND MANIPULATING AUTHORITY

Central-government politics form a basis for power by providing the abstract authoritarian rhetoric needed to establish powerful positions, which are duplicated down through the bureaucratic institutions.[18] The actual exercise of power in Bin Shen, however, is largely unaffected by official state ideologies. Bureaucratic office is perceived as an individual privilege by officials and subjects alike. Entrepreneurs never attempted to use their association to articulate or enforce their rights. The charismatic officeholders somehow earn the respect of all, disregarding their means, since might is usually right. The persistence of established practices has hitherto been silently accepted by higher levels of the state bureaucracy, presumably as a prerequisite for maintaining national integration. Grave cases have been attacked by the central government and also given much publicity,[19] but national policy and everyday practice differ. In a local community such as Bin Shen, the numerous rectification campaigns are merely faint signals. Local power is personalized to a degree where the law is identical with the officials in power, and legality is their specific way of employing personal power. The scope of private entrepreneurship is thus laid down by the practice of local bureaus, which are more concerned with "fairness" than legality. The concept of "fair treatment" (*zhengdang*) is in fact far more commonly used than references to law. Some local officials admitted that these were common principles. When asked about the legality of some of the charges extracted from individual businesses, the head of the ICB local office answered after some contemplation: "I don't think it is a question of whether they are legal [*hefa*] (since this could not be determined), but if they are reasonable [*heli*]." Since the legal foundation for fiscal practices is weak, the struggle is over the amounts paid rather than interpretation of legal codes. Bureaucracy poses a financial obstacle to business, but it is counted as an inevitable overhead.

A theme that permeates all struggle in the local community is the display of conformity. Whether genuine or feigned for strategic purposes, conformity in the outer appearance of things belongs to the shared values of social thought, to some degree resting on a broad, unverbalized consensus. It belongs to "tradition" or the "nature of things," something that can be manipulated, but nevertheless makes up the common platform of public behavior. Fundamental to the display of conformity is the submission to

18. Formal language draws on the morality of central authorities. In this respect, the Confucian tradition, described as "the doctrine of the exemplary center" (e.g., Geertz 1980, 13–15) is continued in the communist moralizing authorities (e.g., Pye 1988), and the state is thus built on moral, rather than legal, order.

19. *Renmin ribao*, September 6, 1989, mentioned, however, that the main fiscal problem was not the rate structure but the administration and collection of taxes.

authority, in domestic affairs as obedience to family elders and in external relations as the recognition of bureaucratic power. This assures those above that their authority can be transformed into privileges, and it provides those below with a recognizable procedure for their own struggle.

Old proverbs and expressions for the administrators' abuse of power are nevertheless many. They stress their lack of morals, ruthlessness, and covetousness. "The officials burn houses, while commoners are not permitted to burn oil lamps." They are the "uncrowned kings" who "divide and rule"; and "when the gods fight, the people suffer." Officials are even compared to old-style landlords in connection with oppressive taxes: "to work for Master Liu" means to work without getting the fruits of your own labor.[20] A long-standing post-Liberation proverb, "The Nationalist party [Guomindang] imposed many taxes; the Communist party [Gongchandang] imposes many meetings," has recently been amended to "the Communist party imposes many taxes and many meetings."

Paralleling conformity within the household, which is tied to respect for authority, conformity in communal affairs revolves around the simultaneous recognition and manipulation of bureaucratic authority. Notwithstanding a certain resistance in recent years, by far the greatest number of shopkeepers still accept and submit to the unwritten codes of the local community. The disciplinary effects of bureaucratic power are obvious, although it is often exercised for purposes other than those intended by the Communist party and government. Ideological control of business people is attempted through the association but carried out by officials not motivated by ideological concerns.

The strategies that individual households adopt toward local bureaucracy are ambiguous. There are certain patterns in these strategies — either conformity and the pursuit of privilege by following the rules set by those in office or, at the other extreme, trying to avoid all personalized relations. This was attempted by a few successful entrepreneurs in the area, who consistently alluded to central-government policies, but the heavy pressure local bureaucrats put on anyone with ample economic resources made it exceedingly difficult. The highly esteemed conformity within the local community means following the rule of custom, rather than the rule of law.

Ideological control over activities of no direct interest to the bureaucracy is indeed limited. The severe shortage of housing and steadily increasing rents are a constant source of exploitation among ordinary people. Landlords frequently break contracts and evict shopkeepers when they get better offers, and the letting of dwellings to private businesspeople is also surrounded by cool calculation. Many incidents were reported of landlords continually

20. Master Liu, a wealthy landlord outside Chengdu, was famous for forcing peasants to work without pay. Now the expression is used of the "people above."

raising the rent, and some even demanded to become full partners in their tenants' businesses, which implied receiving 50 percent of the profits. Such private arrangements are of no interest to the local administration. "Big fish eat small fish, small fish eat shrimp" is a pertinent colloquial expression.

BUREAUCRACY'S IMPACT: OBSTRUCTION OR PROMOTION OF BUSINESS?

Local bureaucratic departments play a considerable position role in defining the bounds for the registration, regulation, and expansion of the private sector. Up to a certain point in time, the three bureaus most important to business — that is, the ICB, street committee, and Tax Bureau — were rated very differently by businesspeople in regard to their attitudes. Being most positive and posing fewer problems, the ICB was to some degree considered a support to businesspeople. In the late 1980s, however, when officials' wages were seriously undermined, this bureau was seen to engage more routinely in the extraction of extralegal fees for issuing and renewing licenses. After 1989, when the entire institutional setup was shaken by popular protests nationwide, the three bureaus were no longer seen to differ. The entire administration was thus as far removed as ever from one based on law.

The two sides followed similar practices: illegal in relation to the "law" as defined by the central government, yet enjoying "conditional acceptance" from the other party. Almost any business practice seems possible if adequately paid for. The reputation for cheating, selling fakes, and so on that the private sector has gained among many ordinary citizens has been steadily nourished by some of its unscrupulous representatives. Many restaurants, for instance, use cooking oil mixed with the oil extracted from pig skin, which is highly unsuitable for consumption, and everybody knows it. Stalls openly sell illegal copies of cassette tapes of famous stars, but the low price matches their quality. Illegal activities are most commonly restrained, not by local authority, but by the immense caution exhibited by customers. Few permanent shops can survive on inferior goods or service. People usually watch out for traveling salesmen, since their tricks are numerous and often sophisticated. Some sell fake medicinal herbs, only staying in the area for a few days before moving on (all sorts of swindlers and con men disappeared for a long period after June 1989). One traveling salesman, a gifted speaker, sold a bicycle-polishing liquid consisting of vinegar and red coloring in fancy-looking bottles. Its effect was limited, and after a few days everyone knew it. Still, he was able to talk strangers passing down the street into buying the stuff, often to the amusement of the nearby shopkeepers, and he made a good profit in spite of being taxed heavily by the collector in the street.

Several shops in Bin Shen sold or processed goods and materials that could not possibly be bought legally by individual households. A local traditional water-pipe workshop molded pipe bodies in a chromium alloy that was in very short supply and only distributed to key state industries. It was procured from a factory in large amounts by a relative and declared to be scrap metal; the finished water pipe sold at a price apparently lower than the world market value of the solid material used. A producer of plastic containers bought his raw materials, also monopolized by the state, through channels that "take a lot more than just good *guanxi*." Another shop sold clothes made for export by a state factory. They were sold on commission for a neighbor who had relatives working at the factory in question. A smithy, on the other hand, could not buy sheet metal at the price determined by the state wholesale department; since it was in high demand, the state shop sold it at a negotiated price (approximately double), making a huge profit. Cigarette sellers in the street have for years openly traded foreign cigarettes purchased on the black market, often connected to illegal money-changing with foreigners.

When confronted with such irregularities, the local bureaucracy remains passive. If it acts, it is only to secure a share of the profit gained through illegal means. While the Tax Bureau denies involvement, its petty officials disclose the practice: in the local free market, the volunteer tax collector willingly admitted that assessments were not made solely according to turnover. The Tax Bureau also embraced "cooperativeness," which in this context may be a way of recognizing local authority; "and if any of them carry out illegal trade we charge them extra—if, for instance, they pump up chickens with water or sell products of inferior quality—in these cases, the tax can be as high as 30 percent of turnover, depending on their political attitude, their agreement with government policies and attitude toward us" (Bruun 1993, 123).

Complaints from people who have been cheated are generally futile. Disputes between residents in the area are mostly sorted out by the volunteer mediators, and only grave cases are transferred to the Bureau of Public Security; this is another example of how petty officials operate as buffers. Cases involving strangers are rarely investigated, as the local public security office claims to lack the power and personnel to operate across administrative boundaries. This was the case when a young woman, who had just started her shop after being unemployed for a number of years, was cheated by two strangers. One day someone posing as a small peasant came to her shop in order to sell her a small quantity of "lotus-root flour," telling her that it was becoming increasingly popular for cooking. He persuaded her to buy a single packet, just to see if she was able to sell it. The next day another man walked by. As he passed her shop, he cried out in joy, pointing to her lotus-root flour. "I have been looking for this for ages," he said. "Can you get me some more? I want to buy a lot." The third day the "small peasant" came back and supplied her with the quantity specified. The woman was stuck with the useless "flour" and lost all her savings. The public security office merely suggested that she be more careful in the future. Similarly, ordinary thefts reported by shopkeepers were rarely investigated.

FORMAL VERSUS INFORMAL HIERARCHIES

The revival of markets and private enterprise and the reduced social control that resulted gave rise to a new set of relations between bureaucracy and private enterprise that were widely recognized on both sides. Both parties reacted to the new sector with self-consciously traditional calculation. How much can a cow be milked? How much can a cart be loaded without killing the horse? Private businesspeople took approaches equally rooted in an earlier era: making optimal use of all household members' positions, paying off officials, doing "social work" to attain privileges, and so on. The two sides shared a strong aversion to the "unknown" — especially intervention in local affairs by higher-level government authorities. In spite of their conflicts, business and bureaucracy had a common interest in resolving conflict locally. History showed external forces to be the most dangerous — when businesses were collectivized on Beijing's orders in the 1950s, businesspeople were deprived of their means of subsistence, and everyone was gradually impoverished. Local people also recalled both the Great Leap Forward, which led to the depression and famine known as the Three Hard Years in 1959–61, when almost every local family experienced deaths, and the atrocities of the centrally ignited Cultural Revolution, when private business was again damned and scapegoated.[21]

The central government's "class struggle" has given way to a struggle over the division of the new material wealth, and over who should "get rich first."[22] With the greater economic opportunities, social hierarchies in the local community became increasingly conspicuous, since power now brought real wealth. Formal authority thus gained importance in the local community, since it could easily be capitalized on through extralegal taxation. The new material means substantiated and invigorated personal followings within the formal structure, which were extended downward by the

21. Almost half of the elderly people in Bin Shen who have returned to private businesses since the reforms told of being seriously molested during the Cultural Revolution: they were dragged through the streets with caps and signs, kicked and beaten up, stabbed with knives, imprisoned, humiliated, and so forth, many to a degree causing permanent physical or mental disablement.

22. This is a far cry from what *Renmin ribao* declared on March 30, 1985, on behalf of the party cadres: "In the situation where some people get rich first and the rest get rich later, in order to let the masses get rich first, we are willing to wait to get rich later. If this may be said to be losing out, then this loss is necessary. If this may be said to be a sacrifice, then this sacrifice is glorious."

involvement of petty officials. Within departments of the local bureaucracy, systems to redistribute locally generated wealth according to rank were either established or strengthened. Although some of the levies extracted from private businesses may be appropriated directly by a particular bureaucrat, a large income is frequently distributed to all officials according to rank within the bureau. Petty bureaucracy apparently also provided its clients with advantages besides political protection.

Considerable wealth was created in private business, enabling some large entrepreneurs to build enterprises with a number of employees, and to bind smaller business owners to them through loans and connections. Private business has developed a clear internal status order, both within the household and in labor relations, where social status carries increasing weight; employers and employees often belong to clearly distinguishable social strata.

The reforms have clearly created alternative career opportunities. Moreover, private business may be seen as the structural continuation of a prerevolutionary informal hierarchy:[23] as its only role is to create wealth, it stands in strong opposition to the bureaucracy, for which political authority and privilege are primary.

State employment and private enterprise may be identified as dual career tracks: "two streams" (*liangge chuan*) that constitute opposed, or competing, routes by which to attain the household's collective ambitions, social ascendence and material satisfaction. One presupposes education, the other skills and ingenuity. One is the ideal approach, the other pragmatic. One is the conventional, the other unorthodox and generally debased. They coincide in treating the attainment of superior positions within hierarchical structures as an important means, either to privileged, formal authority or to informal power based on material wealth. Both are characterized by their principals' undisputed authority and stretch downward into meticulously defined positions. They generate equally coveted values in accordance with Chinese ideals of the good life. It is significant that a sense of "totality" is reached only when they are yoked. A central concern to households is the transfer of surplus from one side to the other: the conversion of material wealth into the education of children, positions of status and authority into material benefits, and so on. For obvious reasons, many households in the contemporary Chinese city aim at connections with both spheres by having members both in government jobs and in some sort of business, or in a position combining the two.

Numerous writers, both Chinese and foreign, still envisage the transformation of Chinese society in terms of the growth of horizontal ties among

---

23. See, e.g., Adshead 1985 on the dual hierarchical structure in Sichuan around 1900. Others have argued that in late imperial China public associations may have evolved without civic power being turned against the state (e.g., Huang 1991, 320c).

ordinary citizens.[24] Yet nothing in my fieldwork indicated attempts by small business people to form alliances and defend their rights, or efforts by the employees in the larger businesses to organize for better wages and working conditions. When we view politics at the level of the local community, there is little evidence of class or group struggle, or abstract ideologies.

While there obviously are differences of interest, it would be grossly misleading to distinguish between business and bureaucracy as separate classes, strata, or underprivileged/elite groups, defending particularistic interests, or espousing radically differing outlooks, since, in drawing a line, such authority is hardly representative of any distinct pattern of behavior as compared to that of the new entrepreneurs, but rather denotes a structurally different institution from a common hold of exchange relations. The connection between the accumulation of capital and the subsequent pursuit of formal status in defense of the gains shows the importance of collective household strategies with respect, for instance, to occupational affiliation.

In a comparative perspective, it seems that anthropological fieldworkers have registered significant "class consciousness" among workers neither in Hong Kong nor in Taiwan. For example, Taiwanese factory women's "perceptions of work . . . involve factors that go beyond the nature of the tasks they perform; and the satisfactions that they find in work derive in large part from the social context they themselves create" (Kung 1981, 209). Usually, such work is regarded as merely an intermediate stage toward a broader family goal (Niehoff 1987). In Bin Shen, businesspeople would cooperate with bureaucrats well aware that this is highly detrimental to their own common group interests. Theories of unconscious subjugation to political domination through formalization of power (e.g., Bloch 1975) appear absurd when one considers both the conscious political actions involved in local petty bureaucracy and the calculating ideologies in the economic field. Answers must be sought in terms of a cultural disposition in favor of vertical rather than horizontal loyalties. The spontaneous creation of local social hierarchies results from the type of loyalties embedded in paternalism, which is consciously reproduced or further developed through the practice of *guanxi* cultivation, and a strong element of conscious competition is ever present (see, e.g., Walder 1983, 1986).

CONCLUSION

In the modernizing Chinese urban areas, all forms of private business play crucial roles in providing "space" for the formation of new ideologies and fa-

24. This is often inspired by Chinese official designation: in 1989, for example, the Chinese media singled out individual business households as a new "middle class" (*zhongchan jieji*) (*Renmin ribao* August 22, 1989).

cilitate the spontaneous development of new forms of social organization.[25] In this respect, private business has the potential for accomplishing what mass campaigns earlier aimed at in the field of modernizing social institutions but were never able to carry through. However, the growth of individual business itself is more truly depicted as an effect of economic and political circumstances, calling for new solutions, rather than an expression of essentially changing values or a growing societal force turned against the state.

After the reforms, business and bureaucracy spontaneously developed into the main political forces in the local community. At least on the surface, however, there is a remarkable consensus on basic ideals in both these sectors, stretching across different social strata: the powerful aspirations of the Chinese household toward ascendence in a total sense, combined with established notions of a given social order, generate dual sources of values and aspirations. Basic social orientations perhaps necessitate a dual hierarchical structure as their counterpart in order to be fully played out. The respective sectors do not determine the individual's identity and permanent economic affiliation.[26] Conformity implies a profound duality: it is the conscious balancing of seemingly contradictory endeavors, and certainly taking care never to reach out too far in any direction. Thus business and bureaucracy reconstituted themselves as complementary strategies, equally known and established in the urban community.

Correspondingly, although the setting in which basic political relations operate has evidently changed, there are reasons to believe that local communities have the potential to reach a new state of balance between political forces, in which certain fundamental values are preserved. Among these are the social prestige derived from official employment, the debasement of small private enterprise, and the household's pursuit of totality in the sense of combined social standing and material wealth.

In the absence of representative democracy and struggle over abstract political issues, bureaucracy as an institution remains the focus of all formal power in the local community. With the emergence of private enterprise as a new source of material wealth, a potential for widened and diversified

25. The stem family, comprising three or more generations under one roof, still serves as the model, at least for the older generation, and is the axis around which variation revolves. Even so, "stem family" describes less than 50 percent of households. Wealthier households exhibit a higher degree of compliance with tradition, but historically, the notion that in earlier times most Chinese lived in large or joint families has been discredited. Apparently, considerable deviation occurred (see, e.g., Hsu 1948), with the "family" varying in both residential patterns and internal economic ties (see, e.g., Cohen 1970), and sometimes consisting merely of a "social unit" without a single set of family relations among its members; profound adaptability is evident (see, e.g., Croll 1987). For a discussion of change in family-continuation patterns, see Whyte 1990.

26. For historical accounts of the perception of social mobility, see Ho 1962; Hu 1933; Kuhn 1984.

political power was created. Judging from the experience in Bin Shen, however, it also created a new interest in local bureaucracy among businesspeople, since the benefits from connections to bureaucratic office tend to be widely dispersed through an informal system of services and rewards. Since street-level bureaucracy is so firmly rooted in history and ideology, it appears to remain qualitatively unchanged by the switch to a market economy. The individual departments have clearly gained greater freedom from their superior institutions through exchanges with and extortion of private business, offering their officials a share of the increased wealth, particularly in urban areas. So even after a critical period of change, it is still worthwhile to be a Chinese official, and in this position at least formally to work to maintain the political status quo.

We should be careful when interpreting changes in Chinese local communities in terms of universalistic concepts, or Western concepts that have a radically different reading when used rhetorically by the Chinese state. Learning from derailed debates on class struggle, revolutions, and modes of production, we should avoid a blinding new conceptualization of Chinese society to make it fit into universalistic categories, created by a sociology molded by analysis of Western revolutionary processes, and thus far more concentrated on prophecies of change than evaluations of continuity.

When investigating the Chinese political process on the level of basic social institutions and political practices, one observes mainly individualized, concrete actions. The individual action gains its political momentum not by itself, however, but through its endless duplication by others, reckoning on "safety in numbers." Within such a system, people will usually either comply with the established order or seek to topple it. The situation I have described may reflect a fundamental political process, which Chinese public authorities at all levels must comply with. For the system to be coherent, the Chinese state must to a large extent absorb, articulate, and reflect common people's values, orientations, and visions. Although local studies like the present one do not permit predictions about the Chinese state, they may nonetheless be indicative of fluctuations in the Chinese national order. The picture of the Chinese state as a repressive, authoritarian, and largely external power defending party-elite interests, in constant danger of being overthrown by "society," is hard to square with the structure of the local community observed in this chapter. One effect of the prevailing hierarchical relations at the local level is that authorities tend to be replaced, not by their opposites, but by their duplicates.

REFERENCES

Adshead, S. A. M. 1985. *Province and Politics in Late Imperial China. Viceregal Government in Szechwan, 1898–1911*. London: Curzon Press.

Bloch, Maurice. 1975. *Political Language and Oratory in Traditional Societies.* London: Academic Press.

Bruun, Ole. 1988. *The Reappearance of the Family as an Economic Unit: A Sample Survey of Individual Households in Workshop Production and Crafts, Chengdu, Sichuan Province, China.* Copenhagen: Center for East and Southeast Asian Studies.

————. 1993. *Business and Bureaucracy in a Chinese City: The Ethnography of Individual Business Households in Contemporary China.* Berkeley: Institute of East Asian Studies, University of California.

Chan, Anita, Richard Madsen, and Jonathan Unger. 1984. *Chen Village: The Recent History of a Peasant Community in Mao's China.* Berkeley and Los Angeles: University of California Press.

Chengdu wanbao, April 13, 1989.

Cohen, Myron L. 1970. "Developmental Process in the Chinese Domestic Group." In *Family and Kinship in Chinese Society,* ed. Maurice Freedman, 21–36. Stanford, Calif.: Stanford University Press.

Croll, Elisabeth. 1987. "New Peasant Family Forms in Rural China." *Journal of Peasant Studies* 14, 4: 485–96.

Geertz, Clifford. 1980. *Negara: The Theatre State in Nineteenth-Century Bali.* Princeton, N.J.: Princeton University Press.

Gold, Thomas B. 1989. "Urban Private Business in China." *Studies in Comparative Communism* 22, 2–3: 187–201.

————. 1990. "Urban Private Business and Social Change." In *China on the Eve of Tiananmen: The Impact of Reform,* eds. Deborah Davis and Ezra F. Vogel, 157–78. Cambridge, Mass.: Harvard University Council on East Asian Studies.

Hankiss, Elemer. 1988. "The "Second Society": Is There an Alternative Model Emerging in Hungary?" *Social Research* 55, 1–2: 13–42.

Hershkovitz, Linda. 1985. "The Fruits of Ambivalence: China's Urban Individual Economy." *Pacific Affairs* 58, 3: 427–50.

Hinton, William. 1966. *Fanshen: A Documentary of Revolution in a Chinese Village.* New York: Monthly Review Press.

Ho Ping-ti. 1962. *The Ladder of Success in Imperial China: Aspects of Social Mobility, 1368–1911.* New York: Da Capo Press. Reprint, 1976.

Hsu, Francis L. K. 1948. *Under the Ancestors' Shadow: Chinese Culture and Personality.* New York: Columbia University Press.

Hu Shi. 1933. *The Chinese Renaissance.* New York: Da Capo Press. Reprint, 1963.

Huang, Philip C. C. 1991. "The Paradigmatic Crisis in Chinese Studies: Paradoxes in Social and Economic History." *Modern China* 17, 3: 299–341.

Kraus, Willy. 1991. *Private Business in China: Revival Between Ideology and Pragmatic Policy.* London: Hurst.

Kuhn, Philip A. 1984. "Chinese Views of Social Classification." In *Class and Social Stratification in Post-Revolution China,* ed. J. L. Watson, 16–28. London: Cambridge University Press.

Kung, Lydia. 1981. "Perceptions of Work Among Factory Women." In *The Anthropology of Taiwanese Society,* ed. Emily Martin Ahern and Hill Gates, 184–211. Stanford, Calif.: Stanford University Press.

Liu, Yia-ling. 1992. "Reform from Below: The Private Economy and Local Politics in the Rural Industrialization of Wenzhou." *China Quarterly*, no. 130 (June): 293–316.

Ma Jisen. 1988. "A General Survey of the Resurgence of the Private Sector of China's Economy." *Social Sciences in China*, no. 3 (September): 78–92.

Manoharan, Thiagarajan. 1990. "Basic Party Units and Decentralized Development." *Copenhagen Papers in East and Southeast Asian Studies*, no. 5: 113–36.

Mosher, Stephen. 1983. *Broken Earth: The Rural Chinese*. New York: Free Press.

Nee, Victor. 1991. "Social Inequalities in Reforming State Socialism: Between Redistribution and Markets in China." *American Sociological Review* 56, 3: 267–82.

Niehoff, Justin D. 1987. "The Villager as Industrialist: Ideologies of Household Manufacturing in Rural Taiwan." *Modern China* 13, 3: 278–309.

Odgaard, Ole. 1992. "Entrepreneurs and Elite Formation in Rural China." *Australian Journal of Chinese Affairs*, no. 28 (July): 89–108.

Potter, Sulamith Heins. 1983. "The Position of Peasants in Modern China's Social Order." *Modern China* 9, 4: 465–99.

Pye, Lucian W. 1988. *The Mandarin and the Cadre: China's Political Cultures*. Ann Arbor: University of Michigan Center for Chinese Studies.

Rosen, Stanley, ed. 1987–88. "The Private Economy." Parts 1 and 2. *Chinese Economic Studies*, 21, 1–2.

Song Bing. 1992. "The Reform of Mainland China's Cadre System: Establishing a Civil Service." *Issues and Studies* 28, 10: 22–43.

Szelényi, Iván. 1988. *Socialist Entrepreneurs: Embourgeoisement in Rural Hungary*. Madison: University of Wisconsin Press.

Taubman, Wolfgang, and Thomas Heberer. 1988. "Die Städtische Privatwirtschaft in der VR China—Second Economy zwischen Markt und Plan." *Bremer Beiträge zur Geographie und Raumplanung*, no. 14. University of Bremen.

Walder, Andrew. 1983. "Organized Dependency and Cultures of Authority in Chinese Industry." *Journal of Asian Studies* 43, 1: 51–76.

———. 1986. *Communist Neo-Traditionalism: Work and Authority in Chinese Industry*. Berkeley and Los Angeles: University of California Press.

Whyte, Martin King. 1990. "Changes in Mate Choice in Chengdu." In *China on the Eve of Tiananmen: The Impact of Reform*, eds. Deborah Davis and Ezra F. Vogel, 181–213. Cambridge, Mass.: Harvard University Council on East Asian Studies.

Whyte, Martin King, and William L. Parish. 1984. *Urban Life in Contemporary China*. Chicago: University of Chicago Press.

Young, Susan. 1989. "Policy, Practice and the Private Sector in China." *Australian Journal of Chinese Affairs*, no. 21 (January): 57–80.

Yudkin, Marcia. 1986. *Making Good: Private Business in Socialist China*. Beijing: Foreign Languages Press.

PART FOUR

Power and Identity in Communities

EIGHT

Everyday Power Relations:
Changes in a North China Village

Yunxiang Yan

In assessing the political consequences of departures from central planning, a key concern is the impact of market-oriented reforms on power relations within socialist redistributive systems. Iván Szelényi's work (1978, 1988) on social stratification in Hungary implies that the power and privilege of socialist redistributors will be undermined by the introduction of market mechanisms. Inspired by Szelényi's insight, Victor Nee (1989) developed a theory of market transition. The core of Nee's theory is that the increased scope of market allocation reduces the scope of bureaucratic redistribution, eroding the power and privilege of officials, who lose their monopoly over resources. This theory has, however, encountered much contrary evidence of the continuing influence of communist cadres at all levels. Jean Oi has proposed an alternative account that emphasizes the cadres' economic role in industrializing villages as the main root of both corruption and their legal power and privilege. She maintains that market allocation in an unreformed political system creates new opportunities for patronage and corruption, altering, but not diminishing, the power and privilege of officials who deal regularly with ordinary citizens (Oi 1989a, 1989b).

Focusing on everyday power relations in a north China village, the present study addresses the same issue, but offers a perspective different from either of the two abovementioned theories. According to Max Weber, power is "the probability that one actor within a social relationship will be in a position to carry out his own will despite resistance, regardless of the basis

This paper is based on field research in 1991 supported by National Science Foundation grant number BNS-9101369. I owe thanks to James L. Watson, the participants of the conference at Arden Homestead, especially Andrew Walder, and an anonymous reviewer for helpful comments on earlier drafts. I am also grateful to Matthew Kohrman for editorial assistance. —YY.

on which this probability rests" (Weber 1947, 152). Following this definition, I examine how people influence the conduct of others in daily life within the boundaries of peasant communities. Changes in power relations are seen as the result of interactions between cadres and ordinary villagers,[1] and attention is thus paid equally to both cadres and ordinary villagers as political actors.

From the perspective of social-exchange theory, I start with a discussion of how rural economic reforms generated a dynamic of change in power relations. Then I consider the political consequences of these changes in two ways — namely, the altered behavior patterns among the grass-root cadres and the political mentality and actions of the villagers. To conclude the essay, I relate this village study to the general impact of reforms on state power, an issue raised by the two aforementioned theories.

Xiajia village, where I conducted my fieldwork from February to August 1991, is located on the southern edge of Heilongjiang Province. It is a farming community with a population of 1,564, growing mostly maize and soybeans. Owing to its poor transport links, there was no rural industry in the village during the collective era, and only a few grain-processing mills exist now, all of them family businesses. According to my survey in 1991, the average net income per capita was 616 yuan in 1990 (the national average was 623 yuan), which places Xiajia at the midpoint economically among Chinese farming communities. In other words, Xiajia will never be designated a government showcase of rural development. It is an ordinary place in every sense except for one thing: I lived in the village for seven years (1971–78) during the collective era and thus know most of its residents' life histories. I revisited Xiajia and carried out a field survey during the spring of 1989, which made it possible to discern the most recent changes when I went back yet again in 1991.

Like most rural communities in China, Xiajia has undergone dramatic social changes over the past four decades. In addition to the influences of the larger social environment, the village's fate was also closely associated

---

1. In this chapter I mainly discuss power relations between the village cadres and peasants. There is no doubt that peasant communities, especially after the reforms, are not isolated universes, and residents have to be involved in power relations with people outside their villages in both economic and social as well as political terms. But these are different kinds of power relations, involving hierarchy and inequality between rural and urban sectors. Moreover, the village cadres are usually treated like ordinary villagers when they go beyond the village boundary, because they are also "rural potatoes" in the eyes of those who are living within the system of state distribution and social welfare. Analytically, it is necessary to distinguish village cadres who do not belong to the state bureaucratic system from cadres in local government or other state organs. Hereafter, by *cadre* I mean village cadres, and I use the term *state officials* to describe the cadres within the state bureaucratic system, which begins at the "township" (*xiang*), the administrative level immediately above the village.

with its leadership. Radical local leadership during the first decade of socialism subjected Xiajia to most, if not all, of the irrational social experiments of the Great Leap Forward. Despite these experiments and the devastation of the 1959–61 famine, by the late 1960s Xiajia had become relatively successful in collective agriculture, and it remained so throughout the 1970s. One of the key factors in the village's achievements, according to many informants, was good management by brigade and team leaders. The collectives in Xiajia were dismantled at the end of 1983.[2] Consequently, the number of cadres at the village level decreased from thirteen to five, including the party secretary, village head, deputy party secretary, village accountant, and head of public security. More important, as shown below, after 1983, these cadres began to play a different role in village politics.

THE BASES OF CADRE POWER IN THE COLLECTIVE ECONOMY

To examine the dynamics of current changes in power relations in village life, we must first understand the structural basis of cadre power prior to the reforms and then see what has happened to this basis since then. In this connection, social-exchange theory provides an instructive perspective.

From a social-exchange point of view, power can be seen as "the ability of persons or groups to impose their will on others despite resistance through deterrence either in the form of withholding regularly supplied rewards or in the form of punishment, inasmuch as the former as well as the latter constitute, in effect, a negative sanction" (Blau 1964, 117). Here the availability and control of resources are crucial for establishing power in social interactions. According to Richard Emerson (1962, 1972), exchange relationships are based on the predicated dependence of two parties upon each other's resources. To the extent that A is unwilling voluntarily to surrender a resource desired by B and able to use this resource to force, coerce, or induce compliance by B, A is said to have power over B. Moreover, if A can monopolize all the resources B needs, B will be dependent on A. Unless B can furnish other kinds of benefits to A as an exchange, this dependence compels B to comply with A's requests. Hence an unbalanced power relationship is established between A and B.

In his analysis of "power-dependence" relations, Emerson presented four ways for a given individual to avoid becoming involved in a power-dependence relationship. When one needs a service another has to offer, one can (a) supply him with another service; (b) obtain the service elsewhere; (c) force him to provide the service; or (d) give up the original

2. Heilongjiang was the last province in China to dismantle the commune system, and the main reason, according to Luo Xiaopeng and others, was the relative success of collective farming. See Luo et al. 1985. For a detailed introduction to Xiajia village, see Yan 1993, 17–39.

demand. If the former is not able to choose any of the four alternatives, he has to become dependent on the latter and accept the latter's power (Emerson 1962, 31–41). Peter Blau reformulated Emerson's schema and applied it further to specify the conditions of social independence, the requirements of power, and their structural implications. According to Blau, the conditions of independence include strategic resources (like money) for starting an exchange relationship, the available ways to escape the other's power, coercive force to compel others, and self-reduction of demands. Among complementary to the conditions of independence the basic strategies to attain and sustain power are indifference to what others offer, monopoly over what others need, law and order, and support of a value system (Blau 1964, 118–24).

Applying this approach to examine the previous structure of power relations in Xiajia, it is evident that because cadres were able to control almost all resources in the collective economy, villagers were left no other choice but to subject themselves to cadre power. Cadre power in the prereform era was based on four main conditions.

First, collectivization provided cadres with the most efficient way to monopolize resources, from the basic means of livelihood to opportunities for upward mobility. In the collectives, Xiajia peasants worked in groups under the supervision of cadres, and their basic needs were distributed annually by the collectives. They had no right to decide what activities they would engage in. During the more radical periods, for all social activities outside the collectives, such as visiting relatives or going to nearby marketplaces, peasants also needed the formal permission of cadres. Complaints about cadres or about state policies were severely punished, and the complainants were often accused of counterrevolutionary activities. In short, peasants were deprived of all rights to basic economic, social-cultural, and political resources (see Oi 1989a, 131–55; Parish and Whyte 1978, 96–114; Zweig 1989).

Second, their loyalty to the party state helped prevent cadres from being seduced by bribery or other forms of corruption, and thus increased their overall ability to exercise power. Owing to the emphasis on political correctness and class origin in cadre recruitment, only those who closely followed the party line and their superiors' instructions could stay in power, and their political loyalty was consistently tested in numerous political campaigns. Political rewards from higher levels of government served to raise their social and political status, bringing psychological rewards and reinforcing their political loyalty. Compared to the current situation, economic corruption was not a serious problem among cadres in the collectives. Many cadres lived in conditions similar to those of ordinary villagers, and the main material privileges they enjoyed were better meals and less manual labor. The revolutionary, honest cadre was a generally accepted ideal. This probity in turn strengthened cadres' capacity to exercise power over team members (see Chan, Madsen, and Unger 1992, 26–30; Huang Shu-min 1989, 105–28; Potter and Potter 1990, 283–95).

Third, state penetration into village society established the legitimacy of cadre authority, and "mass dictatorship" provided a coercive force to compel peasants. Commune officials supervised all village work and always supported village cadres when conflicts occurred between cadres and villagers. Political struggle sessions and the use of village militia are the most common forms of mass dictatorship, and in many cases village cadres took advantage of these means to attack their personal foes (see Friedman, Pickowicz, and Selden 1991; Hinton 1983, 109–201; Oi 1989a; Siu 1989, 189–243).

A fourth source of cadre power was the hegemony of communist ideology. Cadres could enforce their authority by claiming that they represented the party's political line, and their correctness thus could not be questioned by the masses. By resorting to the official ideology, cadres were also able to justify actions that proved to be against the private interests of the peasants, such as eliminating any life chances outside the collectives. "Revolutionary ideologies, which define the progress of a radical movement as inherently valuable for its members, bestow power on the movement's leadership" (Blau 1964, 122). Moreover, the domination of communist ideology made villagers pliant to the dictates of political campaigns that empowered only the movement leaders (see Chan, Madsen, and Unger 1992; Potter and Potter 1990, 270–82; Zweig 1989).

For analytic purposes, the conditions needed for villagers to avoid cadre power are: (1) freedom of physical mobility; (2) a supply of strategic resources able to undermine cadre power; (3) personal ability to resist, or the use of protective networks; and (4) indifference to ideological mobilization. Obviously, none of these conditions existed during the collective era. There was no alternative available to villagers. The household registration system, the ban on rural-urban migration, and the requirement of official certificates to travel, all imprisoned villagers within the boundaries of the collectives (see Potter 1983, 465–99). They had little to offer cadres except bodily service, and what they did have all came from the collectives, which were run by the cadres. Under the totalitarian rulership of the CCP, personal resistance to cadre power or to ideological mobilization was virtually impossible. It would have resulted in grave political trouble.

THE DYNAMICS OF CHANGE AND MARKET-ORIENTED REFORM

The rural reforms brought fundamental changes to this seemingly immutable power structure by creating alternative resources and opportunities outside the bureaucratic redistributive system, and by attenuating the conditions that made villagers dependent upon cadres. There have been four key components of this process of change.

First, decollectivization has undermined the most important basis of cadre power: monopoly over resources. This is mainly because of the distribution of land to families and the shift to household farming. In the eyes of Xiajia residents, the most significant aspect of rural reform was the distribution of land. They always refer to the date of land distribution when discussing recent changes in village life. Farmland in Xiajia was divided into two categories: ration land (*kouliang tian*) and contract land (*chengbao tian*). Every person in the village (regardless of age or sex) was entitled to have two *mu* of ration land, and every adult male labourer received ten *mu* of contract land. Peasants' obligations to provide the state with cheap requisitioned grain and taxes only applied to contract land. The effective duration of land distribution was fifteen years, and within that period no further adjustment would take place.

For ordinary farmers in Xiajia, land is not merely a fundamental means of production; it is the most reliable source of social welfare. Control over land is nothing less than controlling one's fate. From the first day that villagers could make their own decisions about what to plant on their land and how to use the surplus, the very basis of cadre power began to crumble. It was common for villagers to express their feelings about decollectivization with a modern term: freedom (*ziyou*),[3] and they then added a footnote to it by quoting an old popular saying: "People have to obey the person who controls their rice bowls" (*duan shui de wan, fu shui guan*). An old villager once told me: "With a piece of land, you have a rice bowl of your own. It is not the iron bowl that urban people have, but you don't need to beg anybody for a bowl of rice — you dig it up from your own land."

The significance of this change is best illustrated by the simple but profound fact that more than 90 percent of the adult males in Xiajia village now have their own private seals (or "name chops"). In the past this was a privilege enjoyed only by the cadres who ran collectives. Nowadays the peasants need private seals for signing a wide variety of contracts with companies and with local government agencies. The immediate consequence of the departure from collective farming is that they have gained the status of independent legal persons.

Second, as many economists have noted, agricultural productivity surged suddenly after the switch to household farming, and living standards in rural China have generally improved to a remarkable extent. One of the most important consequences of the improvement in villagers' economic

3. It is interesting that peasants in other places, such as Anhui province, also used the word *freedom* to describe their new experience as independent farmers (see Chen 1990, 31).

TABLE 8.1   Economic Status of Xiajia Village Households, 1989

Economic Position / Social Group	Rich Households		Average Households		Poor Households		Total Households
	No.	%	No.	%	No.	%	
Post-1981 cadres	7	54	6	46	0	0	13
Fallen & retired cadres	2	17	6	50	4	33	12
Si shu hu	10	53	8	42	1	5	19
Ordinary peasants of "good class" origins	11	6	121	67	48	27	180
Ordinary peasants of "middle class" origins	8	30	17	63	2	7	27
"Four bad elements"	6	18	25	76	2	6	33
Total	44	16%	183	64%	57	20%	284

NOTE: As the distinction between being "in office" and "out of office" at the time of de-collectivization has resulted in a significant difference for these cadres' postdecollectivization economic performance, I categorize those who have fallen or retired from power before 1982 as a separate group. *Si shu hu* constitute another less-known category, which includes the spouses and children of state cadres, workers, teachers, and military officers, all of whom live in the village and belong to the rural population in the household register system. The "four bad elements" are those who bear negative class labels such as *landlord* or *rich peasant*. (For a detailed explanation of the survey and the classification of the six social groups, see Yan 1992, 3–9.)

circumstances has been the eclipse of the previous social hierarchy by new patterns of economic and social stratification. This is suggested by a household survey of family incomes that I conducted during the spring of 1989 (see table 8.1).

Table 8.1 suggests that while village cadres have taken advantage of the reforms to accumulate private wealth and have become prosperous, a number of ordinary peasants, including some of the formerly disadvantaged, have also benefited both economically and socially. In particular, peasant households of former "middle-peasant" origins have done extremely well. As a result, the previous socialist hierarchy is being replaced by a dual system of social stratification that is characterized by the coexistence of bureaucratic rank with a market-based class order. The emergence of this new structure of social stratification, which echoes what Szelényi (1988) found in rural Hungary, has contributed a great deal to a new pattern of power relations, which was quite visible when I conducted my second field survey of Xiajia in 1991.

The rise of a new group of rich peasants presented a challenge to cadre power in two ways. Many peasants, especially those who have become relatively affluent, suddenly came to possess the strategic resources (money or goods) for social exchange. According to social-exchange theory, "a person who has all the resources required as effective inducements for others to furnish him with the services and benefits he needs is protected against becoming dependent on anyone" (Blau 1964, 119). The shift in control of resources to peasant households constitutes a decline in villagers' dependence on cadres. The rise of peasants' economic well-being further broke the superiority of cadres in the previous social order and made cadres susceptible to material inducements offered by villagers (I shall return to this point later).

The most dramatic fact in general reality is that the common is that the party state has begun to retreat from rural society, and mass dictatorship as a means for controlling society has gradually dissipated. A similar indicator of this change is that the village militia has disappeared although it still exists on paper, the position of militia head has been eliminated. Everyone is so busy trying to advance their economic status that even state officials are no longer interested in monitoring villagers' behavior. In 1991, few state officials came to the village to supervise policy implementation or other work, since the local government's primary concerns were now grain procurement and tax collection.

In contrast to the retreat of the state, social networks made up of connections — referred to in Chinese as *guanxi* — have become increasingly important in village life. It is true that network-building persisted during the collective era, despite the state's efforts to transform traditional patterns of interpersonal relations in China (see Gold 1985; Oi 1989a; Walder 1986). However, since the reforms, the social scope of personal networks has expanded remarkably, involving not only kinship ties but also friends and partners both within and outside the village. As a result, gift exchange, the traditional method of cultivating personal ties, has intensified over the past decade. My survey shows that in 1990, 202 households in Xiajia village (54 percent of the total) spent more than 500 yuan apiece on gifts, with the highest reaching 2,650 yuan. Most of the gift-giving activities took place in the context of institutionalized rituals, such as weddings and funerals. If we take 500 yuan as the average expenditure, this means that most households spent nearly 20 percent of their annual incomes to maintain and expand their social networks (for a detailed account of this change, see Yan 1993).

This recent rise in network-building results from newly emerged demands for cooperation, self-protection, and self-realization among peasants, who have now become independent producers. Today, peasants have to deal with all kinds of problems in agricultural production, from purchasing seeds to selling grain. Mutual assistance during the busy season, financial aid from private loan sources, and social connections outside the village are thus all vital to the peasants' pursuit of a better life. Moreover, a larger web of personal relations provides a stronger protective network for peasants when they come in conflict with village cadres or agents of the local government.

Finally, it is widely recognized that communist ideology no longer provides a compelling basis for the legitimacy of the party state or normative values for organizing society. At the village level, the end of communist ideology is reflected clearly in peasants' cynical attitude toward politics and the state, as well as toward cadre power. They have become indifferent to political campaigns (such as the recent one called "socialist education") and suspicious of cadres' corruption. Paralleling the decline of communist ideology, many new ideas and values have been introduced into rural China, and they play an important role in changing peasant mentalities. Indeed, the flow of information into rural areas today merits much more attention than it currently receives.

Television is one important example. One evening in 1978, I joined several young Xiajia villagers in a five-mile walk to another village in order to watch the first TV set in the area. By 1991, there were 135 TV sets in Xiajia alone, including eight color sets, which translates into one set for every three households. While it is true that the TV stations are under state control, one should note that since the reforms, television programs have changed greatly. In addition to the conventional propaganda, there are many other programs introducing new values and new ideas. For instance, I found myself watching the American TV police series "Hunter" in Xiajia village, the same show having been broadcast in Boston several months before. As a consequence of such programs, during my fieldwork, I was asked to explain such things as how the U.S. Supreme Court works, why an American state governor has no right to control a district judge, and who was fighting for justice in the Gulf War.

In table 8.2, I have summarized the main points discussed above. All the dynamics of change resulted directly or indirectly from rural economic reforms, especially the radical departure from central planning — namely, decollectivization and the restoration of household farming. Each of the dynamics may influence the previous order of social relations in general and thus have structural implications in a broader sense. For instance, household farming may lead to a market economy and privatization, economic development may cause social differentiation, the rapid expansion of personal networks indicates the rise of a social force, and if all these are the case, a postcommunist political culture may well be on its way.[4] Although it is

4. In an earlier essay, Gordon White 1987 discusses the new patterns of power and new axes of political conflict and cooperation generated by the economic reforms. He suggests that a possible political consequence of these changes might be the emergence of a new political process in rural China.

TABLE 8.2   Changes in Power Relations in Xiajia Village

Requirements for Cadre Power before the Reforms	Assumed Conditions for Peasant Independence	Dynamics of Change since the Reforms	Structural Implications for the Future
Collectivization; monopoly of resources	Available alternatives	Decollectivization; private enterprise	Market economy; privatization
Loyalty to the party; political reward	Supply of strategic resources	Economic development, change of cadre ethics	Social differentiation; cadre corruption
State penetration; dictatorship	Capability of personal resistance; protective networks	Retreat of the state; decline of mass dictatorship	Rise of society; new social order
Hegemony of communist ideology	Indifference to ideological mobilization	End of ideology; flow of information	Postcommunist political culture

hard to predict the long-term consequences of these changes, the current political outcomes can be seen clearly in two aspects of village life: changes in the interests and behavior of cadres and the new political mentalities and actions of villagers.

"PLAY THE GAME WISELY": CHANGING PATTERNS OF CADRE BEHAVIOR

Two questions are crucial in assessing changes in village cadres' interests and behavior. What is the criterion of a successful village cadre—political reward from the party state or personal achievement in the family economy? And what is the locus of cadres' legitimacy—the trust of their superiors or the support of the masses? Prior to the rural reforms, neither of these two questions was significant for cadres, because the former answers were the only real choices. During the collective era, the Xiajia leadership was characterized by its strong commitment to the public good, an imperious and despotic style of work, and (for much of the time) relatively successful management of collective agriculture. While enjoying various privileges, including higher work points, most cadres considered political rewards most desirable, and many cadre families were financially on a par with ordinary villagers. The reforms have changed this, however, because alternative resources and opportunities were created outside the bureaucratic system as the collectives were dismantled. Gradually, cadres changed their interests and behavior. The differences among the three party secretaries in charge of Xiajia during various periods are the best example of this.

The party secretary from 1952 to 1960 was considered the worst leader by my informants, because he was extremely loyal to higher-level officials. He endeavored to implement all the irrational policies of the Great Leap Forward, thus making Xiajia residents suffer more than their neighbors during the 1959–61 famine. Relying on the full support of his superiors and the coercive force of the village militia, he controlled Xiajia tyrannically, acquiring the nickname "Big Wolf." An example frequently cited by my informants was that he had ordered a villager tied up and beaten badly just because he had missed a meal in the collective meal hall and complained about it. While the villagers struggled with the threat of hunger in 1959, this party secretary climbed to the highest point in his political career — he was selected as a model grass-roots cadre and invited to participate in an official ceremony at the National Day celebration in Beijing. When I interviewed him about the Great Leap, he was still immersed in happy memories of his glorious past. He went into minute detail, telling me how many cities he had visited during that tour, how happy he was when he met Marshal Zhu De, chairman of the National People's Congress, and how he learned to use flush toilets in fancy hotels. Back home, however, he lived in the same conditions as the village poor, and he was widely recognized as an honest cadre, free of corruption. It seems obvious that he believed in what the party said and worked wholeheartedly for the state, which, by its ideological definition, should also have conformed with the interests of the Xiajia people. For this reason, many villagers have an ambivalent attitude toward this man: on the one hand, they hate him for inflicting famine and poverty on the village; on the other, they respect him for his commitment to public duty and his selfless character.

The party secretary from 1978 to 1987 oversaw the most dramatic turn of events: the dismantling of collectives. Xiajia's collective economy achieved great progress under his leadership during the early 1980s; in the best year (1980), the value of ten work points reached 2.50 yuan. As did his predecessor, he also resorted to coercion to exercise his power and tightly controlled the social life of villagers. He confessed to me that he could not remember how many people he had beaten during his ten-year reign as party secretary. Given this patriarchical tradition among village cadres, it was natural that he and his colleagues first resisted decollectivization and then encountered tremendous difficulties dealing with villagers who were no longer dependent on the cadres' management of production. He told me that after decollectivization, "doing thought work"[5] was no longer ef-

---

5. The term *thought work* can be applied to many means of controlling people, from personal persuasion, informal interrogation, and study workshops to public struggle sessions.

fective, and people did not respect the authority of cadres any more. He tried to organize villagers to carry out such projects as opening a collective enterprise and transforming a dry field into an irrigated rice paddy, but people did not respond to his call. Worse, the party did not appear to appreciate cadres' political achievements, and higher-level state officials withdrew their support of village cadres when the latter needed it most. The most upsetting incident for him was when he became involved in a public conflict with a villager in 1987. Rather than supporting him, the township government pretended to know nothing about it. "It is meaningless to be a cadre now," he said when he explained to me why he had resigned after that incident. Obviously, as a figure mediating two periods, he could not adapt to the new type of power relationships after the reforms and thus had to retreat.

The decline of appreciation for "revolutionary cadres" did not bother the next party secretary, because he simply did not care about political rewards. During one of my interviews in 1989, he gave an interesting explanation of his motives: "Society has changed now. Who cares about the party and the state? Even the top leaders in Beijing are only interested in getting rich, otherwise they should first educate their own children. Why am I doing this job? Simple — for money. I was not interested in the title of party secretary, but I do like the salary of 3,000 yuan per year. In other words, I am working for my children, not for the party." Two years later, I was told that the same cadre had designed his strategy in terms of three "nos": saying nothing, doing nothing, and offending nobody. When I checked this with him myself, he did not hesitate to admit it. His "three-nos" strategy is best illustrated by the way he dealt with a dispute between the village vice head and a peasant, in which the latter blamed and then cursed the former in the village office, where all five cadres were present for a meeting about population control. As I was an invited visitor at the meeting, I witnessed the whole affair and was surprised when the party secretary kept silent until the end. I also found that he did not use the local phrase "sitting on the throne" (*zuo yi di*) to describe his position, even though it was the popular term used by both cadres and villagers for the act of taking the top position in the village. However, he does have something to be proud of: he has advanced his family from one of the poorest to one of the richest in Xiajia, and his two sons' families also moved to the top of the "rich list" in the past two years. This advancement, many informants suggested, was because he was party secretary.

It is clear, in short, that economic benefits have replaced political rewards as the key object of cadres' careers, and these benefits are generated within

---

The ultimate goal of doing thought work is to make the subject comply to the authority of cadres.

the village, not granted by political superiors. Even the party has realized that money now speaks louder than political slogans, and has adopted a market mechanism as a means of maintaining its political control over local cadres. According to Xiajia cadres, the township government has divided their salaries, which draw on local taxes paid by villagers, into a basic salary and bonuses. The bonuses make up four-fifths of their entire incomes, and are linked to the completion of specific tasks. For instance, if they accomplish the work of supervising spring plowing, they may earn one-fifteenth of their annual salaries as a reward, and if they fail they lose the same amount as punishment. Ironically, this method has not raised the cadres' motivation, because many feel manipulated by their party superiors and have thus lost their last vestige of political loyalty. As a cadre commented, "We are treated by our own party as circus dogs—you play a little game well, you get some food in return. Play it one more time, you get another tiny reward."

The locus of cadre legitimacy has also changed remarkably. During the collective era, although in theory village cadres should have been elected by the masses, few attained their positions through such means. No one could stay in power without the trust and support of higher levels of government, and unpopular leaders, like Xiajia's party secretary during the 1950s, were able to hold power as long as they were appreciated by their superiors. Therefore it was out of the question for cadres to put the support of the masses ahead of the demands of their superiors. There was only one known exception in the recent history of Xiajia. Immediately after the fall of the first party secretary in 1960, in an attempt to protect themselves, villagers (through party members) elected a demobilized soldier as the party secretary. He was a well-known anti-authoritarian character and was afraid of no one. This man stayed in power for only a couple of months and was removed from office after he made his first serious effort to resist the orders of the commune party committee. This incident might be seen as failed resistance from below, but it also demonstrates that the authority of village cadres during the collective era depended completely on higher-level officials, and the villagers could do little to affect the power structure in their village.

After the reforms, however, village cadres have gradually come to depend more on support from below than recognition from above. As a result of the reform effort to separate the party committee from government and the polity from the economy, along with the end of political campaigns, village cadres receive fewer administrative instructions and less political support. The recent reform effort to establish "autonomous village committees" based on mass elections also constituted a potential threat to their power base (see Wang 1992). One attempt at free elections was made in 1983 in Xiajia, resulting in the village head being voted out of power by the villagers. That incident scared the cadres so much that they have stifled any kind of election since then.

In addition to the changes in the broader environment, a new feeling of being salaried public servants is also affecting cadres' behavior, because their salaries draw on the money collected from peasant households in the name of "public funding." The cadres, who can no longer claim they are working for the party, feel indebted to the local people, especially when the latter repeatedly make reference to this sensitive subject during public disputes. Moreover, to carry out unpleasant tasks like collecting taxes and grain, or supervising birth control, cadres need the cooperation of their subordinates. As the former party secretary Wang said, "I know that the villagers hate to feed cadres. I would too, if I were them. Collecting grain and money, forcing women to submit to sterilization, all the jobs I do are awful. The most important thing is to play the game nicely. Who knows what is going to happen after you fall out of power?"

Being aware of their newly developed dependence on their subordinates' support, village cadres have lost the incentive to enforce unpopular policies and have instead begun to play a role of mediator or middleman when the state's policies are in direct conflict with local interests, such as in the case of population control. It has long been recognized that the one-child policy causes widespread resentment among peasants. Nonetheless, it should be noted that a broad gap has always existed between this policy and its implementation. From the very beginning, the implementation of the one-child policy encountered resistance from the peasants. In the mid 1980s, the state seemed to retreat silently by allowing couples whose first child was a daughter to have another child in hopes that it would be a boy.

In Xiajia village, the implementation of the single-child policy started at the same time that the rural reforms began. Those who had a second child after April 1980 were fined 700 yuan by the commune government. Fortunately, the village office (the production brigade at that time) showed sympathy to those whose first child was a daughter by giving them a 500 yuan allowance, which meant that the fine was reduced to only 200 yuan, an amount the peasants could afford. But things soon went sour, because the local policy changed in February 1983, and the fine was raised to 1,200 yuan. In the same year, the collectives were also dismantled. Consequently, allowances were no longer available, and those who violated the one-child policy had to pay the entire amount for their second baby. This situation lasted for only one year before state policy changed again. In 1984, women who were over 29 and had a daughter as their first child were permitted to have a second child. To help villagers who wished to have sons, the village cadres had always tried to avoid asking women who had only daughters to submit to sterilization, sometimes by submitting false reports to the government.

To explain the cadres' dilemma, the head of Xiajia village said, "We are peasants, and we know exactly how painful it is for a man to have no son. We don't want to stop anybody's bloodline. This is something that could destroy our own fortune and merit. But we are also cadres, and we have to do our job. So the only way is to have one eye open and another closed [*zheng yi yan, bi yi yan*], to cheat the state while coaxing the villagers."[6] And the current party secretary told me that the secret of doing work now is *yi tuo er bian*, which means to deal with any order or policy from above, one needs first to delay implementation and then to alter it, turning the policy to the interests of the village if possible.[7] As a result of resistance by ordinary peasants and a slowdown by village cadres, the 1990 census in Xiajia village shows that none of the villagers were really affected by the one-child policy during any period. The only difference is that some of them paid for extra children and some did not.

Indeed, the cadres' double-role strategy is well reflected in the phrase "cheating the state and coaxing the villagers" (*pian shangbian, hong xiabian*). Because of increasing demand to protect private interests, cadres have deceived the state in recent years more often than in the earlier 1980s. Moreover, the phenomenon of cheating the state is by no means confined to village cadres; state officials at both township and county levels share the same mentality and strategy—otherwise, many of the village cadres' efforts could not possibly succeed. For instance, in the spring of 1991, the county government required all villages to finish corn planting before April 20. But, as Xiajia village land is located on lower ground, the ground temperature was not warm enough for planting by that date. To meet the deadline, the township cadres indicated that Xiajia cadres had completed the task in time. Although everyone knew that the work could not start until two weeks beyond the deadline, the cadres at the county level were satisfied with the report and dealt with their superiors at the provincial level in the same manner. The cadres at township and village levels were happy too, because they completed their bureaucratic duties without bothering the peasants at all. The group that benefited the most, however, were the peasants, and they did not even know what had happened.

This change can best be demonstrated in a comparison with the collective period. The implementation of government policies in the 1950s and 1960s resembled an inflation process. Cadres at every level would add their own efforts to state policies, because they had only one purpose—to be

6. This kind of mentality is quite common among village cadres in other parts of China. Huang Shu-min reports an interesting story in which the party secretary in a South China village employed a sophisticated strategy to protect some women from abortion, meanwhile meeting the requirements of the upper-level government. See Huang 1989, 185–90.

7. This constitutes a sharp contrast to the attitude of the former party secretary during the 1950s, who told me, "When I was ruling the village [he used precisely the term *ruling*, i.e., *zuo tianxia* in local terms], if the party leader said to do one thing, I would try to complete two, or even three. We believed that if we failed, the landlords would return and take our land away."

appreciated by superiors. A good example of this was the false reports on grain yields among rural cadres during the Great Leap Forward, which eventually caused high procurement of grain and the famine of 1959–61 (see Bernstein 1984). Nowadays, cadres pay much more attention to the reactions from below, and thus policy implementation has become a process of deflation. As rural cadres passively and partially carry out orders from above, central government policies lose their original meaning. This has been captured in a popular saying, "Villages cheat towns, towns cheat counties, it's cheating straight up to the State Council" (*cun pian xiang, xiang pian xian, yizhi pian dao guowuyuan*). In a sense, the new pattern of political behavior among the rural cadres might create an informal mechanism to constrain the unchecked power of central policy.

Another interesting outcome of changes in power relations is that village cadres found themselves involved in more resistance, bargaining, and compromise in the process of exerting their power. While passively carrying out unpopular policies from above, they have become much softer when they have to interfere with the private interests of peasants, in order to avoid open resistance from the latter. A simple indicator is that incidents of cadres beating villagers have declined rapidly since decollectivization; instead, more conflicts have ended up in the reverse: cadres being beaten up by villagers. Imposing fines became the only powerful weapon left in the cadres' hands, and it was applied to almost everything the cadres carried out. However, its efficacy has diminished, because some villagers refused to pay their fines, which again led to direct confrontation between cadres and villagers.

All cadres agreed that compared to neighboring villages, Xiajia was by no means a troublesome place, and in recent years, to get a beating was not the worst of fates for cadres. In neighboring villages, cadres' houses have been set afire by peasants, and at least one cadre was killed by two outraged village youths taking revenge. In many cases, violent conflicts were caused by insignificant incidents that would not have been contemplated if the cadres had still held the same power as during the collective era. While I was doing my fieldwork in Xiajia, two cases of arson occurred, and the victims were both cadres. It seems that the local government could do little to protect the village cadres, except to compensate them economically. After the two arson cases, the township government proposed to raise the local taxes paid by villagers and use the money to buy personal insurance for village cadres, in the hope that this would make the villagers reluctant to attack the cadres' property.

In addition to the loss of their monopoly over resources, economic corruption has weakened village cadres' ability to exercise power. In one case I witnessed, a villager's application for a loan to buy chemical fertilizer was rejected by the village cadres, because funds for agricultural loans had already been diverted to pay the debts of the village. Misappropriation of state funds was nothing unusual at the village level, and the rejection of this personal application would ordinarily have been viewed as a small incident. To the surprise of all, the villager was outraged and started a public dispute with the party secretary on the street. When many people gathered to watch their dispute, the villager suddenly said that he knew where the agricultural loan had gone — it had been lent out as usury by the son of the party secretary. He also accused the village office of collecting extra taxes over the previous year and threatened to report the case to the county government. The party secretary left the spot without saying a word to defend himself. A few days later, I learned that the villager had been allowed to borrow some money from the village office, which was actually a gift to him, because both sides knew the loan would probably never be returned.

Interestingly enough, the same cadre was well known for both his bad temper toward villagers and his commitment to central policy when he was a team leader during the 1970s. People often said that, for this cadre, to curse or beat someone was as normal as eating a bowl of noodles. Despite all complaints, the villagers still supported him and recognized his authority, because he was also responsible for improving the management of the collective. During its successful period of collective farming, most cadres in Xiajia were this type of "iron fist." They ran the village in the style in which a tyrannical father controlled his family in traditional China, and their brutality was justified by their sincere devotion to central policy. Today none of the five current cadres (all of whom were in power before the reform) can boast of being "corruption free," and it is no accident that they have all improved their tempers to a remarkable extent.[8]

It is true that cadre corruption, which surged markedly after the reforms (Gold 1985; Meaney 1991), reveals that cadres still control resources in many ways and can thereby impose their wills on their subordinates (Oi 1989b; Rocca 1992). Nevertheless, the current rise of cadre corruption does not necessarily strengthen cadre power, for two reasons. First, economic corruption should be distinguished from political corruption. As Gong Xiaoxia writes: "It is after the reforms that cadre corruption began to appear more and more in economic forms. . . . Since China was a highly politicized society prior to the reforms, cadre corruption during that time

8. In their follow-up research, the authors of *Chen Village* found a similar trend of character change among the cadres. For instance, Chen Longyong, once a tyrannical party secretary who controlled the villagers' life tightly, turned himself into a private entrepreneur and "had softened with the years" (Chan, Madsen, and Unger 1992, 315). His successor, the current party secretary, Baodai, "is fully aware that a leader's power to exact cowed compliance from the peasantry is a thing of the past, and he generally intrudes on the affairs of his neighbors only when mediation is called for" (1992, 320).

presented itself mainly in political forms" (Gong 1992, 52). In the case of Xiajia, many cadres during the collective era were free of economic corruption, but they abused the villagers in more obvious ways than the current cadres. Economic corruption may increase cadres' personal wealth, but it does not allow them to compel obedience from their subordinates.

Second, corruption based on exchange of resources should be distinguished from that based on distributing resources. Because people involved in social exchange need to observe the norm of reciprocity (see Gouldner 1960), the recipient of a gift or a favor is obligated or in a position inferior to the donor until the "debt" is repaid (see Mauss 1967). This is well captured in a Chinese proverb: "Eating from others, one's mouth becomes soft; taking from others, one's hands become short" (chi ren zui ruan, na ren shou duan). It is obvious that when a cadre receives gifts from his subordinates, his superiority is weakened, because such exchanges reduce the recipient to a position of mutual dependence. Moreover, the obligation of reciprocity implies that corruption based on exchange of resources will benefit both sides: the giver as well as the recipient. This is something quite different from transactions based on the more one-sided dependence of the collective era, when cadres distributed resources to villagers who had no real alternatives.

"LEAVE ME ALONE":
POLITICAL MENTALITY AND ACTION AMONG VILLAGERS

The village power game is played out by both cadres and ordinary villagers. These days village cadres must play the game more wisely, because as indicated above, the economic reforms have broken the previous pattern of dependence and raised the position of villagers. More important, market reforms have changed the villagers' mentality as well as their living standard. New attitudes toward cadre power and authority, the rise of individualism, and an emerging conception of personal rights have also served to redefine the power game in Xiajia.

The most dramatic change is in villagers' perception of cadre power and authority. As I have explained elsewhere (Yan 1992), social life in Xiajia was previously far from "egalitarian": the collectives were perhaps no less hierarchical than the prerevolutionary community. When the cadres stood on the top of the social pyramid, fear dominated popular perceptions of cadre power. Nevertheless, villagers still placed their hopes on good leadership and respected those who led the collective to prosperity. Because cadres controlled all resources and opportunities, they represented the only hope for collective betterment. This is well captured in a popular saying of the collective era: "It's better to have a good team leader than to have a good father" (you ge hao baba, bu ru you ge hao duizhang).

Villagers' fear and respect of cadre power came to an end when the collectives were dismantled in 1983. By the time I conducted my first field survey in early 1989, anger and discontent over cadre corruption had reached a peak. Complaints about various kinds of local taxes and accusations of cadre misconduct were common subjects during my interviews with villagers. To my knowledge, at least two anonymous letters have been sent to the county government in an attempt to bring corrupt cadres into court. Conflicts between cadres and villagers occurred frequently when the latter felt unfairly treated, and quite often a conflict ended in violence. One such public fight in 1987, as noted above, forced the party secretary to resign. This vividly symbolizes the collapse of the authority and power of all village cadres. At that time, many villagers started showing disrespect by refusing to present gifts to cadres in ritual situations, such as weddings or funerals. The village office lost its prestige in the eyes of ordinary farmers, and the focus of public life has gradually moved from the brigade headquarters to the village retail store (for more details see Yan 1992, 15–16; Yan 1993, 167–78).

Obviously, the major reason for the sudden eruption of dissatisfaction with cadre behavior resulted from the advent of family farming, which allows villagers to control their own livelihood. A further reason is that in recent years, the diversification of life chances has raised villagers' sense of individualism and thus changed their views of cadre authority.[9] A widely cited saying in both urban and rural China is now: "A fish has its way, and a shrimp has its way, too" (*yu you yu lu, xia you xia lu*). Here, "way," *lu* in Chinese, may indicate back doors, social connections, personal skills, and so on — all the means needed to make oneself affluent. During my fieldwork, I heard both rich and poor villagers quoting this popular saying when talking about somebody who had done well economically. In Xiajia, many capable individuals have found a way to make money, such as growing cash crops, developing family sidelines, or working in the cities. One of the best chances for financial advancement in the past two years was created by the establishment of a milk-products factory owned jointly by the local government and the Nestlé company of Switzerland. Five people in the village found jobs in the factory and earned a high salary (300 yuan per month versus an average annual income of 616 yuan per capita). Several dozen villagers responded to the new demand for milk by raising dairy cows and have subsequently gained considerable benefits.

In the place of fear and respect, the villagers began to view the cadres' credibility critically, and few still trust leaders unconditionally. In the eyes of my informants, the good cadre has become a myth. When the story of Baogong, an upright and honest official of the Song dynasty, was shown on

9. For an instructive study of public perceptions about life chances and the political implications for China, see Whyte 1985.

TV, many commented cynically that Baogong could not survive in today's environment, because his honesty would hurt the interests of other cadres, and he would thus soon be removed from power or forced into corruption.

The suspicion of cadres is so strong that it sometimes causes unnecessary trouble. In a case I witnessed during my fieldwork, three men came to Xiajia to purchase pigs and cheated villagers by using a platform scale rigged to reduce the weight. Their cheating was discovered, but the villagers did not dare to claim compensation, because these three men came in a military truck and stated that they were soldiers. Finally, the village head intervened in the name of the village office and made the three cheaters return the money to the pig farmers. The villagers were not satisfied with this solution and demanded that the cheaters be punished. When the three men left, I was surprised to see some villagers accuse the village head of making a secret deal. They insisted that the village head must have accepted a bribe from the culprits.

When I asked the accusers why they were so critical of the village head, who deserved some credit for handling the problem, I was told that it was his job to resolve problems like this. After all, they said, he earned 2,600 yuan a year, and his salary was extracted from their incomes. "He is fed by us," one said. Here the practice of paying various local taxes in a direct and open way has given the peasants a new perspective from which to view their relationship with cadres. As I indicated earlier, such an awareness of themselves as tax payers not only diminishes villagers' fear of cadres, but also results in cadres realizing that they are, in fact, employed by the villagers.

In 1991, I also found an increasing cynicism about cadre behavior. While some villagers still complained and even directly confronted cadres if their private interests were challenged, their words of discontent rarely turned into action. Most villagers were tired of complaining about cadre corruption and did not even care about the size of cadre salaries. In response to my inquiries about this newly found complacency, I was frequently met with the popular saying, "It is not proper to refuse paying the taxes and procured grain; you cart them away, and leave me my freedom" (*huang liang guo shui, bu jiao bu dui; ni na ti liu, gei wo zi you*). Indeed, the typical view among Xiajia residents was put into three words by an informant: "Leave me alone" (*bie guan wo*). And the most common strategy adopted by them was to fulfill their prescribed obligations to the state and local government without question and then to protect their personal interests against any additional levies.

In the early stages of my fieldwork, I took this "Leave me alone" mentality as the villagers' passive reaction to the social problems they encountered, and as a sign of their indifference to village politics, including cadre behavior. After a few months of observation, however, I became convinced that this posture concealed other meanings. "Leave me alone" conveyed a strong message — namely, awareness of personal rights and an intention to protect them. Given the heritage of patriarchal authority in Chinese culture and the influence of totalitarian rule under the party, it is not easy for the peasants to tell cadres, "Leave me alone." It could not possibly have happened during the collective period, when the only acceptable demand a peasant could make was for better leadership, and a refusal to accept cadre leadership could lead to accusations of the most serious crime — counterrevolution. It could not have happened immediately after the decollectivization either, because the peasants were still living under the shadow of socialist culture, which conferred patriarchal status on cadres. Such an expression itself symbolizes the development of a consciousness of independence and the rise of political self-confidence among the villagers.

In this regard, the increasing flow of information through TV programs and other means has, as noted above, provided the villagers with new conceptions of economic and political rights and thus encouraged them to resist the imposing power of cadres should their interests be violated. This is best illustrated in their confrontations with state officials from the township government, which usually require more courage and strength. For example, in a case of conflict with the township officials, a villager was detained by the township policemen for a few days. He was so angry that he finally refused to leave the detention room when the township cadres grew tired of him and wanted to send him away. He accused the local policemen of "violating the law and human rights" because they did not have an arrest warrant. I met him in the county seat where he was demanding justice from the county government. He showed me a booklet about the criminal law, and we also talked about the American TV detective Hunter.

It should be noted that rural cadres generally do not welcome the diffusion of political information, especially about personal rights. A state official in the township government, who was a village cadre a few years ago, complained to me that the "education of legal knowledge" was a stupid campaign launched by the state. "From ancient times, the policemen have had the right to beat people," he said. "This is the way it works. The ordinary people are just slaves, pigs. They can be ruled only by whips. Look at what is happening now. Everyone wants to have his rights, and the law protects the tough guys. The result is that these tricky people never commit crimes, but they never stop making trouble either. It just annoys the police department to death, and puts the court on the spot" (*da cuo bu fan, xiao cuo bu duan; qi si gong an ju, nan si fa yuan*).

In another interesting case I witnessed, a widow was suspected of stealing public trees. When two local policemen tried to confiscate a motorcycle from her family as a fine, a physical confrontation occurred between the two parties. The widow accused the policemen of beating her and threatened to use her personal connections in the county police department to punish the offenders. Although no one knew whether she had relatives in power or not, the local policemen decided not to risk offending higher authorities and encouraged the Xiajia village office to give the widow 50 yuan in compensation. The policemen did not, however, want to lose face in the village; and so two weeks later they detained the widow's son on a four-month old charge of gambling, and asked the widow to pay a fine of 300 yuan to free her son. Everyone, including me, thought the widow was defeated when she paid up, but, to the surprise of all, she went to the county seat and came back with a note from municipal in the county government requesting that the local police department return her money.

Many studies of the *guanxi* complex in China have focused on the instrumental function of these personal connections (see e.g., Gold 1985, Huang Kwang-kuo 1987; King 1991). The Xiajia case demonstrates that the recent expansion of *guanxi* networks may have something to do with changes in power relations and, in some circumstances, personal networks may give peasants a way to impose their will on cadres. This parallels Mayfair Yang's argument that the gift economy and personal networks have created a distribution channel outside of the bureaucratic distribution system, and thus constitute a counterforce to the power of the state (see Yang 1989; Yan 1993).

Along with their altered perception of cadre power and newly developed political self-confidence, Xiajia residents' attitudes toward the authority of the party state have also changed. They attribute all social problems, such as inflation, cadre corruption, and public disorder, to high-level state leaders. The best example is perhaps their reaction to the campaign of socialist education launched nationwide in 1990 and 1991 in rural areas. The purpose of this campaign was to clear up problems of village finance and to reeducate peasants about socialism. Xiajia was selected as one of the first villages to launch this campaign, and, as during the collective era, a work team was sent down from the county seat. When I arrived in the spring of 1991, the campaign had been under way for several months, but nothing had happened except that some slogans and posters had been placed on the walls of the village office. Not even a single meeting had been held for the campaign. When I discussed this unusually quiet campaign with my informants, they regarded it as a joke. They maintained that it was a trick by the top leaders to put the masses in the hot seat and thereby hide the serious mistakes made in Beijing. One villager put it this way: "When the people at the top fall sick, they force those at the bottom to take medicine" (*shang bian de bing, gei xia bian chi yao*). We did nothing wrong. Why do they always want to educate us?"

This attitude constitutes a sharp contrast to the ways peasants reacted to state campaigns during the collective period. At that time they told themselves: "The scriptures [state policies] were good, but the monks [the cadres at lower levels] are reciting them wrongly" (*jing dou shi haojing, xia bian de heshang gei nian wai le*). As some informants recalled, even during the famine of 1959–61, few people doubted the correctness of policies from above, and they directed all their discontent toward the village cadres. When relief grain was finally allocated to the villagers, who had suffered from hunger for several months, their first reaction was to thank the party state and Chairman Mao. In their own terms, they once had "good feelings" (*gan qing*) toward the state, but these feelings are now gone.

CONCLUDING REMARKS

Now let me return to the issue raised in the beginning of this chapter. How shall we understand and assess the impact of reforms on cadre power in Xiajia, and how does the Xiajia case relate to current debates about this issue? According to Nee's theory of market transition, if the allocation of goods and services is shifted to marketplaces rather than monopolized by the cadres in the socialist redistributive system, power "becomes more diffused in the economy and society" (Nee 1991, 267). "Therefore, the transition from redistribution to markets involves a transfer of power favoring direct producers relative to redistributors" (Nee 1989, 666). This theory is based on survey data of peasant income collected in 1985, and Nee's key argument relies on the discovery that "current cadre status, following a shift to marketlike conditions, has no effect on a household's chances of being in the top income quintile, nor in its avoidance of poverty, nor in the rate of increase of household income" (Nee 1991, 280).

It is at this point, however, that Oi (1989b) found evidence demonstrating that cadres did take advantage of the reforms by exercising their remaining power. Focusing on the policy context in which the reforms were implemented, Oi conducted a structural analysis of cadre corruption and abuse of power, and offered an instructive counterinterpretation to what Nee proposed: "The most obvious conclusion is that a freer market environment does not necessarily lead to the end of bureaucratic control nor the demise of cadre power" (Oi 1989b, 233). Oi also noted that postreform rural politics remained clientelist in nature (ibid., 231).

It seems to me that in addition to their different conclusions, Nee and Oi also differ from each other in the ways they examine the issue. While defining power as "control over resources" and equating relative income with relative power, Nee emphasizes personal income as the criterion by which to evaluate gain and loss among cadres. In contrast, Oi pays more attention to the institutional aspect of power, with a focus on cadre corruption, and takes the extent to which cadres abuse their power in pursuing personal interest as the standard by which to measure the role of cadres after the reforms.

Applying these perspectives to Xiajia, both seem to have a basis in fact, but neither is sufficient to explain the tremendous changes in power relations. As indicated above, the power of Xiajia cadres has declined to a great extent, and they have lost much of their superiority in social and political terms. But my survey in 1989 also demonstrated that 54 percent of the cadres who were in power on the eve of decollectivization have become affluent, while only 9 percent of the villagers became rich (see table 8.1). This suggests a correlation between cadres' status and their postreform economic achievements. Furthermore, this indicates that neither income nor corruption can be employed as the definitive index of cadre power in the postreform era.

An useful dimension, which may be more useful in examining this issue, is the degree of peasant dependence or, to put it another way, the degree of control cadres have over resources. In studies of state socialism, it has long been recognized that the party state's power and authority are based on its monopoly over resources and opportunities, which is maintained and reinforced by the new ruling class of officials (Djilas 1957; Szelényi 1978). Such a monopoly leads to citizen dependence upon officials for the satisfaction of material needs and social mobility, a social phenomena characterized as a form of "organized dependence" by Andrew Walder (1983, 1986). In the context of village society, the fundamental feature of cadre power was villagers' dependence on cadres for the resources under their control. "Men are powerful when many want what they, the few, are able to supply or many fear what they, the few, are able to withhold," George Homans notes (1974, 197). Among many other things, the resources of living, working, resting, socializing, and self-expression are the basic needs of everyday life. These basic resources were, until the reform era, tightly controlled by village cadres, in a situation where villagers were highly dependent. It follows that by examining what happened to these control mechanisms and the degree to which ordinary peasants depend on resources controlled by cadres, one can obtain a better understanding of recent changes in power relations.

My findings from Xiajia lead me to conclude that market reforms have changed the previous balance of villagers' dependence on their leaders and, in some respects, have made cadres dependent on villagers for their incomes. The reforms have eroded cadres' previous power and privilege by breaking their monopoly over resources and by creating new income opportunities that make the accumulation of personal wealth more attractive than the political rewards offered by the party state. Their political role in village society has also changed from that of the tyrannical "local emperor" ruling the village as the agent of the party state to prudent middlemen who negotiate between the state and village society. For villagers, the reforms have ended their dependence on the collectives and the cadres who ran them, and have thereby to a great extent freed them from cadre domination. While cadres have benefited economically from the reforms, villagers have gained much more in social and political terms — that is, they have attained new individual rights (the right to work, rest, move away, and speak out). Even though the ratio of rich households to ordinary villagers is lower than that to cadres, the reforms have opened the way for the former to compete with the latter in the same market order. In short, the most significant change in power relations has been the erosion of cadres' former monopolized superiority in village life.

The Xiajia case, however, has particularities that speak to important issues of regional variation. Xiajia was and still is a farming community, with an economy characterized by agricultural production. Peasant income still derives mainly from farming and family sidelines. Unlike parts of southeastern China, the trend of marketization and commercialization has yet to play an influential role in the Xiajia economy. Nevertheless, as everyone in farming relies on similar resources, and as land — the primary means of production — was distributed evenly among villagers at the time of decollectivization, the reforms may have produced a more profound political impact on Xiajia than on other industrial or more prosperous areas where a diversified commercial economy has emerged since the reforms. As Ákos Róna-Tas has observed in the case of Hungary, a shift to a market economy tends to have a more egalitarian effect in household farming than in larger enterprises, because agricultural production requires less political and social capital (1990, 205–7). Had there been collective enterprises in Xiajia, or if the majority of its residents had engaged in nonagricultural business, the village cadres would probably have had more resources on hand, and thus might have been able to compel or induce the villagers to respond to their power (see Oi 1990). This contradicts the prediction that the significant weakening of cadre power should coincide with a rather mature development of market transactions (see Nee 1989, 1991).

Among the various dynamics contributing to this fundamental change in power relations in Xiajia, decollectivization and the cessation of mass dictatorship have been the most crucial. As this chapter has shown, collectivization was the key institution through which cadres monopolized all economic, social, and political resources and thus controlled the life of villagers. Mass dictatorship, supported by the state and communist ideology, provided the most powerful instrument for cadres to maintain their monopoly of resources and suppress any resistance. These two mechanisms existed everywhere in rural China prior to the reforms and have subsequently eroded. I therefore regard the Xiajia case as illustrative of recent events in rural communities in China and believe that my study has implications that go well beyond Xiajia's boundaries.

REFERENCES

Bernstein, Thomas B. 1984. "Stalinism, Famine, and Chinese Peasants: Grain Procurement During the Great Leap Forward." *Theory and Society* 13, 3: 339–77.

Blau, Peter M. 1964. *Exchange and Power in Social Life.* New York: John Wiley & Sons.

Chan, Anita, Richard Madsen, and Jonathan Unger. 1992. *Chen Village under Mao and Deng.* Expanded and updated edition. Berkeley and Los Angeles: University of California Press.

Chen Yizi. 1990. *Zhongguo: Shinian gaige yu bajiu minyun* (China: Ten Years of Reforms and the Democracy Movement in 1989). Taipei: Lianjing Press.

Djilas, Milovan. 1957. *The New Class: An Analysis of the Communist System of Power.* New York: Praeger.

Emerson, Richard M. 1962. "Power Dependence Relations." *American Sociological Review* 27, 1: 31–41.

———. 1972. "Exchange Theory." In *Sociological Theory in Progress,* eds. J. Berger and M. Zelditch. Boston: Houghton Mifflin.

Friedman, Edward, Paul Pickowicz, and Mark Selden, with Kay Ann Johnson. 1991. *Chinese Village, Socialist State.* New Haven, Conn.: Yale University Press.

Gold, Thomas. 1985. "After Comradeship: Personal Relations in China since the Cultural Revolution." *China Quarterly,* no. 104 (December): 657–75.

Gong Xiaoxia. 1992. "Ganbu xingwei fangshi de bianhua he Zhongguo gongmin shehui de xingqi" (Changes in Patterns of Cadre Behavior and the Rise of Civil Society in China). *Zhongguo zhi chun* (China Spring) 106 (April): 52–54.

Gouldner, Alvin W. 1960. "The Norm of Reciprocity: A Preliminary Statement." *American Sociological Review* 25, 2: 161–78.

Hinton, William. 1983. *Shenfan.* New York: Random House, Vintage Books.

Homans, George. 1974. *Social Behavior: Its Elementary Forms.* New York: Harcourt Brace Jovanovich.

Huang, Kwang-kuo. 1987. "Face and Favor: The Chinese Power Game." *American Journal of Sociology* 92, 4: 944–74.

Huang, Shu-min. 1989. *The Spiral Road: Change in a Chinese Village Through the Eyes of a Communist Party Leader.* Boulder, Colo.: Westview Press.

King, Ambrose Yeo-chi. 1991. "Kuan-hsi and Network Building: A Sociological Interpretation." *Daedalus* 120, 2: 63–84.

Luo Xiaopeng et al. 1985. "Lishixing de zhuanbian" (The Historic Change). In *Nongcun, jingji yu shehui* (Countryside, Economy, and Society), 3: 121–31. Beijing: Knowledge Press.

Mauss, Marcel. 1967. *The Gift.* New York: Norton.

Meaney, Connie Squires. 1991. "Market Reform and Disintegrative Corruption in Urban China." In *Reform and Reaction in Post-Mao China: The Road to Tiananmen,* ed. Richard Baum, 124–42. New York: Routledge.

Nee, Victor. 1989. "A Theory of Market Transition: From Redistribution to Markets in State Socialism." *American Sociological Review* 54, 5: 663–81.

———. 1991. "Social Inequalities in Reforming State Socialism: Between Redistribution and Markets in China." *American Sociological Review* 56, 3: 267–82.

Oi, Jean. 1989a. *State and Peasant in Contemporary China: The Political Economy of Village Government.* Berkeley and Los Angeles: University of California Press.

———. 1989b. "Market Reform and Corruption in Rural China." *Studies in Comparative Communism* 22, 2–3: 221–33.

———. 1990. "The Fate of the Collective after the Commune." In *Chinese Society on the Eve of Tiananmen: The Impact of Reform*, eds. Deborah Davis and Ezra Vogel, 15–36. Cambridge, Mass.: Harvard University Press.

Parish, William L., and Martin King Whyte. 1978. *Village and Family in Contemporary China*. Chicago: University of Chicago Press.

Potter, Sulamith Heins. 1983. "The Position of Peasants in Modern China's Social Order." *Modern China* 9, 3. 465–99.

Potter, Sulamith, and Jack Potter. 1990. *China's Peasants: The Anthropology of a Revolution*. New York: Cambridge University Press.

Rocca, Jean-Louis. 1992. "Corruption and Its Shadow: An Anthropological View of Corruption in China." *China Quarterly*, no. 130 (June): 402–16.

Róna-Tas, Ákos. 1990. "The Second Economy in Hungary: The Social Origins of the End of State Socialism." Ph.D. diss., Department of Sociology, University of Michigan.

Siu, Helen. 1989. *Agents and Victims in South China: Accomplices in Rural Revolution*. New Haven, Conn.: Yale University Press.

Szelényi, Iván. 1978. "Social Inequalities under State Socialist Redistributive Economies." *International Journal of Comparative Sociology* 19, 1–2: 61–78.

———. 1988. *Socialist Entrepreneurs: Embourgeoisement in Rural Hungary*. Madison: University of Wisconsin Press.

Walder, Andrew G. 1983. "Organized Dependency and Cultures of Authority in Chinese Industry." *Journal of Asian Studies* 43, 1: 51–76.

———. 1986. *Communist Neo-Traditionalism: Work and Authority in Chinese Industry*. Berkeley and Los Angeles: University of California Press.

Wang, Zhenyao. 1992. "Construction of Village Committees: Background, Current Situation, and Guidance of the Government Policy." Paper presented at the 1992 annual meeting of the Association for Asian Studies, Washington, D.C.

Weber, Max. 1947. *The Theory of Social and Economic Organization*. New York: Free Press.

White, Gordon. 1987. "The Impact of Economic Reforms in the Chinese Countryside: Toward the Politics of Social Capitalism?" *Modern China* 13, 4: 411–40.

Whyte, Martin King. 1985. "The Politics of Life Chances in the People's Republic of China." In *Power and Policy in the PRC*, ed. Yu-ming Shaw, 244–65. Boulder, Colo.: Westview Press.

Yan, Yun-xiang. 1992. "The Impact of Rural Reform on Economic and Social Stratification in a Chinese Village." *Australian Journal of Chinese Affairs*, no. 27 (January): 1–23.

———. 1993. "The Flow of Gifts: Reciprocity and Social Networks in a Chinese Village." Ph.D. diss., Department of Anthropology, Harvard University.

Yang, Mayfair Mei-Hui. 1989. "The Gift Economy and State Power in China." *Comparative Studies in Society and History* 31, 1: 25–54.

Zweig, David. 1989. *Agrarian Radicalism in China, 1968–1981*. Cambridge, Mass.: Harvard University Press.

NINE

Economy and Ethnicity:
The Revitalization of a Muslim Minority
in Southeastern China

Dru C. Gladney

One of the unexpected consequences of economic reforms in China has been ethnic revitalization.[1] Economic reforms initiated in minority areas were designed to improve the living conditions of minorities and hasten their general development, thereby encouraging their integration into the Chinese Han majority mainstream.[2] Marxist theories have long held that socioeconomic development leads to the erosion, and eventual disappearance, of class differences, as well as national and ethnic loyalties. Economic reforms, by stimulating growth in the economies of state-identified minority groups, were therefore expected to promote the assimilation of minorities into the broader Han majority culture. In China, not unlike the former Soviet Union, the opposite has occurred: as minorities developed economically, so did their ethnic consciousness.

1. This study is based on three years of field research between 1982 and 1986 in the People's Republic of China, with brief return visits in 1987, 1988, 1989, 1990, 1991, 1993, and 1994, funded by the Committee on Scholarly Communication with the People's Republic of China, Fulbright, the Wenner-Gren foundation, UNESCO, and the East-West Center, and with sponsorship from the Central Institute of Nationalities, the Ningxia Academy of Social Sciences, the Fujian Academy of Social Sciences, and Xiamen University. While the data for this study derive from earlier field research and appear at greater length in Gladney 1991, this chapter more specifically addresses the unintended social and political consequences of economic reform among Hui in the community under study.
2. According to the 1990 census, there are fifty-six official "nationalities" (*minzu*) in China, with the Han majority nationality comprising 92 percent of the population, and minorities 8 percent, totaling 91.2 million in population. The Hui nationality, with which this chapter is primarily concerned, is the second largest minority nationality (after the Zhuang), and the most numerous of the so-called "Muslim" nationalities. There are ten nationalities whose main religion is Islam, the Hui, Uygur, Kazakh, Kyrgyz, Uzbek, Tatar, Salar, Dongxiang, Baoan, and Tadjik, altogether numbering about 20 million (17.5 million according to the 1990 census; see Gladney 1991, 1993; Heberer 1989; Pillsbury 1981).

Until the dismantling of the Soviet Union in 1991, it was generally thought by Soviet and Western scholars that minority peoples were gradually "modernizing" and becoming more "Russian" (on "Russification," see Allworth 1980; Dunlop 1983; Olcott 1987). In China, it has been widely believed that minority peoples were inexorably becoming assimilated to the Han Chinese (on "Sinification," see Ch'en 1966; Lai 1988). If economic reforms in minority areas are in fact contributing to ethnic revitalization, this may have important implications for China's continued national unity. By examining economic reform in one southeastern lineage community, I examine the ways in which economic liberalization contributes to ethnic (and in this case even religious) resurgence.

UNINTENDED CONSEQUENCES OF ECONOMIC REFORMS
IN MINORITY AREAS

Ding Yongwei beeped me. On a February 1994 visit to Quanzhou city in southern Fujian province, Ding called me from his private car on his cellular phone. I received the call on a beeper (*bi pi ji*) he had lent me (and had to show me how to use, since I had never used one before).[3] When I first met Ding in 1984, I had just begun to study the collection of villages where the people surnamed Ding, officially recognized as members of the Hui minority nationality in 1979 (see Gladney 1991, 290–95), resided. The villagers at that time still depended primarily on agriculture and aquaculture for their living, and they had only just begun to experience the rapid rise in income that would lead to Ding Yongwei lending me his beeper just ten years later. In a formal interview, Liu Zhengqing, the vice-mayor of Chendai township, told me that the Ding villagers were so wealthy that in one village of 600 households, there were 700 telephones, most of them cellular. When I asked my old friend Ding Yongwei if he was doing well, he held out his cellular phone and declared: "If I weren't wealthy, could I be holding this?" (*bu fu de hua, zheige nadeqi ma?*). He later explained that the government's decision to recognize the Ding community as members of the Hui minority in 1979 was primarily responsible, not only for their newfound economic prosperity, but also for a tremendous subsequent fascination with their ethnic and religious roots. In this case, the Ding claim to be descended from foreign Muslim traders who settled in Quanzhou in the ninth century. When I first began learning about this area in the early 1980s, these Hui

3. The visit was owing to participation in a UNESCO-sponsored conference, "Contributions of Islamic Culture on China's Maritime Silk Route," Quanzhou, Fujian, February 21–26, 1994. The conference was hosted by the Fujian Academy of Social Sciences and the Fujian Maritime Museum. I thank Chen Dasheng and the museum's director, Wang Lianmao, for inviting me to the conference, and the East-West Center for providing travel support.

were known, not only as among the least developed people in southern Fujian, but also as those most assimilated into the local Han Chinese culture (Zhuang 1993).

Recent travelers to northwestern China have also been surprised to discover that although the overall significance of the ancient Silk Road for East-West trade has declined since its zenith during the Han dynasty, one can still find many of the indigenous peoples along its routes engaging in activities strikingly similar to those of their forebears. From Kashgar to Xi'an, and even from Shanghai to Guangzhou, Muslim and other minority traders are flourishing in local marketplaces, often dominating village and township economies to a degree disproportionate to their relatively low numbers visàvis the Han majority.[4] This flourishing of traditional ethnic economies reverses an earlier trend under Stalinist economic planning in which the scope of private enterprise and other forms of local economic autonomy were severely limited (see Stark and Nee 1989). In this chapter, I argue that a closer examination of specific changes in economic policies toward the Hui nationality will reveal that this departure from central planning led specifically to ethnic revitalization. The rise of ethnic consciousness stimulated by these new economic policies has local ethnic groups asserting themselves in what I have termed a "new politics of difference" in China (Gladney 1994b).

From the early period of the People's Republic, the communists made good on promises made to groups encountered during the Long March and in Yan'an to provide assistance to them and reward them for supporting the revolution. These promises required first that minorities be identified according to Stalinist criteria. Out of over 400 applicant groups in the early 1950s, China's preeminent anthropologist, Fei Xiaotong, informs us that a total of 55 minority nationalities were eventually recognized (Fei 1981, 60). Minorities were then accorded the following entitlements: greater flexibility in local economic practices, increased state funding for local development projects, disproportional access to political office, priority in educational advancement, exemption for most minorities from birth-planning restrictions, and more local control over distribution of tax revenues in "autonomous" minority areas (Dreyer 1976). In many cases, these "privileges" were often token in nature and often honored only in the breach. More important, the entitlements were meant to be temporary, until minority develop-

4. The Han are the majority nationality in every frontier minority region except Tibet, with the following Han percentages in border areas: Heilongjiang, 85 percent; Inner Mongolia, 83 percent; Ningxia, 68 percent; Guangxi, 61 percent; Guangdong, 58 percent; Liaoning, 52 percent; Xinjiang, 49 percent; Yunnan, 48 percent; Qinghai, 46 percent (*Renmin ribao*, November 14, 1990, 3; see also Heberer 1989, 44).

ment could reach that of the Han, and were rarely extended to more "developed" minorities, such as the Koreans and Manchu.

During times of political conservatism, such as the Anti-Rightist Campaign (1957–58) and Cultural Revolution (1966–76), these privileges were often rescinded as "ethnic" (*minzu*), and "local nationalisms" (*difang minzu zhuyi*) were thought to be "feudal remnants" with no place in the "new China." People were often afraid to admit their minority background, or reluctant to take advantage of the entitlement programs. After 1978, however, under Deng Xiaoping's economic and political liberalization, these entitlements once again took on increased importance in minority regions. Minorities quickly took advantage of the economic reforms to press for further economic and political opportunities on the basis of their ethnic status. Minorities were in fact among the first to take advantage of the economic reforms and to benefit from them. As token privileges led to real economic growth, political clout, and larger families in minority areas, other groups began to claim ethnic minority status and the corresponding entitlements. One notable consequence of this dramatic change was the rapid growth of the minority population, which increased 35 percent between the 1982 and 1990 censuses, whereas the Han majority grew only 10 percent (Gladney 1991, 222). This was owing not only to their having more children than the Han but also to the dramatic increase in those previously classified as "Han" who successfully had themselves reclassified as members of minority groups, indicating the increasing desirability of minority status. I shall show that for at least one community in southeastern China, changes in the economy — new opportunities for entrepreneurship, increased international sources of investment, and the revival of private trade — both contributed to and benefited from changes in government policy toward their ethnic status.

Departures from central planning have set in motion important processes of social and political change in minority areas. First, there is increased economic as well as political autonomy, because local cadres have much to gain from supporting local minority interests, often at the expense of the state. By politically identifying the minorities as "nationalities" in the early 1950s, with "autonomous" regions, provinces, counties, and even villages, the state set in motion a process of legitimate political activity, no matter how token initially, that was later difficult to limit. As a result, subsequent economic participation of minorities in the marketplace, in their autonomous districts, and in their own areas of specialization was legitimized by their state-assigned political status. Such participation could be exercised more easily during more politically "open" or reform periods, and although not immune, was less subject to repression during conservative periods.

Secondly, there has been a growing enrichment of certain minorities, often at the expense of the majority, even to the point of surpassing Han neighbors in some regions. This may be a result of the preferential policies outlined above, which were originally designed to spur economic development and "national unity." In some regions, this preferential treatment has led to increased jealousy on the part of Han neighbors, ethnic rivalry, and even conflicts with the state, as well as growing numbers of Han people who wish to claim minority status.

Third, cultural and educational programs designed to hasten the unification of China's minorities with the Han majority have led to a revitalization of ethnic and religious heritages, trade, household economics, and even religious movements (e.g., Islamic revitalization, Tibetan Buddhist assertiveness, and Mongol interest in Genghis Khan). Through the teaching of minority history, dance, music, and cultural practices in the schools and by public media, China has encouraged "cultural nationalism" despite its eventual goal of assimilating minorities into the Han mainstream (see Gladney 1994a).

Fourth, the state's increasing international trade with Middle Eastern nations has stimulated further religious and economic resurgence among China's Muslims in particular, while limiting the state's ability to repress Islamic movements and Muslim separatism. This is a quite different situation than that of Tibet, where China has little to lose in real economic and political terms on the international front from repressive measures. No foreign nation, including India and Nepal, has curtailed trade with China over the Tibetan issue. China has to be much more careful, however, in terms of the treatment of its nearly twenty million Muslims. The increasing importance of the Middle East for the export of cheap Chinese labor, low-grade weaponry, and agricultural produce, coupled with a growing reliance on Middle Eastern oil, has led to a corresponding increase in the importance of China's domestic policy toward its Muslim population (see Gladney 1994c). If China treats its Muslim minority peoples too severely, it might jeopardize key trade relations with several Middle Eastern governments, who have often expressed concern about the treatment of China's Muslims. At the same time, the growing participation of China's Muslims, collectively and individually, in international trade relations with Middle Eastern governments, has contributed to a validation of Islamic identity and the economic power of Islam.

Fifth, encouraging minorities to exploit their ethnic identities in the local and national political economy has led to increasing *transnational* connections between ethnic groups within China and their relatives abroad. This "globalization of local identity," to quote Arjun Appadurai, has led to strengthened connections among ethnic groups in China and their kinsmen, primarily in Southeast Asia and Taiwan. These networks become sources of funds, capital investment, and institutional alliances that lie well outside the centrally planned economy.

Finally, the minority nationality identification and preferential treatment program has led to similar political and economic demands *within the Han majority*. As such, growing Han nationalisms, such as among the Cantonese, Hakka, Subei, and other peoples previously thought of as Han, with only regional differences, can be seen as an unintended consequence of the state's departure from its original economic development program, initiated to stimulate integration, not economic and ethnic decentralization.

NATIONALITY, SOCIETY, AND STATE

Having one foot in the Muslim world and another well planted in Chinese civilization, the Hui Muslim nationality (now numbering 8.4 million according to the 1990 census) were traditionally well situated to serve as cultural and economic mediators within Chinese society, as well as between the Han Chinese majority and other non-Han minorities in Chinese society. This traditional role was severely curtailed, and in some cases completely eliminated, after the collectivization and religious reform campaigns in the late 1950s and early 1960s. With the relaxation of restrictions on private enterprise and ethnic expression in the early 1980s, the state was not prepared for, nor did it envision, the speed and vitality with which Muslims returned to their ethnoreligious roots and exploited opportunities to advance themselves and their community.

This point was made to me first when I was traveling in Tibet in February 1985. At any given time of the year, there were on average 10–20,000 Hui merchants from northwestern China temporarily residing in Tibet, trading small manufactured goods such as carpets, plastic articles, and shoes for television sets, radios, watches, and other luxury items brought in from India through Nepal. At any other port of entry in China, Hui and often Uygur Muslims can be seen engaged in this kind of barter-trade.[5] Local Tibetan cadres explained to me that "free trade" was encouraged around the Jokhang temple in order to "fill the cracks of socialism" and improve the lot of Tibet's "majority" people, the Tibetans (who are over 90 percent of the population). They thus made extra efforts to assist local Tibetan and Hui Muslim businesses at the expense of the Han Chinese, in what David Wank in chapter 6 describes as a "symbiotic clientelism" between entrepreneurs and local officials against the state and broader society. The liberaliza-

5. Hui Muslim traders in Tibet are vividly and somewhat derogatorily portrayed in the 1985 Tian Zhuangzhuang film *Horsethief* (*Dao ma zei*). This chapter primarily addresses the role of the Hui as economic middlemen; more extensive discussion of the Uygur and their trading practices is to be found in Gladney 1990, 1992.

tion of state policy with regard to private enterprise and the expression of minority national identity gave the Hui a unique opportunity to engage in a traditional activity that has long historical and cultural roots, roots that Hui in Fujian are only beginning to discover. As Jean Oi has argued elsewhere (Oi 1989), this alliance between local officials and entrepreneurs has allowed patronage and corruption, but in forms that avoid prosecution precisely because of the general assistance policies directed toward minorities, as well as cadre fear of stirring up minority anti-Han sentiment.

Hui Muslims have been known throughout China.... known as specialists in such areas as transport, the wool trade, jewelry, and vending food from small stands. Specializations ranged widely in scale and varied regionally according to the ancient.......... tradition of this..... in urban or rural settings. Before 1949, "Hui" referred to any person claiming to be Muslim or of Muslim descent. At Yan'an and later during the first Chinese census in 1953, it came to designate one "nationality" (*minzu*), which distinguished the Hui from the nine other identified Muslim nationalities in China (Uygur, Kazakh, Kirghiz, etc.), as well as from the Han majority and fifty-four other minority "nationalities." Chairman Mao and the early Yan'an communists eventually only promised autonomy, and not the possibility of secession, to the minority regions who submitted to state authority (see Gladney 1991, 87–93; Heberer 1989, 40–46). "The Communist government of China may be said to have inherited a policy of trying to facilitate the demise of nationality identities through granting self-government to minorities," June Dreyer has noted (1976, 17). Economic reforms have increased the autonomy of these peoples and made it increasingly difficult to carry out an "inherited" policy intended to assimilate them.

Hui Muslim traditional specializations were virtually lost after the 1955 collectivization reforms but have rapidly returned since the 1978 economic liberalization policy. Here we see an important shift in economic institutions. Prior to 1979, one could rarely find a Hui-run private enterprise, restaurant, or shop in China, although that was what they were known for prior to 1949. The centrally planned economy drove Hui out of private business into factory work in the cities, and into farming in the countryside. Although Hui engaged in these activities prior to 1949, they were primarily known for small business, craftsmanship, and entrepreneurialism, which disappeared under Mao. Under Deng, not only in the ancient Silk Road maritime port of Quanzhou, where this chapter begins, but throughout the villages and towns where Muslims now live, Hui have prospered at a rapid rate through strong participation in small private businesses and industry — in many places far surpassing their Han neighbors.

While Western theorists have often regarded "ethnic entrepreneurialism" as either detrimental to free enterprise or counterproductive to economic development in the larger economy (Bonacich 1973; Piore 1973), recent studies have argued that ethnic-based enterprises often exploit non-economic resources and are ideally suited to small and medium-sized urban and small-town economies (Waldinger 1983; Wong 1987; Zenner 1991). In his survey of "middlemen minorities," Walter Zenner (1991, 24) argues that minorities often play an important role in bridging diverse communities through cultural and economic brokering. These groups often develop communal solidarities, according to Zenner (1991, 19–20), banning out-group marriage, residing in closed communities, using kin ties for capital investment, following ethnic occupational specializations, establishing language and cultural schools for children, participating in nonmajority religious rites, avoiding local politics that are not important to their ethnic group, and maintaining formal ethnic community organizations, often with ties to groups beyond national boundaries.

These characteristics reflected much of Hui Muslim life before the late 1950s. Hui lived in what one frequent traveler to Muslim areas throughout China described as "little Muslim worlds," in almost total isolation from the non-Muslims among whom they lived. Since the major migrations of Muslims in the fourteenth century, Muslim communities throughout China had maintained their own self-sufficient villages and ethnic enclaves, with schools, restaurants, and mosques, meeting non-Muslims primarily in the marketplace. Following the late 1950s collectivization campaigns in the countryside and Socialist Reconstruction of Industry campaigns in urban areas, Hui villages were often redistricted to be included in larger multiethnic collectives. In the urban areas, Hui were assigned residence according to workplace, thus dispersing the community to a large degree. Now that post-1979 reforms and market liberalizations have been promoted for the sake of economic development, Hui communities are once again beginning to reflect the characteristics Zenner (1991) describes, returning to their traditional ethnic lifestyles. This will be illustrated by an examination of one Hui community in Fujian.

ECONOMIC PROSPERITY AND MUSLIM MINORITY IDENTITY IN A FUJIANESE LINEAGE COMMUNITY

In May 1984, when I first sought to visit the Hui lineage community on the outskirts of Quanzhou city in southern Fujian, I was told by local officials that the area was economically too "backward" (luohou), and that it would be "inconvenient" (bu fangbian) for me to visit their homes in Chendai township. Instead, members of the Hui lineage who shared the single surname Ding arranged to visit me in Quanzhou city. They were eager to tell me how it was that in 1979 they had been recognized as members of the Hui minority nationality, and that their community was beginning to change as a result. I was told that if I had been allowed to visit their coastal villages, I would have found communities that still derived most of their income from farming, fishing, and coastal clam cultivation. In the summer of 1986, I spent two months in Quanzhou, and on frequent visits to Chendai, I noticed that while the farming and fishing were still present, small factories were beginning to spring up, producing plastic shoes, bags, and containers, as well as medicine and other sundries. I also noticed the large, recently refurbished lineage hall, shrines to local deities, and numerous pigs scavenging for food.

By February 1991, I saw little evidence of fishing or farming; rather, the township was characterized by many new factories and huge three- and four-storey houses, and there was an almost complete absence of pigs. Adjacent to the lineage hall, a new mosque had just been completed to serve a growing local community of believers. In 1994, these changes, both economic and religious, were even more dramatic. These dramatic transformations are owing to economic reforms that have made the Chendai Hui begin to resemble their Muslim ancestors of ancient Quanzhou.

Near what is now Quanzhou city, there existed an ancient Silk Road maritime port known as "Zaitun," which Marco Polo called "one of the largest and most commodious ports in the world." At the southern entrance to the ancient harbor, there are thirteen villages with the single surname Ding, whose inhabitants, numbering over sixteen thousand and called the *wan ren Ding* (ten thousand Ding), claim descent from the earliest Muslim traders who settled on China's southeastern coast. However, since the descendants of Muslim ancestors in Quanzhou had begun to assimilate to southern Fujianese culture as early as the Ming dynasty (1368–1644), the vast majority of the Ding now follow local folk religious observances in their daily rituals and health care, no longer practicing Islam or Muslim dietary restrictions. Absent Islamic Hui culture, they were not recognized as members of the Hui nationality.

I have documented the process of identification whereby several Hui descent groups in Quanzhou maneuvered politically to be recognized as members of the Hui minority elsewhere (Gladney 1991, 286–90). It is important to note here that these Hui provided the perfect example of Chinese Stalinist nationality policy: they thought of themselves as Hui ethnically, but were not Muslim in religion. Because these Hui did not fit the cultural criteria established elsewhere in China, where Hui are often devout or at least titular Muslims and generally abstain from pork, they had difficulty justifying their claim to Hui nationality status. The state only recognized them when proof of their Muslim ancestry was found in local family genealogies, and a well-organized grass-roots association pressed the local government for recognition. It was economic and political liberalization under Deng that provided the impetus for their group mobilization. "We knew that if we were going to take advantage of the new economic reforms," one Ding lineage member told me in 1985, "we had to get recognized as Hui." This is not to deny the ethnic feeling for their ancestry the Ding shared prior to 1979. Rather, it only indicates that in 1979 it became possible and important enough for them to press for recognition of that ancestry.

The state did not, however, envision that recognizing the Ding and other groups as Hui would lead, not only to economic prosperity, but to a revitalized interest in Islam and ethnoreligious expression. Although this community still maintains a lineage hall and might be described anthropologically as a single-surname lineage community, there are now other Ding in southeastern China, as well as thousands of others claiming descent from Muslim ancestors, perhaps due to local awareness of the Ding's prosperity.

The Ding have lived in Chendai since the Wanli period of the Ming dynasty (1573–1620), supposedly having fled there from Quanzhou to avoid persecution. Since that time, they have been known for their specialized aquacultural economy. The town of Chendai is on the Fujian coast and well suited for cultivating the razor clams for which the Ding lineage are famous. Before 1949, they were not only engaged in this industry, but also produced opium and had many small factories that made woven bags and sundry goods. These goods were exported extensively and led to the migration of many Ding Hui to Southeast Asia, Taiwan, and Hong Kong in their business endeavors. After 1955, when private industries were collectivized in China, these small factories were either curtailed or transferred to the larger commune, of which the Ding lineage constituted seven brigades.

Since 1979, and the implementation of the economic reform policies in the countryside, the Ding have been recognized as members of the Hui nationality, and have once again begun operating small private factories producing athletic shoes and plastic goods, like the brightly colored plastic sandals, rugs, and other sundries found in most Chinese department stores. Of the 3,350 households in the seven villages (former brigades) in Chendai (which are 92 percent Hui), over 60 ran small factories in 1991. By 1994, the majority of all households derived their primary incomes from these "sideline" enterprises. In the larger factories, there may be over a hundred workers; in smaller ones, often only ten or so. Workers can work as long as they wish, which is usually eight to ten hours a day, seven days a week.

As a result of these many factories and their hard work, the Ding have begun to do extremely well. Several Ding families have registered as *wanyuanhu* (10,000-yuan families). One family banked at least 100,000 yuan (U.S. $33,000) in 1986. That was an extraordinary amount then, but in 1994 it became commonplace. The average annual income in the predominately Hui Chendai township in 1983 was 611 yuan per person, whereas in the larger, Han-dominated Jinjiang county, it was only 402 yuan in 1982 (People's Republic of China 1987, 175). By 1984, Chendai income reached 837 yuan per person for the town, while the Hui within Chendai averaged 1,100 yuan. Their income increased 33 percent in 1985. By 1989, the entire township's income had jumped to an average annual income of 1,000 yuan per person (Ding 1990, 3). This indicates a substantial increase in local Hui income over Han income in the county as well as the township. It is clear that the economic success was not limited to the Hui, as Han in Fujian also prospered during this period. Income from factories and industrial enterprises increased in the entire township from 1.4 million yuan in 1979 to 620 million yuan in 1993 (see table 9.1).[6]

The argument here is that economic reforms allowed minorities to assert their access to certain privileges, also encouraged under the economic reforms, which enabled them to prosper relatively faster than the Han. The increase of Hui over Han income was mainly owing to the encouragement of Hui-owned businesses, the permitted political mobilization of the Hui community, and the reestablishment of Hui overseas family connections, all of which were still being discouraged among the Han in the late 1970s and early 1980s. These activities became commonplace along the southeastern coast in the late 1980s, but my informants said that Han cadres in Jinjiang county were reluctant to encourage such practices among the Han until the Hui proved successful with them without political repercussions.

Finally, income from sideline enterprises in agriculture and small industry has also grown at an incredibly rapid rate (see table 9.2). Although the Hui only constitute one-seventh of the town's population, they account for over one-third of the income (township records). In 1984, Chendai was the first town in Fujian province to become a *yiyuan zhen* (100,000,000-yuan town). Color television sets are owned by almost every household, and there were over 550 motorcycles in the seven all-Hui villages in 1991. Over half of the Hui in the town have their own two- to four-level homes, paid for with cash from their savings. Many of the multi-level homes that I visited had small piecework factories on the first level (making tennis shoe soles here, the linings there, laces elsewhere, and so on), while the various stem family branches lived on the other levels. For example, Ding Yongwei, mentioned at the beginning of this chapter, has two sons. On the first level of his four-storey stone-block home, he has a small factory that produces the stretchy fabric that is used to line the insides of athletic shoes. He obtains the materials from a distant relative in the Philippines. His youngest son and wife live on the second floor. His oldest son, wife, and two children live on the third floor (as a Hui, Ding's son is allowed to have two children). Ding Yongwei and his wife occupy the top floor.

It is clear that during this period, economic reorganization occurred as a

6. Note that the 1989 figures are based on Ding 1990, whereas the 1979–93 records are derived from my field notes and township records.

TABLE 9.1 Income from Factory and Industrial
Enterprises, Chendai Township, 1979–1993
(in yuan)

Year	Income
1979	1,440,000
1980	3,220,000
1981	5,630,000
1982	6,150,000
1983	8,780,000
1984	29,040,000
1985	36,240,000
1986	41,450,000
1987	46,880,000
1988	56,720,000
1989	68,410,000
1990	92,200,000
1991	156,140,000
1992	334,540,000
1993	620,170,000

SOURCES: 1994 township records; 1989 figures from Ding 1990, 3.

TABLE 9.2 Income from Agricultural and Industrial
Sideline Enterprises, Chendai Township, 1979–1993
(in yuan)

Year	Income
1979	4,490,000
1980	4,920,000
1981	7,460,000
1982	11,770,000
1983	13,880,000
1984	17,770,000
1988	60,940,000
1989	74,010,000
1990	92,200,000
1991	173,820,000
1992	353,490,000
1993	639,690,000

SOURCES: 1994 township records; 1989 figures from Ding 1990, 3.

TABLE 9.3   Composition of the Labor Force,
Chendai Township, 1978–1992
(%)

	Agriculture	Industry
1978	69.9%	30.1%
1984	19.9	80.1
1985	14.0	86.0
1989	13.0	87.0
1992	7.0	93.0

SOURCES: 1994 township records; 1989 figures from Ding 1990, 3.

result of the economic reforms. Prior to 1978, the majority of the labor force (69.9 percent) in Chendai were engaged in agriculture, and only 30 percent were involved in industry. By 1992, this had shifted dramatically, with 93 percent of the labor force engaged in industry (table 9.3). Income from sideline enterprises has increased eight times over 1979. The Ding believe that this was because of their recognition as Hui. Whatever the reason, it is clear that economic reforms and their skill in turning their ethnicity to their own advantage led to dramatic changes in the political economy of the area.

ETHNIC POLITICS AND ECONOMIC PROSPERITY

Ding Hui do not attribute their prosperity to industriousness alone. When they were recognized as part of the Hui nationality in 1979, they became eligible for assistance as members of an underprivileged minority. They have received several government subsidies that have spurred their economy. Between 1980 and 1984, the government gave over 200,000 yuan to the seven Hui teams, which they spent on a running-water system, ponds for raising fish, and expansion of their razor-clam industry. The Ministry of Education has given 40,000 yuan to build a middle school, and 33,000 yuan for a primary school. As a minority nationality the Hui also receive preference in high school and college admission, and they are allowed to have one more child per family than the Han. Hui representation in the local government is also disproportionately higher than their percentage of the population. Two of the ten party committee representatives (*changwei*) were surnamed Ding in 1985, as was the town's party secretary.

Perhaps more important, the Ding have exploited their transnational connections to relatives abroad, and started to do so earlier than the Han in their area, leading to increased sources of capital investment. Over 50 percent of the Ding lineage members have overseas relatives, mainly in the Philippines, Indonesia, and Singapore — a higher proportion than their

Han neighbors (see Li 1990, 337–46). They have reestablished communications with these relatives and have been assisted by frequent remittances. One of the reasons Hui and Han alike are eager to exploit overseas connections is that joint ventures are not subject to the same government taxes as other private industries. With both their minority status and overseas connections, the Hui are in a much stronger position to exploit these favorable conditions than the Han.

This outside income is an important factor in the rapid economic development of the seven Ding villages. All seven Hui villages have elementary schools, thanks to donations from overseas relatives averaging 20,000 yuan each. Neighboring Han villages have one elementary school for every three or four villages. The Ding say that their close and frequent contact with overseas relatives is a result of their strong feeling of ethnic identity, which they say surpasses that of neighboring Han lineages, with their overseas relations. It is interesting, however, that one wealthy village family that maintained extensive overseas relations revealed that overseas relatives are often reluctant to admit their Islamic heritage! While it is not true of all Ding, in this case, it is clear that many villagers and their overseas relatives are exploiting a favorable minority nationality policy even when they may not share strong ethnic feelings about their past.

These government subsidies and special benefits are important factors in the Ding Hui claim to ethnic minority status. The manipulation of ethnic identity for special favored treatment has been well documented by anthropologists as an example of "situational" ethnicity, where ethnic groups frequently maneuver and reposition themselves for political and economic advantages (Barth 1969; Wallerstein 1987). This is certainly an important factor in understanding why the Ding lineage's ethnic identity has become even more relevant under Deng's economic reforms. Changes in socioeconomic conditions and the local political economy are conducive to rapid ethnic change. Even before such policies were promulgated, however, Ding Hui occupied a distinct ecological and commercial niche, which they had maintained for generations.

This indicates that for the Ding, their ethnic attachment to certain economic practices is not merely situational, but belongs to a more deeply ingrained identity, which has been part of their collective memory for generations (Geertz 1973; Keyes 1981). Even when they have been prevented from openly expressing those traditions, they have been preserved privately through family and communal ritual. It is significant that in ancestor worship, where pork is the most highly prized of all ancestral offerings, the Ding did not offer pork to their ancestors precisely because they remembered them to be Muslim, even though they themselves for the most part are no longer Muslim and include pork in their diet. Part of the *jipin* (requirements of remembrance) stipulated in their genealogy was the offering of razor clams to their ancestors (Ding Clan Genealogy 1980, 30). This indicates that ethnic specialization of labor was maintained in southern Fujian, where Hui are known to have been involved in specific aquacultural industries. These specializations were interrupted by PRC collectivist policies but have reappeared with the economic reforms.

Economic reforms encouraged private enterprise and dismantling of centrally planned economies, allowing for the rise of local associations and ethnic mobilization for economic goals. These associations in turn led to increased ethnic and even religious revitalization in this community as well as the reestablishment of international networks. Central-state policy accords special economic and political privileges to these recently recognized Hui along the southeastern coast and encourages their interaction with foreign Muslim governments. This has had a significant impact on their ethnic identity. Fujian provincial and local municipal publications proudly proclaim Quanzhou to be the site of the third most important Islamic holy grave and the fifth most important mosque in the world.[7] Religious and government representatives from over thirty Muslim nations were escorted to Muslim sites in Quanzhou as part of a state-sponsored delegation in spring 1986. The successful promotion of Quanzhou's place on the ancient Silk Route and in Islamic history led to two UNESCO-sponsored conferences in 1991 and 1994, with substantial international participation, as part of UNESCO's ongoing study of the Silk Route as a medium of intercultural exchange.

In February 1991, the UNESCO-sponsored Silk Roads Expedition arrived in Quanzhou, which became its main port of entry on China's "Maritime Silk Route," virtually bypassing the traditional stopping-place, Guangzhou. During the four-day conference and Silk Road festivities, in which I participated, foreign guests and Muslim dignitaries were brought to a Chendai Ding village as part of their orientation in order to highlight the recent economic prosperity and government support for the modern descendants of the ancient Muslim maritime traders. At the 1994 conference, not only were academic papers presented, but participants were offered the possibility of paying to go on a tour of "Islamic Maritime Sites" following the

---

7. The tombs are said to hold the remains of Imam Sayid and Imam Waggas from Medina, two reputed cousins of the Prophet Muhammad, sent to China by the Prophet with two other missionaries, Wahb Abu Kabcha, who is said to be buried in Guangzhou's bell tomb, and another saint, buried in Yangzhou. According to He Qiaoyuan's 1629 history of Fujian (the *Minshu*), these four missionary saints visited China during the Wu De period of the Tang emperor Gao Zu (A.D. 618–26), which is hardly possible, since Islam dates to Muhammad's famous Hijra (or "journey") from Mecca to Medina in 622 and the Prophet died in 632. For the debate over the authenticity of the tombs, and the 1009–10 dating of the Quanzhou mosque, see Chen 1984, 95–101. For the claim that Quanzhou is an Islamic pilgrimage site, see Yang 1985.

conference, including visits to mosques and Muslim cemeteries in Hang-zhou, Suzhou, Shanghai, Xi'an, and Beijing. During the 1994 conference in Quanzhou, on the fifteenth day of the Chinese New Year, participants were taken to several Hui-run factories, as well as to the Ding lineage's cemetery, where Ding elders remembered their ancestors by performing such rites as burning incense, bowing three times, reading portions of the genealogy, and, in a newly "invented" tradition, presenting flowers to their ancestors' graves. In reflection of their ancestors' Islamic heritage, the Ding invited their local imam to read a passage of the Quran in front of the graves. Afterward, he invited the few foreign and local Muslims to join him in a Quranic recitation. The ceremony was followed by statements by local officials, including a strong expression of support from Hei Böll, the former chairman of the Ningxia Hui Autonomous Region and current vice-chairman of the People's Political Consultative Congress. Foreign Muslims, including the director of the UNESCO project and officials and scholars from Iran, Kuwait, Turkey, and Malaysia also made public statements of support.

Partly as a result of these and earlier official and international Islamic contacts, construction of the Xiamen international airport was completely underwritten by a low-interest loan from the government of Kuwait in the mid 1980s. The Kuwaitis also assisted in the building of a large hydroelectric dam project along the Min River outside Fuzhou. A Jordanian businessman visiting in spring 1986 offered to donate U.S. $1.5 million to rebuild the Qingjing mosque in Quanzhou, established in the year 1009. China claims that the many Islamic relics in Quanzhou are evidence of a long history of friendly exchanges between China and the Muslim world. As a result of China's growing trade with Third World Muslim nations, it is only natural that these historical treasures should be displayed and made available to foreign Muslim visitors. It is also not surprising that the descendants of these early foreign Muslim residents in Quanzhou — the Ding, Guo, Huang, Jin, and other Hui lineages — are interested in further interaction with distant foreign Muslim relations.

International Islamic attention has had an impact upon the self-perception of the Ding lineage as Hui descendants. It has also led to a kind of ethnic revitalization and rediscovery of their Muslim heritage. In 1984, construction of a mosque was proposed in Chendai so that the Hui there could begin to learn more about Islam. The Quanzhou mosque is too far from Chendai (fifteen kilometers) to be of practical use to them, and it is now without a resident imam. When the new mosque was completed in Chendai in 1990, it attracted many villagers interested in learning more about Islam. Quranic study courses have been conducted, and some vil-lagers have begun to learn Arabic. In 1991, they invited an imam from Inner Mongolia, and eighteen students from the Ding lineage have gone to

Huhehot to study with the Chendai imam's teacher in order to become future imams, including two women. There are four other mosques in Fujian, which formerly had imams from Ningxia and Gansu, who came at the invitation of the provincial Islamic Association between 1982 and 1989, but they all eventually returned to their more familiar homes in the Islamic northwest, and now Chendai is the only mosque with an imam in all of Fujian province. This is particularly ironic, since the mosque in Chendai is the newest mosque in Fujian, established among villagers who have only recently begun to practice the Islamic faith.

In November 1984, a grass-roots organization of Ding Hui leaders was recognized by the government as the "Jinjiang County Chendai Town Commission for Hui Affairs." This is quite significant, in that formal voluntary associations outside of initial government sponsorship are generally considered illegal in China, and in this case the state recognized the organization well after it was established. One of the commission's first acts was to establish a small museum in the ancestral hall, which now displays articles substantiating their foreign Muslim ancestry, their recognition as members of the Hui nationality in 1979, their recent economic success, and the visits of foreign Muslims and foreign dignitaries, including a picture of the author's 1986 visit! The ancestral hall museum possesses the usual ritual objects and ancestral tablets on the domestic altar, as do other southern Fujianese temples, but the hall is no longer used in the worship of ancestors. Locals affirmed that daily rituals of the domestic cult, lighting incense on a daily basis, and providing special offerings on festivals and feast days, were similar to those of other Fujianese families. The main difference here is that no pork was admitted into the ancestral hall. Ding members told me that they often rinsed their mouths with tea before making offerings to their ancestors, as a way of cleansing pork residue that might be offensive to them. Perhaps more important, this ancestral hall received special township-level support and approval. Ancestral halls are now allowed in China but are generally not patronized by the state. The township provided some funding for the ancestral hall, reasoning that it also contained a historical museum of the history of the Hui, and thus of foreign relations in China. I have never seen another ancestral hall containing a museum, and it was the nicest hall that I visited in Fujian.[8]

8. In 1990, the commission sponsored and completed construction of an "Islamic prayer hall" (*qingzhen libaitang*) adjacent to the lineage village. This "prayer hall" was built exactly like a mosque, with a qibla (niche identifying orientation toward Mecca) and worship area, in Arab architectural style. The commission was not officially allowed at the time to call it a mosque (*qingzhensi* or *masjdid*), however, as the China Islamic Association had not approved its construction. In Beijing, I was told by representatives of the association in 1991 that they were uncomfortable about giving their imprimatur to a mosque situated in a village of Hui who were not entirely Islamic and practiced Minnan folk religion. Nevertheless, a growing number

The Ding Hui commission has also asked that Jinjiang county be recognized as an autonomous minority county, but this has not worked out, according to one official, because of "redistricting difficulties." Other Hui have told me the state would never risk recognizing an autonomous Hui county that was not Islamic for fear of antagonizing conservative national and international Muslim opinion. The community apparently celebrated the Ramadan fast in 1989 and 1990 by giving up pork for the month. This possible creation of a new Islamic identity for the Hui in Chendai is important to watch as it becomes increasingly relevant for them in their altered social context. It is also important to note that the reforms and prosperity that have come to Ding villagers as a result of their pressing for recognition as members of the Hui nationality and descendants of the ancient Silk Road Muslim traders have not been restricted to the Muslim Hui Ding; they have benefited the entire township. Chendai township not only has a substantial Han population, but there are also many among the Ding who do not believe in Islam, including folk religionists, and even about eighty households of Christians, who were nevertheless registered as members of the so-called Hui "Muslim" nationality! These Ding converted in the 1930s under the influence of a Western Protestant missionary, and they too have recently rebuilt their church, possibly because the local government allowed the construction of the Islamic prayer hall.

Prosperity has come to the Ding lineage partly as a result of government minority assistance, through tax breaks, development incentives, and permission to engage in small business, and partly as a result of the local Hui taking aggressive advantage of opportunities for collective action, economic enterprise, and increased contacts with overseas relatives. As noted above, although the Ding lineage only constitutes one-seventh of the town's population, it accounts for over one-third of the entire area's annual income. Economic prosperity has been accompanied by ethnic and even religious revival. These lineages have always maintained a Hui identity that in conjunction with recent events is only now beginning to take on a decidedly Islamic commitment, something quite unforeseen when the state chose to institute economic reforms in the late 1970s. It is clear that the Ding pressed for recognition as members of the Hui nationality just at the time of Deng's economic liberalization policies, and then quickly took advantage of them as an ethnic minority — a minority whose main cultural trait was defined as "entrepreneurialism." Here, ethnic revitalization can be seen as a direct consequence of shifts in economic policy. The earlier centrally planned

---

of Hui villagers attend the mosque for regular prayer and Quranic study. In late 1991, they invited the imam to come to the prayer hall, and now it is officially recognized as a mosque (*qingzhensi*).

economy prevented ethnic specialization, entrepreneurialism, and exploitation of individual and corporate overseas ties. Now that economic planning has been decentralized, it will be very difficult to put these revitalized
aspects of Ding ethnicity back in the box.

MUSLIM TRADERS, CHINESE STATE

This chapter has demonstrated that the Hui have dramatically resurrected
entrepreneurial traditions handed down to them from their Muslim ancestors. The Chinese state has played an important role in allowing these tradi
tions to flourish, as in the past decade, or in restricting them, as during the
two decades from 1958 to 1978. Nevertheless, while the state can restrict or
support trade, it cannot control the consequences of its economic policies,
which have a direct influence on nationality policy and ethnic identity. The
Hui, Uygur, and other Muslim communities bring to their economic en-
gagements an interest in trading and a desire to maximize their opportunities for advancement. Whether their motivations be personal enrichment, religious enhancement, or strengthening community solidarity, their
marginalized position in Chinese society has put them in a position where
trade and mediation are important skills needed for survival and self-
strengthening, developed over years of relative isolation among the Chinese
majority or in opposition to a non-Muslim state. Economic reforms have not
only allowed the reestablishment of these "ethnic" traditions but have directly stimulated them.

This is particularly true of the Hui, whose "cultural makeup" is said to
predispose them to entrepreneurialism. The recognition of the unique contribution Hui entrepreneurial abilities might make to economic development represents a dramatic shift from past criticisms of these characteristics
as capitalistic and feudal. Perhaps to seek historical support for this state
policy, Lai Cunli, in his 312-page survey of Hui economic history, commis-
sioned by the China Minority Nationality Research Office of the State Commission for Nationality Affairs, argues, after a detailed historical review of
the entrepreneurial role Hui have played throughout Chinese history, that
their "minority culture" is uniquely entrepreneurial compared to those of
other nationalities in China, and that this "business culture" has been responsible for making major contributions to the development of China's
economy (Lai 1988, 3, 283). "One can see," he concludes, "that the business activity of the early Hui ancestors was an extremely great influence on
the formation of the Hui nationality" (ibid., 276). Similarly, the well-known
Hui historian Ma Tong argues that the fact that the early ancestors of the
Hui were primarily traders, businessmen, and soldiers had a profound influence on their later formation as a nationality:

Based on the analysis of historical records, Arab, Persian, Central Asian, and other foreign businessmen, soldiers, officials, and missionaries who believed in Islam and came to China were the ancestors of the Hui nationality; since they resided in China and even married Han women, they gradually formed into the Hui nationality, and [it] became an important member of our country's great multinational family. . . . From the very earliest period, the vast majority of Islamic disciples in China were engaged in trade and business activity. (Ma [1981] 1983, 06, 07)

Although the state has sought to exploit entrepreneurial traditions among the Hui to encourage economic development in rural and urban areas, as well as to make use of an "Islamic card" in its international relations, it has not been able to prevent the full expression of Hui ethnoreligious identity, which is inextricably linked to Islam. With economic privatization has come ethnoreligious revitalization and a growing awareness of Muslim links to the outside Islamic world. Just as the state has encouraged and courted investment from foreign Muslim governments in China, only to find that foreign Muslims have generally preferred to build mosques rather than factories, so among the Hui, the state has not been able to divorce national from religious interests, or economic development from Islamic awareness.

I have argued elsewhere that prior to the founding of the PRC, Hui identity, like the term "Hui," was ill defined at best. To be Hui meant to be Muslim, and it bore little connection to ethnic or nationality status. A foreign Muslim was a Hui, as well as a Uygur, Kazakh, or Chinese-speaking Muslim — a policy still maintained in Taiwan, which does not recognize the Hui as a separate nationality, only as a religious group (Pillsbury 1981, 35). With the identification of the Hui as a nationality (*minzu*) by the early Chinese communists in Yan'an and then officially in 1953, Muslims had legitimate economic and political incentives to define themselves as members of the Hui or other Muslim minorities. These economic and political privileges that the early communists held out to their early Muslim supporters led directly to the rise of their collective identity as a nationality. The Hui nationality experienced a "crystallization" and even, perhaps, invention of national identity that has had far-reaching consequences for their development. Not only are Hui in Fujian rediscovering their Islamic roots, but Hui throughout China are exploiting every potential privilege attached to their minority nationality status. Economic prosperity has only served to support these tendencies — developments that the early Chinese communists could never have envisioned. For the Hui in Quanzhou, recognition in 1979 as Hui did not cause their economic prosperity, but it certainly helped it. By the same token, potential economic prosperity was not the only reason for their reassertion of ethnicity, but it certainly was an important incentive. It is clear from this study, however, that economic reforms had much to do with the ethnic transformations in the Quanzhou countryside.

THE LEGITIMIZATION OF ETHNICITY IN CHINA

This chapter has not yet established why it is that the sight of ethnic and religious nationalism rapidly expanding along with the economy in minority, especially Muslim, areas has not led the PRC to reverse its policy. If the Chinese communist state is aware, as it clearly must be, that "a push for reformation from below" (Szelényi 1988) contributed to the Hungarian communists' fall from power, why does it not simply rescind its recognition of minority nationality identity and declare then communal differences, like class differences, have been eradicated in China? Since economic reforms have not only stimulated the local economy in minority regions, as intended, but have also inadvertently led to ethnic and religious revitalization, continued economic growth might very well lead to increased ethnic separatism and religious conflict. Why tie economic and other privileges to ethnicity in China, rather than just repudiating ethnic and religious differences altogether? This was certainly done during the Cultural Revolution and earlier radical periods. Yet it has not occurred under Deng Xiaoping, who has allowed, if not encouraged, ethnicity and religion through a liberalized economy. Why do leaders listen to interest groups and their demands? Why not ignore them?

By linking entrepreneurialism and privatization with nationality status, ethnicity in China has gained an increased legitimacy and legality. In state socialist societies, identity is not just something you maintain about yourself, which is open to debate, self-definition, and other-definition; rather, it is a right you possess, legislated and enforced by the state, marked in your passport, and determined at birth (or at nationality registration in the case of mixed parentage). Nationality becomes a registered, public association, to which one belongs by law, unlike other voluntary associations, which may be severely restricted in such societies. In this way, one sees a legalization and essentialization of ethnicity, a state-sponsored primordialization, to use Edward Shils's (1957) term, by giving ethnicity state authority, legality, and the aura of legitimacy. This both diminishes the power of the state (i.e., local cadres, who cannot object to ethnic assertions of interest) and at the same time legitimates the state's power to define which groups constitute nationalities and which groups do not (see Kornai 1992, 52). The state does derive benefits from permitting entrepreneurialism among minority nationalities, particularly through gaining wider ethnic support, as well as the "symbolic capital" China enjoys in the international arena through portraying itself as multinational, with the Han in the vanguard of national socioeconomic development and modernity. The state also establishes itself as a benefactor and teacher of the "backward" minority peoples, who should eventually "evolve" and assimilate, with appropriate support and leadership provided by the Communist party.

There are many consequences of this legitimation of decentralized economic reforms and entrepreneurialism among national minorities in socialist states. First, there is a clear devolving downward of power and authority, from the state and majority nationality to the ethnic minority leaders and their followers. Second, in the other direction, there is an enhanced ability of minorities to influence government officials, as well as a reluctance on the part of those officials to interfere with minority "rights." Third, there is a relative decline in the authority of local officials to enforce central policy, especially in areas where minorities constitute large population concentrations. Fourth, and perhaps most important, there is an increase in collective self-identities as *minzu* (nationalities), a rise in the numbers of those who wish to be considered as such, and perhaps even a desire among the Han majority to exploit cultural differences for personal gain. For example, minority art and romanticization of ethnic "primitivity" is growing in popularity among the broader populace (see Gladney 1994a). The 1990 census revealed that in China, fewer people want to be known as Han. We now find that even among the majority Han population, increasing numbers of "sub-Han" peoples, such as the Cantonese (self-proclaimed "Wu" and "Tang" peoples), Sichuanese, Hakka, and Fujianese, are beginning to assert their distinctiveness, maintaining local languages, and even claiming ethnic difference from the Han majority.

Fifth, identity becomes further linked economically to nationality. One cannot get a job in the formal sector or enter school without registering one's nationality. And, finally, there are now new types of political and economic competition that are often ethnic and subethnic, whereas before ethnicity was not arguably the main divide for political conflict (in official dogma, it was class), or at least it was more restricted by the state, which believed ethnicity to be transitory and superstructural. While ethnicity is certainly much more than a state-recognized categorization, in state socialist societies, the power and authority of ethnicity becomes sanctioned, indeed legalized, by the state, and is stimulated and legitimated by economic reforms. Unlike corruption, ethnic revitalization that results from economic liberalization cannot be restricted or criminalized.

Events in Yugoslavia and Romania (Kligman 1990) suggest that the categories of nationality established under state socialism, while in some cases helping to undermine that very system, have nevertheless gained a power and legitimacy of their own, which is not easily denied once attained. This chapter has shown how such an identity, given by the state to one lineage in southern Fujian through its recognition as one of fifty-five official minority nationalities, has allowed its emergence as a vibrant ethnic group, which is now asserting itself in the economic and political sphere, both domestically and internationally. Economic reforms under Deng have served to strengthen and enhance ethnic differences. Although minority recognition was part of the original Leninist-Stalinist-inspired central plan, the state (and perhaps the minorities themselves) never imagined what they would become, where the state would take them, or they the state.

REFERENCES

Allworth, Edward. 1980. "Ambiguities in Russian Group Identity and Leadership of the RSFSR." In *Ethnic Russia in the USSR. The Dilemma of Dominance*, ed. Edward Allworth, 17-18. New York: Pergamon Press.

Barth, Fredrik. 1969. "Introduction." In *Ethnic Groups and Boundaries: The Social Organization of Cultural Difference*, ed. Fredrik Barth, 9–38. Boston: Little, Brown.

Bonacich, Edna. 1973. "A Theory of Middlemen Minorities." *American Sociological Review* 37: 583–94.

Chen Dasheng, ed. 1984. *Islamic Inscriptions in Quanzhou*. Translated by Chen En-ming. Yinchuan: Ningxia People's Publishing Society; Quanzhou: Fujian People's Publishing Society.

Chen Guoqiang, ed. 1990. *Chendai Huizushi yanjiu* (Research on Chendai Hui Nationality History). Beijing: China Academy of Social Sciences Press.

Ch'ên Yüan. 1966. *Western and Central Asians in China under the Mongols: Their Transformation into Chinese*. Monumenta Serica, monograph 15. Los Angeles: Monumenta Serica at the University of California.

Connor, Walker. 1984. *The National Question in Marxist-Leninist Theory and Strategy*. Princeton: Princeton University Press.

"Ding Clan Genealogy." 1980. In *Quanzhou wenxian congkan di san zong* (Quanzhou Documents Collection, no. 13). Quanzhou: Quanzhou Historical Research Society.

Ding Xiancao. 1990. "Chendai: The Past and the Present." In *Chendai Huizushi yanjiu* (Research on Chendai Hui Nationality History), ed. Chen Guoqiang, 1–6. Beijing: China Academy of Social Sciences Press.

Dreyer, June. 1976. *China's Forty Million: Minority Nationalities and National Integration in the People's Republic of China*. Cambridge, Mass.: Harvard University Press.

Dunlop, John B. 1983. *The Faces of Contemporary Russian Nationalism*. Princeton: Princeton University Press.

Fan Changjiang. [1936] 1980. *Zhongguo de xibei jiao* (China's Northwest Corner). 1st ed., edited by the Chinese Academy of Social Sciences, Tianjin: Public Publishing House. Reprint Beijing: New China Publishing Society.

Fei Xiaotong. 1981. "Ethnic Identification in China." In *Toward a People's Anthropology*, ed. Fei Xiaotong, 60–77. Beijing: New World Press.

Geertz, Clifford. 1973. "The Integrative Revolution: Primordial Sentiments and Civil Politics in the New States." In *The Interpretation of Cultures*, ed. Clifford Geertz, 255–310. New York: Basic Books.

Gladney, Dru C. 1990. "The Ethnogenesis of the Uighur." *Central Asian Survey* 9, 1: 1–28.

———. 1991. *Muslim Chinese: Ethnic Nationalism in the People's Republic.* Cambridge, Mass.: Harvard University Press for the Council on East Asian Studies.

———. 1992. "Transnational Islam and Uighur National Identity: Salman Rushdie, Sino-Muslim Missile Deals, and the Trans-Eurasian Railway." *Central Asian Survey* 11, 3: 1–18.

———. 1993. "The Muslim Face of China." *Current History* 92, 575: 275–80.

———. 1994a. "Representing Nationality in China: Refiguring Majority/Minority Identities." *Journal of Asian Studies* 53, 1: 1–34.

———. 1994b. "Ethnic Identity in China: The New Politics of Difference." In *China Briefing, 1994*, ed. William A. Joseph, 171–92. Boulder, Colo.: Westview Press.

———. 1994c. "Sino-Middle Eastern Perspectives since the Gulf War: Views from Below." *International Journal of Middle Eastern Studies* 26, 4: 677–92.

Heberer, Thomas. 1989. *China and Its National Minorities: Autonomy or Assimilation?* New York: M. E. Sharpe.

Keyes, Charles F. 1981. "The Dialectics of Ethnic Change." In *Ethnic Change*, ed. Charles F. Keyes, 4–30. Seattle: University of Washington Press.

Kligman, Gail. 1990. "Reclaiming the Public: A Reflection on Creating Civil Society in Romania." *East European Politics and Societies* 4, 3: 393–438.

Kornai, János. 1992. *The Socialist System: The Political Economy of Socialism.* Princeton, N.J.: Princeton University Press.

Lai Cunli. 1988. *Huizu shangye shi* (A History of Hui Nationality Mercantilism). Beijing: Zhongguo Shangye Chubanshe.

Li Tianxi. 1990. "Tradition of Patriotism and Village-Love of the Overseas Chinese of the 'Ding' Clan of Chendai." In *Chendai Huizushi yanjiu* (Research on Chendai Hui Nationality History), ed. Chen Guoqiang, 337–46. Beijing: China Academy of Social Sciences Press.

Ma Tong. [1981] 1983. *Zhongguo Yisilan jiaopai yu Menhuan zhidu shilue* (A History of Muslim Factions and the Menhuan System in China). Yinchuan: Ningxia People's Publishing Society.

Ningxia Hui Autonomous Region Population Census Office. 1983. *Ningxia Huizu zizhiqu di san ci renkou pucha* (Ningxia Hui Autonomous Region Third Population Census). Beijing: n.p.

Oi, Jean. 1989. "Market Reform and Corruption in Rural China." *Studies in Comparative Communism* 22, 2–3: 221–33.

Olcott, Martha Brill. 1987. *The Kazakhs.* Stanford, Calif.: Hoover Institution Press.

People's Republic of China. Population Census Office of the State Council and the Institute of Geography of the Chinese Academy of Sciences. 1987. *The Population Atlas of China.* Oxford: Oxford University Press.

Pillsbury, Barbara L. K. 1981. "The Muslim Population of China: Clarifying the Question of Size and Ethnicity." *Institute for Muslim Minority Affairs Journal* 3, 2: 35–58.

Piore, Michael. 1973. "The Role of Immigration in Industrial Growth: A Case Study of the Origins and Character of Puerto Rican Migration to Boston." MIT Department of Economics, Working Paper no. 112.

Shils, Edward. 1957. "Primordial, Personal, Sacred and Civil Ties." *British Journal of Sociology* 8, 2: 130–45.

Stark, David. 1989. "Privatization in Hungary: From Plan to Market or from Plan to Clan?" *Eastern European Politics and Societies* 4, 3: 351–92.

Stark, David, and Victor Nee. 1989. "Toward an Institutional Analysis of State Socialism." In *Remaking the Economic Institutions of Socialism: China and Eastern Europe*, eds. Victor Nee and David Stark, 1–31. Stanford, Calif.: Stanford University Press.

Szelényi, Iván. 1988. *Socialist Entrepreneurs: Embourgeoisement in Rural Hungary.* Madison: University of Wisconsin Press.

Waldinger, Roger. 1983. "Ethnic Enterprise and Industrial Change· A Case Study of the New York Garment Industry." Ph.D. diss., Harvard University.

Wallerstein, Immanuel. 1987. "The Construction of Peoplehood: Racism, Nationalism, Ethnicity." *Sociological Forum* 2, 2: 373–88.

Wong, Bernard. 1987. "The Role of Ethnicity in Enclave Enterprises: A Study of the Chinese Garment Factories in New York City." *Human Organization* 4, 2: 120–30.

Yang Hongxun. 1985. "A Preliminary Discussion on the Building Year of Quanzhou Holy Tomb and the Authenticity of Its Legend." In *The Islamic Historic Relics in Quanzhou*, ed. Committee for Protecting Islamic Historical Relics in Quanzhou and the Research Centre for the Historical Relics of Chinese Culture, 1–15. Quanzhou: Fujian People's Publishing House.

Zenner, Walter P. 1991. *Minorities in the Middle: A Cross-Cultural Analysis.* Albany: State University of New York Press.

Zhuang Jinghui. 1993. "Chendai Dingshi Huizu Hanhua de yanjiu" (Research on Han Assimilation of the Ding Lineage in Chendai). *Haijiaoshi yanjiu* 34, 2: 93–107.

INDEX

Agriculture, Chinese: in Chendai, 254; collective, 9, 217; effect of market economy on, 239; household, 6, 11, 220, 223, 239; increases in production, 220

Agriculture, Hungarian: collective, 36, 37; commercialization of, 40; effect of foreign exchange reform on, 140; household, 36, 47, 65; private plots in, 41, 47; in second economy, 39–40

Allocative efficiency: and corruption, 215; effect of banking reform on, 120; of Hungarian labor markets, 116, 145; in socialist politics, 35, 116

Anti-Rightist Campaign (China, 1957-58), 245

Artisans, Hungarian: organization of, 77n11; in second economy, 68

Assets: ownership of, 7; productive, 19

Assets, allocation of, 1; by Communist Party, 7; by Hungarian Socialist Workers' Party, 35, 56; in socialist systems, 30–31

Association Law (Hungary, 1989), 28, 34; legalization of capital ownership, 141; legalization of private enterprise, 53

Authoritarianism: agencies of, 91; of Chinese central government, 202; of communist regimes, 1; and departures from central planning, 18

Authority: in central planning, 87; citizens' exercise of, 16; citizens' resistance to, 14, 17, 42; Communist Party's basis of, 7; of Hungarian party state, 54, 135, 143; in local governments, 14–16; manipulation

by Chinese entrepreneurs, 202–4; role in central planning, 87; role of volunteer work in, 195

Autonomy: of Chinese local governments, 244; for Chinese minorities, 248; of citizens, 4; in Hungarian second economy, 38; of interest groups, 62; role in state intervention, 90; in Stalinist period, 35

Banking, Chinese: control by local governments, 102; loans to entrepreneurs, 162

Banking, Hungarian: central regulation of, 122; foreign-exchange licenses in, 135; loans to entrepreneurs, 49, 53; two-tiered system of, 119, 120–22. *See also* Commercial banks, Hungarian

Banking reform, Hungarian, 115–19, 143, 145; risks of, 120–22; role of HSWP in, 122–23

Bao (obligation), 168

Bargaining: and emergence of civil society, 16; by Hungarian workers, 43, 117, 127, 132

Bartlett, David, 4, 5–6

Bin Shen (Chengdu, Sichuan Province): bureaucratic institutions in, 197; compulsory fees in, 198; cooperation between business and bureaucracy in, 201, 202, 208, 210; criminal gangs in, 194n12; during Cultural Revolution, 206n21; exchange relations in, 201; household strategies of, 190–91; illegal business in,

67; industrial production in, 64, 123; managers in, 128; market competition in, 52; privatization of, 33n8; reform of, 10; scope of, 30n3

Entrepreneurs, Chinese: access to profit, 160–64; access to protection, 164–66, 207; access to real estate, 161; bank loans to, 162; as clients, 155; conspicuous consumption by, 188, 201; cooperation with officials, 154, 155, 201–4, 248, dependence on officials, 154, 158–60, 185; domestic organization among, 192; effect of central state policies on, 165; foreign trade by, 160; fraud against, 205–6, gifts to officials, 167–69, 172–73; harassment of, 164–65, 174; incentives for, 96; influence on officials, 166–72; levels of support for, 173–75; living standards of, 176; manipulation of authority, 202–4; minorities among, 245, 259, 262; networks among, 208; partnerships with public enterprise, 163, 171–72; party membership of, 177; patronage of officials, 176–77; as petty bureaucrats, 200; prosecution for kickbacks, 175; protection from bureaucratic campaigns, 165–66; protection from regulation, 158; in Self-employed Laborers' Association, 195; social status of, 201, 207; social work of, 196, 206; and student movement, 176n14; support by local officials, 160–66, 175–76; tax evasion by, 164; urban strategies of, 190; use of kinship ties, 170–71, 175; use of passive resistance, 190, 198–200; use of payoffs, 166–69; volunteer work by, 195–96; of Xiamen, 157, 176n14. See also Private enterprise, Chinese

Entrepreneurs, Hungarian: capital for, 49; cooperative partnerships among, 33; effect of 1982 reforms on, 34; legalization of, 54; officials among, 29; under recentralization, 39; taxation of, 128–29. See also Private enterprise, Hungarian

Entrepreneurs' Party (Hungary), 54

Ethnicity: legitimization of, 262–64; role in Chinese economic reform, 254–62

Ethnic revitalization, Chinese, 10, 15, 242–43; in Chendai, 257, 258; politics of, 254–60, 262; role in economic reform, 259–60, 263

Exchange relationships, 217, 218

Extrabudgetary funds (China), 88, 93–99; and capital construction, 106; central control over, 99–102; effect of *tanpai* on, 102; expansion under decentralization, 95–99; incentive function of, 95, 100–102; local governments' use of, 92, 99, 101, 107; managers' use of, 95, 100–101; under Mao Zedong, 95; ownership of, 98–99, proportion to budgetary funds, 103–5; sources of, 96; in state extractive capacity, 90, 92; taxation of, 100. See also Second budget, Chinese

Extractive capacity, 88; indicators of, 90; political constraints on, 91; role of budgetary funds in, 92, 93. See also State capacity

Extractive capacity, Chinese: decline of, 103–5, 109; political consequences of decline, 105–9; and rise of second budget, 103; role of local officials in, 154

Fair treatment (*zhengdang*), 202

Families, Chinese: petty bureaucrats in, 194; in private enterprise, 190–93; "stem," 209n25; submission to authority in, 189, 202–3. See also Household enterprise, Chinese; Kinship, Chinese

Famines, 12, 237

Fangbian. See Gift-giving

Fangquan rangli (devolution of control), 96

Fei Xiaotong, 244

Foreign exchange, Hungarian, 114, 115, 118, 135–36, 138, 140; control of National Bank over, 138

Foreign-exchange liberalization, Hungarian, 135–36, 146–47; effect of Western investors in, 140–41, 144, 146, 147; effect on hard currency, 137; effect on household sector, 138–40, 144; effect on HSWP, 140–42; effect on private enterprise, 137–38; political consequences of, 141–42; role of HSWP in, 118

Foreign investment: Chinese, 157; in Hungary, 10, 64, 136, 140–41, 142, 144, 146, 147

Foreign trade: in China, 160, 170; Hungarian terms of, 64, 129

Foreign Trade Bureau (China), 170

Forint, Hungarian: devaluation of, 136–37; surpluses of, 116

Fujian Province: ancestral halls of, 258; cooperative enterprises in, 156n2; Hui in,

Ma Tong, 260

Mencius, 193n11

Mining industry, Hungarian, 123–24, 146

Ministry of Education (China), 254

Ministry of Finance (Hungary): and 1989 Association Law, 34; and 1982 property rights reform, 41, 51n30, 53; and second economy, 54, 65, 67

Ministry of Industry (Hungary), 123–24; negotiations with Trade Union Council, 130; and steel industry, 125

Ministry of Planning (Hungary), reformers in, 40

Minorities, Chinese: assimilation of, 246; criteria for identification, 244–45; during Cultural Revolution, 245; under Deng Xiaoping, 245, 264; effect of economic reform on, 242–49, 252, 254–62; exemption from birth-planning restrictions, 244; growth in, 245, 263; influence over government officials, 263; preferential treatment of, 244, 259, 261; prosperity of, 254; role in society, 249; in township economies, 244; use of networks, 246–47. See also Ding family (Hui); Hui nationality (China)

Monopolies, national, 8, 9; as characteristic of central planning, 87, 88; effect on production, 43n19

Mosques, 261; in Chendai township, 257, 258; prosperity of, 16; in Quanzhou, 256, 257. See also Islam

Muslims: connections with Hui, 256; foreign aid to China, 257, 261; missionaries, 256n7; traders, 244, 256, 259. See also Islam

Muslims, Chinese, 4, 6, 15, 242n2; diversity among, 261; domestic policy towards, 246; as traders, 243, 260

Nagy, Imre, 37; negotiation with HSWP, 132

Nagy, Sándor, 130

National Bank of Hungary: bad loans by, 120–21; control of money supply, 119, 137–38; credit policy of, 122–23; devaluation of currency, 136; monopoly on credit, 115–16, 119

National Bank of Yugoslavia, 120

National Council of Trade Unions (Hungary), 73; alliance with local party secretaries, 130; challenges to HSWP, 130–34,

135, 144, 146; May Day demonstration (1989), 133; organization of strikes, 133, 136; political change within, 129–31; political influence of, 130; on work partnerships, 76–77. See also Trade unions, Hungarian

Nationalist Party (Guomindang, China), 203

National Organization of Artisans (Hungary), 77n11

National Planning Office (Hungary), 38, 40; reform proposals of, 46, 50

Nee, Victor, 4, 154; theory of market transition, 215, 297

Networks, Chinese: and bureaucratic institutions, 196; changes in, 177–79; ethnic minorities in, 246–47; importance to village life, 222–23. See also Personal ties (*guanxi*)

Networks, Hungarian: in second economy, 38, 40, 56

New Economic Mechanism (Hungary, 1968), 37, 51; and demand for labor, 44; as departure from central planning, 79, 115; early phases of, 116, 119; labor demand under, 127–28; private sector response to, 38, 41; suspension of (1972), 130

Obligation (*bao*), 168

Officials, party: alternative sources of revenue for, 13–14; autonomy from superiors, 14; and decline of party state, 16; dependency among, 12; living standards of, 12; sources of income, 17; ties to entrepreneurs, 16–17

Officials, party (China): abuse of power, 202–3; access to capital, 162; allocation of resources by, 153, 154, 185, 215; attitude towards village cadres, 226; clientelism of, 155, 179–80; competition among, 174, 175; cooperation with entrepreneurs, 154, 155, 201, 202–4, 248; corruption among, 107–8; criticism of, 200; discretion concerning entrepreneurs, 165–66, 173, 180–81; economic crimes of, 179n18; employment in private firms, 166, 169–71; and extrabudgetary funds, 100–101; extralegal privileges for, 200; gifts to, 167–69, 172–73; and growth of private enterprise, 172–76; incentives under central planning, 87; influence of en-

Compositor:	Keystone Typesetting, Inc.
Text:	10/12 Baskerville
Display:	Baskerville
Printer and Binder:	Thomson-Shore, Inc.